R00512 94953

CHILTON'S Repair and Tune-Up Guide

Datsun
1973–78

ILLUSTRATED

Prepared by the
Automotive Editorial Department
Chilton Book Company
Chilton Way
Radnor, Pa. 19089
215—687-8200

president and chief executive officer **WILLIAM A. BARBOUR;** executive vice president **RICHARD H. GROVES;** vice president and general manager **JOHN P. KUSHNERICK;** managing editor **KERRY A. FREEMAN, S.A.E.;** senior editor **RICHARD J. RIVELE;** editor **ROBERT F. KING**

CHILTON BOOK COMPANY   RADNOR, PENNSYLVANIA

Copyright © 1978 by Chilton Book Company
All Rights Reserved
Published in Radnor, Pa. by Chilton Book Company
and simultaneously in Ontario, Canada
by Thomas Nelson & Sons, Ltd.

Manufactured in the United States of America

34567890   765432109

Chilton's Repair & Tune-Up Guide: Datsun 1973–78
ISBN 0-8019-6694-9 pbk.

Library of Congress Catalog Card No. 77-90862

Chilton Book Company thanks Nissan Motor Corporation in U.S.A., Gardena, California 90247, for assistance in the preparation of this book.

Although the information in this guide is based on industry sources and is as complete as possible at the time of publication, the possibility exists that the manufacturer made later changes which could not be included here. While striving for total accuracy, Chilton Book Company cannot assume responsibility for any errors, changes, or omissions that may occur in the compilation of this data.

SAFETY NOTICE

Proper service and repair procedures are vital to the safe, reliable operation of all motor vehicles, as well as the personal safety of those performing repairs. This book outlines procedures for servicing and repairing vehicles using safe, effective methods. The procedures contain many NOTES, CAUTIONS and WARNINGS which should be followed along with standard safety procedures to eliminate the possibility of personal injury or improper service which could damage the vehicle or compromise its safety.

It is important to note that repair procedures and techniques, tools and parts for servicing motor vehicles, as well as the skill and experience of the individual performing the work vary widely. It is not possible to anticipate all of the conceivable ways or conditions under which vehicles may be serviced, or to provide cautions as to all of the possible hazards that may result. Standard and accepted safety precautions and equipment should be used when handling toxic or flammable fluids, and safety goggles or other protection should be used during cutting, grinding, chiseling, prying, or any other process that can cause material removal or projectiles.

Some procedures require the use of tools specially designed for a specific purpose. Before substituting another tool or procedure, you must be completely satisfied that neither your personal safety, nor the performance of the vehicle will be endangered.

Contents

Chapter 1 General Information and Maintenance 1

How To Use This Book, 1
Tools and Equipment, 2
History, 2
Serial Number Identification, 2
Routine Maintenance, 3
Air Cleaner, 3
Positive Crankcase Ventilation Valve, 4
Evaporative Emissions System, 5
Belts, 5
Air Conditioning, 6
Fluid Level Checks, 8
Capacities, 11
Tires, 11
Fuel Filter, 12
Lubrication, 13
Oil and Fuel Recommendations, 13
Oil Changes, 13
Pushing, Towing and Jump Starting, 15
Jacking, 16

Chapter 2 Tune-Up and Troubleshooting 17

Tune-Up Procedures, 17
Spark Plugs, 17
Tune-Up Specifications, 18
Spark Plug Heat Range, 21
Breaker Points and Condenser, 23
Dwell Angle, 27
Datsun Electronic Ignition, 28
Ignition Timing, 32
Valve Lash, 33
Carburetor, 35
Electronic Fuel Injection—810, 37
Troubleshooting, 38

Chapter 3 Engine and Engine Rebuilding 53

Engine Electrical, 53
Distributor, 53
Firing Order, 54
Alternator, 54
Regulator, 56
Starter, 58
Battery and Starter Specifications, 60
Engine Mechanical, 61
Design, 61
Engine I.D. Table, 62
General Engine Specifications, 63
Crankshaft and Connecting Rod Specifications, 64
Piston and Ring Specifications, 65
Valve Specifications, 65
Torque Specifications, 66
Engine Removal and Installation—all engines except F10, 66
Engine Removal and Installation—F10, 67
Cylinder Head, 68
Intake Manifold, 72
Exhaust Manifold, 73
Timing Chain Cover, 73
Timing Chain and Camshaft, 75
Timing Chain and Tensioner, 76
Camshaft, 77
Pistons and Connecting Rods, 78
Engine Lubrication, 79
Oil Pan, 79
Rear Main Oil Seal, 79
Oil Pump, 79
Engine Cooling, 80
Radiator, 80
Water Pump, 81
Thermostat, 82
Engine Rebuilding, 83

Chapter 4 Emission Controls and Fuel System 105

Emission Controls, 105
Crankcase Emission Controls, 105
Evaporative Emission Control System, 108
Spark Timing Control System Dual Point Distributor, 108
Early Fuel Evaporation System, 111
Boost Control Deceleration Device, 111
Automatic Temperature Controlled Air Cleaner, 112
Exhaust Gas Recirculation, 113
Transmission Controlled Spark System, 115
Air Injection Reactor System, 115
Electric Choke, 117
Catalytic Converter, 118
Fuel System, 119
Fuel Pump—all except 810, 119
Fuel Pump—F10, 119
Carburetor, 121
Electronic Fuel Injection System, 126

iv CONTENTS

Chapter 5 Chassis Electrical 128

Understanding and Troubleshooting Electrical Systems, 128
Heater, 130
Heater Assembly, 130
Heater Core, 135
Radio, 135
Windshield Wiper Motor and Linkage, 139
Instrument Cluster, 140
Headlights, 144
Fuse Locations, 144

Chapter 6 Clutch and Transmission 145

Manual Transmission, 145
Clutch, 149
Clutch Specifications, 151
Clutch Master Cylinder, 153
Clutch Slave Cylinder, 153
Bleeding the Clutch Hydraulic System, 155
Automatic Transmission, 155

Chapter 7 Drive Train 157

Driveline, 157
Driveshaft and Universal Joints, 157
Rear Axle, 161
Axle Shaft, 161
Axle Driveshafts, 162

Chapter 8 Suspension and Steering 165

Front Suspension, 165
Strut, 165
Ball Joint, 168
Hub Assembly, 169
Front End Alignment, 171
Wheel Alignment Specifications, 172
Rear Suspension, 175
Springs, 179
Shock Absorber, 181
Steering, 182
Steering Wheel, 182
Turn Signal Switch, 183
Steering Lock, 183
Steering Gear, 183

Chapter 9 Brakes 187

Brake System, 187
Adjustment, 187
Hydraulic System, 187
Master Cylinder, 187
System Bleeding, 190
Front Disc Brakes, 191
Disc Brake Pads, 191
Calipers and Brake Discs, 193
Wheel Bearing Adjustment, 195
Rear Drum Brakes, 195
Brake Shoes, 195
Parking Brake, 198
Brake Specifications, 200

Chapter 10 Body 201

Doors, 201
Door Panels, 202
Hood, Trunk and Tailgate, 202
Fuel Tank, 202

Appendix 211

Chapter One

General Information and Maintenance

How To Use This Book

Chilton's Repair and Tune-Up Guide for the Datsun is intended to teach you more about the inner workings of your automobile and save you money in its upkeep. The first two chapters will be the most used, since they contain maintenance and tune-up information and procedures. The following seven chapters concern themselves with the more complex systems of the Datsun. Operating systems from engine through brakes are covered to the extent that we feel the average do-it-yourselfer should get involved. Chilton's *Datsun 2* won't explain rebuilding the transmission for the simple reason that the expertise required and the investment in special tools make this task uneconomical. We will tell you how to change your own brake pads and shoes, replace points and plugs, and many more jobs that will save you money, give you personal satisfaction, and help you avoid problems.

Before loosening any bolts, please read through the entire section and the specific procedure. This will give you the overall view of what will be required as far as tools, supplies, and you. There is nothing more frustrating than having to walk to the bus stop on Monday morning because you were short one metric bolt during your Sunday afternoon repair. So read ahead and plan ahead.

The sections begin with a brief discussion of the system and what it involves. Adjustments and/or maintenance are then discussed, followed by removal and installation procedures and then repair or overhaul procedures where they are feasible. When repair is considered to be out of your league, we tell you how to remove the part and then how to install the new or rebuilt replacement. In this way you at least save the labor costs. Backyard repair of such components as the alternator are just not practical.

Two basic mechanic's rules should be mentioned here. One, whenever the left-side of the car is referred to, it is meant to specify the driver's side of the car. Conversely, the right-side of the car means the passenger's side of the car. Second, most screws and bolts are removed by turning counterclockwise and tightened by turning clockwise. Safety is always the most important rule. Constantly be aware of the dangers involved in working on an automobile and take the proper precautions. Use jackstands when working under a raised vehicle. Don't smoke or allow an exposed flame to come near the battery or any part of the fuel system. Always use the proper tool and use it correctly; bruised knuckles and skinned fingers aren't a mechanic's standard equipment. Always take your time and have patience; once you have some experience and gain confidence, working on your car will become an enjoyable hobby.

Tools And Equipment

The following list is the basic requirement to perform most of the procedures described in this guide. Your Datsun is fastened together with metric screws and bolts; if you don't already have a set of metric wrenches—buy them. Standard wrenches are either too loose or too tight a fit on metric fasteners.

1. Metric sockets, also a $^{13}/_{16}$ in. spark plug socket. If possible, buy various length socket drive extensions. One break in this department is that the metric sockets available in the US will all fit the ratchet handles and extensions you may already have (¼, ⅜, and ½ in. drive).
2. Set of metric combination (one end open and one box) wrenches.
3. Spark plug wire gauge.
4. Flat feeler gauge for breaker points and valve lash checking.
5. Slot and phillips heads screwdrivers.
6. Timing light, preferably a DC battery hook-up type.
7. Dwell/tachometer.
8. Torque wrench. This assures proper tightening of important fasteners and avoids costly thread stripping (too tight) or leaks (too loose).
9. Oil can filler spout.
10. Oil filter strap wrench. Makes removal of a tight filter much simpler. Never use to install filter.
11. Pair of channel lock pliers. Always handy to have.
12. Two sturdy jackstands—cinder blocks, bricks, and other makeshift supports are just not safe.

History

The first Datsun automobile was produced in 1913. The original name of the company, D.A.T., was derived from the last initials of the three founders. Datson, for son of D.A.T., was used later and finally evolved into Datsun. Since the first few cars were imported in 1960, Datsun has moved up to third place in imported sales.

This guide covers all Datsun coupes, sedans, and station wagons from 1973 to 1978. Separate books are available for the 240-280Z sports cars, and the pickup trucks. Years and models covered in this book are the 510 for 1973, the 1200 for 1973, the B210 from 1974 to 1978, the 610 from 1973 to 1976, and the 710 from 1974 to 1977. Also covered are the F10 for 1977 and 1978, the 810 from 1977 to 1978, the 200SX for 1977 and 1978, and the new 510 for 1978.

Serial Number Identification

CHASSIS

The chassis serial number is stamped into the firewall. The model designation, such as B210, precedes the serial number. The chassis number is also located on a dashboard plate which is visible through the windshield.

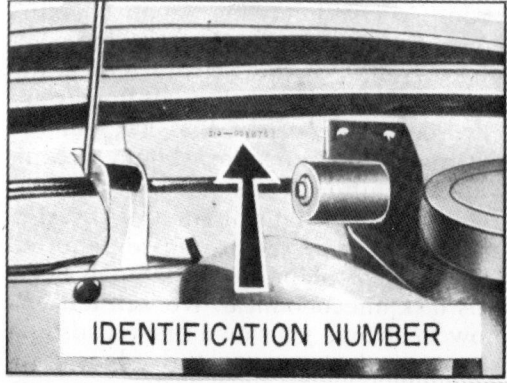

VEHICLE IDENTIFICATION PLATE

The vehicle identification plate is attached to the firewall. This plate gives the vehicle model, engine displacement

GENERAL INFORMATION AND MAINTENANCE

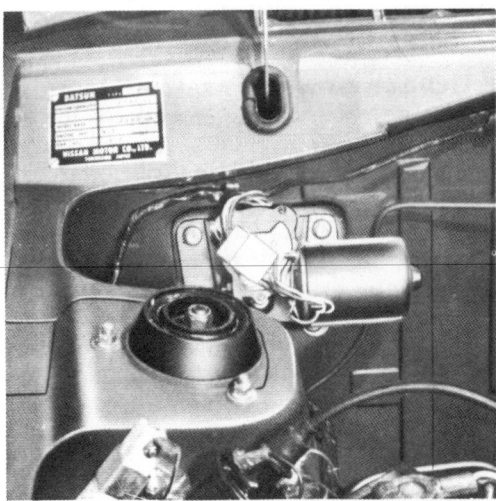

Vehicle identification plate

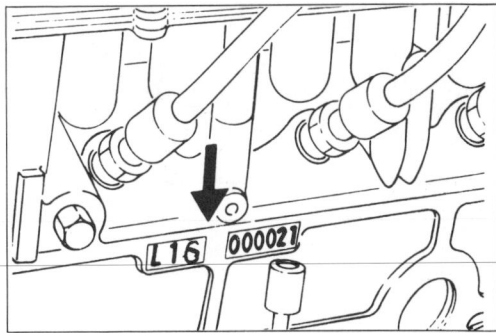

Engine serial number

in cc, SAE horsepower rating, wheelbase, engine number, and chassis number.

ENGINE

The engine number is stamped on the right-side top edge of the cylinder block. The engine serial number is preceded by the engine model code.

Routine Maintenance

AIR CLEANER

All Datsuns covered in this guide are equipped with a disposable paper cartridge air cleaner element. At every tuneup, or sooner if the car is operated in a dusty area, undo the wingnut, remove the housing top, and withdraw the element. Check the element. Replace the filter if it is extremely dirty. Loose dust can sometimes be removed by striking the filter

If the old filter is dirty, replace it

4 GENERAL INFORMATION AND MAINTENANCE

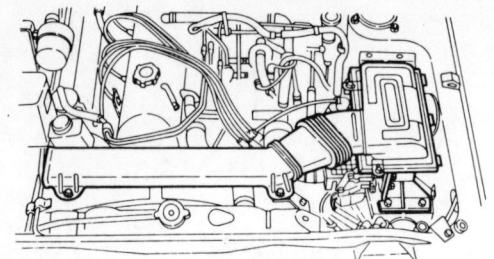

810 air filter

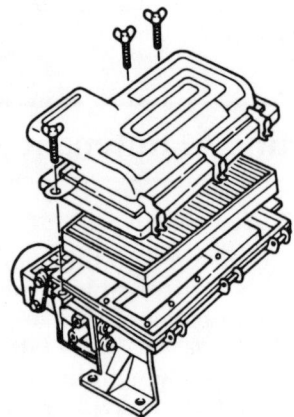

810 air filter showing wing nuts

POSITIVE CRANKCASE VENTILATION VALVE

This valve meters crankcase blow-by gases into the intake manifold to be burned with the normal air/fuel mixture. The PCV valve should be replaced every 24,000 miles. Make sure that all PCV connections are tight. Check that the connecting hoses are clear and not clogged. Replace any brittle or broken hoses.

To replace the valve, which is located in the intake manifold directly below the carburetor:

1. Squeeze the hose clamp with pliers and remove the hose.

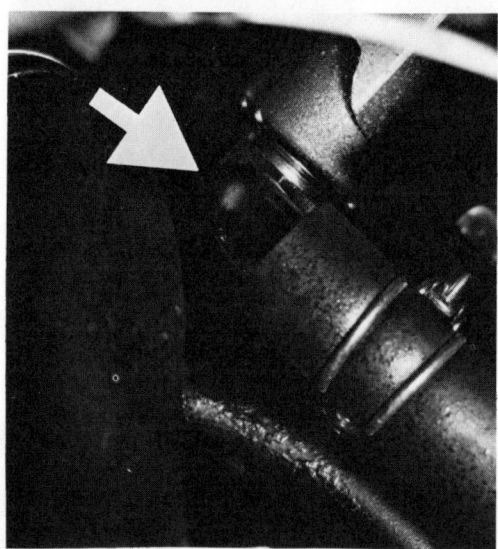

against a hard surface several times. The filter should be replaced every 24,000 miles. Before installing either the original or a replacement filter, wipe out the inside of the air cleaner housing with a clean rag or paper towel. Install the paper air cleaner filter, seat the top cover on the bottom housing, and tighten the wing nut.

PCV valve (arrow). On the late models, there are so many hoses in the way, the valve is hard to spot

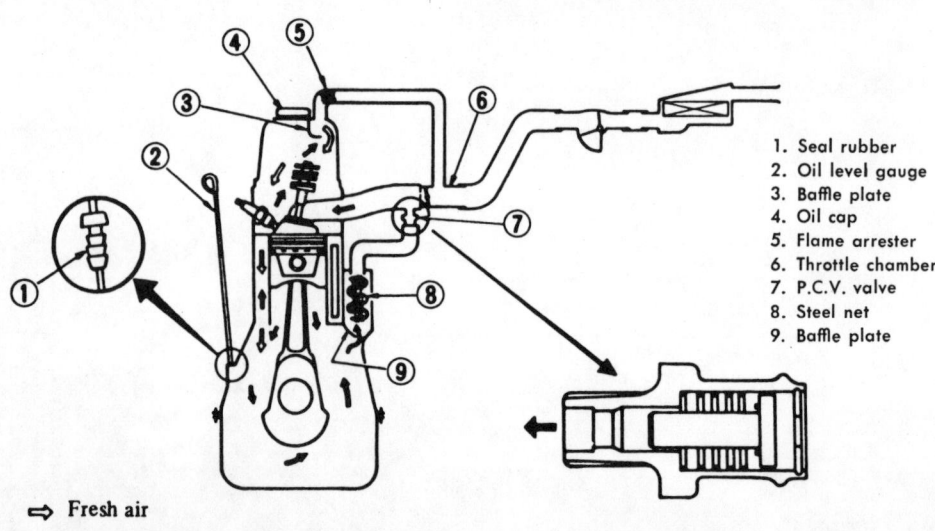

1. Seal rubber
2. Oil level gauge
3. Baffle plate
4. Oil cap
5. Flame arrester
6. Throttle chamber
7. P.C.V. valve
8. Steel net
9. Baffle plate

⇨ Fresh air
➡ Blow-by gas

810 PCV valve location—others similar

GENERAL INFORMATION AND MAINTENANCE

2. Using a wrench, unscrew the PCV valve and remove the valve.

3. Disconnect the ventilation hoses and flush with solvent.

4. Install the new PCV valve and replace the hoses and clamp.

EVAPORATIVE EMISSIONS SYSTEM

Check the evaporative emissions system every 12,000 miles. Check the fuel and vapor lines for proper connection and correct routing as well as condition. Replace damaged or deteriorated parts as necessary. Remove and check the operation of the check valve in the following manner:

1. With all hoses disconnected from the valve, apply air pressure to the fuel tank side of the valve. The air should flow through the valve and exit the crankcase side of the valve. If the valve does not operate as outlined above, replace it.

2. Apply air pressure to the crankcase side of the valve. Air should not pass to either of the other two outlets.

3. When air pressure is applied to the carburetor side of the valve, the air should pass through to exit out the fuel tank and/or the crankcase side of the valve.

BELTS

Tension Checking, Adjusting, and Replacement

Push in on the drive belt about midway between the crankshaft pulley and the alternator. If the belt deflects more than 9/16 in. or less than 3/8 in., it's too

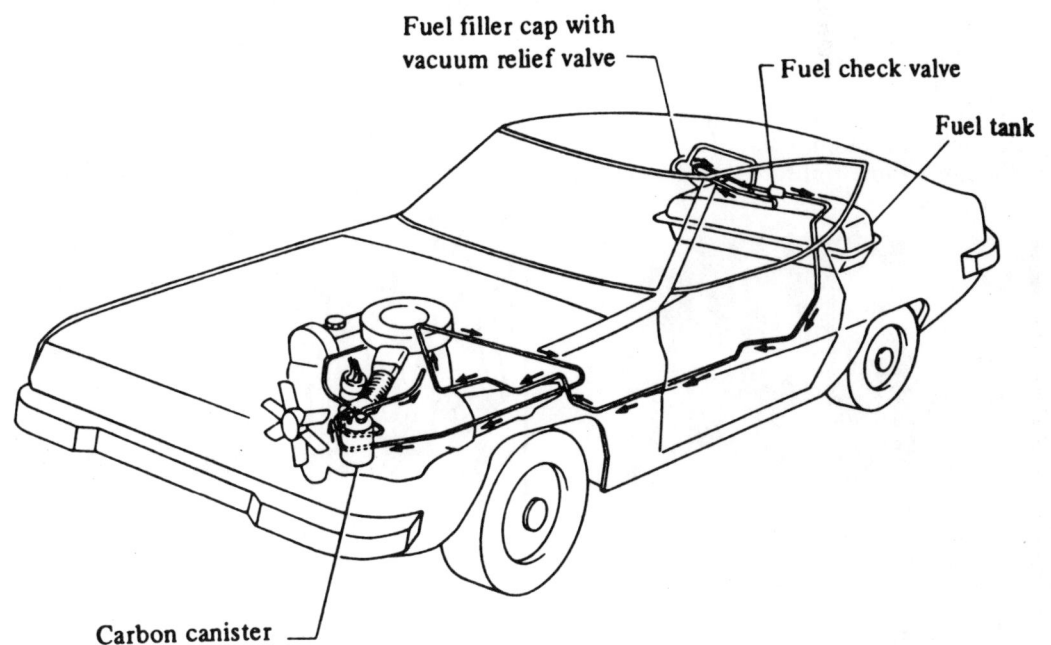

Evaporative emissions schematic

GENERAL INFORMATION AND MAINTENANCE

Evaporative emissions canister

loose or too tight. If the belt is frayed or cracked, replace it. Adjust belt tension as follows:

1. Loosen both nuts on the bracket.
2. When replacing the belt, pry the alternator toward the engine and slip the belt from the pulleys.
3. Carefully pry the alternator out with a bar, such as a ratchet handle or broom handle, and then tighten the alternator bracket nuts.
4. Recheck the tension.

The alternator drive belt also operates the water pump. It might be good insurance to carry an extra belt in the trunk.

NOTE: *The optional air conditioning drive belt is adjusted in a similar fashion.*

Loosen the alternator bracket nuts to adjust belt tension

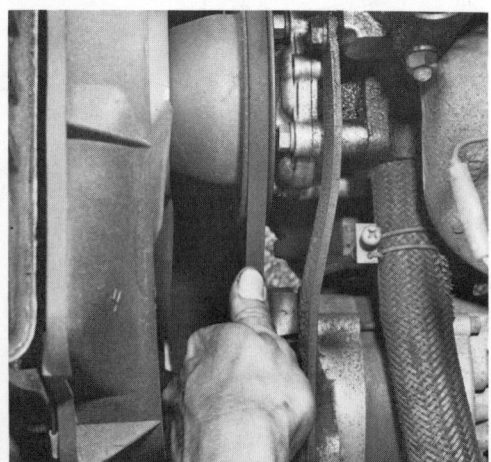

Checking belt deflection

AIR CONDITIONING

This book contains no repair or maintenance procedures for the air conditioning

GENERAL INFORMATION AND MAINTENANCE

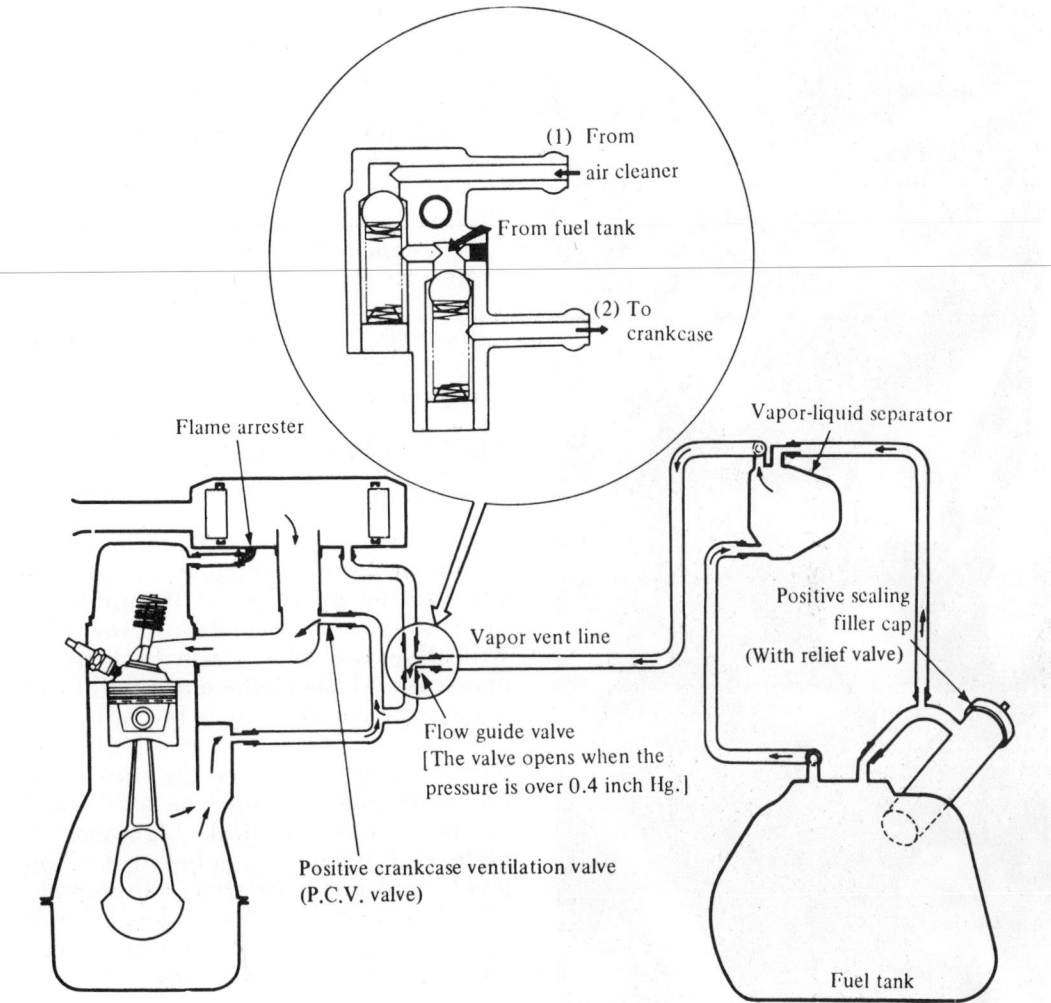

Typical 1973–74 evaporative control system showing location of check valve

system. It is recommended that any such repairs be left to the experts, whose personnel are well aware of the hazards and who have the proper equipment.

CAUTION: *The compressed refrigerant used in the air conditioning system expands into the atmosphere at a temperature of −21.7° F or lower. This will freeze any surface, including your eyes, that it contacts. In addition, the refrigerant decomposes into a poisonous gas in the presence of flame. Do not open or disconnect any part of the air conditioning system.*

Sight Glass Check

You can safely make a few simple checks to determine if your air conditioning system needs service. The tests work best if the temperature is warm (about 70° F).

1. Place the automatic transmission in Park or the manual transmission in Neutral. Set the parking brake.
2. Run the engine at a fast idle (about 1,500 rpm) either with the help of a friend, or by temporarily readjusting the idle speed screw.
3. Set the controls for maximum cold with the blower on high.
4. Locate the sight glass in one of the system lines. Usually it is on the left alongside the top of the radiator.
5. If you see bubbles, the system must be recharged. Very likely there is a leak at some point.
6. If there are no bubbles, there is either no refrigerant at all or the system is fully charged. Feel the two hoses going

GENERAL INFORMATION AND MAINTENANCE

The sight glass is located in the head of the receiver-dryer (arrow)

to the belt-driven compressor. If they are both at the same temperature, the system is empty and must be recharged.

7. If one hose (high-pressure) is warm and the other (low-pressure) is cold, the system may be alright. However, you are probably making these tests because you think there is something wrong, so proceed to the next step.

8. Have an assistant in the car turn the fan control on and off to operate the compressor clutch. Watch the sight glass.

9. If bubbles appear when the clutch is disengaged and disappear when it is engaged, the system is properly charged.

10. If the refrigerant takes more than 45 seconds to bubble when the clutch is disengaged, the system is overcharged. This usually causes poor cooling at low speeds.

CAUTION: *If it is determined that the system has a leak, it should be corrected as soon as possible. Leaks may allow moisture to enter and cause a very expensive rust problem.*

NOTE: *Exercise the air conditioner for a few minutes, every two weeks or so, during the cold months. This avoids the possibility of the compressor seals drying out from lack of lubrication.*

FLUID LEVEL CHECKS

Engine Oil

The best time to check the engine oil is before operating the engine or after it has been sitting for at least 10 minutes in order to gain an accurate reading. This will allow the oil to drain back in the crankcase. To check the engine oil level, make sure that the vehicle is resting on a level surface, remove the oil dipstick, wipe it clean and reinsert the stick firmly for an accurate reading. The oil dipstick has two marks to indicate high and low oil level. If the oil is at or below the "low level" mark on the dipstick, oil should be added as necessary. The oil level should be maintained in the safety margin, neither going above the "high level" mark or below the "low level" mark.

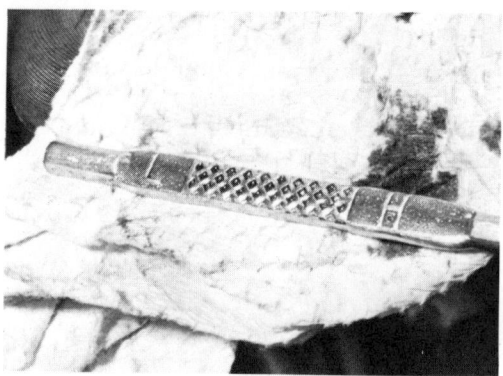

Oil dipstick markings

Transmission

MANUAL

Check the level of the lubricant in the transmission every 3,000 miles. The lubricant level should be maintained to the bottom of the filler hole. Hold in on the

GENERAL INFORMATION AND MAINTENANCE

filler plug when unscrewing it. When you are sure that all of the threads of the plug are free of the transmission case, move the plug away from the case slightly. If lubricant begins to flow out of the transmission, then you know it is full. If not, add SAE90 gear oil as necessary. It is recommended that the transmission lubricant be changed every 24,000 miles.

AUTOMATIC

Check the level of the automatic transmission fluid every 2,000 miles. There is a dipstick at the right rear of the engine under the hood. It has a scale on each side, one for COLD and the other for HOT. The transmission is considered hot after 15 miles of highway driving.

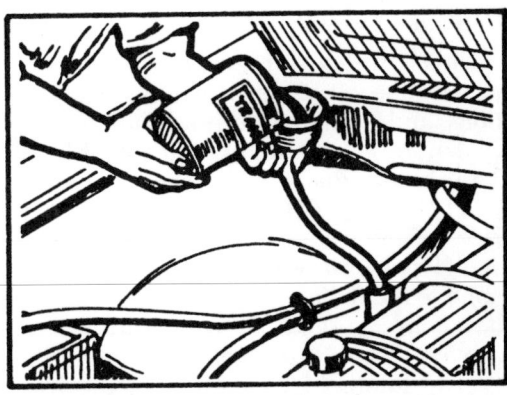

Add automatic transmission fluid through the dipstick tube

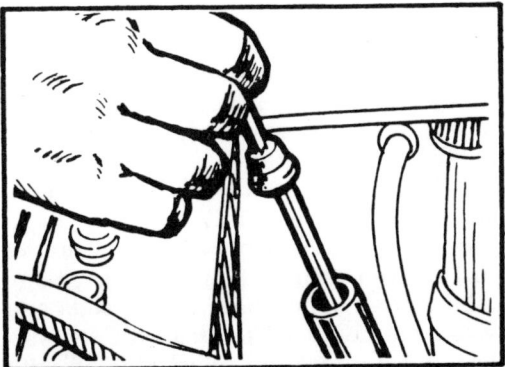

Remove the automatic transmission dipstick with engine warm and idling in Park

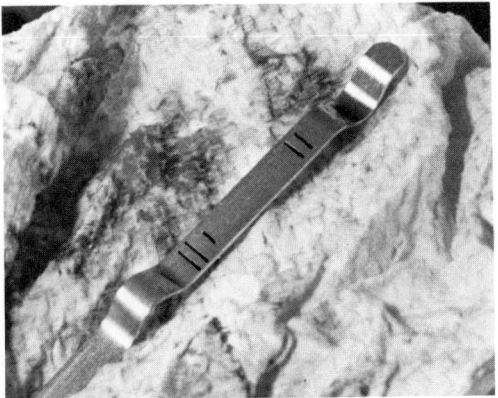

Automatic transmission dipstick markings

Park the car on a level surface with the engine running. If the transmission is not hot, shift into Drive, Low, then Neutral or Park. Set the handbrake and block the wheels.

Remove the dipstick, wipe it clean, then reinsert it firmly. Remove the dipstick and check the fluid level on the appropriate scale. The level should be at the "Full" mark.

If the level is below the "Full" mark, add Type A or Dexron® type automatic transmission fluid as necessary, with the engine running, through the dipstick tube. Do not overfill, as this may cause the transmission to malfunction and damage itself.

Brake and Clutch Master Cylinder

Check the levels of brake fluid in the brake and clutch master cylinder reservoirs every 3,000 miles. The fluid level should be maintained to a level not below the bottom line on the reservoirs and not above the top line. Any sudden decrease in the level in either of the three reservoirs (two for the brakes and one for the clutch) indicates a probable leak in that particular system and the possibility of a leak should be checked out.

Remove the cap to add hydraulic fluid

Coolant

Check the coolant level every time you change the oil. Check for loose connections and signs of deterioration of the coolant hoses. Maintain the coolant level 3 in. below the level of the filler neck when the engine is cold. Add a mixture of 70% to 50% water and 30% to 50% ethylene glycol antifreeze as necessary. Never remove the radiator cap when the vehicle is hot or overheated. Wait until it has cooled. Place a thick cloth over the radiator cap to shield yourself from the heat and turn the radiator cap *slightly* until the sound of escaping pressure can be heard. *Do not turn any more.* Allow the pressure to release gradually. When no more pressure can be heard escaping, then remove the cap with the heavy cloth *cautiously.* Never add cold water to an overheated engine while the engine is not running. Run the engine until it reaches normal operating temperature after filling the radiator to make sure that the thermostat has opened and all air is bled from the system.

Rear Axle

Check the rear axle lubricant every 6,000 miles. Remove the filler plug in the axle housing. The lubricant should be up to the bottom of the filler hole with the vehicle resting on a level surface. Add SAE90 gear oil as necessary to bring the lubricant up to the proper level.

Steering Gear

Check the level of the lubricant in the steering gear every 12,000 miles. If the level is low, check for leakage. An oily film is not considered a leak; solid grease must be present. Change the lubricant every 36,000 miles. Use steering gear lubricant. The lubricant is added and checked through the filler plug hole in the top of the steering gear.

Battery

The battery is located in the engine compartment. Routinely check the battery electrolyte level and specific gravity. A few minutes occasionally spent monitoring battery condition is worth saving hours of frustration when your car won't start due to a dead battery. Only distilled water should be used to top up the battery, as tap water, in many areas, contains harmful minerals. Two tools which will facilitate battery maintenance are a hydrometer and a squeeze bulb filler. These are cheap and widely available at automotive parts stores, hardware stores, etc. The specific gravity of the electrolyte should be between 1.27 and 1.20. Keep the top of the battery clean, as a film of dirt can sometimes completely discharge a battery. A solution of baking soda and water may be used to clean the top surface, but be careful to flush this off with clear water and that none of the solution enters the filler holes. Clean the battery posts and clamps with a wire brush to eliminate corrosion deposits. Special clamp and terminal cleaning brushes are available for just this purpose. Lightly coat the posts and clamps with petroleum

Check the rubber gasket on the cap when checking coolant level

Keep battery top and posts clean

GENERAL INFORMATION AND MAINTENANCE

Capacities

Model	Engine Crankcase With Filter	Engine Crankcase Without Filter	Transmission (pts) 4-Spd	Transmission (pts) 5-Spd	Automatic (total capacity)	Drive Axle (pts)	Gas Tank (gals)	Cooling System (qts)
1973 510	5.2	4.4	4.4	—	11.4	1.75	11.9	7.2
1973 1200	3.4	2.7	2.5	—	11.8	1.8	9.3	5.7
1973 610	5.0	4.5	4.25	—	11.8	1.75/2.75 (wagon)	13.8	9.0
1974 B210	4.25	3.75	2.5	—	11.8	1.8	11.5	5.5
1974 610	4.5	4.0	4.25	—	11.8	1.75/2.2 (wagon)	14.5/13.5 (wagon)	7.25
1974 710	4.5	4.0	3.5	—	11.8	2.75	13.25/11.8 (wagon)	7.25
1975 B210	4.2	3.7	3.7	—	12.00	2.0	11.5	5.7
1975 610	4.5	4.0	4.25	—	11.8	1.75/2.75 (wagon)	14.5/13.7 (wagon)	7.25
1975 710	4.5	4.0	4.25	—	11.8	2.75	13.2/11.8 (wagon)	7.25
1976–78 B210	3.8	3.4	2.75	3.6	11.8	1.8	11.5	6.25
1976 610	4.5	4.0	4.25	—	11.8	1.75/2.2 (wagon)	14.5/13.75 (wagon)	7.25
1976–77 710	4.5	4.0	4.25	—	11.8	2.75	13.25/11.8 (wagon)	7.25
1977–78 810	6.0	5.25	3.6	—	11.8	2.75/2.2 (wagon)	15.9/14.5 (wagon)	11
1977–78 F10	3.6	3.2	4.9	4.9	—	—	10.6	7
1977–78 200SX	4.5	4.0	—	3.6	11.8	2.75	15.9	7.9
1978 510	4.5	4.0	3.6	3.6	11.8	2.75	13.2	9.4

jelly or chassis grease after cleaning them.

TIRES

Check the air pressure in your tires every few weeks. Make sure that the tires are cool, as you will get a false reading when the tires are heated because air pressure increases with temperature. A decal tells you the proper tire pressure for the standard equipment tires. Naturally, when you replace tires you will

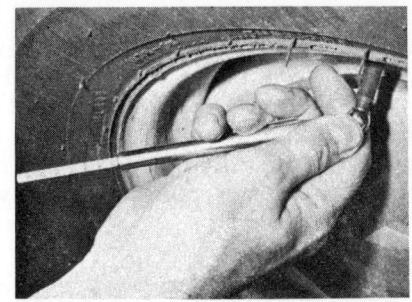

Frequently check your tire pressure with a reliable gauge

GENERAL INFORMATION AND MAINTENANCE

want to get the correct tire pressures for the new ones from the dealer or manufacturer. It pays to buy a tire pressure gauge to keep in the car, since those at service stations are usually inaccurate or broken.

While you are checking the tire pressure, take a look at the tread. The tread should be wearing evenly across the tire. Excessive wear in the center of the tread indicates overinflation. Excessive wear on the outer edges indicates underinflation. An irregular wear pattern is usually a sign of incorrect front wheel alignment or wheel balance. A front end that is out of alignment will usually pull the car to one side of a flat road when the steering wheel is released. Incorrect wheel balance will produce vibration in the steering wheel, while unbalanced rear wheels will result in floor or trunk vibration.

Rotating the tires every 6,000 miles or so will result in increased tread life. Use the correct pattern for your tire switching. Most automotive experts agree that radial tires are better all around performers, giving longer wear and better handling. An added benefit which you should consider when purchasing tires is that radials have less rolling resistance and can give up to a 10% increase in fuel economy over a bias-ply tire.

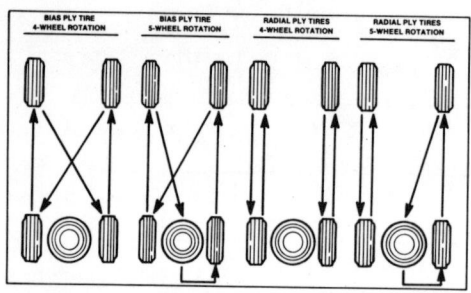

Tire rotation patterns

Tires of different construction should never be mixed. Always replace tires in sets of four or five when switching tire types and never substitute a belted tire for a bias-ply, a radial for a belted tire, etc. An occasional pressure check and periodic rotation could make your tires last much longer than a neglected set and maintain the safety margin which was designed into them.

FUEL FILTER

The fuel filter on all models is a disposable plastic unit. It's located on the right inner fender. The filter should be replaced at least every 24,000 miles. A dirty filter will starve the engine and cause poor running.

Fuel filter (arrow). This is a 1978 510; others are similar

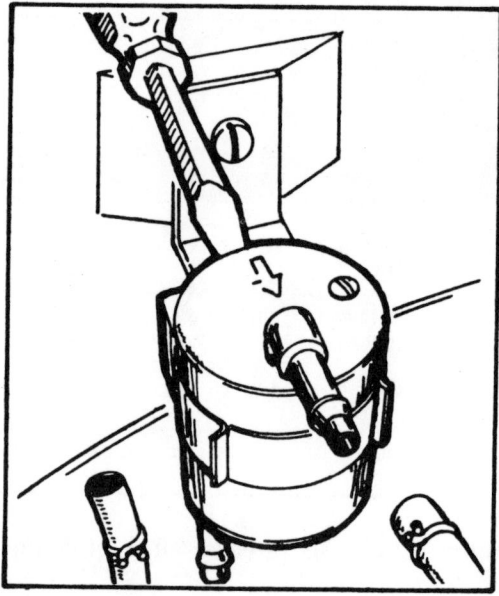

Push the old filter out of the clamp

Replacement

1. Locate fuel filter on right-side of the engine compartment.
2. Disconnect the inlet and outlet hoses from the fuel filter. Make certain that the inlet hose (bottom) doesn't fall

GENERAL INFORMATION AND MAINTENANCE

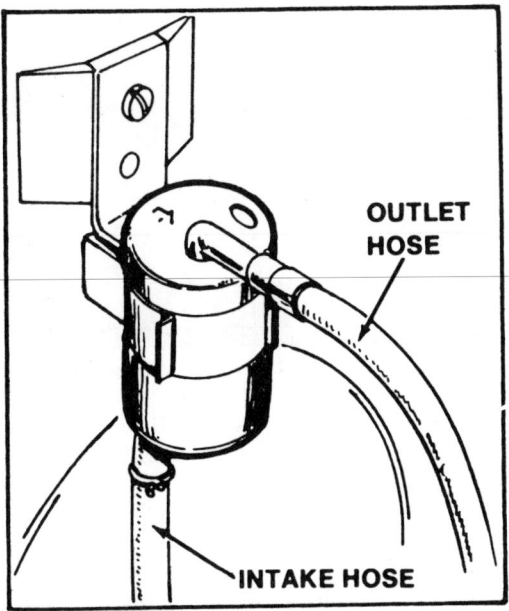

Be sure to reattach the hoses correctly

below the fuel tank level or the gasoline will drain out.

3. Pry the fuel filter from its clip and replace the assembly.

4. Replace the inlet and outlet lines; secure the hose clamps to prevent leaks.

5. Start the engine and check for leaks.

Lubrication

OIL AND FUEL RECOMMENDATIONS

Your Datsun is designed to operate on regular low lead or lead-free fuel. The octane ratings are listed on the inside of the fuel filler door, but these need only be checked when traveling outside of the United States. Should you find the regular gasoline available, say in Mexico, to be of too low an octane, mix enough Premium to raise the octane level. No benefit will be derived from running a higher octane gasoline than that recommended.

Oil must be selected with regard to the anticipated temperatures during the period before the next oil change. Using the chart, select the oil viscosity for the lowest expected temperature and you will be assured of easy cold starting and sufficient engine protection. The oil you pour into your Datsun engine should have the designation "SE" marked on the top of its container. Under the classification system adopted by the American Petroleum Institute (API) in May, 1970, "SE" is the highest designation for passenger car use. The "S" stands for passenger car and the second letter denotes a more specific application. "SA" oil, for instance, contains no additives and is suitable only for very light-duty usage. Oil designated "MS" (motor severe) may also be used, since this was the highest classification under the old API rating system.

Oil Viscosity Selection Chart

	Anticipated Temperature Range	SAE Viscosity
Multi-grade	Above 32° F	10W—40 10W—50 20W—40 20W—50 10W—30
	May be used as low as −10° F	10W—30 10W—40
	Consistently below 10° F	5W—20 5W—30
Single-grade	Above 32° F	30
	Temperature between +32° F and −10° F	10W

OIL CHANGES

The mileage figures given in your owner's manual are the Datsun recommended intervals for oil and filter changes assuming average driving. If your Datsun is being used under dusty, polluted, or off-road conditions, change the oil and filter sooner than specified. The same thing goes for cars driven in stop-and-go traffic or only for short distances.

Always drain the oil after the engine has been running long enough to bring it to operating temperature. Hot oil will flow easier and more contaminants will be removed along with the oil than if it were drained cold. You will need a large capacity drain pan, which you can pur-

14 GENERAL INFORMATION AND MAINTENANCE

chase at any store which sells automotive parts. Another necessity is containers for the used oil. You will find that plastic bottles, such as those used for bleach or fabric softener, make excellent storage jugs. One ecologically desirable solution to the used oil disposal problem is to find a cooperative gas station owner who will allow you to dump your used oil into his tank. Another is to keep the oil for use around the house as a preservative on fences, railroad tie borders, etc.

Datsun recommends changing both the oil and filter during the first oil change and the filter every other oil change thereafter. For the small price of an oil filter, it's cheap insurance to replace the filter at every oil change. One of the larger filter manufacturers points out in its advertisements that not changing the filter leaves one quart of dirty oil in the engine. This claim is true and should be kept in mind when changing your oil.

Changing Your Engine Oil

1. Run the engine until it reaches normal operating temperature.
2. Jack up the front of the car and support it on safety stands.
3. Slide a drain pan of at least 6 quarts capacity under the oil pan.
4. Loosen the drain plug. Turn the plug out by hand. By keeping an inward

The oil filter on L-series engines is easily located on the right hand side of the block

pressure on the plug as you unscrew it, oil won't escape past the threads and you can remove it without being burned by hot oil.

5. Allow the oil to drain completely and then install the drain plug. Don't

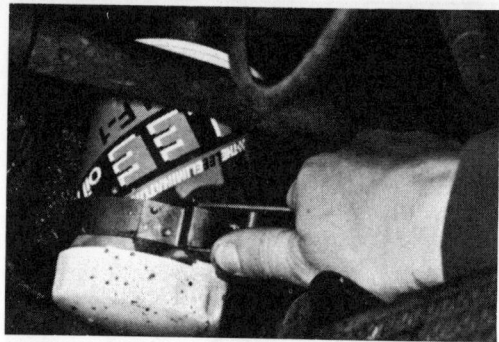

A strap wrench will make oil filter removal easier

overtighten the plug, or you'll be buying a new pan or a trick replacement plug for buggered threads.

6. Using a strap wrench, remove the oil filter. Keep in mind that it's holding about one quart of dirty, hot oil.

NOTE: *You can remove the oil filter on 510, 610, and 710 models from above.*

7. Empty the old filter into the drain pan and dispose of the filter.
8. Using a clean rag, wipe off the filter adapter on the engine block. Be sure that the rag doesn't leave any lint which could clog an oil passage.
9. Coat the rubber gasket on the filter with fresh oil. Spin it onto the engine *by hand;* when the gasket touches the adapter surface give it another ½–¾ turn. No more, or you'll squash the gasket and it will leak.
10. Refill the engine with the correct amount of fresh oil. See the "Capacities" chart.

Lightly oil the rubber gasket on the filter before installation

11. Crank the engine over several times and then start it. If the oil pressure "idiot light" doesn't go out or the pres-

GENERAL INFORMATION AND MAINTENANCE

sure gauge shows zero, shut the engine down and find out what's wrong.

12. If the oil pressure is OK and there are no leaks, shut the engine off and lower the car.

Transmission

MANUAL

Change the transmission lubricant in your manual transmission every 36,000 miles as follows:

1. Park the car on a level surface and apply the parking brake. Jack up the car and support it on stands.
2. Remove the oil filler plug (the upper one).
3. Place a drain pan under the drain plug in the transmission bottom pan.
4. Slowly remove the drain plug keeping an upward pressure on it until you can quickly pull it out.
5. Allow all of the old gear oil to drain and then replace the plug. Don't overtighten it.
6. Fill the transmission with SAE 90 gear oil. Refill with the quantity shown in the "Capacities" chart. An oil suction gun or squeeze bulb filler are handy for this chore and can be used for the rear axle, too.
7. Replace the filler plug and lower the car.

AUTOMATIC

The transmission fluid in an automatic transmission should be changed every 24,000 miles of normal driving or every 12,000 miles of driving under abnormal or severe conditions. The fluid should be drained immediately after the vehicle has been driven, but before it has had the chance to cool. Follow the procedure given below:

1. Drain the automatic transmission fluid from the transmission into a large drain pan, by removing the transmission bottom pan screws, pan, and gasket.
2. Thoroughly clean the bottom pan and position a new gasket on the pan mating surface. Use petroleum jelly on the gasket to seal it. Install the bottom pan and secure it with the attaching screws, tightening them to 3–5 ft lbs.
3. Pour the same amount of Type A Dexron® automatic transmission fluid, which was drained from the oil pan, in through the filler pipe. Make sure that the funnel, container, hose, or any other item used to assist in filling the transmission is clean.
4. Start the engine. Do NOT race it. Allow the engine to idle for a few minutes.
5. Place the selector lever in Park and apply the parking brake. With the transmission fluid at operating temperatures, check the fluid level; add fluid to bring the level to the "FULL" mark on the dipstick.

Rear Axle

Change the gear oil in the rear axle every 36,000 miles as follows:

1. With the car on a level surface, jack up the rear and support it with stands.
2. Slide a drain pan under the drain plug, remove the plug, and allow the oil to drain out.
3. Install the drain plug, but don't overtighten it. Remove the filler plug.
4. Refill the rear axle with SAE 90 gear oil up to the level of the filler plug.
5. Install the filler plug and lower the car.

CHASSIS GREASING

Datsun doesn't install lubrication fittings in lube points on the steering linkage or suspension. You can buy metric threaded fittings to grease these points or use a pointed, rubber tip end on your grease gun. Lubricate all joints equipped with a plug every 24,000 miles. Replace the plugs after lubrication.

Pushing, Towing and Jump Starting

If your Datsun is equipped with a manual transmission, it may be push started in an extreme emergency. It should be recognized that there is the possibility of damaging bumpers and/or fenders of both cars. Make sure that the bumpers of both cars are evenly matched. Depress the clutch pedal, select Second or Third gear, and switch the ignition On. When the car reaches a speed of approximately 10 or 15 mph, release the clutch to start

GENERAL INFORMATION AND MAINTENANCE

the engine. DO NOT ATTEMPT TO PUSH START AN AUTOMATIC DATSUN.

Both manual and automatic Datsuns may be towed for short distances and at no more than 20 mph. If the car must be towed a great distance, it should be done with either the rear wheels off the ground or the driveshaft disconnected.

Jump starting is the favored method of starting a car with a dead battery. Make sure that the cables are properly connected, negative-to-negative and positive-to-positive, or you stand a chance of damaging the electrical systems of both cars. Keep the engine running in the donor car. If the car still fails to start, call a garage—continual grinding on the starter will overheat the unit and make repair or replacement necessary.

Jacking

Never use the tire changing jack for anything other than that. If you intend to use this tool to perform your own maintenance, a good scissors or small hydraulic jack and two sturdy jackstands would be a wise purchase. Always chock the wheels when changing a tire or working beneath the car. It cannot be overemphasized, CLIMBING UNDER A CAR SUPPORTED BY JUST THE JACK IS EXTREMELY DANGEROUS.

Chapter Two

Tune-Up and Troubleshooting

The following procedures are specific ones for your Datsun. At the back of the chapter, there is a general "Tune-Up" section along with a "Troubleshooting" section to help you should the car need more than a regular tune-up.

Tune-Up Procedures

The following procedures will show you exactly how to tune your Datsun. Datsun recommends a tune-up, including points and plugs, at 12,000 mile intervals. If you're experiencing some specific problem, turn to the "Troubleshooting" section at the end of the chapter and follow the programmed format until you pinpoint the trouble. If you're just doing a tune-up to restore your Datsun's pep and economy, proceed with the following steps.

It might be noted that the tune-up is a good time to take a look around the engine compartment for beginning problems and head them off before they get expensive. Look for oil and fuel leaks, deteriorating radiator or heater hoses, loose and/or frayed fan belt, etc. These little items have the tendency to develop into major headaches, so don't overlook anything.

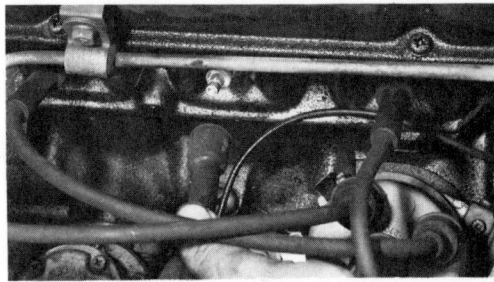

Pull on the spark plug boot not the wire

SPARK PLUGS

A typical spark plug consists of a metal shell surrounding a ceramic insulator. A metal electrode extends downward through the center of the insulator and protrudes a small distance. Located at the end of the plug and attached to the side of the outer metal shell is the side electrode. The side electrode bends in at a 90 degree angle so that its tip is even with, and parallel to, the tip of the center electrode. The distance between these two electrodes (measured in thousandths of an inch) is called the spark plug gap. The spark plug in no way produces a spark but merely provides a gap across which the current can arc. The coil produces anywhere from 20,000 to 40,000 volts, which travels to the distributor where it is distributed through the spark plug wires to the spark plugs. The current passes along the center electrode and

Tune-Up Specifications

When analyzing compression test results, look for uniformity among cylinders, rather than specific pressures.

Year	Model	SPARK PLUG Type	Gap (in.)	DISTRIBUTOR Point Dwell (deg)	Point Gap (in.)	IGNITION TIMING (deg) MT	AT	Fuel Pump Pressure (psi)	IDLE SPEED (rpm) MT	AT①	VALVE CLEARANCE (in.) In	Ex	Percentage of CO at idle
1973	510	BP-6ES	0.028–0.031	49–55	0.018–0.022	5B @ 800	5B @ 650	2.6–3.4	800	650	0.008 cold, 0.010 hot	0.010 cold, 0.012 hot	1.5
1973	1200	BP-5ES	0.032–0.036	49–55	0.020	5B @ 700	5B @ 600	NA	700	600	0.010 cold, 0.014 hot	0.010 cold, 0.014 hot	1.5
1973	610	BP-6ES	0.028–0.031	49–55	0.018–0.022	5B @ 800	5B @ 650	2.6–3.4	800	650	0.008 cold, 0.010 hot	0.010 cold, 0.012 hot	1.5
1974	610	B6ES	0.028–0.031	49–55	0.017–0.022	12B @ 750	12B @ 650	3–3.8	750	650	0.010 hot	0.012 hot	3
1974	710	B6ES	0.028–0.031	49–55	0.017–0.022	12B @ 800	12B @ 650	2.6–3.4	800	650	0.010 hot	0.012 hot	1.5
1974	B210	BP5ES	0.031–0.035	49–55	0.017–0.022	5B @ 800	5B @ 650	3.4	800	640	0.014 hot	0.014 hot	1.5
1975	B210 (Federal)	BP-5ES	0.031–0.035	49–55	0.017–0.022	10B	10B	3.8	700	650	0.014 hot	0.014 hot	2.0
1975	610	BP-6ES	0.031–0.035	49–55	0.017–0.022	12B	12B	3.8	750	650	0.010 hot	0.012 hot	2.0

TUNE-UP AND TROUBLESHOOTING

Year	Model	Spark Plug	Gap	Point Gap/Type	Point Dwell	Timing	Idle Speed (M/T)	Idle Speed (A/T)	Valve Clearance Intake	Valve Clearance Exhaust	Fuel Pump Pressure
1975	710	BP-6ES	0.031–0.035	49–55	0.017–0.022	12B	12B	3.8	750	650	0.010 hot	0.012 hot	2.0
1975	B210 (California)	BP-6ES	0.031–0.035	Electronic	②	10B	10B	3.8	750	650	0.014 hot	0.014 hot	2.0
1975	710, 610 (California)	BP-6ES	0.031–0.035	Electronic	②	12B	12B	3.8	750	650	0.010 cold	0.012 cold	2.0
1976	B210 (Federal)	BP-5ES	0.031–0.035	49–55	0.017–0.022	10B	10B	3.8	700	650	0.014 hot	0.014 hot	2.0
1976	B210 (California)	BP-5ES	0.031–0.035	Electronic	②	10B	10B	3.8	700	650	0.014 hot	0.014 hot	2.0
1976	610, 710 (Federal)	BP-6ES	0.031–0.035	49–55	0.018–0.022	12B	12B	3.8	750	650	0.010 hot	0.012 hot	2.0
1976	610, 710 (California)	BP-6ES	0.031–0.035	Electronic	②	12B	12B	3.8	750	650	0.010 hot	0.012 hot	2.0
1977	B210 (Federal)	BP-5ES	0.039–0.043	49–55	0.018–0.022	10B	8B	3.8	700	650	0.014 hot	0.014 hot	2.0
1977	B210 (California)	BP-5ES	0.039–0.043	Electronic	②	10B	10B	3.8	700	650	0.014 hot	0.014 hot	2.0
1977	710 (Federal)	BP-6ES	0.031–0.035	49–55	0.018–0.022	12B	12B	3.8	750	650	0.010 hot	0.012 hot	2.0
1977–78	F10 (Federal)	BP-5ES	0.039–0.043	49–55②	0.018–0.022 ②	10B	10B	3.8	700	700	0.014 hot	0.014 hot	2.0
1977–78	F10 (California)	BP-5ES	0.039–0.043	Electronic	②	10B	10B	3.8	700	700	0.014 hot	0.014 hot	2.0

Tune-Up Specifications (cont.)

When analyzing compression test results, look for uniformity among cylinders, rather than specific pressures.

Year	Model	SPARK PLUG Type	SPARK PLUG Gap (in.)	DISTRIBUTOR Point Dwell (deg)	DISTRIBUTOR Point Gap (in.)	IGNITION TIMING (deg) MT	IGNITION TIMING (deg) AT	Fuel Pump Pressure (psi)	IDLE SPEED (rpm) MT	IDLE SPEED (rpm) AT①	VALVE CLEARANCE (in.) In	VALVE CLEARANCE (in.) Ex	Percentage of CO at idle
1977–78	200SX (Federal)	BP-6ES	0.039–0.043	49–55②	0.019②	9	12	3.8	600	600	0.010 hot	0.012 hot	1.0
1977–78	810	B6ES	0.039–0.043	Electronic	②	10	10	3.6	700	650	0.010 hot 0.008 cold	0.012 hot 0.010 cold	1.0/0.5 Cal.
1978	510 (Federal)	BP-6ES	0.039–0.043	Electronic	②	9	12	3.8	600	600	0.010 hot	0.012 hot	1.0
1977–78	200SX (California)	BP-6ES	0.039–0.043	Electronic	②	9	12	3.8	600	600	0.010 hot	0.012 hot	1.0
1978	510 (California)	BP-6ES	0.039–0.043	Electronic	②	10	12	3.8	600	600	0.010 hot	0.012 hot	1.0

NOTE: Emission control requires a very precise approach to tune-up. Timing and idle speed are peculiar to the engine and its application, rather than to the engine alone. Data for the particular application is on a sticker in the engine compartment on all late models. If the sticker disagrees with this chart, use the sticker figure. The results of any adjustments or modifications should be checked with a CO meter.

① In Drive
② Some models have electronic ignition—reluctor gap 0.008–0.016 in.

TUNE-UP AND TROUBLESHOOTING

jumps the gap to the side electrode, and, in so doing, ignites the air/fuel mixture in the combustion chamber.

Spark plug life and efficiency depend upon the condition of the engine and the temperatures to which the plug is exposed. Combustion chamber temperatures are affected by many factors such as compression ratio of the engine, air/fuel mixtures, exhaust emission equipment, and the type of driving you do. Spark plugs are designed and classified by number according to the heat range at which they will operate most efficiently.

SPARK PLUG HEAT RANGE

While spark plug heat range has always seemed to be somewhat of a mystical subject for many people, in reality the entire subject is quite simple. Basically, it boils down to this; the amount of heat the plug absorbs is determined by the length of the lower insulator. The longer the insulator (or the farther it extends into the engine), the hotter the plug will operate; the shorter the insulator the cooler it will operate. A plug that absorbs little heat and remains too cool will quickly accumulate deposits of oil and carbon since it is not hot enough to burn them off. This leads to plug fouling and consequently to misfiring. A plug that absorbs too much heat will have no deposits, but, due to the excessive heat, the electrodes will burn away quickly and in some instances, preignition may result. Preignition takes place when plug tips get so hot that they glow sufficiently to ignite the fuel/air mixture before the actual spark occurs. This early ignition will usually cause a pinging during low speeds and heavy loads. In severe cases, the heat may become high enough to start the fuel/air mixture burning throughout the combustion chamber rather than just to the front of the plug as in normal operation. At this time, the piston is rising in the cylinder making its compression stroke. The burning mass is compressed and an explosion results, forcing the piston back down in the cylinder while it is still trying to go up. Obviously, something must go, and it does—pistons are often damaged.

The general rule of thumb for choosing the correct heat range when picking a spark plug is: if most of your driving is long distance, high speed travel, use a colder plug; if most of your driving is stop and go, use a hotter plug. Factory-installed plugs are, of course, compromise plugs, since the factory has no way of knowing what sort of driving you do. It should be noted that most people never have occasion to change their plugs from the factory-recommended heat range.

Removal and Installation

1. Grasp the spark plug boot and pull it straight out. Don't pull on the wire. If the boot(s) are cracked, replace them.
2. Place the spark plug socket firmly on the plug. Turn the spark plug out of the cylinder head in a counterclockwise direction.

NOTE: *The Datsun cylinder head is aluminum, which is easily stripped. Remove plugs only when the engine is cold.*

If removal is difficult, loosen the plug only slightly and drip penetrating oil onto the threads. Allow the oil time enough to work and then unscrew the plug. Proceeding in this manner will prevent damaging the threads in the cylinder head. Be sure to keep the socket straight to avoid breaking the ceramic insulator.

3. Continue and remove the remaining spark plugs.
4. Inspect the plugs using the "Troubleshooting" section illustrations and then clean or discard them according to condition.

New spark plugs come pre-gapped, but double check the setting or reset them if you desire a different gap. The recommended spark plug gap is listed in the "Tune-Up Specifications" chart. Use a

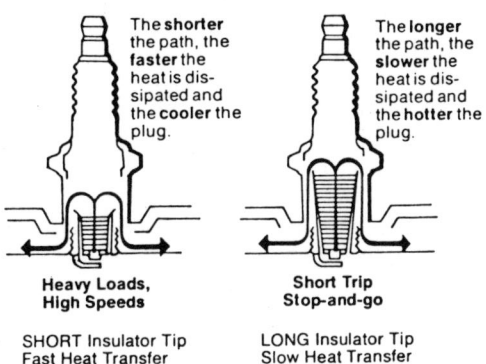

Spark plug heat range

TUNE-UP AND TROUBLESHOOTING

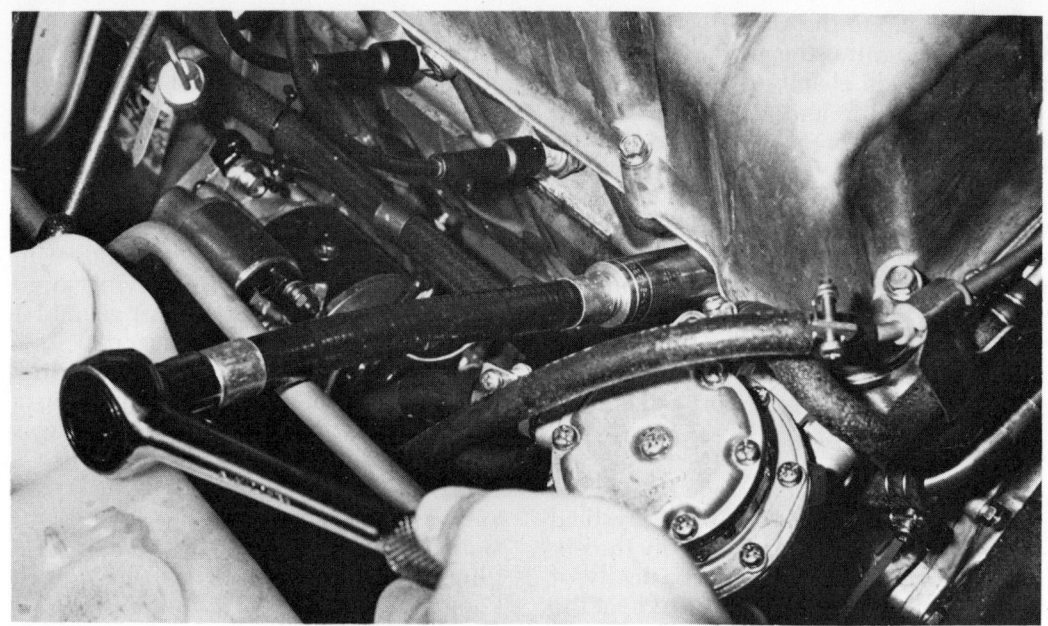

Keep the socket straight on the plug to avoid breaking it

spark plug wire gauge for checking the gap. The wire should pass through the electrode with just a slight drag. Using the electrode bending tool on the end of the gauge, bend the side electrode to ad-

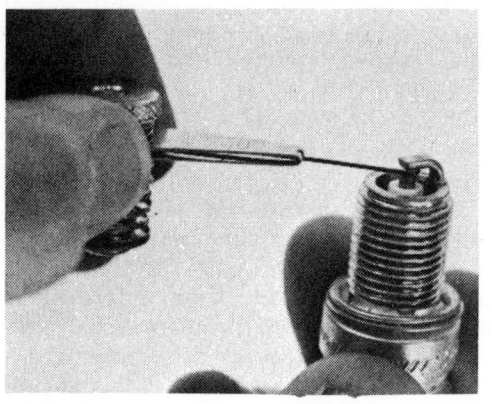

Gap the spark plug with a wire gauge

just the gap. Never attempt to adjust the center electrode. Lightly oil the threads of the replacement plug and install it hand-tight. It is a good practice to use a torque wrench to tighten the spark plugs on any car and especially on the Datsun, since the head is aluminum. Torque the spark plugs to 14–22 ft lbs. Install the ignition wire boots firmly on the spark plugs.

Checking and Replacing Spark Plug Cables

Visually inspect the spark plug cables for burns, cuts, or breaks in the insulation. Check the spark plug boots and the nipples on the distributor cap and coil. Replace any damaged wiring. If no physical damage is obvious, the wires can be checked with an ohmmeter for excessive resistance. Remove the distributor cap and leave the wires connected to the cap. Connect one lead of the ohmmeter to the corresponding electrode inside the cap and the other lead to the spark plug terminal (remove it from the spark plug for the test). Replace any wire which shows over 50,000 ohms. Generally speaking, however, resistance should not run over 35,000 ohms and 50,000 ohms should be considered the outer limits of acceptability. Test the coil wire by connecting the ohmmeter between the center contact in the cap and either of the primary terminals at the coil. If the total resistance of the coil and cable is more than 25,000 ohms, remove the cable from the coil and check the resistance of the cable alone. If the resistance is higher than 15,000 ohms, replace the cable. It should be remembered that wire resistance is a function of length, and that the longer the cable, the greater the resistance. Thus, if the cables on your car are longer than the

TUNE-UP AND TROUBLESHOOTING

factory originals, resistance will be higher and quite possibly outside of these limits.

When installing a new set of spark plug cables, replace the cables one at a time so there will be no mixup. Start by replacing the longest cable first. Install the boot firmly over the spark plug. Route the wire exactly the same as the original. Insert the nipple firmly into the tower on the distributor cap. Repeat the process for each cable.

BREAKER POINTS AND CONDENSER

Different distributors have been used through the years on various models. The following chart should aid you in determining which one you have.

Year	Model	Points	Condenser Location
1973	510	Dual	Outside distributor
	1200	Single	Outside distributor
	610	Dual	Outside distributor
1974-78	All	Single①	Inside distributor

① Except California models with breakerless ignition.

The dual breaker point distributor was used on the 510 and 610 in 1973 as part of the emissions control system. The point sets are wired parallel in the primary ignition circuit. The two sets have a phase difference of 7°, making one a retard set and the other an advance. Ignition timing is advanced or retarded depending on which set is switching. Which set the engine operates on is controlled by a relay which in turn is connected to throttle position, temperature, and transmis-

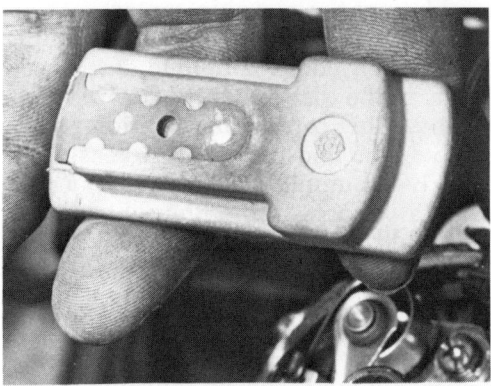

Pull the rotor straight off to remove it

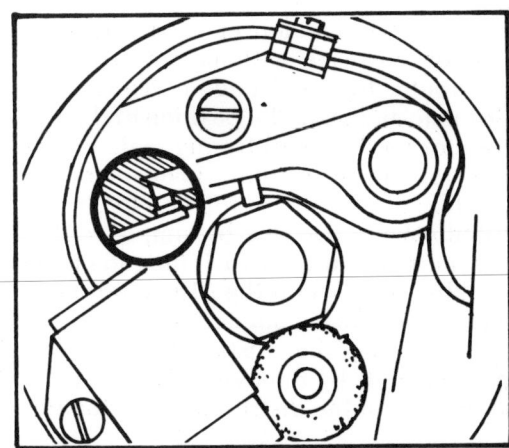

Carefully check the point contact surfaces

sion switches. The dual points are adjusted with a feeler gauge in the same manner as the single point distributor.

Inspection of the Points

1. Disconnect the high-tension wire from the top of the distributor and the coil.
2. Remove the distributor cap by prying off the spring clips on the sides of the cap.
3. Remove the rotor from the distributor shaft by pulling it straight up. Examine the condition of the rotor. If it is cracked or the metal tip is excessively worn or burned, it should be replaced. Clean the tip with fine emery paper.
4. Pry open the contacts of the points with a screwdriver and check the condition of the contacts. If they are excessively worn, burned or pitted, they should be replaced.
5. If the points are in good condition, adjust them and replace the rotor and the distributor cap. If the points need to be replaced, follow the replacement procedure given below.

Replacement of the Breaker Points and Condenser

1. Remove the coil high-tension wire from the top of the distributor cap. Remove the distributor cap and place it out of the way. Remove the rotor from the distributor shaft.
2. On single point distributors, remove the condenser from the distributor body. On early dual-point distributors, you will

TUNE-UP AND TROUBLESHOOTING

find that one condenser is virtually impossible to reach without removing the distributor from the engine. To do this, first note and mark the position of the distributor on the small timing scale on the front of the distributor. Then mark the position of the rotor in relation to the distributor body. Do this by simply replacing the rotor on the distributor shaft and marking the spot on the distributor body where the rotor is pointing.

3. Remove the distributor on dual point models by removing the small bolt at the rear of the distributor. Lift the dis-

Adjusting the point gap

tributor out of the block. It is now possible to remove the rear condenser.

4. On single point distributors, remove the points assembly attaching screws and then remove the points. A magnetic screwdriver or one with a holding mechanism will come in handy here, so that you don't drop a screw into the distributor and have to remove the entire distributor to retrieve it. After the points are removed, wipe off the cam and apply new cam lubricant. If you don't, the points will wear out in a few thousand miles.

5. On dual point distributors, you will probably find it easier to simply remove the points assemblies while the distributor is out of the engine. Install the new points and condensers. You can either set the point gap now or later after you have reinstalled the distributor.

6. On dual point models, install the distributor, making sure the marks made earlier are lined up. Note that the slot for the oil pump drive is tapered and will only fit one way.

7. On single point distributors, slip the new set of points onto the locating dowel and install the screws that hold the assembly onto the plate. Don't tighten them all the way yet, since you'll only have to loosen them to set the point gap.

8. Install the new condenser on single point models and attach the condenser lead to the points.

9. Set the point gap and dwell (see the following sections).

Adjustment of the Breaker Points with a Feeler Gauge

SINGLE POINT DISTRIBUTOR

1. If the contact points of the assembly are not parallel, bend the stationary contact so that they make contact across the entire surface of the contacts. Bend only the stationary bracket part of the point assembly; not the movable contact.

2. Turn the engine until the rubbing block of the points is on one of the high points of the distributor cam. You can do this by either turning the ignition switch to the start position and releasing it quickly ("bumping" the engine) or by using a wrench on the bolt which holds the crankshaft pulley to the crankshaft.

3. Place the correct size feeler gauge between the contacts. Make sure that it is parallel with the contact surfaces.

4. With your free hand, insert a screwdriver into the eccentric adjusting screw, then twist the screwdriver to either in-

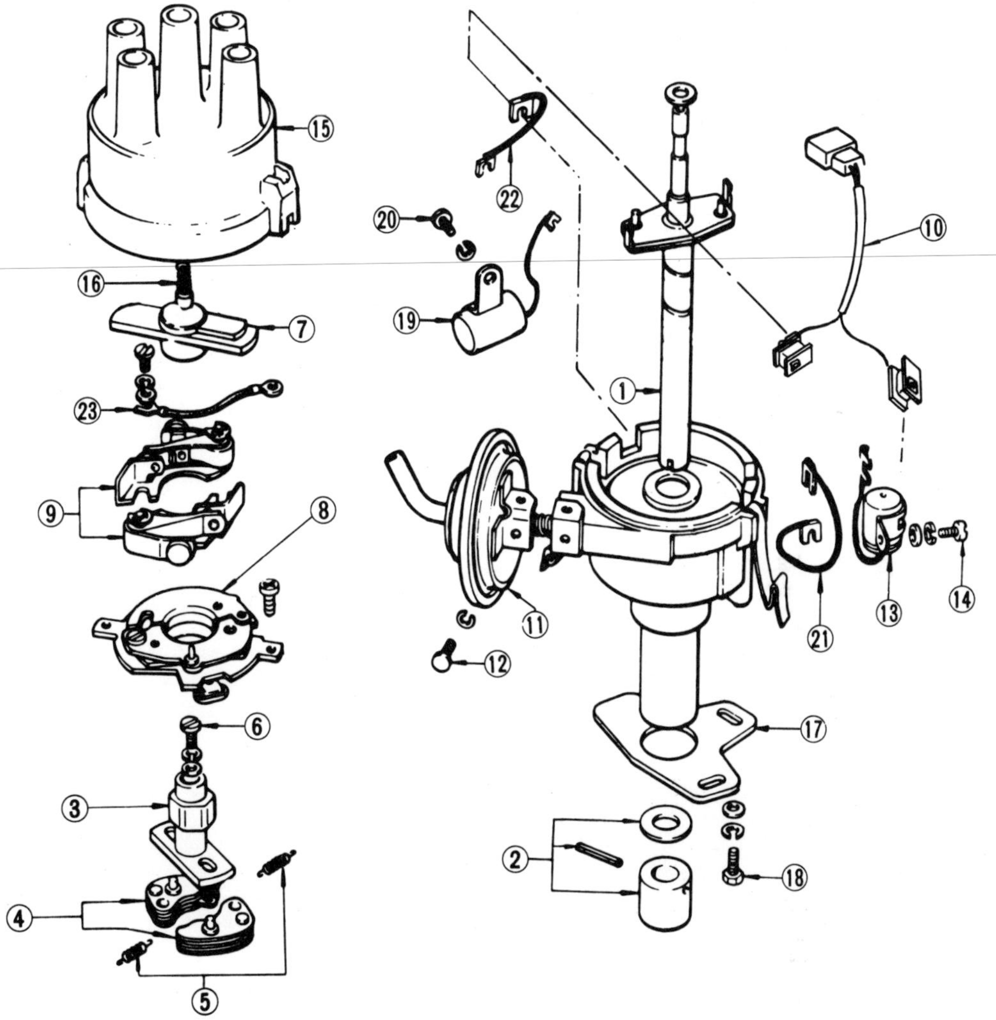

TUNE-UP AND TROUBLESHOOTING

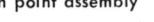

Dual point distributor components (1973—510 and 610)

1. Shaft assembly
2. Collar set assembly
3. Cam assembly
4. Governor weight assembly
5. Governor spring set
6. Screw
7. Rotor
8. Breaker plate
9. Breaker points
10. Connector assembly
11. Vacuum control assembly
12. Screw
13. Condenser
14. Screw
15. Distributor cap
16. Carbon point assembly
17. Retaining plate
18. Bolt
19. Condenser
20. Screw
21. Lead wire
22. Lead wire
23. Ground wire

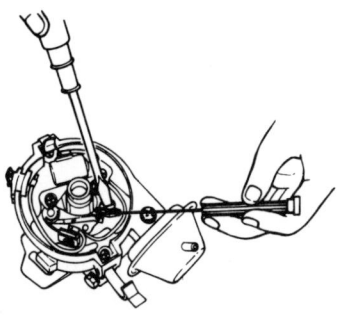

All single point distributor gap is adjusted with the eccentric screw

crease or decrease the gap to the proper setting.

5. Tighten the adjustment lockscrew and recheck the contact gap to make sure that it didn't change when the lockscrew was tightened.

6. Replace the rotor and distributor cap, and the high-tension wire which connnects the top of the distributor and the coil. Make sure that the rotor is firmly seated all the way onto the distributor shaft and that the tab of the rotor is

TUNE-UP AND TROUBLESHOOTING

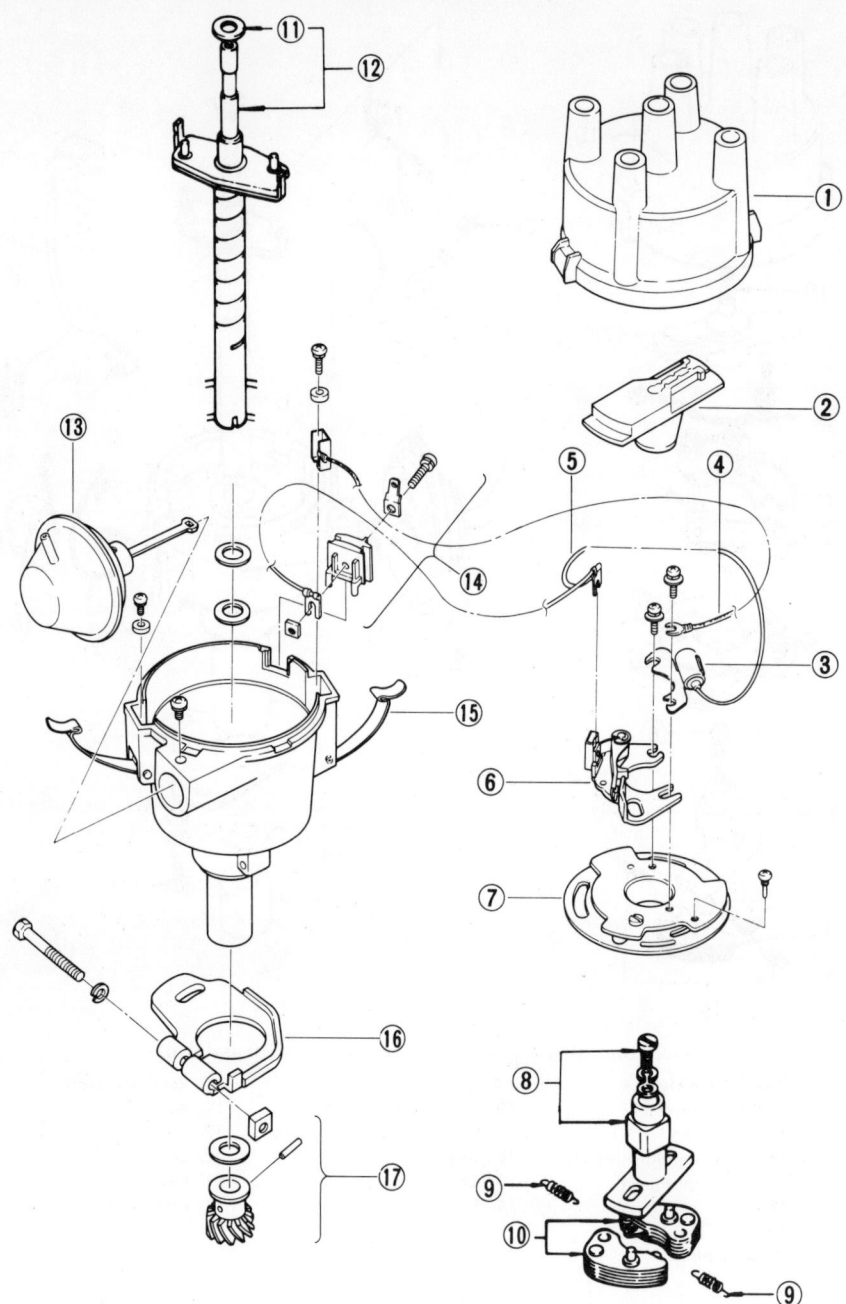

Single point distributor components

1. Cap
2. Rotor
3. Condenser
4. Ground wire
5. Lead wire
6. Breaker points
7. Breaker plate
8. Cam assembly
9. Governor spring
10. Governor weight
11. Thrust washer
12. Shaft assembly
13. Vacuum control assembly
14. Terminal assembly
15. Clamp
16. Retaining plate
17. Gear set

aligned with notch in the shaft. Align the tab in the base of the distributor cap with the notch in the distributor body. Make sure that the cap is firmly seated on the distributor and that the retainer clips are in place. Make sure that the end of the high-tension wire is firmly placed in the top of the distributor and the coil.

TUNE-UP AND TROUBLESHOOTING 27

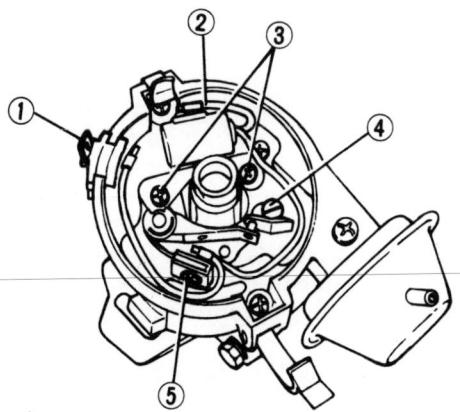

Single point distributor

1. Primary lead terminal
2. Ground lead wire
3. Set screw
4. Adjuster
5. Screw

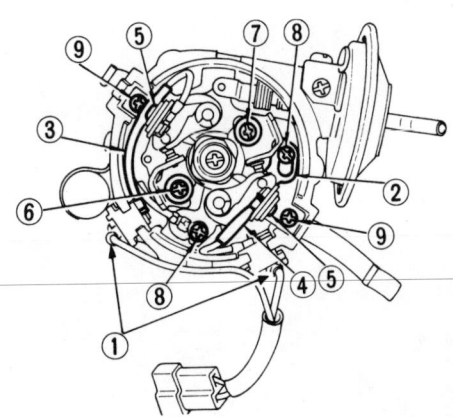

Dual point distributor. Do not disturb screws (8) when replacing or adjusting points.

1. Lead wire terminal set screws
2. Adjuster plate
3. Primary lead wire—advanced points
4. Primary lead wire—retarded points
5. Primary lead wire set screw
6. Set screw—advanced points
7. Set screw—retarded points
8. Adjuster plate set screws
9. Breaker plate set screws

DUAL POINT DISTRIBUTOR

The two sets of breaker points are adjusted with a feeler gauge in the same manner as those in a single point distributor, except that you do the actual adjusting by twisting a screwdriver in the point set notch. Check the "Tune-Up Specifications" chart for the correct setting; both are set to the same opening.

DWELL ANGLE

The dwell angle or cam angle is the number of degrees that the distributor cam rotates while the points are closed. There is an inverse relationship between dwell angle and point gap. Increasing the point gap will decrease the dwell angle and vice versa. Checking the dwell angle with a meter is a far more accurate method of measuring point opening than the feeler gauge method.

After setting the point gap to specification with a feeler gauge as described above, check the dwell angle with a meter. Attach the dwell meter according to the manufacturer's instruction sheet. A typical dwell meter hook-up is illustrated in the "Tune-Up" section at the end of the chapter. The negative lead is grounded and the positive lead is connected to the primary wire terminal which runs from the coil to the distributor. Start the engine, let it idle and reach operating temperature, and observe the dwell on the meter. The reading should fall within the allowable range. If it does not, the gap will have to be reset or the breaker points will have to be replaced.

Adjustment of the Breaker Points with a Dwell Meter

SINGLE POINT DISTRIBUTOR

1. Adjust the points with a feeler gauge as previously described.
2. Connect the dwell meter to the ignition circuit as according to the manufacturer's instructions. One lead of the meter is connected to a ground and the other lead is connected to the distributor post on the coil. An adapter is usually provided for this purpose.

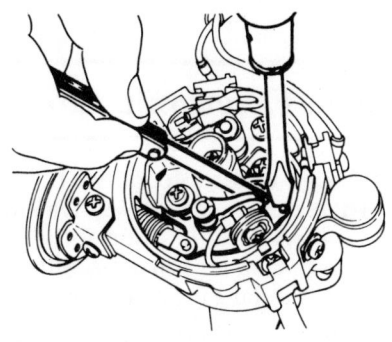

Point gap on the dual point distributor is adjusted by twisting a screwdriver in the notch

TUNE-UP AND TROUBLESHOOTING

Later models have a rubber cap over the distributor terminals

3. If the dwell meter has a set line on it, adjust the meter to zero the indicator.
4. Start the engine.
NOTE: *Be careful when working on any vehicle while the engine is running. Make sure that the transmission is in Neutral and that the parking brake is applied. Keep hands, clothing, tools and the wires of the test instruments clear of the rotating fan blades.*
5. Observe the reading on the dwell meter. If the reading is within the specified range, turn off the engine and remove the dwell meter.
NOTE: *If the meter does not have a scale for 4 cylinder engines, multiply the 8 cylinder reading by two.*
6. If the reading is above the specified range, the breaker point gap is too small. If the reading is below the specified range, the gap is too large. In either case, the engine must be stopped and the gap adjusted in the manner previously covered.
After making the adjustment, start the engine and check the reading on the dwell meter. When the correct reading is obtained, disconnect the dwell meter.
7. Check the adjustment of the ignition timing.

DUAL POINT DISTRIBUTOR

Adjust the point gap of a dual point distributor with a dwell meter as follows:
1. Disconnect the wiring harness of the distributor from the engine wiring harness.
2. Using a jumper wire, connect the black wire of the engine side of the harness to the black wire of the distributor side of the harness (advance points).
3. Start the engine and observe the reading on the dwell meter. Shut the engine off and adjust the points accordingly as previously outlined for single point distributors.
4. Disconnect the jumper wire from the black wire of the distributor side of the wiring harness and connect it to the yellow wire (retard points).
5. Adjust the point gap as necessary.
6. After the dwell of both sets of points is correct, remove the jumper wire and connect the engine-to-distributor wiring harness securely.

Datsun Electronic Ignition

In 1975, in order to cope with California's stricter emissions laws, Datsun introduced electronic ignition for all models sold in that state. For 1978, electronic ignition is standard for all cars in the Datsun lineup.
The Datsun electronic ignition system operates on the same principles as other

TUNE-UP AND TROUBLESHOOTING

Electronic ignition distributor—cap and rotor removed

factory-installed electronic ignition systems. As in other systems, Datsun electronic ignition differs from its conventional counterpart only in the distributor component area. The secondary side of the ignition system is exactly the same as a conventional system.

The components of the electronic ignition system include: the transistor ignition unit (also called an amplifier or an electronic module); a ballast resistor; a reluctor; and a magnetic pickup coil. The function of these components will be discussed in the following paragraph.

The system operates as follows: Instead of coil current being switched on and off by mechanical means (the breaker points), this function is taken over by a transformer (the transistor ignition unit). Inside the distributor, in place of the normal points and condenser, there is a toothed wheel (the reluctor). The reluctor, which resembles a gear slightly, is attached to the distributor shaft and has one tooth for each cylinder in the engine—four teeth for four-cylinder engines and six teeth for six-cylinder engines. When the teeth of the rotating reluctor approach the magnetic pickup coil (which is attached to the distributor base plate), they induce a voltage which tells the externally-mounted amplifier to turn the coil primary off. A timing circuit in the amplifier, which is located in the passenger compartment on either the right or left hand side, will turn the current back on again after the coil field has collapsed. When the ignition switch is on and the reluctor is rotating, the primary current flows through the primary windings of the coil and through the transistor ignition unit to ground. When the current is turned off (by the transistor ignition unit or amplifier), the magnetic field built up in the coil is allowed to collapse, inducing a high voltage in the secondary windings of the coil. This high voltage is then sent through the coil high tension lead to the distributor cap where it is distributed to the spark plugs through the rotor. Dwell, of course, is electronically controlled and non-adjustable.

TUNE-UP AND TROUBLESHOOTING

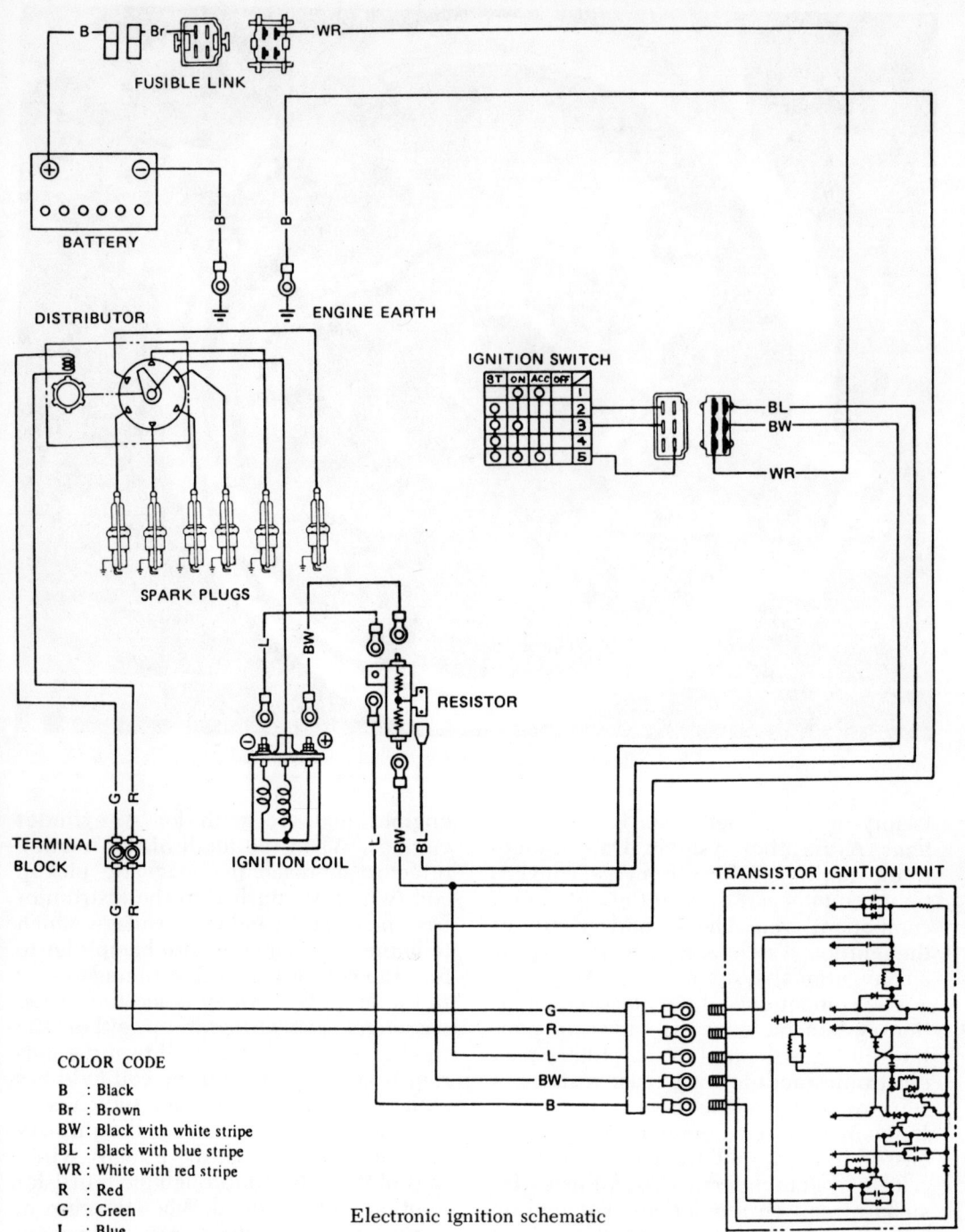

Electronic ignition schematic

COLOR CODE
B : Black
Br : Brown
BW : Black with white stripe
BL : Black with blue stripe
WR : White with red stripe
R : Red
G : Green
L : Blue

Maintenance and adjustment procedures on the electronic ignition system are somewhat simpler than on a conventional system. Since there are no points and condenser to replace at tune-up time, a number of steps have been eliminated. Also, since dwell is electronically controlled, the ignition timing should never need adjustment. However, Datsun still recommends checking the timing at 12,000 mile intervals. The electronic control unit itself, being completely solid-state, should be maintenance-free.

Air Gap Adjustment—Electronic Ignition

The only adjustment Datsun recommends on the electronic ignition system

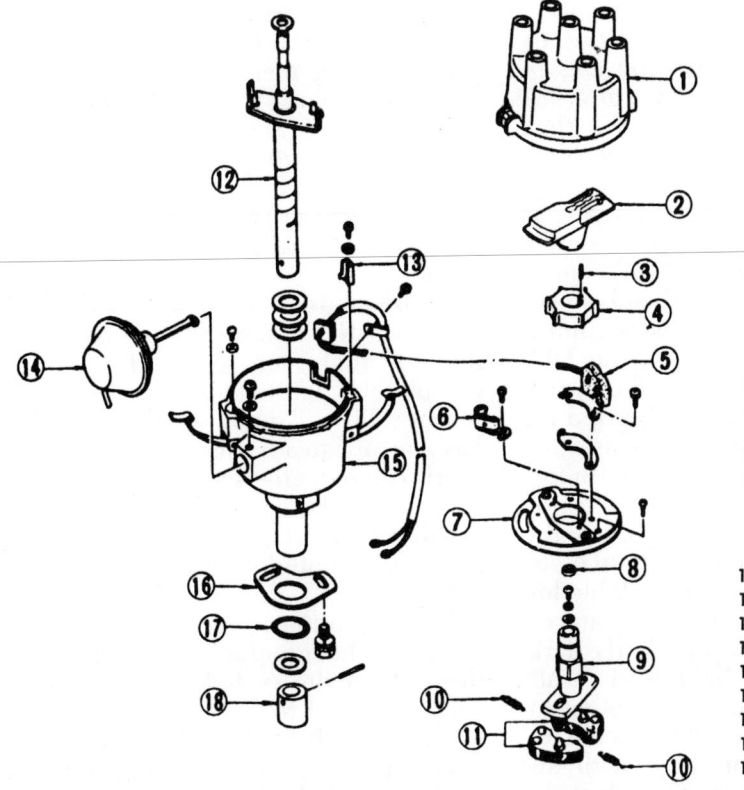

TUNE-UP AND TROUBLESHOOTING 31

1. Cap assembly
2. Rotor head assembly
3. Roll pin
4. Reluctor
5. Pick-up coil
6. Contactor
7. Breaker plate assembly
8. Packing
9. Rotor shaft
10. Governor spring
11. Governor weight
12. Shaft assembly
13. Cap setter
14. Vacuum controller
15. Housing
16. Fixing plate
17. O-ring
18. Collar

Exploded view—electronic ignition distributor

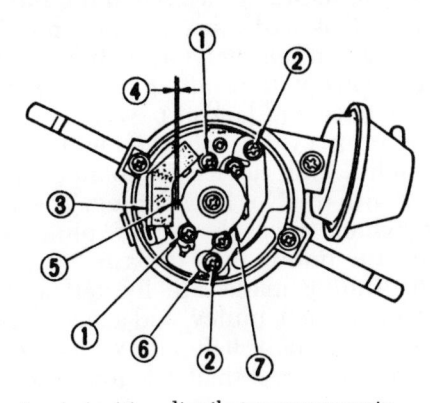

Electronic ignition distributor components

1. Pick-up coil set screws (air gap)
2. Adjuster plate set screws
3. Pick-up coil
4. Air gap
5. Pole piece
6. Adjuster plate
7. Reluctor

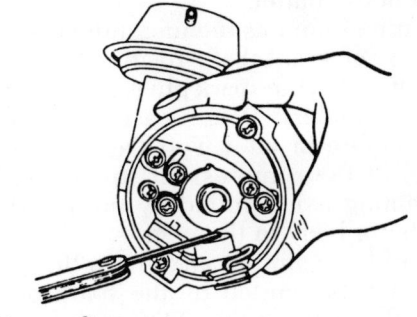

Air gap adjustment

is adjustment of the air gap between the reluctor and the pickup coil. This should be checked, and adjusted, if necessary, at the normal tune-up intervals.

1. Remove the distributor cap and rotor.
2. Using a *non-magnetic* feeler gauge, check the gap between the pickup coil and the reluctor. One of the reluctor teeth and the coil must be aligned. You can do this by bumping the engine over until you get the correct alignment. The correct clearance is 0.008–0.016 in.
3. If the gap needs adjusting, loosen the pickup coil screws and move the pickup coil until the correct clearance is obtained. Tighten the screws.

TUNE-UP AND TROUBLESHOOTING

IGNITION TIMING

CAUTION: *When performing this or any other operation with the engine running, be very careful of the alternator belt and pulleys. Make sure that your timing light wires don't interfere with the belt.*

Ignition timing is an important part of the tune-up. It is always adjusted after the points are gapped (dwell angle changed), since altering the dwell affects the timing. Three basic types of timing lights are available, the neon, the DC, and the AC powered. Of the three, the DC light is the most frequently used by professional tuners. The bright flash put out by the DC light makes the timing marks stand out on even the brightest of days. Another advantage of the DC light is that you don't need to be near an electrical outlet. Neon lights are available for a few dollars, but their weak flash makes it necessary to use them in a fairly dark work area. One neon light lead is attached to the spark plug and the other to the plug wire. The DC light attaches to the spark plug and the wire with an adapter and two clips attach to the battery posts for power. The AC unit is similar, except that the power cable is plugged into a house outlet.

Ignition timing is the measurement, in degrees of crankshaft rotation, of the point at which the spark plugs fire in each of the cylinders. It is measured in degrees before or after Top Dead Center (TDC) of the compression stroke. Ignition timing is controlled by turning the distributor body in the engine.

Ideally, the air/fuel mixture in the cylinder will be ignited by the spark plug just as the piston passes TDC of the compression stroke. If this happens, the piston will be beginning its downward motion of the power stroke just as the compressed and ignited air/fuel mixture starts to expand. The expansion of the air/fuel mixture then forces the piston down on the power stroke and turns the crankshaft.

Because it takes a fraction of a second for the spark plug to ignite the mixture in the cylinder, the spark plug must fire a little before the piston reaches TDC. Otherwise, the mixture will not be completely ignited as the piston passes TDC and the full power of the explosion will not be used by the engine.

The timing measurement is given in degrees of crankshaft rotation before the piston reaches TDC (BTDC). If the setting for the ignition timing is 5° BTDC, the spark plug must fire 5° before each piston reaches TDC. This only holds true, however, when the engine is at idle speed.

As the engine speed increases, the pistons go faster. The spark plugs have to ignite the fuel even sooner if it is to be completely ignited when the piston reaches TDC. To do this, the distributor has a means to advance the timing of the spark as the engine speed increases. This is accomplished by centrifugal weights within the distributor and a vacuum diaphragm, mounted on the side of the distributor.

If the ignition is set too far advanced (BTDC), the ignition and expansion of the fuel in the cylinder will occur too soon and tend to force the piston down while it is still traveling up. This causes engine ping. If the ignition spark is set too far retarded, after TDC (ATDC), the piston will have already passed TDC and started on its way down when the fuel is ignited. This will cause the piston to be forced down for only a portion of its travel. This will result in poor engine performance and lack of power.

The timing is best checked with a timing light. This device is connected in series with the No. 1 spark plug. The current which fires the spark plug also causes the timing light to flash.

The timing marks are located at the front crankshaft pulley and consist of a notch on the crankshaft pulley and a scale of degrees of crankshaft rotation attached to the front cover.

When the engine is running, the timing light is aimed at the marks on the flywheel pulley and the pointer.

Ignition Timing Adjustment

NOTE: *Refer to Chapter 4 "Emission Controls and Fuel System" for the procedure to check and adjust the phase timing of the two sets of points on 1973 models.*

TUNE-UP AND TROUBLESHOOTING

The timing light flash will "stop" the pulley so that you can check ignition timing

1. Set the dwell to the proper specification.
2. Locate the timing marks on the crankshaft pulley and the front of the engine.
3. Clean off the timing marks so that you can see them.
4. Use chalk or white paint to color the mark on the crankshaft pulley and the mark on the scale which will indicate the correct timing when aligned with the notch on the crankshaft pulley.
5. Attach a tachometer to the engine.
6. Attach a timing light to the engine, according to the manufacturer's instructions.
7. Leave the vacuum line connected to the distributor vacuum diaphragm.
8. Check to make sure that all of the wires clear the fan and then start the engine. Allow the engine to reach normal operating temperature.
9. Adjust the idle to the correct setting.

Timing marks—L-series engines

10. Aim the timing light at the timing marks. If the marks that you put on the pulley and the engine are aligned when the light flashes, the timing is correct. Turn off the engine and remove the tachometer and the timing light. If the marks are not in alignment, proceed with the following steps.
11. Turn off the engine.
12. Loosen the distributor lockbolt just enough so that the distributor can be turned with a little effort.
13. Start the engine. Keep the wires of the timing light clear of the fan.
14. With the timing light aimed at the pulley and the marks on the engine, turn the distributor in the direction of rotor rotation to retard the spark, and in the opposite direction of rotor rotation to advance the spark. Align the marks on the pulley and the engine with the flashes of the timing light. Tighten the hold-down bolt.

VALVE LASH

Valve adjustment determines how far the valves enter the cylinder and how long they stay open and closed.

If the valve clearance is too large, part of the lift of the camshaft will be used in removing the excessive clearance. Consequently, the valve will not be opening as far as it should. This condition has two effects: the valve train components will emit a tapping sound as they take up the excessive clearance and the engine will perform poorly because the valves don't open fully and allow the proper amount of gases to flow into and out of the engine.

If the valve clearance is too small, the intake valves and the exhaust valves will open too far and they will not fully seat on the cylinder head when they close. When a valve seats itself on the cylinder head, it does two things: it seals the combustion chamber so that none of the gases in the cylinder escape and it cools itself by transferring some of the heat it absorbs from the combustion in the cylinder to the cylinder head and to the engine's cooling system. If the valve clearance is too small, the engine will run poorly because of the gases escaping from the combustion chamber. The valves will also become overheated and

TUNE-UP AND TROUBLESHOOTING

will warp, since they cannot transfer heat unless they are touching the valve seat in the cylinder head.

NOTE: *While all valve adjustments must be made as accurately as possible, it is better to have the valve adjustment slightly loose than slightly tight, as a burned valve may result from overly tight adjustments.*

Valve Adjustment—1200, B210, and F10

1. Run the engine until it reaches normal operating temperature. Oil temperature, not water temperature, is critical to valve adjustment. With this in mind, make sure the engine is fully warmed up since this is the only way to make sure the parts have reached their full expansion. Generally speaking, this takes around fifteen minutes. After the engine has reached normal operating temperature, shut it off.

2. Purchase a new valve cover gasket before removing the valve cover. The new silicone gasket sealers are just as good or better if you can't find a gasket.

3. Note the location of any hoses or wires which may interfere with valve cover removal, disconnect them and move them aside. Then, remove the bolts which hold the valve cover in place.

4. After the valve cover has been removed, the next step is to get the number one piston at TDC on the compression stroke. There are at least two ways to do it; you can bump the engine over with the starter or turn it over by using a wrench on the front pulley attaching bolt. The easiest way to find TDC is to turn the engine over slowly with a wrench (after first removing no. 1 plug) until the piston is at the top of its stroke and the TDC timing mark on the crankshaft pulley is in alignment with the timing mark pointer. At this point, the valves for no. 1 should be closed.

5. With no. 1 piston at TDC of the compression stroke, check the clearance on valves Nos. 1, 2, 3, and 5 (counting from the front to the rear).

6. To adjust the clearance, loosen the locknut with a wrench and turn the adjuster with a screwdriver while holding the locknut. The correct size feeler gauge should pass with a slight drag between the rocker arm and the valve stem.

7. Turn the crankshaft one full revolution to position the no. 4 piston at TDC of the compression stroke. Adjust valves nos. 4, 6, 7, and 8 in the same manner as the first four.

8. Replace the valve cover.

Valve Adjustment—510, 610, 710, 200SX

1. The valves are adjusted with the engine at normal operating temperature. Oil temperature, and the resultant parts expansion, is much more important than water temperature. Run the engine for at least fifteen minutes to ensure that all the parts have reached their full expansion. After the engine is warmed up, shut it off.

2. Purchase either a new gasket or some silicone gasket seal before removing the camshaft cover. Note the location of any wires and hoses which may interfere with cam cover removal, disconnect them and move them aside. Then remove the bolts which hold the cam cover in place and remove the cam cover.

3. Place a wrench on the crankshaft pulley bolt and turn the engine over until the valves for No. 1 cylinder are closed. When both cam lobes are pointing up,

Adjusting 1200, B210, and F10 valve clearance

Valve lash adjustment—L-series engines

TUNE-UP AND TROUBLESHOOTING

the valves are closed. If you have not done this before, it is a good idea to turn the engine over slowly several times and watch the valve action until you have a clear idea of just when the valve is closed.

4. Check the clearance of the intake and exhaust valves. You can differentiate between them by lining them up with the tubes of the intake and exhaust manifolds. The correct size feeler gauge should pass between the base circle of the cam and the rocker arm with just a slight drag. Be sure the feeler gauge is inserted *straight* and not on an angle.

5. If the valves need adjustment, loosen the locking nut and then adjust the clearance with the adjusting screw. You will probably find it necessary to hold the locking nut while you turn the adjuster. After you have the correct clearance, tighten the locking nut and recheck the clearance. Remember, it's better to have them too loose than too tight, especially exhaust valves.

6. Repeat this procedure until you have checked and/or adjusted all the valves. Keep in mind that all that is necessary is to have the valves closed and the camshaft lobes pointing up. It is not particularly important what stroke the engine is on.

7. Install the cam cover gasket, the cam cover, and any wires and hoses which were removed.

Valve Adjustment—810

The engine must be "overnight" cold before beginning. It must not be operated for about eight hours before adjusting the valves. Then, proceed as follows:

1. Note the locations of all hoses or wires that would interfere with valve cover removal, disconnect them and move them aside. Then, remove the six bolts which hold the valve cover in place.

2. Bump one end of the cover sharply to loosen the gasket and then pull the valve cover off the engine vertically.

3. Crank the engine with the starter until both No. 1 cylinder valves (No. 1 is at the front) are closed (the lobes are pointed upward), and the timing mark on the crankshaft pulley is lined up approximately as it would be when the No. 1 spark plug fires.

4. Adjust the No. 1 cylinder intake valve to 0.008 in. (0.20 mm). First loosen the pivot locking nut and then insert the feeler gauge between the cam and cam follower. Adjust the pivot screw until there is a slight pull on the gauge when it is inserted *straight* between the cam and follower. Then, tighten the locking nut, recheck the adjustment, and correct as necessary.

5. Repeat the procedure for the No. 1 cylinder exhaust valve, but use a 0.010 in. (0.25 mm) gauge.

You can differentiate between the intake and exhaust valves by lining them up with the tubes of the intake and exhaust manifolds.

6. Repeat Steps 4 and 5 for the other cylinders, going in the firing order of 1-5-3-6-2-4. Turn the engine ahead ⅓ turn before adjusting the valves for each cylinder so that the lobes will point upward.

7. Reinstall the valve cover gasket and hoses, start the engine, and operate it until it is fully warmed up.

8. Repeat the entire valve adjustment procedure using the gauges specified in the "Tune-Up" chart, but do not loosen the locking nuts unless the gauge indicates that adjustment is required.

9. When all valves are at hot specifications, clean all traces of old gasket material from the valve cover and the head. Install the new gasket in the valve cover with sealer and install the valve cover. Tighten the valve cover bolts evenly in several stages going around the cover to ensure a good seal. Reconnect all hoses and wires securely and operate the engine to check for leaks.

CARBURETOR

This section contains only tune-up adjustment procedures for carburetors. Descriptions, adjustments, and overhaul procedures for carburetors can be found in Chapter 4.

When the engine in your Datsun is running, the air-fuel mixture from the carburetor is being drawn into the engine by a partial vacuum which is created by the movement of the pistons downward on the intake stroke. The amount of air-fuel mixture that enters into the engine is controlled by the throttle plate(s) in the bottom of the carburetor. When the engine is not running the throttle plate(s)

TUNE-UP AND TROUBLESHOOTING

is closed, completely blocking off the bottom of the carburetor from the inside of the engine. The throttle plates are connected by the throttle linkage to the accelerator pedal in the passenger compartment of the Datsun. When you depress the pedal, you open the throttle plates in the carburetor to admit more air-fuel mixture to the engine.

When the engine is not running, the throttle plates are closed. When the engine is idling, it is necessary to have the throttle plates open slightly. To prevent having to hold your foot on the pedal when the engine is idling, an idle speed adjusting screw was added to the carburetor linkage.

The idle adjusting screw contacts a lever (throttle lever) on the outside of the carburetor. When the screw is turned, it either opens or closes the throttle plates of the carburetor, raising or lowering the idle speed of the engine. This screw is called the curb idle adjusting screw.

Idle Speed and Mixture Adjustment

1. Start the engine and run it until it reaches operating temperature.
2. Allow the engine idle speed to stabilize by running the engine at idle for at least one minute.
3. If it hasn't already been done, check and adjust the ignition timing to the proper setting.
4. Turn off the engine and connect a tachometer to the engine.
5. Remove the air cleaner and start the engine. With the transmission in Neutral, check the idle speed on the tachometer. If the reading on the tachometer is correct, continue on to Step 6. If it is not correct, turn the idle adjusting screw with a screwdriver clockwise to increase the idle speed and counterclockwise to decrease it.
6. With an automatic transmission in Drive (wheels chocked and parking brake applied) and a manual transmission in Neutral, turn the mixture screw out until the engine rpm starts to drop due to an overly rich mixture.
7. Turn the screw in past the starting point until the engine rpm start to drop because of a too lean mixture.
8. Turn the mixture screw back out to the point midway between the two extreme positions where the engine began losing rpm to achieve the fastest and smoothest idle.
9. Adjust the curb idle speed to the proper specification.
10. Remove the tachometer and install the air cleaner.

NOTE: *To be sure that the vehicle complies with emission laws, have the exhaust checked with a "CO" meter. The percentage of CO is given in the "Tune-Up Specifications" chart.*

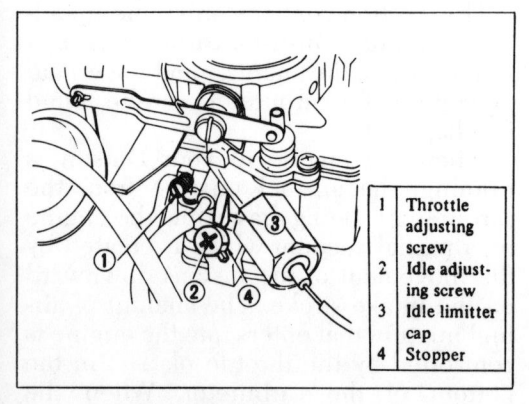

1	Throttle adjusting screw
2	Idle adjusting screw
3	Idle limitter cap
4	Stopper

Carburetor adjusting screws

Mixture screw (arrow). Note limiter tab

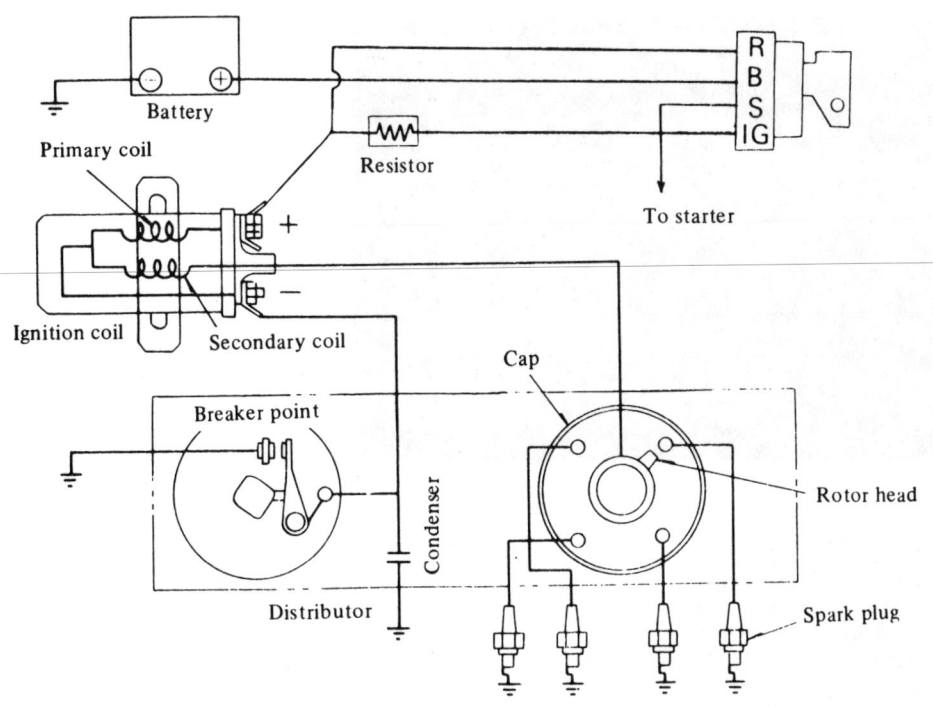

TUNE-UP AND TROUBLESHOOTING

Conventional ignition circuit

ELECTRONIC FUEL INJECTION–810

Idle speed is the only adjustment necessary on these fuel injected cars. Warm the engine to normal temperature and hook-up a tachometer. Automatic transmission cars are adjusted with selector in Drive, so be sure that parking is on and the wheels blocked for safety. Adjust the speed to specifications using the adjusting screw. The idle speed adjusting screw is located in the throttle chamber near the distributor. Idle mixture cannot be set without the use of a CO meter.

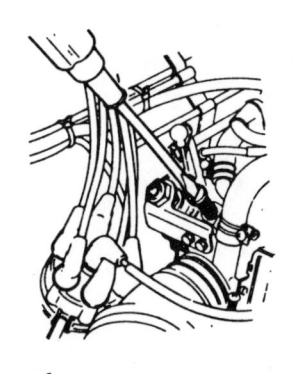

Idle speed screw (arrow)

810 idle speed screw

Trouble-shooting

The following section is designed to aid in the rapid diagnosis of engine problems. The systematic format is used to diagnose problems ranging from engine starting difficulties to the need for engine overhaul. It is assumed that the user is equipped with basic hand tools and test equipment (tach-dwell meter, timing light, voltmeter, and ohmmeter).

Troubleshooting is divided into two sections. The first, *General Diagnosis*, is used to locate the problem area. In the second, *Specific Diagnosis*, the problem is systematically evaluated.

General Diagnosis

PROBLEM: Symptom	Begin diagnosis at Section Two, Number ——
Engine won't start:	
Starter doesn't turn	1.1, 2.1
Starter turns, engine doesn't	2.1
Starter turns engine very slowly	1.1, 2.4
Starter turns engine normally	3.1, 4.1
Starter turns engine very quickly	6.1
Engine fires intermittently	4.1
Engine fires consistently	5.1, 6.1
Engine runs poorly:	
Hard starting	3.1, 4.1, 5.1, 8.1
Rough idle	4.1, 5.1, 8.1
Stalling	3.1, 4.1, 5.1, 8.1
Engine dies at high speeds	4.1, 5.1
Hesitation (on acceleration from standing stop)	5.1, 8.1
Poor pickup	4.1, 5.1, 8.1
Lack of power	3.1, 4.1, 5.1, 8.1
Backfire through the carburetor	4.1, 8.1, 9.1
Backfire through the exhaust	4.1, 8.1, 9.1
Blue exhaust gases	6.1, 7.1
Black exhaust gases	5.1
Running on (after the ignition is shut off)	3.1, 8.1
Susceptible to moisture	4.1
Engine misfires under load	4.1, 7.1, 8.4, 9.1
Engine misfires at speed	4.1, 8.4
Engine misfires at idle	3.1, 4.1, 5.1, 7.1, 8.4

PROBLEM: Symptom	Probable Cause
Engine noises: ①	
Metallic grind while starting	Starter drive not engaging completely
Constant grind or rumble	*Starter drive not releasing, worn main bearings
Constant knock	Worn connecting rod bearings
Knock under load	Fuel octane too low, worn connecting rod bearings
Double knock	Loose piston pin
Metallic tap	*Collapsed or sticky valve lifter, excessive valve clearance, excessive end play in a rotating shaft
Scrape	*Fan belt contacting a stationary surface
Tick while starting	S.U. electric fuel pump (normal), starter brushes
Constant tick	*Generator brushes, shreaded fan belt
Squeal	*Improperly tensioned fan belt
Hiss or roar	*Steam escaping through a leak in the cooling system or the radiator overflow vent
Whistle	*Vacuum leak
Wheeze	Loose or cracked spark plug

①—It is extremely difficult to evaluate vehicle noises. While the above are general definitions of engine noises, those starred (*) should be considered as possibly originating elsewhere in the car. To aid diagnosis, the following list considers other potential sources of these sounds.

Metallic grind:
Throwout bearing; transmission gears, bearings, or synchronizers; differential bearings, gears; something metallic in contact with brake drum or disc.

Metallic tap:
U-joints; fan-to-radiator (or shroud) contact.

Scrape:
Brake shoe or pad dragging; tire to body contact; suspension contacting undercarriage or exhaust; something non-metallic contacting brake shoe or drum.

Tick:
Transmission gears; differential gears; lack of radio suppression; resonant vibration of body panels; windshield wiper motor or transmission; heater motor and blower.

Squeal:
Brake shoe or pad not fully releasing; tires (excessive wear, uneven wear, improper inflation); front or rear wheel alignment (most commonly due to improper toe-in).

Hiss or whistle:
Wind leaks (body or window); heater motor and blower fan.

Roar:
Wheel bearings; wind leaks (body and window).

38

TUNE-UP AND TROUBLESHOOTING

Specific Diagnosis

This section is arranged so that following each test, instructions are given to proceed to another, until a problem is diagnosed.

INDEX

Group		Topic
1	*	Battery
2	*	Cranking system
3	*	Primary electrical system
4	*	Secondary electrical system
5	*	Fuel system
6	*	Engine compression
7	**	Engine vacuum
8	**	Secondary electrical system
9	**	Valve train
10	**	Exhaust system
11	**	Cooling system
12	**	Engine lubrication

*—The engine need not be running.
**—The engine must be running.

SAMPLE SECTION

Test and Procedure	Results and Indications	Proceed to
4.1—Check for spark: Hold each spark plug wire approximately ¼" from ground with gloves or a heavy, dry rag. Crank the engine and observe the spark.	→ If no spark is evident:	→ 4.2
	→ If spark is good in some cases:	→ 4.3
	→ If spark is good in all cases:	→ 4.6

DIAGNOSIS

1.1—Inspect the battery visually for case condition (corrosion, cracks) and water level.	If case is cracked, replace battery:	1.4
	If the case is intact, remove corrosion with a solution of baking soda and water (CAUTION: *do not get the solution into the battery*), and fill with water:	1.2
1.2—Check the battery cable connections: Insert a screwdriver between the battery post and the cable clamp. Turn the headlights on high beam, and observe them as the screwdriver is gently twisted to ensure good metal to metal contact. *Testing battery cable connections using a screwdriver*	If the lights brighten, remove and clean the clamp and post; coat the post with petroleum jelly, install and tighten the clamp:	1.4
	If no improvement is noted:	1.3
1.3—Test the state of charge of the battery using an individual cell tester or hydrometer. Spec. Grav. Reading — Charged Condition 1.260-1.280 — Fully Charged 1.230-1.250 — Three Quarter Charged 1.200-1.220 — One Half Charged 1.170-1.190 — One Quarter Charged 1.140-1.160 — Just About Flat 1.110-1.130 — All The Way Down *State of battery charge* *The effect of temperature on the specific gravity of battery electrolyte*	If indicated, charge the battery. NOTE: *If no obvious reason exists for the low state of charge (i.e., battery age, prolonged storage), the charging system should be tested*:	1.4

Test and Procedure	Results and Indications	Proceed to
1.4—Visually inspect battery cables for cracking, bad connection to ground, or bad connection to starter.	If necessary, tighten connections or replace the cables:	2.1

Tests in Group 2 are performed with coil high tension lead disconnected to prevent accidental starting.

Test and Procedure	Results and Indications	Proceed to
2.1—Test the starter motor and solenoid: Connect a jumper from the battery post of the solenoid (or relay) to the starter post of the solenoid (or relay).	If starter turns the engine normally:	2.2
	If the starter buzzes, or turns the engine very slowly:	2.4
	If no response, replace the solenoid (or relay). If the starter turns, but the engine doesn't, ensure that the flywheel ring gear is intact. If the gear is undamaged, replace the starter drive.	3.1 3.1
2.2—Determine whether ignition override switches are functioning properly (clutch start switch, neutral safety switch), by connecting a jumper across the switch(es), and turning the ignition switch to "start".	If starter operates, adjust or replace switch:	3.1
	If the starter doesn't operate:	2.3
2.3—Check the ignition switch "start" position: Connect a 12V test lamp between the starter post of the solenoid (or relay) and ground. Turn the ignition switch to the "start" position, and jiggle the key.	If the lamp doesn't light when the switch is turned, check the ignition switch for loose connections, cracked insulation, or broken wires. Repair or replace as necessary:	3.1
	If the lamp flickers when the key is jiggled, replace the ignition switch.	3.3

Checking the ignition switch "start" position

Test and Procedure	Results and Indications	Proceed to
2.4—Remove and bench test the starter, according to specifications in the car section.	If the starter does not meet specifications, repair or replace as needed:	3.1
	If the starter is operating properly:	2.5
2.5—Determine whether the engine can turn freely: Remove the spark plugs, and check for water in the cylinders. Check for water on the dipstick, or oil in the radiator. Attempt to turn the engine using an 18" flex drive and socket on the crankshaft pulley nut or bolt.	If the engine will turn freely only with the spark plugs out, and hydrostatic lock (water in the cylinders) is ruled out, check valve timing:	9.2
	If engine will not turn freely, and it is known that the clutch and transmission are free, the engine must be disassembled for further evaluation:	Next Chapter

TUNE-UP AND TROUBLESHOOTING 41

Tests and Procedures	Results and Indications	Proceed to
3.1—Check the ignition switch "on" position: Connect a jumper wire between the distributor side of the coil and ground, and a 12V test lamp between the switch side of the coil and ground. Remove the high tension lead from the coil. Turn the ignition switch on and jiggle the key.	If the lamp lights:	3.2
	If the lamp flickers when the key is jiggled, replace the ignition switch:	3.3
	If the lamp doesn't light, check for loose or open connections. If none are found, remove the ignition switch and check for continuity. If the switch is faulty, replace it:	3.3

Checking the ignition switch "on" position

3.2—Check the ballast resistor or resistance wire for an open circuit, using an ohmmeter.	Replace the resistor or the resistance wire if the resistance is zero.	3.3
3.3—Visually inspect the breaker points for burning, pitting, or excessive wear. Gray coloring of the point contact surfaces is normal. Rotate the crankshaft until the contact heel rests on a high point of the distributor cam, and adjust the point gap to specifications.	If the breaker points are intact, clean the contact surfaces with fine emery cloth, and adjust the point gap to specifications. If pitted or worn, replace the points and condenser, and adjust the gap to specifications: NOTE: *Always lubricate the distributor cam according to manufacturer's recommendations when servicing the breaker points.*	3.4
3.4—Connect a dwell meter between the distributor primary lead and ground. Crank the engine and observe the point dwell angle.	If necessary, adjust the point dwell angle: NOTE: *Increasing the point gap decreases the dwell angle, and vice-versa.*	3.6
	If dwell meter shows little or no reading:	3.5

Dwell meter hook-up

Dwell angle

| 3.5—Check the condenser for short: Connect an ohmmeter across the condenser body and the pigtail lead. | If any reading other than infinite resistance is noted, replace the condenser: | 3.6 |

Checking the condenser for short

TUNE-UP AND TROUBLESHOOTING

Test and Procedure	Results and Indications	Proceed to
3.6—Test the coil primary resistance: Connect an ohmmeter across the coil primary terminals, and read the resistance on the low scale. Note whether an external ballast resistor or resistance wire is utilized. *Testing the coil primary resistance*	Coils utilizing ballast resistors or resistance wires should have approximately 1.0Ω resistance; coils with internal resistors should have approximately 4.0Ω resistance. If values far from the above are noted, replace the coil:	4.1
4.1—Check for spark: Hold each spark plug wire approximately $1/4''$ from ground with gloves or a heavy, dry rag. Crank the engine, and observe the spark.	If no spark is evident: If spark is good in some cylinders: If spark is good in all cylinders:	4.2 4.3 4.6
4.2—Check for spark at the coil high tension lead: Remove the coil high tension lead from the distributor and position it approximately $1/4''$ from ground. Crank the engine and observe spark. CAUTION: *This test should not be performed on cars equipped with transistorized ignition.*	If the spark is good and consistent: If the spark is good but intermittent, test the primary electrical system starting at 3.3: If the spark is weak or non-existent, replace the coil high tension lead, clean and tighten all connections and retest. If no improvement is noted:	4.3 3.3 4.4

4.3—Visually inspect the distributor cap and rotor for burned or corroded contacts, cracks, carbon tracks, or moisture. Also check the fit of the rotor on the distributor shaft (where applicable).	If moisture is present, dry thoroughly, and retest per 4.1:
	If burned or excessively corroded contacts, cracks, or carbon tracks are noted, replace the defective part(s) and retest per 4.1:
	If the rotor and cap appear intact, or are only slightly corroded, clean the contacts thoroughly (including the cap towers and spark plug wire ends) and retest per 4.1:
	  If the spark is good in all cases:
	  If the spark is poor in all cases:
		4.1
		
		4.1
		
		4.6
		4.5

4.4—Check the coil secondary resistance: Connect an ohmmeter across the distributor side of the coil and the coil tower. Read the resistance on the high scale of the ohmmeter. *Testing the coil secondary resistance*	The resistance of a satisfactory coil should be between $4K\Omega$ and $10K\Omega$. If the resistance is considerably higher (i.e., $40K\Omega$) replace the coil, and retest per 4.1: NOTE: *This does not apply to high performance coils.*	4.1

TUNE-UP AND TROUBLESHOOTING 43

Test and Procedure	Results and Indications	Proceed to
4.5—Visually inspect the spark plug wires for cracking or brittleness. Ensure that no two wires are positioned so as to cause induction firing (adjacent and parallel). Remove each wire, one by one, and check resistance with an ohmmeter.	Replace any cracked or brittle wires. If any of the wires are defective, replace the entire set. Replace any wires with excessive resistance (over 8000Ω per foot for suppression wire), and separate any wires that might cause induction firing.	4.6
4.6—Remove the spark plugs, noting the cylinders from which they were removed, and evaluate according to the chart below.	See below.	See below.

	Condition	Cause	Remedy	Proceed to
	Electrodes eroded, light brown deposits.	Normal wear. Normal wear is indicated by approximately .001″ wear per 1000 miles.	Clean and regap the spark plug if wear is not excessive: Replace the spark plug if excessively worn:	4.7
	Carbon fouling (black, dry, fluffy deposits).	If present on one or two plugs:		
		Faulty high tension lead(s).	Test the high tension leads:	4.5
		Burnt or sticking valve(s).	Check the valve train: (Clean and regap the plugs in either case.)	9.1
		If present on most or all plugs: Overly rich fuel mixture, due to restricted air filter, improper carburetor adjustment, improper choke or heat riser adjustment or operation.	Check the fuel system:	5.1
	Oil fouling (wet black deposits)	Worn engine components. NOTE: *Oil fouling may occur in new or recently rebuilt engines until broken in.*	Check engine vacuum and compression: Replace with new spark plug	6.1
	Lead fouling (gray, black, tan, or yellow deposits, which appear glazed or cinder-like).	Combustion by-products.	Clean and regap the plugs: (Use plugs of a different heat range if the problem recurs.)	4.7

TUNE-UP AND TROUBLESHOOTING

Condition	Cause	Remedy	Proceed to
Gap bridging (deposits lodged between the electrodes).	Incomplete combustion, or transfer of deposits from the combustion chamber.	Replace the spark plugs:	4.7
Overheating (burnt electrodes, and extremely white insulator with small black spots).	Ignition timing advanced too far.	Adjust timing to specifications:	8.2
	Overly lean fuel mixture.	Check the fuel system:	5.1
	Spark plugs not seated properly.	Clean spark plug seat and install a new gasket washer: (Replace the spark plugs in all cases.)	4.7
Fused spot deposits on the insulator.	Combustion chamber blow-by.	Clean and regap the spark plugs:	4.7
Pre-ignition (melted or severely burned electrodes, blistered or cracked insulators, or metallic deposits on the insulator).	Incorrect spark plug heat range.	Replace with plugs of the proper heat range:	4.7
	Ignition timing advanced too far.	Adjust timing to specifications:	8.2
	Spark plugs not being cooled efficiently.	Clean the spark plug seat, and check the cooling system:	11.1
	Fuel mixture too lean.	Check the fuel system:	5.1
	Poor compression.	Check compression:	6.1
	Fuel grade too low.	Use higher octane fuel:	4.7

Test and Procedure	Results and Indications	Proceed to
4.7—Determine the static ignition timing. Using the crankshaft pulley timing marks as a guide, locate top dead center on the compression stroke of the number one cylinder.	The rotor should be pointing toward the no. 1 tower in the distributor cap, and the armature spoke for that cylinder should be lined up with the stator.	4.8
4.8—Check coil polarity: Connect a voltmeter negative lead to the coil high tension lead, and the positive lead to ground (NOTE: *reverse the hook-up for positive ground cars*). Crank the engine momentarily. **Checking coil polarity**	If the voltmeter reads up-scale, the polarity is correct:	5.1
	If the voltmeter reads down-scale, reverse the coil polarity (switch the primary leads):	5.1

TUNE-UP AND TROUBLESHOOTING

Test and Procedure	Results and Indications	Proceed to
5.1—Determine that the air filter is functioning efficiently: Hold paper elements up to a strong light, and attempt to see light through the filter.	Clean permanent air filters in gasoline (or manufacturer's recommendation), and allow to dry. Replace paper elements through which light cannot be seen:	5.2
5.2—Determine whether a flooding condition exists: Flooding is identified by a strong gasoline odor, and excessive gasoline present in the throttle bore(s) of the carburetor.	If flooding is not evident: If flooding is evident, permit the gasoline to dry for a few moments and restart. If flooding doesn't recur: If flooding is persistant:	5.3 5.6 5.5
5.3—Check that fuel is reaching the carburetor: Detach the fuel line at the carburetor inlet. Hold the end of the line in a cup (not styrofoam), and crank the engine.	If fuel flows smoothly: If fuel doesn't flow (NOTE: *Make sure that there is fuel in the tank*), or flows erratically:	5.6 5.4
5.4—Test the fuel pump: Disconnect all fuel lines from the fuel pump. Hold a finger over the input fitting, crank the engine (with electric pump, turn the ignition or pump on); and feel for suction.	If suction is evident, blow out the fuel line to the tank with low pressure compressed air until bubbling is heard from the fuel filler neck. Also blow out the carburetor fuel line (both ends disconnected): If no suction is evident, replace or repair the fuel pump: NOTE: *Repeated oil fouling of the spark plugs, or a no-start condition, could be the result of a ruptured vacuum booster pump diaphragm, through which oil or gasoline is being drawn into the intake manifold (where applicable).*	5.6 5.6
5.5—Check the needle and seat: Tap the carburetor in the area of the needle and seat.	If flooding stops, a gasoline additive (e.g., Gumout) will often cure the problem: If flooding continues, check the fuel pump for excessive pressure at the carburetor (according to specifications). If the pressure is normal, the needle and seat must be removed and checked, and/or the float level adjusted:	5.6 5.6
5.6—Test the accelerator pump by looking into the throttle bores while operating the throttle.	If the accelerator pump appears to be operating normally: If the accelerator pump is not operating, the pump must be reconditioned. Where possible, service the pump with the carburetor(s) installed on the engine. If necessary, remove the carburetor. Prior to removal:	5.7 5.7
5.7—Determine whether the carburetor main fuel system is functioning: Spray a commercial starting fluid into the carburetor while attempting to start the engine.	If the engine starts, runs for a few seconds, and dies: If the engine doesn't start:	5.8 6.1

TUNE-UP AND TROUBLESHOOTING

Test and Procedures	Results and Indications	Proceed to
5.8—Uncommon fuel system malfunctions: See below:	If the problem is solved: If the problem remains, remove and recondition the carburetor.	6.1

Condition	Indication	Test	Usual Weather Conditions	Remedy
Vapor lock	Car will not restart shortly after running.	Cool the components of the fuel system until the engine starts.	Hot to very hot	Ensure that the exhaust manifold heat control valve is operating. Check with the vehicle manufacturer for the recommended solution to vapor lock on the model in question.
Carburetor icing	Car will not idle, stalls at low speeds.	Visually inspect the throttle plate area of the throttle bores for frost.	High humidity, 32-40° F.	Ensure that the exhaust manifold heat control valve is operating, and that the intake manifold heat riser is not blocked.
Water in the fuel	Engine sputters and stalls; may not start.	Pump a small amount of fuel into a glass jar. Allow to stand, and inspect for droplets or a layer of water.	High humidity, extreme temperature changes.	For droplets, use one or two cans of commercial gas dryer (Dry Gas) For a layer of water, the tank must be drained, and the fuel lines blown out with compressed air.

Test and Procedure	Results and Indications	Proceed to
6.1—Test engine compression: Remove all spark plugs. Insert a compression gauge into a spark plug port, crank the engine to obtain the maximum reading, and record.	If compression is within limits on all cylinders: If gauge reading is extremely low on all cylinders: If gauge reading is low on one or two cylinders: (If gauge readings are identical and low on two or more adjacent cylinders, the head gasket must be replaced.)	7.1 6.2 6.2

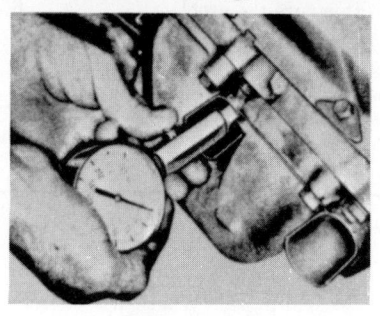

Testing compression
(© Chevrolet Div. G.M. Corp.)

Compression pressure limits
(© Buick Div. G.M. Corp.)

Maxi. Press. Lbs. Sq. In.	Min. Press. Lbs. Sq. In.	Maxi. Press. Lbs. Sq. In.	Min. Press. Lbs. Sq. In.	Max. Press. Lbs. Sq. In.	Min. Press. Lbs. Sq. In.	Max. Press. Lbs. Sq. In.	Min. Press. Lbs. Sq. In.
134	101	162	121	188	141	214	160
136	102	164	123	190	142	216	162
138	104	166	124	192	144	218	163
140	105	168	126	194	145	220	165
142	107	170	127	196	147	222	166
146	110	172	129	198	148	224	168
148	111	174	131	200	150	226	169
150	113	176	132	202	151	228	171
152	114	178	133	204	153	230	172
154	115	180	135	206	154	232	174
156	117	182	136	208	156	234	175
158	118	184	138	210	157	236	177
160	120	186	140	212	158	238	178

TUNE-UP AND TROUBLESHOOTING 47

Test and Procedure	Results and Indications	Proceed to
6.2—Test engine compression (wet): Squirt approximately 30 cc. of engine oil into each cylinder, and retest per 6.1.	If the readings improve, worn or cracked rings or broken pistons are indicated:	Next Chapter
	If the readings do not improve, burned or excessively carboned valves or a jumped timing chain are indicated: NOTE: *A jumped timing chain is often indicated by difficult cranking.*	7.1
7.1—Perform a vacuum check of the engine: Attach a vacuum gauge to the intake manifold beyond the throttle plate. Start the engine, and observe the action of the needle over the range of engine speeds.	See below.	See below

	Reading	Indications	Proceed to
	Steady, from 17-22 in. Hg.	Normal.	8.1
	Low and steady.	Late ignition or valve timing, or low compression:	6.1
	Very low	Vacuum leak:	7.2
	Needle fluctuates as engine speed increases.	Ignition miss, blown cylinder head gasket, leaking valve or weak valve spring:	6.1, 8.3
	Gradual drop in reading at idle.	Excessive back pressure in the exhaust system:	10.1
	Intermittent fluctuation at idle.	Ignition miss, sticking valve:	8.3, 9.1
	Drifting needle.	Improper idle mixture adjustment, carburetors not synchronized (where applicable), or minor intake leak. Synchronize the carburetors, adjust the idle, and retest. If the condition persists:	7.2
	High and steady.	Early ignition timing:	8.2

TUNE-UP AND TROUBLESHOOTING

Test and Procedure	Results and Indications	Proceed to
7.2—Attach a vacuum gauge per 7.1, and test for an intake manifold leak. Squirt a small amount of oil around the intake manifold gaskets, carburetor gaskets, plugs and fittings. Observe the action of the vacuum gauge.	If the reading improves, replace the indicated gasket, or seal the indicated fitting or plug: If the reading remains low:	8.1 7.3
7.3—Test all vacuum hoses and accessories for leaks as described in 7.2. Also check the carburetor body (dashpots, automatic choke mechanism, throttle shafts) for leaks in the same manner.	If the reading improves, service or replace the offending part(s): If the reading remains low:	8.1 6.1
8.1—Remove the distributor cap and check to make sure that the armature turns when the engine is cranked. Visually inspect the distributor components.	Clean, tighten or replace any components which appear defective.	8.2
8.2—Connect a timing light (per manufacturer's recommendation) and check the dynamic ignition timing. Disconnect and plug the vacuum hose(s) to the distributor if specified, start the engine, and observe the timing marks at the specified engine speed.	If the timing is not correct, adjust to specifications by rotating the distributor in the engine: (Advance timing by rotating distributor opposite normal direction of rotor rotation, retard timing by rotating distributor in same direction as rotor rotation.)	8.3
8.3—Check the operation of the distributor advance mechanism(s): To test the mechanical advance, disconnect all but the mechanical advance, and observe the timing marks with a timing light as the engine speed is increased from idle. If the mark moves smoothly, without hesitation, it may be assumed that the mechanical advance is functioning properly. To test vacuum advance and/or retard systems, alternately crimp and release the vacuum line, and observe the timing mark for movement. If movement is noted, the system is operating.	If the systems are functioning: If the systems are not functioning, remove the distributor, and test on a distributor tester:	8.4 8.4
8.4—Locate an ignition miss: With the engine running, remove each spark plug wire, one by one, until one is found that doesn't cause the engine to roughen and slow down.	When the missing cylinder is identified:	4.1

TUNE-UP AND TROUBLESHOOTING

Test and Procedure	Results and Indications	Proceed to
9.1—Evaluate the valve train: Remove the valve cover, and ensure that the valves are adjusted to specifications. A mechanic's stethoscope may be used to aid in the diagnosis of the valve train. By pushing the probe on or near push rods or rockers, valve noise often can be isolated. A timing light also may be used to diagnose valve problems. Connect the light according to manufacturer's recommendations, and start the engine. Vary the firing moment of the light by increasing the engine speed (and therefore the ignition advance), and moving the trigger from cylinder to cylinder. Observe the movement of each valve.	See below	See below

Observation	Probable Cause	Remedy	Proceed to
Metallic tap heard through the stethoscope.	Sticking hydraulic lifter or excessive valve clearance.	Adjust valve. If tap persists, remove and replace the lifter:	10.1
Metallic tap through the stethoscope, able to push the rocker arm (lifter side) down by hand.	Collapsed valve lifter.	Remove and replace the lifter:	10.1
Erratic, irregular motion of the valve stem.*	Sticking valve, burned valve.	Recondition the valve and/or valve guide:	Next Chapter
Eccentric motion of the pushrod at the rocker arm.*	Bent pushrod.	Replace the pushrod:	10.1
Valve retainer bounces as the valve closes.*	Weak valve spring or damper.	Remove and test the spring and damper. Replace if necessary:	10.1

*—When observed with a timing light.

Test and Procedure	Results and Indications	Proceed to
9.2—Check the valve timing: Locate top dead center of the No. 1 piston, and install a degree wheel or tape on the crankshaft pulley or damper with zero corresponding to an index mark on the engine. Rotate the crankshaft in its direction of rotation, and observe the opening of the No. 1 cylinder intake valve. The opening should correspond with the correct mark on the degree wheel according to specifications.	If the timing is not correct, the timing cover must be removed for further investigation:	

TUNE-UP AND TROUBLESHOOTING

Test and Procedure	Results and Indications	Proceed to
10.1—Determine whether the exhaust manifold heat control valve is operating: Operate the valve by hand to determine whether it is free to move. If the valve is free, run the engine to operating temperature and observe the action of the valve, to ensure that it is opening.	If the valve sticks, spray it with a suitable solvent, open and close the valve to free it, and retest. If the valve functions properly: If the valve does not free, or does not operate, replace the valve:	 10.2 10.2
10.2—Ensure that there are no exhaust restrictions: Visually inspect the exhaust system for kinks, dents, or crushing. Also note that gasses are flowing freely from the tailpipe at all engine speeds, indicating no restriction in the muffler or resonator.	Replace any damaged portion of the system:	11.1
11.1—Visually inspect the fan belt for glazing, cracks, and fraying, and replace if necessary. Tighten the belt so that the longest span has approximately ½" play at its midpoint under thumb pressure.	Replace or tighten the fan belt as necessary:	11.2

Checking the fan belt tension
(© Nissan Motor Co. Ltd.)

11.2—Check the fluid level of the cooling system.	If full or slightly low, fill as necessary: If extremely low:	11.5 11.3
11.3—Visually inspect the external portions of the cooling system (radiator, radiator hoses, thermostat elbow, water pump seals, heater hoses, etc.) for leaks. If none are found, pressurize the cooling system to 14-15 psi.	If cooling system holds the pressure: If cooling system loses pressure rapidly, re-inspect external parts of the system for leaks under pressure. If none are found, check dipstick for coolant in crankcase. If no coolant is present, but pressure loss continues: If coolant is evident in crankcase, remove cylinder head(s), and check gasket(s). If gaskets are intact, block and cylinder head(s) should be checked for cracks or holes. If the gasket(s) is blown, replace, and purge the crankcase of coolant: NOTE: *Occasionally, due to atmospheric and driving conditions, condensation of water can occur in the crankcase. This causes the oil to appear milky white. To remedy, run the engine until hot, and change the oil and oil filter.*	11.5 11.4 12.6

TUNE-UP AND TROUBLESHOOTING 51

Test and Procedure	Results and Indication	Proceed to
11.4—Check for combustion leaks into the cooling system: Pressurize the cooling system as above. Start the engine, and observe the pressure gauge. If the needle fluctuates, remove each spark plug wire, one by one, noting which cylinder(s) reduce or eliminate the fluctuation. **Radiator pressure tester** (© American Motors Corp.)	Cylinders which reduce or eliminate the fluctuation, when the spark plug wire is removed, are leaking into the cooling system. Replace the head gasket on the affected cylinder bank(s).	
11.5—Check the radiator pressure cap: Attach a radiator pressure tester to the radiator cap (wet the seal prior to installation). Quickly pump up the pressure, noting the point at which the cap releases. **Testing the radiator pressure cap** (© American Motors Corp.)	If the cap releases within ± 1 psi of the specified rating, it is operating properly:	11.6
	If the cap releases at more than ± 1 psi of the specified rating, it should be replaced:	11.6
11.6—Test the thermostat: Start the engine cold, remove the radiator cap, and insert a thermometer into the radiator. Allow the engine to idle. After a short while, there will be a sudden, rapid increase in coolant temperature. The temperature at which this sharp rise stops is the thermostat opening temperature.	If the thermostat opens at or about the specified temperature:	11.7
	If the temperature doesn't increase: (If the temperature increases slowly and gradually, replace the thermostat.)	11.7
11.7—Check the water pump: Remove the thermostat elbow and the thermostat, disconnect the coil high tension lead (to prevent starting), and crank the engine momentarily.	If coolant flows, replace the thermostat and retest per 11.6:	11.6
	If coolant doesn't flow, reverse flush the cooling system to alleviate any blockage that might exist. If system is not blocked, and coolant will not flow, recondition the water pump.	—
12.1—Check the oil pressure gauge or warning light: If the gauge shows low pressure, or the light is on, for no obvious reason, remove the oil pressure sender. Install an accurate oil pressure gauge and run the engine momentarily.	If oil pressure builds normally, run engine for a few moments to determine that it is functioning normally, and replace the sender.	—
	If the pressure remains low:	12.2
	If the pressure surges:	12.3
	If the oil pressure is zero:	12.3

TUNE-UP AND TROUBLESHOOTING

Test and Procedure	Results and Indications	Proceed to
12.2—Visually inspect the oil: If the oil is watery or very thin, milky, or foamy, replace the oil and oil filter.	If the oil is normal:	12.3
	If after replacing oil the pressure remains low:	12.3
	If after replacing oil the pressure becomes normal:	—
12.3—Inspect the oil pressure relief valve and spring, to ensure that it is not sticking or stuck. Remove and thoroughly clean the valve, spring, and the valve body.	If the oil pressure improves:	—
	If no improvement is noted:	12.4
Oil pressure relief valve (© British Leyland Motors)		
12.4—Check to ensure that the oil pump is not cavitating (sucking air instead of oil): See that the crankcase is neither over nor underfull, and that the pickup in the sump is in the proper position and free from sludge.	Fill or drain the crankcase to the proper capacity, and clean the pickup screen in solvent if necessary. If no improvement is noted:	12.5
12.5—Inspect the oil pump drive and the oil pump:	If the pump drive or the oil pump appear to be defective, service as necessary and retest per 12.1:	12.1
	If the pump drive and pump appear to be operating normally, the engine should be disassembled to determine where blockage exists:	Next Chapter
12.6—Purge the engine of ethylene glycol coolant: Completely drain the crankcase and the oil filter. Obtain a commercial butyl cellosolve base solvent, designated for this purpose, and follow the instructions precisely. Following this, install a new oil filter and refill the crankcase with the proper weight oil. The next oil and filter change should follow shortly thereafter (1000 miles).		

Chapter Three

Engine and Engine Rebuilding

Engine Electrical

DISTRIBUTOR

Removal

1. Remove the high-tension wires from the distributor cap terminal towers, noting their positions to assure correct reassembly.
2. Disconnect the distributor wiring harness.
3. Disconnect the vacuum line(s).
4. Unlatch the two distributor cap retaining clips and remove the distributor cap.
5. Note the position of the rotor in relation to the base. Scribe a mark on the base of the distributor and on the engine block to facilitate reinstallation. Align the marks with the direction the metal tip of the rotor is pointing.
6. Remove the bolt which holds the distributor to the engine.
7. Lift the distributor assembly from the engine.

Installation

1. Insert the distributor shaft and assembly into the engine. Line up the mark on the distributor and the one on the engine with the metal tip of the rotor. Make sure that the vacuum advance diaphragm is pointed in the same direction as it was pointed originally. This will be done automatically if the marks on the engine and the distributor are lined up with the rotor.
2. Install the distributor hold-down bolt and clamp. Leave the screw loose enough so that you can move the distributor with heavy hand pressure.
3. Connect the primary wire to the coil. Install the distributor cap on the distributor housing. Secure the distributor cap with the spring clips.
4. Install the spark plug wires. Make sure that the wires are pressed all the way into the top of the distributor cap and firmly onto the spark plug.
5. Adjust the point dwell and set the ignition timing.

NOTE: *If the crankshaft has been turned or the engine disturbed in any manner (i.e., disassembled and rebuilt) while the distributor was removed, or if the marks were not drawn, it will be necessary to initially time the engine. Follow the procedure given below.*

Installation—Engine Disturbed

1. It is necessary to place the No. 1 cylinder in the firing position to correctly install the distributor. To locate this position, the ignition timing marks on the crankshaft front pulley are used.
2. Remove the No. 1 cylinder spark

53

plug. Turn the crankshaft until the piston in the No. 1 cylinder is moving up on the compression stroke. This can be determined by placing your thumb over the spark plug hole and feeling the air being forced out of the cylinder. Stop turning the crankshaft when the timing marks that are used to time the engine are aligned.

3. Oil the distributor housing lightly where the distributor bears on the cylinder block.

4. Install the distributor so that the rotor, which is mounted on the shaft, points toward the No. 1 spark plug terminal tower position when the cap is installed. Of course you won't be able to see the direction in which the rotor is pointing if the cap is on the distributor. Lay the cap on the top of the distributor and make a mark on the side of the distributor housing just below the No. 1 spark plug terminal. Make sure that the rotor points toward that mark when you install the distributor.

5. When the distributor shaft has reached the bottom of the hole, move the rotor back and forth slightly until the driving lug on the end of the shaft enters the slots cut in the end of the oil pump shaft and the distributor assembly slides down into place.

6. When the distributor is correctly installed, the breaker points should be in such a position that they are just ready to break contact with each other. This is accomplished by rotating the distributor body after it has been installed in the engine. Once again, line up the marks that you made before the distributor was removed from the engine.

7. Install the distributor hold-down bolt.

8. Install the spark plug into the No. 1 spark plug hole and continue from Step 3 of the preceding distributor installation procedure.

ALTERNATOR

Alternator Precautions

To prevent damage to the alternator and regulator, the following precautionary measures must be taken when working with the electrical system.

1. Never reverse battery connections.
2. Booster batteries for starting must

Firing Order

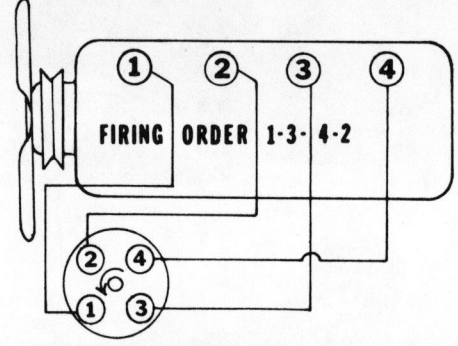

510, 610, 710, and 200SX

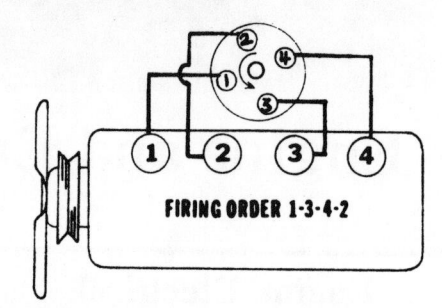

1200, B210, and F10

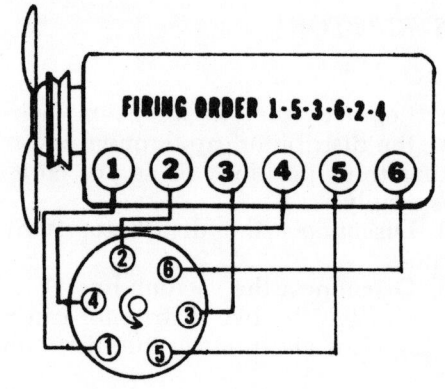

810

be connected properly. Make sure that the positive cable of the booster battery is connected to the positive terminal of the battery that is getting the boost. This applies to both negative and ground cables.

3. Disconnect the battery cables before using a fast charger; the charger has a tendency to force current through the diodes in the opposite direction for which they were designed. This burns out the diodes.

4. Never use a fast charger as a booster for starting the vehicle.

5. Never disconnect the voltage regulator while the engine is running.

ENGINE AND ENGINE REBUILDING 55

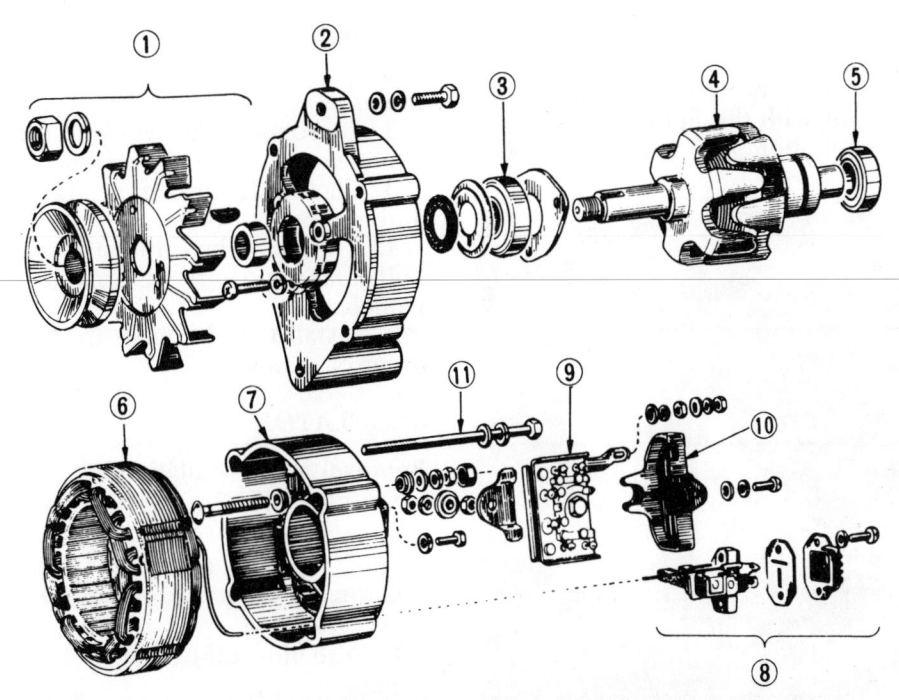

Exploded view of 1200, B210, and F10 alternator

1. Pulley assembly
2. Front cover
3. Front bearing
4. Rotor
5. Rear bearing
6. Stator
7. Rear cover
8. Brush assembly
9. Diode set plate assembly
10. Diode cover
11. Through-bolt

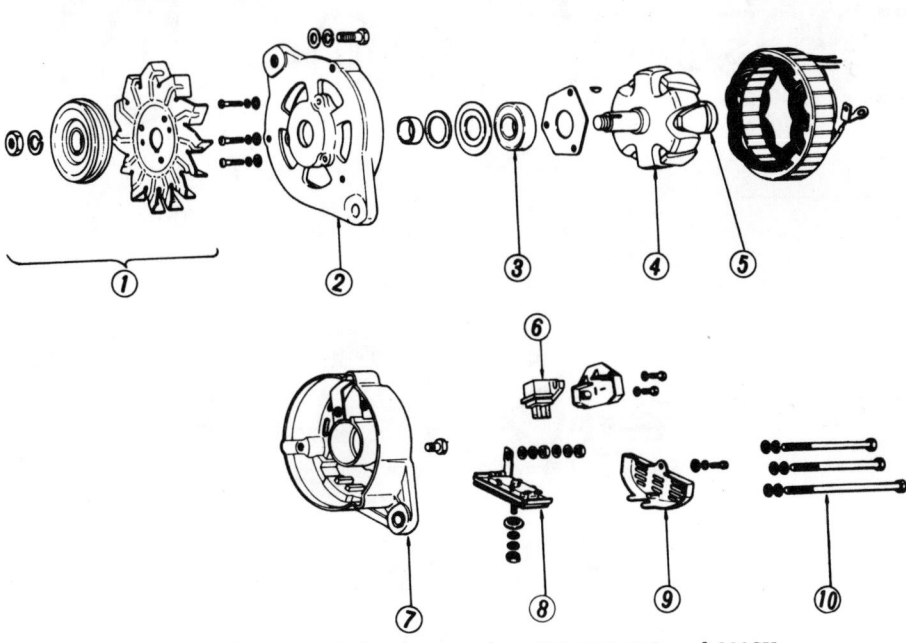

Exploded view of alternator used on 510, 610, 710, and 200SX

1. Pulley assembly
2. Front cover
3. Front bearing
4. Rotor
5. Rear bearing
6. Brush assembly
7. Rear cover
8. Diode set plate assembly
9. Diode cover
10. Through-bolts

56 ENGINE AND ENGINE REBUILDING

6. Do not ground the alternator output terminal.

7. Do not operate the alternator on an open circuit with the field energized.

8. Do not attempt to polarize an alternator.

Alternator connections—integral regulator alternator

Removal and Installation

1. Disconnect the negative battery terminal.
2. Disconnect the two lead wires and connector from the alternator.
3. Loosen the drive belt adjusting bolt and remove the belt.
4. Unscrew the alternator attaching bolts and remove the alternator from the vehicle.
5. Install the alternator in the reverse order of removal.

REGULATOR

Removal and Installation

NOTE: *1978 models are equipped with integral regulator alternators. Since the regulator is part of the alternator, no adjustments are possible or necessary.*

1. Disconnect the negative battery terminal.
2. Disconnect the electrical lead connector of the regulator.
3. Remove the two mounting screws

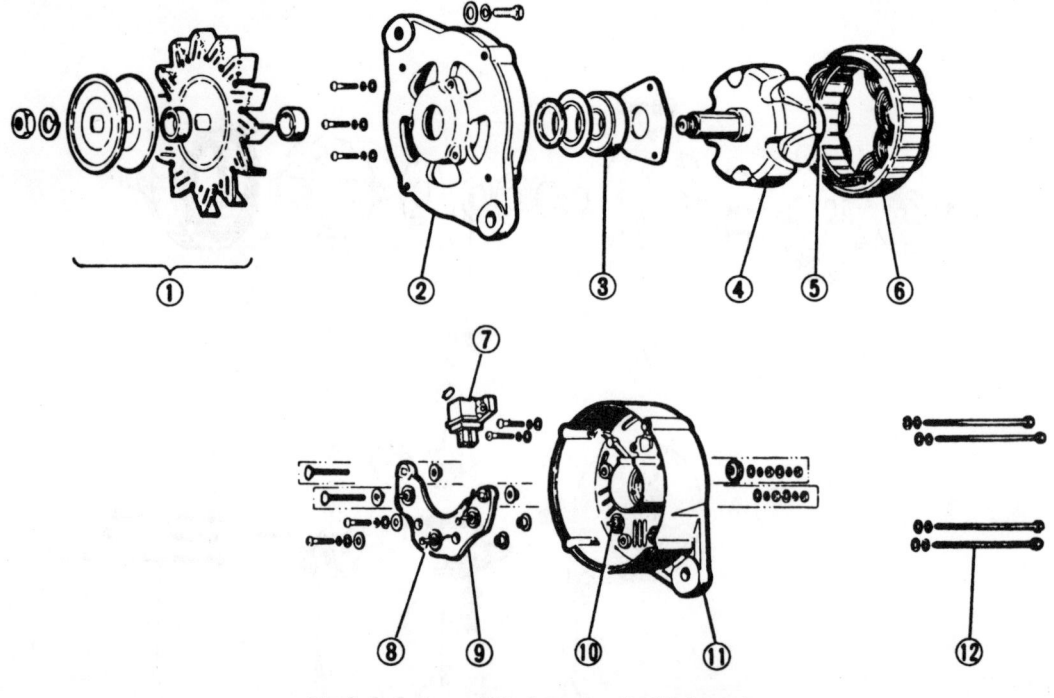

Exploded view—810 alternator (1977 shown)

1. Pulley assembly
2. Front cover
3. Front bearing
4. Rotor
5. Rear bearing
6. Stator assembly
7. Brush assembly
8. Diode
9. SR holder
10. Diode
11. Rear cover
12. Through bolts

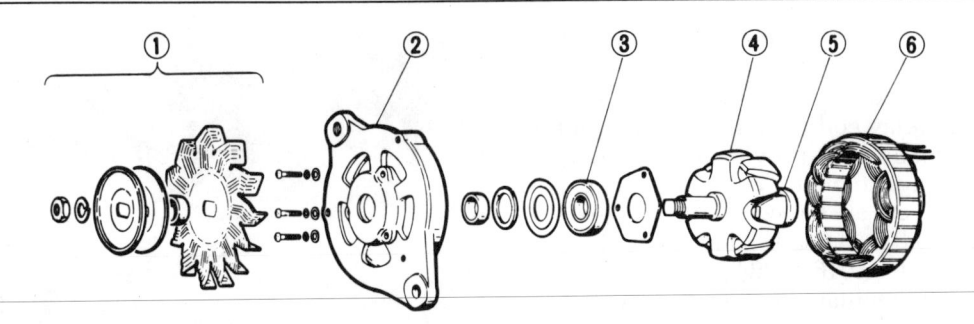

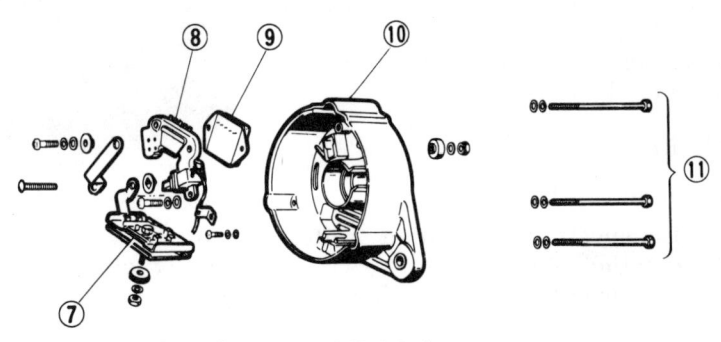

ENGINE AND ENGINE REBUILDING 57

Integral regulator alternator—1978 510 shown

1. Pulley assembly
2. Front cover
3. Front bearing
4. Rotor
5. Rear bearing
6. Stator
7. Diode (Set plate) assembly
8. Brush assembly
9. IC voltage regulator
10. Rear cover
11. Through bolt

and remove the regulator from the vehicle.

4. Install the regulator in the reverse order of removal.

Adjustment

1. Adjust the voltage regulator core gap by loosening the screw which is used to secure the contact set on the yoke, and move the contact up or down as necessary. Retighten the screw. The gap should be 0.024–0.039 in.

2. Adjust the point gap of the voltage regulator coil by loosening the screw used to secure the upper contact and

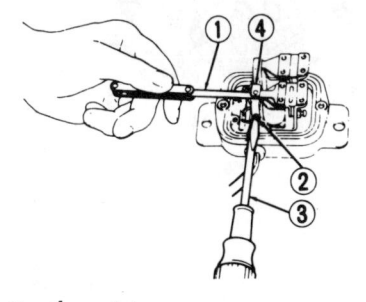

Adjusting the point gap
1. Feeler gauge
2. Screw
3. Phillips screwdriver
4. Upper contact

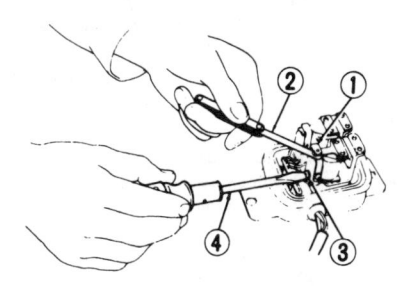

Adjusting the core gap
1. Contacts
2. Feeler gauge
3. Adjusting screw
4. Phillips screwdriver

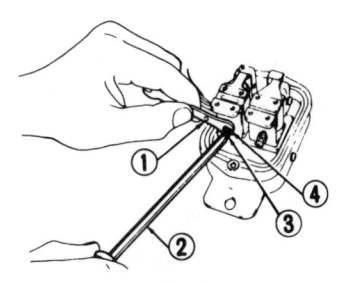

Adjusting the regulated voltage
1. Wrench
2. Phillips screwdriver
3. Adjusting screw
4. Locknut

move the upper contact up or down. The gap should be 0.012–0.016 in.

3. The core gap and point gap on the charge relay coil is or are adjusted in the same manner as previously outlined for the voltage regulator coil. The core gap is to be set at 0.032–0.039 in. (except B210—0.031–0.035 in.) and the point gap adjusted to 0.016–0.024 in.

4. The regulated voltage is adjusted by loosening the locknut and turning the adjusting screw clockwise to increase, or counterclockwise to decrease the regulated voltage. The voltage should be between 14.3–15.3 volts at 68° F.

STARTER

Removal and Installation

1. Disconnect the negative battery cable from the battery.
2. Disconnect the starter wiring at the starter, taking note of the positions for correct reinstallation.
3. Remove the bolts attaching the

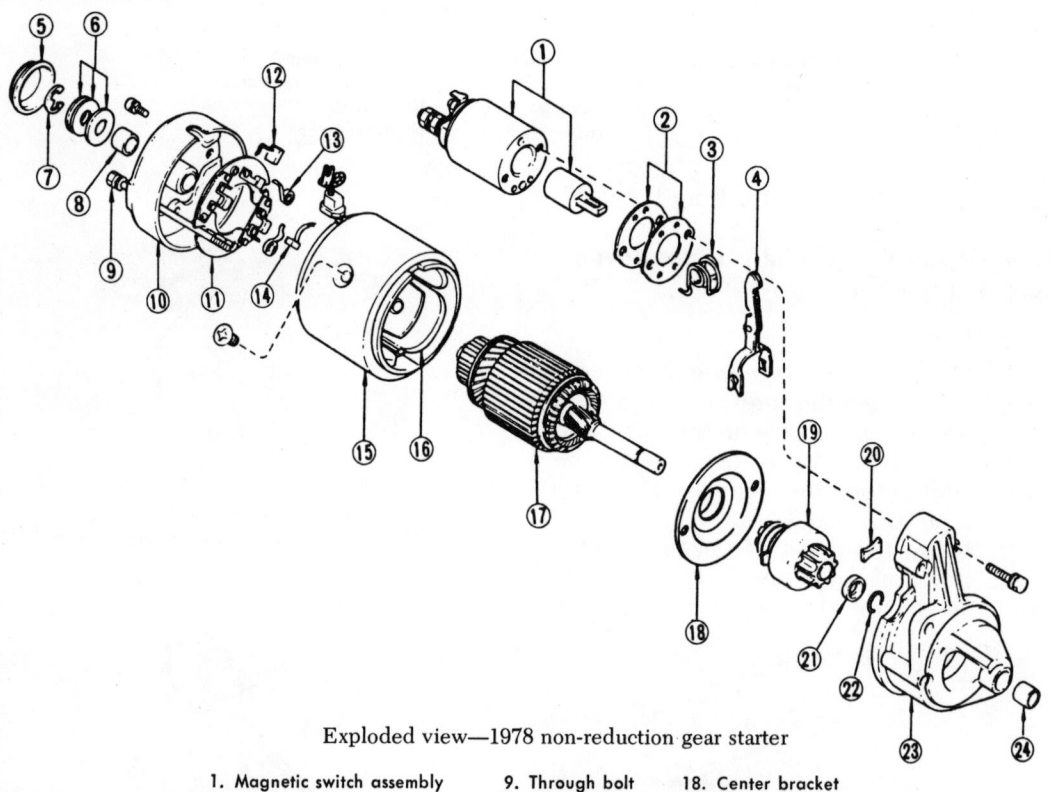

Note the wire locations before removing the starter

Exploded view—1978 non-reduction gear starter

1. Magnetic switch assembly
2. Dust cover
   (Adjusting washer)
3. Torsion spring
4. Shift lever
5. Dust cover
6. Thrust washer
7. E-ring
8. Rear cover metal
9. Through bolt
10. Rear cover
11. Brush holder
12. Brush (—)
13. Brush spring
14. Brush (+)
15. Yoke
16. Field coil
17. Armature
18. Center bracket
19. Pinion assembly
20. Dust cover
21. Pinion stopper
22. Stopper clip
23. Gear case
24. Gear case metal

ENGINE AND ENGINE REBUILDING 59

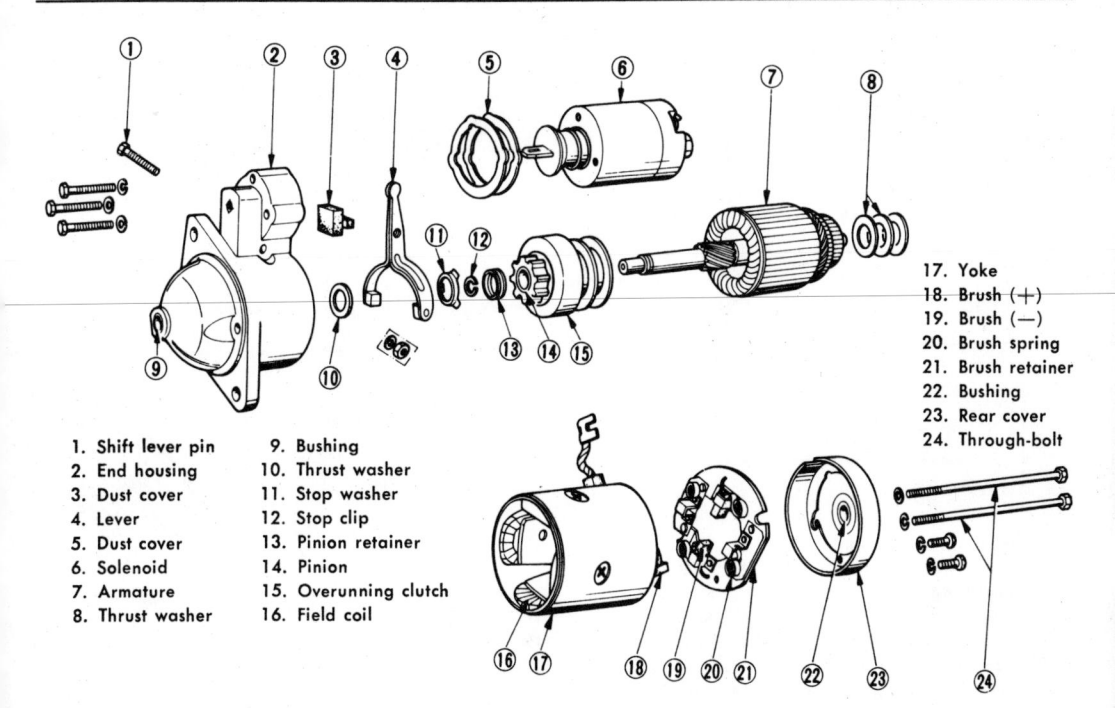

1. Shift lever pin
2. End housing
3. Dust cover
4. Lever
5. Dust cover
6. Solenoid
7. Armature
8. Thrust washer
9. Bushing
10. Thrust washer
11. Stop washer
12. Stop clip
13. Pinion retainer
14. Pinion
15. Overrunning clutch
16. Field coil
17. Yoke
18. Brush (+)
19. Brush (−)
20. Brush spring
21. Brush retainer
22. Bushing
23. Rear cover
24. Through-bolt

Exploded view of 510, 610, and 710 starter

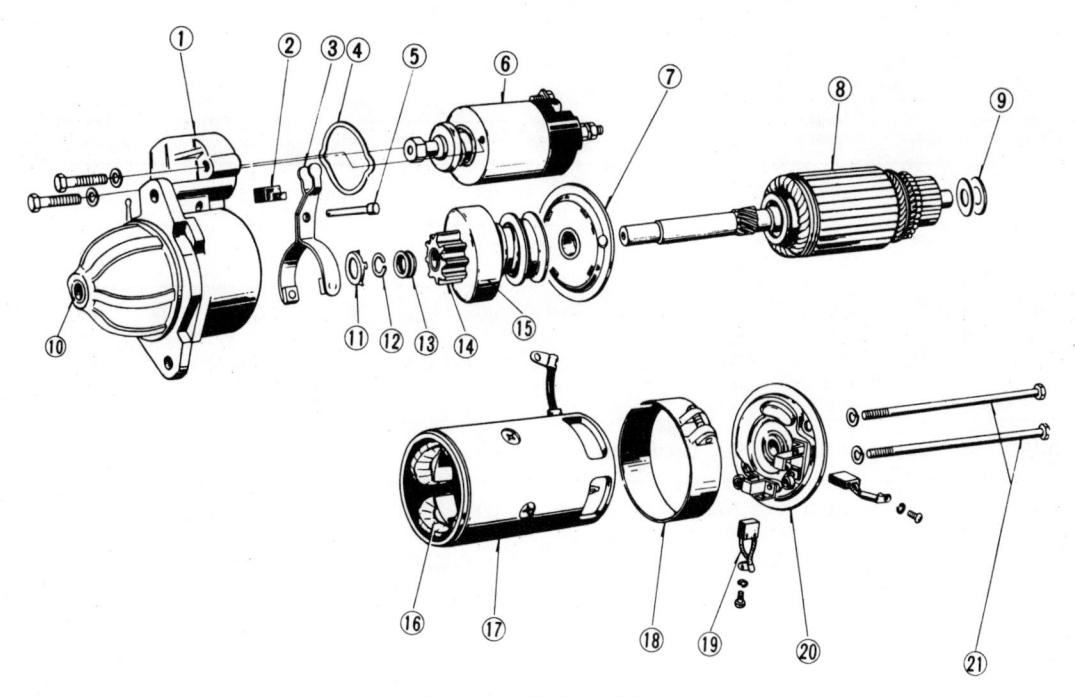

Exploded view of 1200 and B210 starter

1. End housing
2. Dust cover
3. Lever
4. Dust cover
5. Pin
6. Solenoid
7. Center bracket
8. Armature
9. Thrust washer
10. Bushing
11. Stop washer
12. Stop clip
13. Pinion retainer
14. Pinion
15. Overrunning clutch
16. Field coil
17. Yoke
18. Brush cover
19. Brush
20. Rear cover
21. Through-bolt

60 ENGINE AND ENGINE REBUILDING

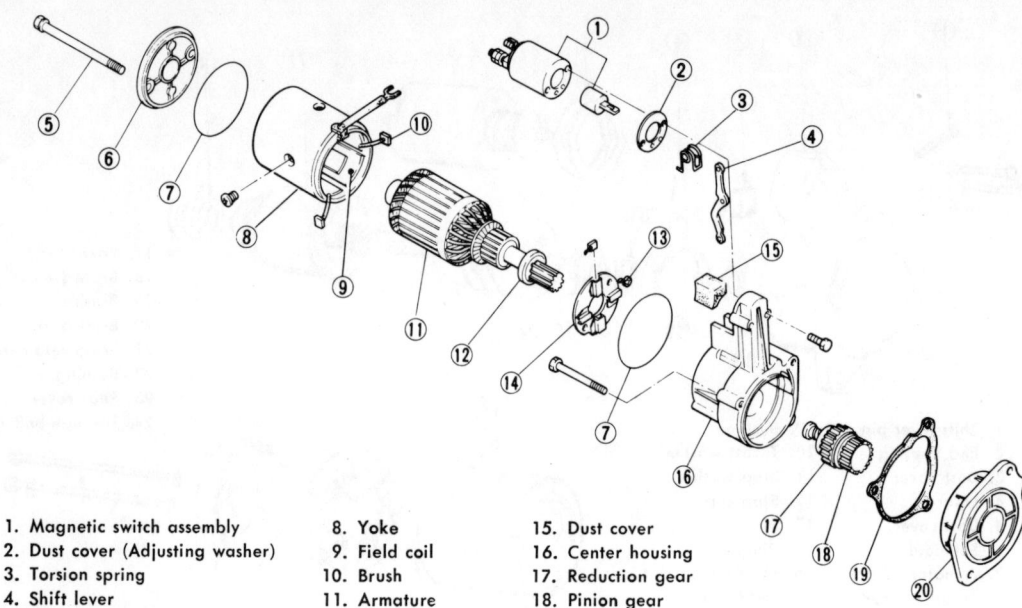

1. Magnetic switch assembly
2. Dust cover (Adjusting washer)
3. Torsion spring
4. Shift lever
5. Through bolt
6. Rear cover
7. O-ring
8. Yoke
9. Field coil
10. Brush
11. Armature
12. Center bearing
13. Brush spring
14. Brush holder
15. Dust cover
16. Center housing
17. Reduction gear
18. Pinion gear
19. Packing
20. Gear case

Reduction gear starter

Battery and Starter Specifications

Year	Model	Battery Amp Hour Capacity	STARTER LOCK TEST Amps	Volts	Torque (ft/lbs)	NO LOAD TEST Amps	Volts	RPM	Brush Spring Tension (oz)	Minimum Brush Length (in.)
1973	510	50, 60	420	6.0	7.9	60	12	7,000	62	0.28
1973	1200	NA	420	6.3	6.5	60	12	7,000	62	0.37
All	610, 710	NA	430 (MT)	6.0	6.3	60	12	7,000	49–64	0.47
			540 (AT)	5.0	6.0	60	12	6,000	49–64	0.47
All	200SX	NA	Not Recommended			60	12	7,000	49–64	0.47
All	B210 F10	NA	Not Recommended			60	12	7,000	49–64	0.47
All	810	NA	Not Recommended			60	12	7,000	49–64	0.47
1978	510	NA	Not Recommended			60	12	7,000	49–64 (non-reduction) 52–70 (reduction gear)	0.47 0.47

MT Manual Transmission
AT Automatic Transmission
NA Not Available

ENGINE AND ENGINE REBUILDING

starter to the engine and remove the starter from the vehicle.

4. Install the starter in the reverse order of removal.

Brush Replacement

1. With the starter out of the vehicle, remove the bolts holding the solenoid to the top of the starter and remove the solenoid.
2. To remove the brushes, remove the two thru-bolts and the two rear cover attaching screws and remove the rear cover.
3. Disconnect the brush electrical leads and remove the brushes.
4. Install the brushes in the reverse order of removal.

Starter Drive Replacement

1. With the starter motor removed from the vehicle, remove the solenoid from the starter.
2. Remove the two thru-bolts and separate the gear case from the yoke housing.
3. Remove the pinion stopper clip and the pinion stopper.
4. Slide the starter drive off the armature shaft.
5. Install the starter drive and reassemble the starter in the reverse order of removal.

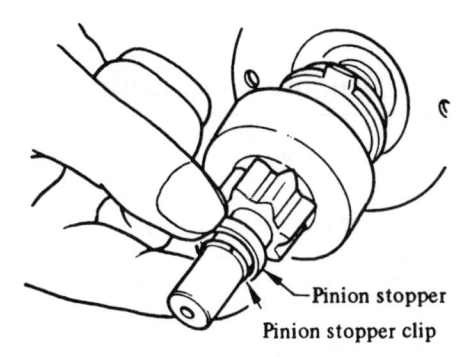

Pinion stopper removal

Engine Mechanical

DESIGN

There are three different engine families used in the models covered in this book. All of the engines are of the inline, water-cooled variety, and all of them utilize a cast iron block and an aluminum cylinder head.

The A12, A13 and A14 series of engines are used in the 1200, the B210, and the F10. The major difference between these engines is the increased displacement of the A13 and the A14, achieved through a longer stroke. All the A series engines are overhead valve engines. The camshaft is placed high in the cylinder block allowing short pushrods; therefore, valve train reciprocating weight is reduced and higher engine speeds are possible. Like the L-series engines, the A-series has a five main bearing crankshaft with thrust taken on the center bearing.

The L16, and L18, and L20B engines are used in the 510 (both old and new), the 610, and the 710. These engines are all overhead camshaft designs, and like the A-series engines, are all essentially the same engine with differences in displacement. The larger L18 and L20 were developed from the L16 engine used in the original 510. The L18 is a bored and stroked L16 and was first used in the 1973 610 and then in the 710. For the 1974 610, the stroke was further increased for the 1952 cc displacement of the L20B. Currently, the L20B engine is used in the new (1978) 510 series, the 710, and the 200SX, as well as the pickup trucks. These engines utilize a five main bearing crankshaft with the thrust taken on the center bearing.

The 810 is the only one of the Datsun sedans to use a six-cylinder engine, sport-

L24 engine—early model. 810's are fuel injected

ENGINE AND ENGINE REBUILDING

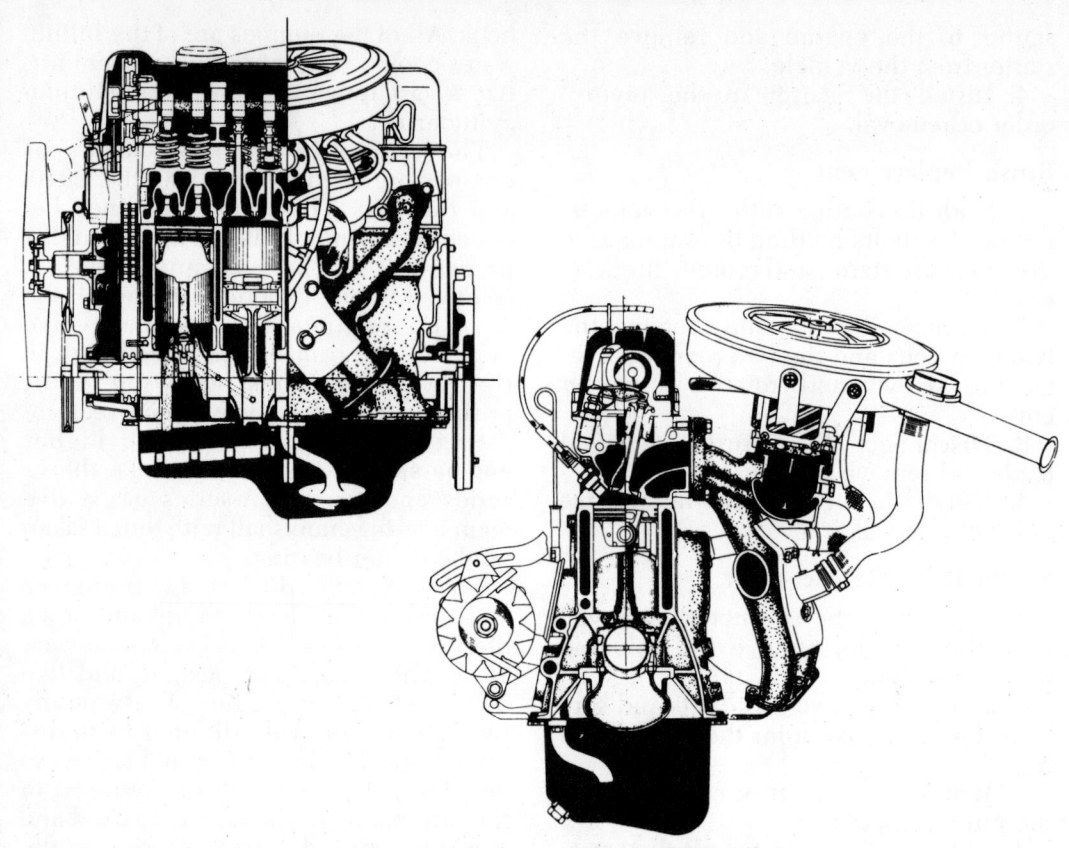

Cutaway of L16 engine (L18, L20B similar)

ing as it does a smaller version of the engine found in the Z-car. This engine is known as the L24 engine and is an overhead camshaft inline six-cylinder. Datsun's six-cylinder engines were developed from their OHC four cylinders, and share a great many similarities. Essentially, the L24 engine is a stretched version of the L20B found in the sedans. Besides the extra two cylinders, the major difference is that the L24 engine is fuel-injected while the others are carbureted. Like the others, the L24 utilizes a cast-iron block and an aluminum cylinder head.

Engines are referred to by model designation codes throughout this book. Use the "Engine Identification" chart for identification of engines by model, number of cylinders, displacement, and camshaft location.

Engine I.D. Table

Number of Cylinders	Displacement cu in. (cc)	Type	Engine Model Code
4	97.3 (1,595)	OHC	L16
4	71.5 (1,171)	OHV	A12
4	108.0 (1,770)	OHC	L18
4	78.59 (1,288)	OHV	A13
4	119.1 (1,952)	OHC	L20B
4	85.24 (1,397)	OHV	A14
6	146 (2,393)	OHC	L24

ENGINE AND ENGINE REBUILDING 63

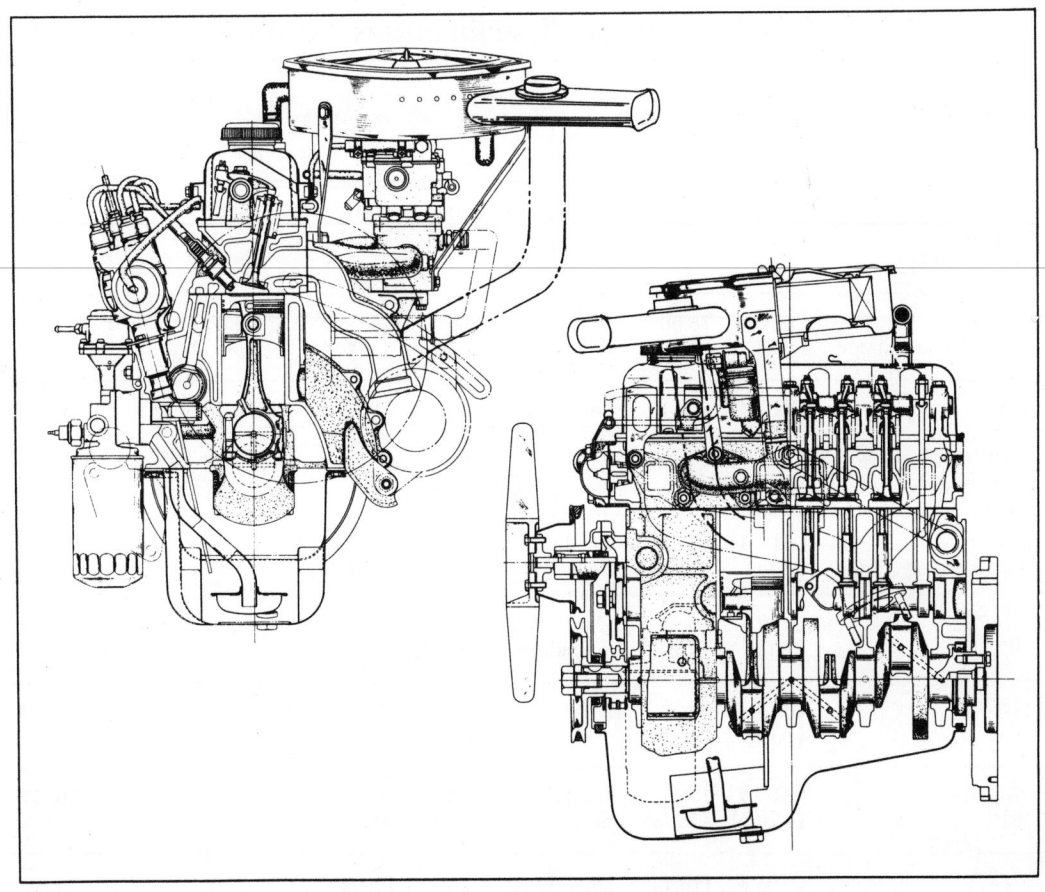

Cutaway of A12 engine (A13, A14 similar)

General Engine Specifications

Year and Model	Type (model)	Engine Displacement cu in. (cc)	Carburetor Type	Horse-power (SAE) @ rpm	Torque @ rpm (ft lbs)	Bore x Stroke (in.)	Compression Ratio	Normal Oil Pressure (psi)
1973 510 1600 Sedan	OHC 4 (L16)	97.3 (1595)	Dual throat downdraft	96 @ 5,600	100 @ 3,600	3.27 x 2.90	8.5 : 1	54–57
1973 1200 Sedan 1200 Coupe	OHV 4 (A12)	71.5 (1171)	Dual throat downdraft	69 @ 6,000	70 @ 4,000	2.87 x 2.76	8.5 : 1	54–60
1973 610 1800 Sedan 610 1800 Hardtop 610 1800 Wagon	OHC 4 (L18)	108.0 (1770)	Dual throat downdraft	100 @ 5,600	100 @ 3,600	3.35 x 3.307	8.5 : 1	50–57
1974–75 610 Sedan 610 Hardtop 610 Wagon	OHC 4 (L20B)	119.1 (1952)	Dual throat downdraft	112 @ 5,600	108 @ 3,600	3.35 x 3.39	8.5 : 1	50–57

General Engine Specifications (cont.)

Year and Model	Type (model)	Engine Displacement cu in. (cc)	Carburetor Type	Horsepower (SAE) @ rpm	Torque @ rpm (ft lbs)	Bore x Stroke (in.)	Compression Ratio	Normal Oil Pressure (psi)
1974 710 Sedan 710 Hardtop	OHC 4 (L18)	108 (1770)	Dual throat downdraft	100 @ 5,600	100 @ 3,600	3.35 x 3.07	8.5 : 1	50–57
1974 B210 Sedan, Coupe	OHV 4 (A13)	78.59 (1288)	Dual throat downdraft	78 @ 6,000	75 @ 4,000	2.87 x 3.03	8.5 : 1	43–50
1975 710 Sedan 710 Hardtop 710 Wagon	OHC 4 (L20B)	119.1 (1952)	Dual throat downdraft	100 @ 5,600	100 @ 3,600	3.35 x 3.39	8.5 : 1	50–57
1975 B210 Sedan, Coupe	OHV 4 (A14)	85.24 (1397)	Dual throat downdraft	78 @ 6,000	75 @ 4,000	3.09 x 3.03	8.5 : 1	43–50
1976–78 B210	OHV 4 (A14)	85.2 (1397)	Dual throat downdraft	80 @ 6,000	83 @ 3,600	2.79 x 3.03	8.5 : 1	43–50
1977–78 F10	OHV 4 (A14)	85.2 (1397)	Dual throat downdraft	80 @ 6,000	83 @ 3,600	2.79 x 3.03	8.5 : 1	43–50
1976 610	OHC 4 (L20B)	119.1 (1952)	Dual throat downdraft	112 @ 5,600	108 @ 3,600	3.35 x 3.39	8.5 : 1	50–57
1976–77 710	OHC 4 (L20B)	119.1 (1952)	Dual throat downdraft	100 @ 5,600	100 @ 5,600	3.35 x 3.39	8.5 : 1	50–57
1977–78 200SX	OHC 4 (L20B)	119.1 (1952)	Dual throat downdraft	97 @ 5,600	102 @ 3,200	3.35 x 3.39	8.5 : 1	50–57
1978 510	OHC 4 (L20B)	119.1 (1952)	Dual throat downdraft	97 @ 5,600	102 @ 3,200	3.35 x 3.39	8.5 : 1	50–57
1977–78 810	OHC 6 (L24)	146 (2393)	Electronic Fuel Injection	154 @ 5,600	155 @ 4,400	3.27 x 2.90	8.6 : 1	50–57

Crankshaft and Connecting Rod Specifications

Engine Model	CRANKSHAFT Main Brg Journal Dia	Main Brg Oil Clearance	Shaft End-Play	Thrust on No.	CONNECTING ROD BEARINGS Journal Dia	Oil Clearance	Side Clearance
L16	2.1631–2.1636	0.001–0.003	0.002–0.006	3	1.9670–1.9675	0.001–0.003	0.008–0.012
A12	1.9671–1.9668	0.001–0.002	0.002–0.006	3	1.7701–1.7706	0.001–0.002	0.008–0.012
L18	2.1631–2.1636	0.001–0.002	0.002–0.007	3	1.9670–1.9675	0.001–0.002	0.008–0.012
L20B	2.333–2.360	0.0008–0.002	0.002–0.007	3	1.9660–1.9670	0.001–0.002	0.008–0.012

ENGINE AND ENGINE REBUILDING

Crankshaft and Connecting Rod Specifications (cont.)

Engine Model	CRANKSHAFT Main Brg Journal Dia	Main Brg Oil Clearance	Shaft End-Play	Thrust on No.	CONNECTING ROD BEARINGS Journal Dia	Oil Clearance	Side Clearance
L18 (710)	2.3599–2.360	0.0008–0.002	0.002–0.007	3	1.967–1.9675	0.001–0.002	0.008–0.012
A13	1.966–1.967	0.0008–0.002	0.002–0.006	3	1.7701–1.7706	0.0008–0.002	0.008–0.012
A14	1.966–1.967	0.0008–0.002	0.002–0.006	3	1.7701–1.7706	0.0008–0.002	0.008–0.012
L24	2.1631–2.1636	0.001–0.003	0.002–0.007	Center	1.9670–1.9675	0.001–0.002	0.008–0.012

Piston and Ring Specifications

All measurements in inches

Engine Model	Piston Clearance	RING GAP Top Compression	Bottom Compression	Oil Control	RING SIDE CLEARANCE Top Compression	Bottom Compression	Oil Control
L16	0.001–0.002	0.009–0.015	0.006–0.012	0.006–0.012	0.002–0.003	0.001–0.003	0.001–0.003
A12	0.001–0.002	0.008–0.014	0.008–0.014	0.010–0.014	0.002–0.003	0.002–0.003	0.002–0.003
L18	0.001–0.002	0.014–0.022	0.012–0.020	0.012–0.035	0.002–0.003	0.002–0.003	0.002–0.003
A13	0.001–0.002	0.008–0.010	0.008–0.010	0.010–0.030	0.002–0.003	0.002–0.003	—
L20B	0.001–0.002	0.010–0.020	0.010–0.020	0.010–0.020	0.002–0.003	0.002–0.003	—
L20B 1975–78	0.001–0.002	0.010–0.016	0.012–0.020	0.012–0.022	0.002–0.003	0.001–0.003	—
A14 1975–78	0.0009–0.002	0.008–0.014	0.006–0.012	0.012–0.035	0.002–0.003	0.001–0.002	Combined ring
L24	0.001–0.002	0.009–0.015	0.006–0.012	0.006–0.012	0.002–0.003	0.001–0.003	0.001–0.003

— Not applicable

Valve Specifications

Engine Model	Seat Angle (deg)	VALVE SPRING PRESSURE (lbs @ in.) Outer	Inner	VALVE SPRING FREE LENGTH (in.) Outer	Inner	STEM TO GUIDE CLEARANCE (in.) Intake	Exhaust	Valve Guide Removable
L16	45	105 @ 1.21 64 @ 1.53	56 @ .96 27 @ 1.38	2.05	1.77	0.001–0.002	0.002–0.003	Yes
A12	45	66 @ 1.52 135 @ 1.23	—	1.80	—	0.001–0.002	0.002–0.003	Yes

ENGINE AND ENGINE REBUILDING

Valve Specifications (cont.)

Engine Model	Seat Angle (deg)	VALVE SPRING PRESSURE (lbs @ in.) Outer	Inner	VALVE SPRING FREE LENGTH (in.) Outer	Inner	STEM TO GUIDE CLEARANCE (in.) Intake	Exhaust	Valve Guide Removable
L18	45	108 @ 1.16	56 @ .97	1.97	1.77	0.001–0.002	0.002–0.003	Yes
A13	45	129 @ 1.19	—	1.831	—	0.0006–0.0018	0.0016–0.0028	Yes
L20B	45	108 @ 1.16	56 @ 0.965	1.968	1.766	0.0008–0.0021	0.0016–0.0029	Yes
L20B 1975–78	45½	108 @ 1.16	56 @ 0.965	1.968	1.766	0.0008–0.002	0.0016–0.002	Yes
A14 1975–78	45	129 @ 1.19	—	1.831	—	0.0006–0.002	0.0016–0.003	Yes
L24	45	47 @ 1.57 / 108 @ 1.16	56 @ 0.96	1.97	1.76	0.001–0.002	0.002–0.003	Yes

— Not applicable

Torque Specifications
All readings in ft lbs

Engine Model	Cylinder Head Bolts	Main Bearing Bolts	Rod Bearing Bolts	Crankshaft Pulley Bolt	Flywheel to Crankshaft Bolts
L16	40	33–40	20–24	116–130	69–76
A12	33–35	36–38	25–26	108–116	47–54
L18	47–62	33–40	33–40	87–116	101–116
A13	54–58	36–43	23–27	108–145	54–61
L20B	47–61	33–40	33–40	87–116	101–116
A14	51–54	36–43	23–27	108–145	54–61
L24	47–61	33–40	20–24	116–130	101

ENGINE REMOVAL AND INSTALLATION–ALL ENGINES EXCEPT F10

The engine and transmission are removed together and then separated when out of the car.

1. Mark the location of the hinges on the hood. Unbolt and remove the hood.
2. Disconnect the battery cables. Remove the battery from models with the L16 engine.
3. Drain the coolant and automatic transmission fluid.
4. Remove the grille on 510, 610, and 710 models. Remove the radiator after disconnecting the automatic transmission coolant tubes.
5. Remove the air cleaner.
6. Remove the fan and pulley.

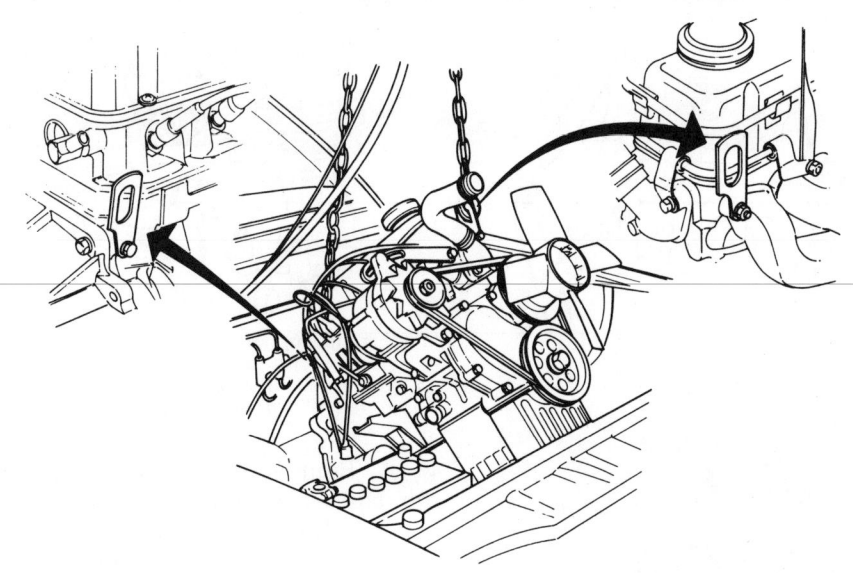

Removing the engine. The A13 is shown, but all engines are removed in a similar manner.

7. Disconnect:
   a. water temperature gauge wire;
   b. oil pressure sending unit wire;
   c. ignition distributor primary wire;
   d. starter motor connections;
   e. fuel hose;
   f. alternator leads;
   g. heater hoses;
   h. throttle and choke connections.
8. Disconnect the power brake booster hose from the engine.
9. Remove the clutch operating cylinder and return spring.
10. Disconnect the speedometer cable from the transmission. Disconnect the backup light switch and any other wiring or attachments to the transmission. On cars with the L18 and L20B engine, disconnect the parking brake cable at the rear adjuster.
11. Disconnect the column shift linkage. Remove the floorshift lever. On 1200 and B210 models, remove the boot, withdraw the lock pin, and remove the lever from inside the car.
12. Detach the exhaust pipe from the exhaust manifold. Remove the front section of the exhaust system.
13. Mark the relationship of the driveshaft flanges and remove the driveshaft.
14. Place a jack under the transmission. Remove the rear crossmember. On 1200 and B210 models, remove the rear engine mounting nuts.
15. Attach a hoist to the lifting hooks on the engine (at either end of the cylinder head). Support the engine.
16. Unbolt the front engine mounts. Tilt the engine by lowering the jack under the transmission and raising the hoist.
17. Reverse the procedure to install the engine.

ENGINE REMOVAL AND INSTALLATION—F10

The engine and transmission must be removed as a single unit. Since the F10 is a front wheel drive car, this is a fairly involved procedure.

1. Mark the location of the hinges on the hood and then remove the hood.
2. Disconnect the battery cables and remove the battery.
3. Drain the coolant from the radiator and remove the radiator and radiator hoses.

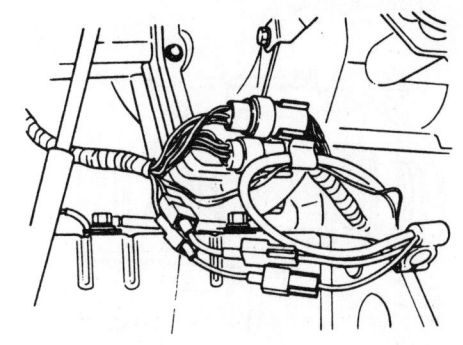

F10 engine harness connector

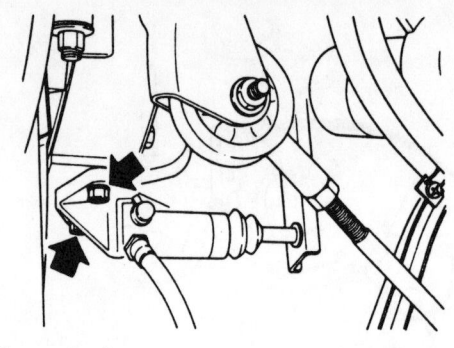

ENGINE AND ENGINE REBUILDING

Slave cylinder

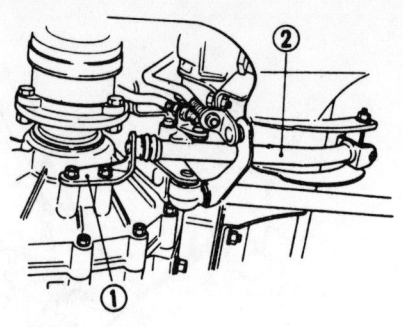

Radius link support
1. Link support
2. Radius link

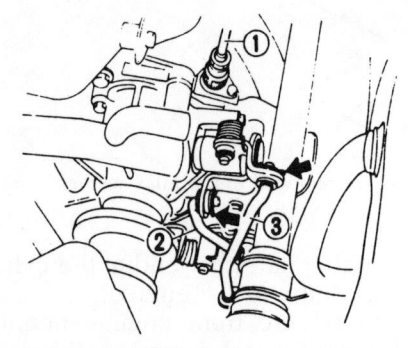

Speedometer cable and shift rod removal
1. Speedometer cable
2. Shift rod
3. Select rod

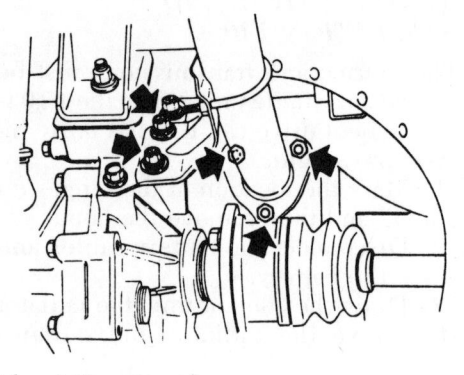

Exhaust pipe removal

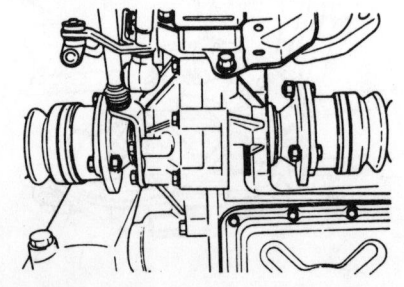

Axle shaft removal

4. Remove the air cleaner and all attendant hoses and lines.
5. Disconnect the following:
 a. Ignition coil ground wire and high tension lead
 b. Wires to the distributor at the block connector
 c. Carburetor throttle linkage
 d. Fusible links
 e. Engine harness connectors
 f. Fuel line to the carburetor and the fuel return hose
 g. Heater hoses on all vacuum hoses
 h. Air pump hoses
6. Remove the slave cylinder from the clutch housing.
7. Unhook the speedometer cable from the transmission and remove the shift linkage from the transmission.
8. Unbolt the exhaust pipe from the exhaust manifold. There are three bolts which attach the pipe to the manifold and two bolts which attach the pipe support to the engine.
9. Unbolt the axle shafts from the differential.
10. Remove the left and right buffer rods from the engine. Do not alter the length of the rods.
11. Unbolt the engine from the engine mounts. Unbolt the transmission mount.
12. Attach a sling to the engine and remove it.
13. Installation is the reverse of removal. If the buffer rod length has not been altered, it should still be correct.

CYLINDER HEAD

Removal and Installation

NOTE: *To prevent distortion or warping of the cylinder head, allow the*

ENGINE AND ENGINE REBUILDING 69

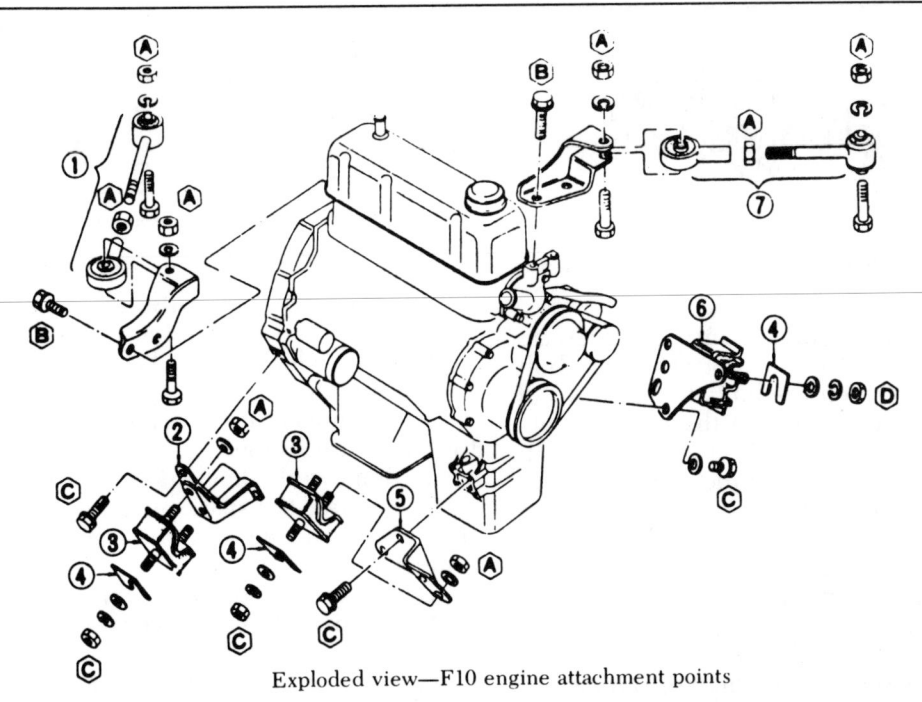

Exploded view—F10 engine attachment points

1. Buffer rod assembly (R.H.)
2. Engine support bracket (R.H.)
3. Front engine mounting insulator
4. Engine mounting shim
5. Engine support bracket (L.H.)
6. Rear engine mounting insulator
7. Buffer rod assembly (L.H.)

engine to cool completely before removing the head bolts.

A12, A13, AND A14 OVERHEAD VALVE ENGINES

To remove the cylinder head on OHV engines:
1. Drain the coolant.
2. Disconnect the battery ground cable.
3. Remove the upper radiator hose. Remove the water outlet elbow and the thermostat.
4. Remove the air cleaner, carburetor, rocker arm cover, and both manifolds.
5. Remove the spark plugs.
6. Disconnect the temperature gauge connection.
7. Remove the head bolts and remove the head and rocker arm assembly

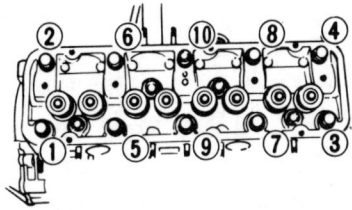

A12, 13 and 14 cylinder head bolt loosening sequence

together. Rap the head with a mallet to loosen it from the block. Remove the head and discard the gasket.
8. Remove the pushrods, keeping them in order.

To replace the cylinder head on OHV engines:
1. Make sure that head and block surfaces are clean. Check the cylinder head surface with a straightedge and a feeler gauge for flatness. If the head is warped more than 0.003 in., it must be trued. If this is not done, there will probably be a leak. The block surface should also be checked in the same way. If the block is warped more than 0.003 in., it must be trued.
2. Install a new head gasket. Most gaskets have a TOP marking. Make sure that the proper head gasket is used on the A12 so that no water passages are blocked off.
3. Install the head. Install the pushrods in their original locations. Install the rocker arm assembly. Loosen the rocker arm adjusting screws to prevent bending pushrods when tightening the head bolts. Tighten the head bolts finger-tight. The single bolt marked T must go in the No. 1 position on the center right-side of the engine.

ENGINE AND ENGINE REBUILDING

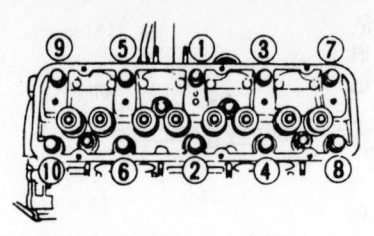

A-series cylinder head torque tightening sequence

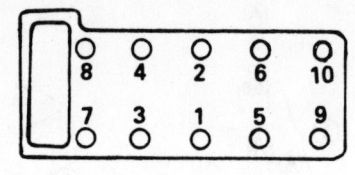

L-series head torque tightening sequence (4 cylinders)

4. Refer to the "Torque Specifications" chart for the correct head bolt torque. Tighten the bolts to one third of the specified torque in the order shown in the head bolt tightening sequence illustration. Torque the rocker arm mounting bolts to 15–18 ft lbs.
5. Tighten the bolts to two thirds of the specified torque in sequence.
6. Tighten the bolts to the full specified torque in sequence.
7. Adjust the valves to the cold setting.
8. Reassemble the engine. Intake and exhaust manifold bolt torque is 7–10 ft lbs. Fill the cooling system. Start the engine and run it until normal temperature is reached. Remove the rocker arm cover. Torque the bolts in sequence once more. Check the valve clearances.
9. Retorque the head bolts after 600 miles of driving. Check the valve clearances after torquing, as this may disturb the settings.

L16, L18, AND L20B OVERHEAD CAMSHAFT ENGINES

NOTE: *Any of the following procedures that involve removing or disturbing the timing chain on the overhead cam engine make use of the factory procedure to support the chain. This procedure involves the use of a factory approved wooden wedge to hold the timing chain in place. Unfortunately, personal experience reveals that while the factory procedure works fine in theory, in practice, you may find that it is somewhat difficult. A longer, but ultimately less frustrating alternative is to remove the front cover anytime you have to work on the timing chain.*

1. Crank the engine until the No. 1 piston is TDC of the compression stroke and disconnect the negative battery cable, drain the cooling system and remove the air cleaner and attending hoses.
2. Remove the alternator.
3. Disconnect the carburetor throttle linkage, the fuel line and any other vacuum lines or electrical leads, and remove the carburetor.
4. Disconnect the exhaust pipe from the exhaust manifold.
5. Remove the fan and fan pulley.
6. Remove the spark plugs to protect them from damage. Lay the spark plugs aside and out of the way.
7. Remove the rocker cover.
8. Remove the water pump.
9. Remove the fuel pump.
10. Remove the fuel pump drive cam.
11. Mark the relationship of the camshaft sprocket to the timing chain with paint or chalk. If this is done, it will not be necessary to locate the factory timing marks. Before removing the camshaft sprocket, it will be necessary to wedge the chain in place so that it will not fall down into the front cover. The factory procedure is to wedge the timing chain in place with the wooden wedge shown here. The problem with this procedure is that it may allow the chain tensioner to move out far enough to cock itself against the chain. If this happens, you'll find that the chain won't go back over the sprocket after you've put the sprocket back on. In this case, you'll have to remove the front cover and push the tensioner back. After you've wedged the chain, unbolt the camshaft sprocket and remove it.
12. Loosen and remove the cylinder head bolts. You will need a 10 mm allen wrench to remove the head bolts. Keep

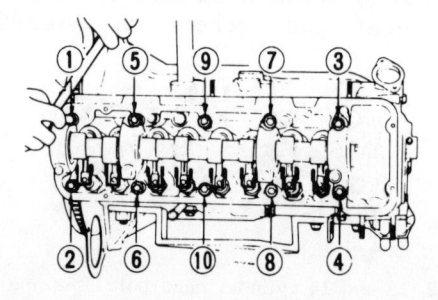

L-series engine cylinder head bolt loosening sequence

the bolts in order since they are different sizes. Lift the cylinder head assembly from the engine. Remove the intake and exhaust manifolds as necessary.

13. Thoroughly clean the cylinder block and head mating surfaces and install a new cylinder head gasket. Do not use sealer on the cylinder head gasket.

14. With the crankshaft turned so that the No. 1 piston is at TDC of the compression stroke (if not already done so as mentioned in Step 1), make sure that the camshaft sprocket timing mark and the oblong groove in the plate are aligned.

15. Place the cylinder head in position on the cylinder block, being careful not to allow any of the valves to come in contact with any of the pistons. Do not rotate the crankshaft or camshaft separately because of possible damage which might occur to the valves.

16. Temporarily tighten the two center right and left cylinder head bolts to 14.5 ft lbs.

17. Install the camshaft sprocket together with the timing chain to the camshaft. Make sure the marks you made earlier line up with each other. If you get into trouble, see "Timing Chain Removal and Installation" for timing procedures.

18. Install the cylinder head bolts. Note that there are two sizes of bolts used; the longer bolts are installed on the driver's side of the engine with a smaller bolt in the center position. The remaining small bolts are installed on the opposite side of the cylinder head.

19. Tighten the cylinder head bolts in three stages: first to 29 ft lbs, second to 43 ft lbs, and lastly to 47–62 ft lbs.

Tighten the cylinder head bolts on all models in the proper sequence.

20. Install and assemble the remaining components of the engine in the reverse order of removal.

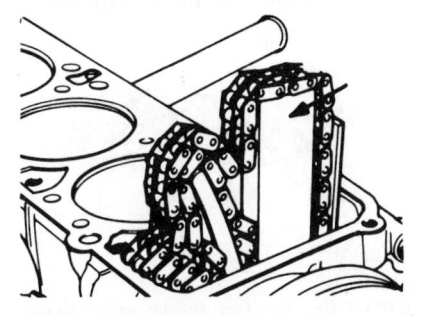

Wedge the chain with a wooden block (arrow). If you don't, you'll be fishing for the chain in the crankcase

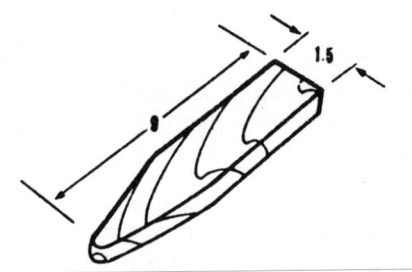

Dimensions for fabricating wooden wedge (used to hold chain in place)

L24 OVERHEAD CAMSHAFT ENGINE

NOTE: *Any of the following procedures that involve removing or disturbing the timing chain on the overhead cam engine make use of the factory procedure to support the chain. This procedure involves the use of a factory approved wooden wedge to hold the timing chain in place. Unfortunately, personal experience reveals that while the factory procedure works fine in theory, in practice, you may find that it is somewhat difficult. A longer, but ultimately less frustrating alternative is to remove the front cover anytime you have to work on the timing chain.*

1. Crank the engine until the No. 1 piston is at TDC of the compression stroke, disconnect the battery, and drain the cooling system.

2. Remove the radiator hoses and the heater hoses. Unbolt the alternator mounting bracket and move the alternator to one side.

3. If the car is equipped with air-conditioning, unbolt the compressor and place it to one side. *Do not disconnect the compressor lines. Severe injury could result.*

4. Remove the fan and the fan pulley. Remove the power steering pump.

5. Remove the water pump. Remove the spark plug leads from the spark plugs.

6. Remove the cold start valve and the fuel pipe as an assembly. Remove the throttle linkage.

7. Remove all lines and hoses from the intake manifold. Mark them first so you will know where they go.

8. Unbolt the exhaust manifold from the exhaust pipe. The cylinder head can be removed with both the intake and exhaust manifolds in place.

9. Remove the camshaft cover.

10. Mark the relationship of the cam-

ENGINE AND ENGINE REBUILDING

shaft sprocket to the timing chain with paint. There are timing marks on the chain and the sprocket which should be visible when no. 1 piston is at TDC, but the marks are quite small and not particularly useful.

11. Before removing the camshaft sprocket, it will be necessary to wedge the chain in place so that it will not fall down into the front cover. The factory procedure is to wedge the timing chain in place with the wooden wedge shown here. The problem with this procedure is that it may allow the chain tensioner to move out far enough to cock itself against the chain. If this happens, you'll find that the chain won't go back over the sprocket after you've put the sprocket back on. In this case, you'll have to remove the front cover and push the tensioner back. After you've wedged the chain, unbolt the camshaft sprocket and remove it.

12. Remove the cylinder head bolts. They require an allen wrench type socket adapter. Keep the bolts in order as two different sizes are used.

13. Lift off the cylinder head. You may have to tap it *lightly* with a hammer.

To install the cylinder head:

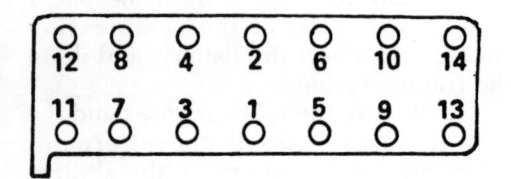

L24 head torque sequence

14. Install a new head gasket and place the head in position on the block.
15. Install the head bolts in their original locations.
16. Torque the head bolts in three stages: first to 29 ft lbs, then to 43 ft lbs, then to 62 ft lbs.
17. Reinstall the camshaft sprocket in its original location. The chain is installed at the same time as the sprocket. Make sure the marks you made earlier line up. If the chain has slipped, or the engine has been disturbed, correct the timing as described under "Timing Chain Removal and Installation".
18. Reinstall all ancillary parts, coolant, etc.
19. Adjust the valves as described in chapter 2.

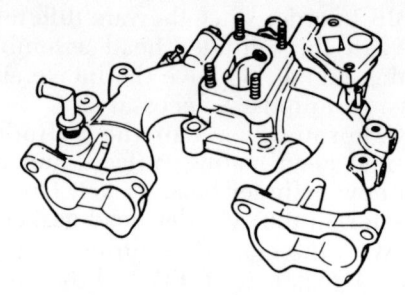

A-series engine intake manifold

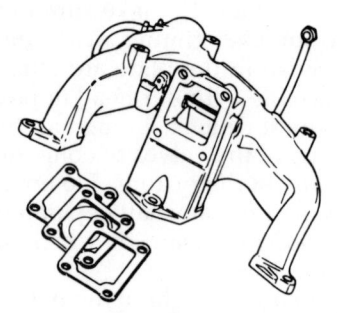

A-series engine exhaust manifold

20. After 600 miles of driving, retorque the head bolts and readjust the valves.

Overhaul

Cylinder head overhaul should be referred to a competent automotive machine shop. Valve guides and seats are removable and oversizes are available from Datsun.

INTAKE MANIFOLD

Removal and Installation—All Except 810

1. Remove the air cleaner assembly together with all of the attending hoses.
2. Disconnect the throttle linkage and fuel and vacuum lines from the carburetor.
3. The carburetor can be removed from the manifold at this point or can be removed as an assembly with the intake manifold.

Removing the A-series intake and exhaust manifolds as a unit

ENGINE AND ENGINE REBUILDING

L-series engine intake manifold

4. On the A12, A13, and A14 engines, disconnect the intake and exhaust manifold unless you are removing both. Loosen the intake manifold attaching nuts, working from the two ends toward the center, and then remove them.

5. Remove the intake manifold from the engine.

6. Install the intake manifold in the reverse order of removal.

L24 Engine (810) Intake Manifold Removal and Installation

1. Disconnect all hoses to the air cleaner and remove the air cleaner.

2. Disconnect all air, water vacuum and fuel hoses to the intake manifold. Remove the cold start valve and fuel pipe as an assembly. Remove the throttle linkage.

3. Remove the B.P.T. valve control tube from the intake manifold. Remove the EGR hoses.

4. Disconnect all electrical wiring to the fuel injection unit. Note the location of the wires and mark them in some manner to facilitate reinstallation.

5. Make sure all wires, hoses, lines, etc. are removed. Unbolt the intake manifold. Keep the bolts in order since they are of two different sizes.

6. Installation is the reverse of removal. Use a new gasket, clean both sealing surfaces, and torque the bolts in several stages, working from the center outward.

EXHAUST MANIFOLD

Removal and Installation

1. Remove the air cleaner assembly.

2. Disconnect the exhaust pipe from the exhaust manifold. Disconnect the intake manifold from the exhaust manifold (on A12, A13, and A14 engines) unless you are removing both.

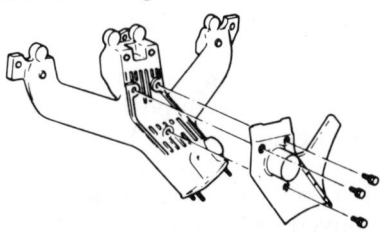

L-series engine exhaust manifold

3. Loosen and remove the exhaust manifold attaching nuts and remove the manifold from the engine.

4. Install the exhaust manifold in the reverse order of removal.

TIMING CHAIN COVER

Removal and Installation

A12, A13, AND A14 OVERHEAD VALVE ENGINES

1. Remove the radiator. Loosen the alternator adjustment and remove the belt.

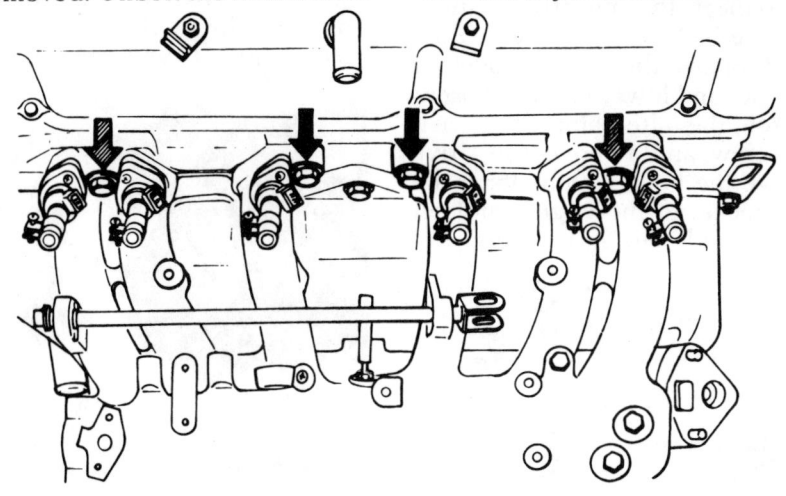

L24 engine intake manifold securing bolts

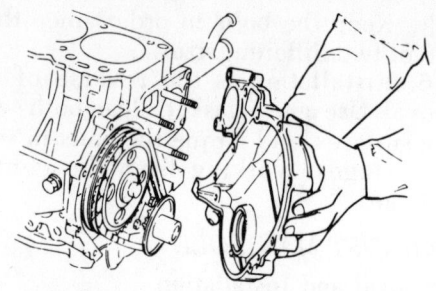

ENGINE AND ENGINE REBUILDING

Removing the A-series engine timing cover

Loosen the air pump adjustment and remove the belt on engines with the air pump system.

2. Remove the fan and water pump.
3. Bend back the locktab from the crankshaft pulley nut. Remove the nut by affixing a heavy wrench and rapping the wrench with a hammer. The nut must be unscrewed in the opposite direction of normal engine rotation. Pull off the pulley.
4. It is recommended that the oil pan be removed or loosened before the front cover is removed.
5. Unbolt and remove the timing chain cover.
6. Replace the crankshaft oil seal in the cover. Most models use a felt seal.
7. Reverse the procedure to install, using new gaskets. Apply sealant to both sides of the timing cover gasket. Front cover bolt torque is 4 ft lbs, water pump bolt torque is 7–10 ft lbs, and oil pan bolt torque is 4 ft lbs.

L16, L18, L20B, AND L24 OVERHEAD CAMSHAFT ENGINES

1. Disconnect the negative battery cable from the battery, drain the cooling system, and remove the radiator together with the upper and lower radiator hoses.
2. Loosen the alternator drive belt adjusting screw and remove the drive belt. Remove the bolts which attach the alternator bracket to the engine and set the alternator aside out of the way.

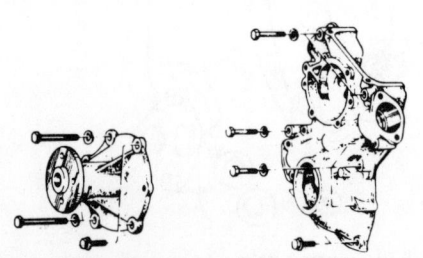

L-series engine front cover bolts

3. Remove the distributor.
4. Remove the oil pump attaching screws, and take out the pump and its drive spindle.
5. Remove the cooling fan and the fan pulley together with the drive belt.
6. Remove the water pump.
7. Remove the crankshaft pulley bolt and remove the crankshaft pulley.
8. Remove the bolts holding the front cover to the front of the cylinder block, the four bolts which retain the front of the oil pan to the bottom of the front cover, and the two bolts which are screwed down through the front of the cylinder head and into the top of the front cover.
9. Carefully pry the front cover off the front of the engine.
10. Cut the exposed front section of the oil pan gasket away from the oil pan. Do the same to the gasket at the top of the front cover. Remove the two side gaskets and clean all of the mating surfaces.
11. Cut the portions needed from a new oil pan gasket and top front cover gasket.
12. Apply sealer to all of the gaskets and position them on the engine in their proper places.
13. Apply a light coating of grease to the crankshaft oil seal and carefully mount the front cover to the front of the engine and install all of the mounting bolts.
   Tighten the 8 mm bolts to 7–12 ft lbs and the 6 mm bolts to 3–6 ft lbs. Tighten the oil pan attaching bolts to 4–7 ft lbs.
14. Before installing the oil pump, place the gasket over the shaft and make sure that the mark on the drive spindle faces (aligned) with the oil pump hole.

When removing the A-series engine timing cover it is necessary to loosen or remove the oil pan

ENGINE AND ENGINE REBUILDING

Install the oil pump so that the projection on the top of the shaft is located in the exact position as when it was removed or in the 11:25 o'clock position with the piston in the No. 1 cylinder placed at TDC on the compression stroke, if the engine was disturbed since disassembly. Tighten the oil pump attaching screws to 8–10 ft lbs. See "Oil Pump Removal and Installation."

TIMING CHAIN AND CAMSHAFT

Removal and Installation

A12, A13, AND A14 OVERHEAD VALVE ENGINES

It is recommended that this operation be done with the engine removed from the vehicle.

1. Remove the timing chain cover.
2. Unbolt and remove the chain tensioner.
3. Remove the camshaft sprocket retaining bolt.
4. Pull off the camshaft sprocket, easing off the crankshaft sprocket at the same time. Remove both sprockets and chain as an assembly. Be careful not to lose the shims and oil slinger from behind the crankshaft sprocket.
5. Remove the distributor, distributor drive spindle, and pushrods.

Remove the oil pump and pump driveshaft.

6. Unbolt and remove the camshaft locating plate.
7. Remove the camshaft carefully. This will be easier if the block is inverted to prevent the lifters from falling down. The lifters are of the mushroom type and cannot be removed until the camshaft has been removed. It may be necessary to remove the oil pan to reach the lifters for removal.
8. The camshaft bearings can be pressed out and replaced. They are available in undersizes, should it be necessary to regrind the camshaft journals.
9. Reinstall the camshaft. If the locating plate has an oil hole, it should be to the right of the engine. The locating plate is marked with the word LOWER and an arrow. Locating plate bolt torque is 3–4 ft lbs. Be careful to engage the drive pin in the rear end of the camshaft with the slot in the oil pump driveshaft.
10. Camshaft end-play can be measured after temporarily replacing the camshaft sprocket and securing bolt.

End-play should be no more than 0.001–0.003 in. If end-play is excessive, replace the locating plate. They are available in several sizes.

11. If the crankshaft or camshaft has been replaced, install the sprockets temporarily and make sure that they are parallel. Adjust by shimming under the crankshaft sprocket.
12. Assemble the sprockets and chain, aligning them.
13. Turn the crankshaft until the keyway and the No. 1 piston is at top dead center. Install the sprockets and chain. The oil slinger behind the crankshaft sprocket must be replaced with the concave surface to the front. If the chain and sprocket installation is correct, the sprocket marks must be aligned between the shaft centers when the No. 1 piston is at top dead center. Engine camshaft sprocket retaining bolt torque is 33–36 ft lbs.
14. The rest of the reassembly proce-

A-series engine camshaft locating plate correctly installed

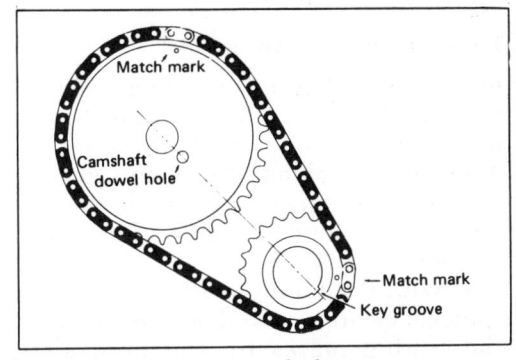

A-series engine timing mark alignment

ENGINE AND ENGINE REBUILDING

dure is the reverse of disassembly. Engine chain tensioner bolt torque is 4–6 ft lbs.

TIMING CHAIN AND TENSIONER
Removal and Installation
L16, L18, L20B, AND L24 OVERHEAD CAMSHAFT ENGINES

1. Before beginning any disassembly procedures, position the no. 1 piston at TDC on the compression stroke.
2. Remove the front cover as previously outlined. Remove the camshaft cover.
3. With the No. 1 piston at TDC, the timing marks on the camshaft sprocket and the timing chain should be visible. Mark both of them with paint. Also mark the relationship of the camshaft sprocket

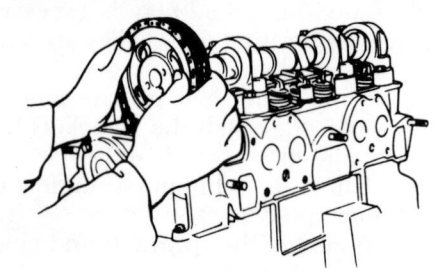

Removing the camshaft sprocket

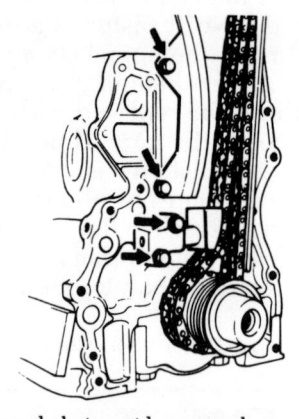

Tensioner and chain guide removal

to the camshaft. At this point you will notice that there are three sets of timing marks and locating holes in the sprocket. They are for making adjustments to compensate for timing chain stretch. See the following "Timing Chain Adjustment" for more details.

4. With the timing marks on the cam sprocket clearly marked, locate and mark the timing marks on the crankshaft sprocket. Also mark the chain timing

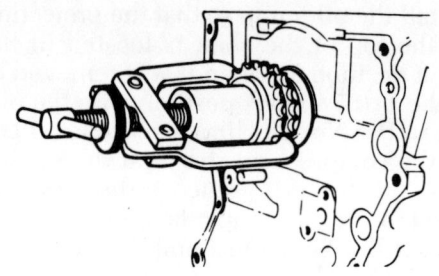

Crankshaft sprocket removal

mark. Of course, if the chain is not to be re-used, marking it is useless.

5. Unbolt the camshaft sprocket and remove the sprocket along with the chain. As you remove the chain, hold it where the chain tensioner contacts it. When the chain is removed, the tensioner is going to come apart. Hold on to it and you won't lose any of the parts. There is no need to remove the chain guide unless it is being replaced.

6. Install the timing chain and the camshaft sprocket together after first positioning the chain over the crankshaft sprocket. Position the sprocket so that the marks made earlier line up. This is assuming that the engine has not been disturbed. The camshaft and crankshaft keys should both be pointing upward. If a new chain and/or gear is being installed, position the sprocket so that the timing marks on the chain align with the marks on the crankshaft sprocket and the camshaft sprocket (with both keys pointing up). The marks are on the right-hand side of the sprockets as you face the engine. Engines up to 1974 have 42 pins between the mating marks of the chain and sprockets when the chain is installed correctly. 1975 and later engines, *except the L24*, have 44 pins. The L24 engine used in the 810 has 42 pins between timing

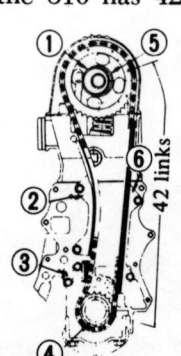

1. Fuel pump drive cam
2. Chain guide
3. Chain tensioner
4. Crank sprocket
5. Cam sprocket
6. Chain guide

Timing chain and sprocket alignment—L-series engine

ENGINE AND ENGINE REBUILDING

marks. The factory manual refers to the pins as links, but in American terminology this is incorrect. Count the pins. There are two pins per chain link. *This is an important step. If you do not get the exact number of pins between the timing marks, valve timing will be incorrect and the engine will either not run at all or run very badly.*

7. Install the chain tensioner. Install the remaining components in the reverse order of disassembly.

Timing Chain Adjustment

L16, L18, L20B AND L24 OVERHEAD CAMSHAFT ENGINES

When the timing chain stretches excessively, the valve timing will be adversely affected. There are three sets of holes and timing marks on the camshaft sprocket. The first two are used for the four-cylinder engines, and the third one is only of use for the L24 engine.

If the stretch of the chain roller links is excessive, adjust the camshaft sprocket location by transferring the set position of the camshaft sprocket from the factory position of no. 1 to one of the other positions as follows:

1. Turn the crankshaft until the no. 1 piston is at TDC on the compression stroke. Examine whether the camshaft sprocket location notch is to the left of the oblong groove on the camshaft retaining plate. If the notch in the sprocket is to the left of the groove in the retaining plate, then the chain is stretched and needs adjusting.

2. Remove the camshaft sprocket together with the chain and reinstall the sprocket and chain with the locating dowel on the camshaft inserted into either the no. 2 or 3 hole of the sprocket (depending on whether the engine is a four or six cylinder). The timing mark on the timing chain must be aligned with the mark on the sprocket. The amount of modification is 4 degrees of crankshaft rotation for each mark.

3. Recheck the valve timing as outlined in Step 1. The notch in the sprocket should be to the right of the groove in the camshaft retaining plate.

4. If and when the notch cannot be brought to the right of the groove, the timing chain is worn beyond repair and must be replaced.

CAMSHAFT

Removal and Installation

L16, L18, L20B, AND L24 OVERHEAD CAMSHAFT ENGINES

1. Removal of the cylinder head from the engine is optional. Remove the camshaft sprocket from the camshaft together with the timing chain.

2. Loosen the valve rocker pivot locknut and remove the rocker arm by pressing down on the valve spring.

3. Remove the two retaining nuts on the camshaft retainer plate at the front of the cylinder head and carefully slide the camshaft out of the camshaft carrier.

4. Lightly coat the camshaft bearings with clean motor oil and carefully slide

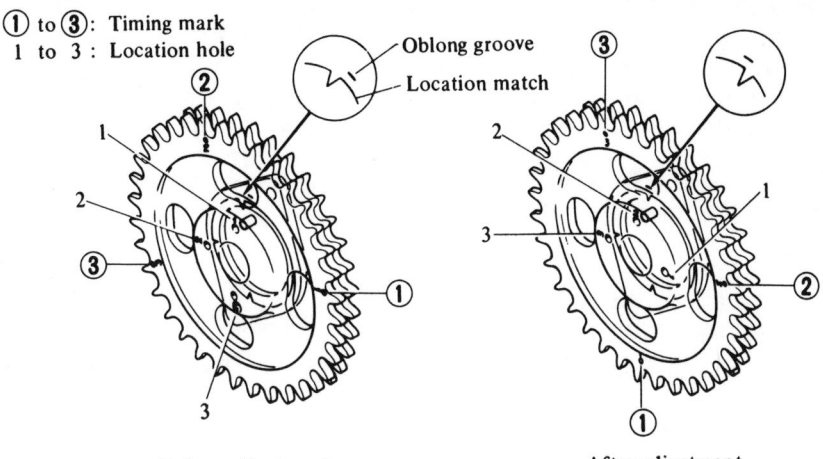

① to ③: Timing mark
1 to 3 : Location hole

Before adjustment

After adjustment

Timing chain adjustment

the camshaft in place in the camshaft carrier.

5. Install the camshaft retainer plate with the oblong groove in the face of the plate facing toward the front of the engine.

6. Check the valve timing as outlined under "Timing Chain Removal and Installation" and install the timing sprocket on the camshaft, tightening the bolt together with the fuel pump cam to 86–116 ft lbs.

7. Install the rocker arms by pressing down the valve springs with a screwdriver and install the valve rocker springs.

8. Install the cylinder head, if it was removed, and assemble the rest of the engine in the reverse order of removal.

PISTONS AND CONNECTING RODS
Removal and Installation
ALL ENGINES

1. Remove the cylinder head.
2. Remove the oil pan.
3. Remove any carbon buildup from the cylinder wall at the tope end of the piston travel with a ridge reamer tool.
4. Position the piston to be removed at the bottom of its stroke so that the connecting rod bearing cap can be reached easily from under the engine.
5. Unscrew the connecting rod bearing cap and remove the cap and lower half of the bearing.
6. Push the piston and connecting rod up and out of the cylinder block with a length of wood. Use care not to scratch the cylinder wall with the connecting rod or the wooden tool.
7. Keep all of the components from each cylinder together and install them in the cylinder from which they were removed.
8. Coat the bearing face of the connecting rod and the outer face of the pistons with engine oil.
9. Turn the top compression ring to bring its gap to about the 1:30 o'clock position. Set the remaining rings so that their gaps are positioned 180° apart around the piston. The oil ring gap will be directly under the top compression ring gap.
10. Turn the crankshaft until the rod journal of the particular cylinder you are working on is brought to the TDC position.

11. With the piston and rings clamped in a ring compressor, the notched mark on the head of the piston toward the front of the engine, and the oil hole side of the connecting rod toward the fuel pump side of the engine, push the piston and connecting rod assembly into the cylinder bore until the big bearing end of the connecting rod contacts and is seated on the rod journal of the crankshaft. Use care not to scratch the cylinder wall with the connecting rod.

12. Push down farther on the piston and turn the crankshaft while the connecting rod rides around on the crankshaft rod journal. Turn the crankshaft until the crankshaft rod journal is at BDC (bottom dead center).

13. Align the mark on the connecting rod bearing cap with that on the connecting rod and tighten the bearing cap bolts to the specified torque.

14. Install all of the piston/connecting rod assemblies in the manner outlined above and assemble the oil pan and cylinder head to the engine in the reverse order of removal.

Piston and Connecting Rod Identification and Positioning

The pistons are marked with a number or "F" in the piston head. When installed in the engine the number or "F" markings are to be facing toward the front of the engine.

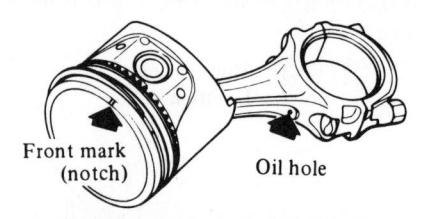

Piston and rod positioning—L-series engines

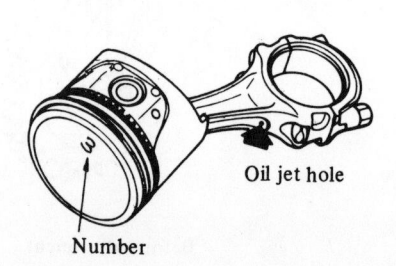

Piston and rod positioning—A-series engines

ENGINE AND ENGINE REBUILDING

The connecting rods are installed in the engine with the oil hole facing toward the fuel pump side (right) of the engine.

NOTE: *It is advisable to number the pistons, connecting rods, and bearing caps in some manner so that they can be reinstalled in the same cylinder, facing in the same direction from which they are removed.*

Engine Lubrication

OIL PAN

Removal and Installation

ALL ENGINES

To remove the oil pan it will be necessary to unbolt the motor mounts and jack the engine to gain clearance. Drain the oil, remove the attaching screws, and remove the oil pan and gasket. Install the oil pan in the reverse order with a new gasket, tightening the screws to 4–7 ft lbs.

REAR MAIN OIL SEAL

Replacement

In order to replace the rear main oil seal, the rear main bearing cap must be removed. Removal of the rear main bearing cap requires the use of a special rear main bearing cap puller. Also, the oil seal is installed with a special crankshaft rear oil seal drift. Unless these or similar tools are available to you, it is recommended that the oil seal be replaced by a Datsun service center.

1. Remove the engine and transmission assembly from the vehicle.
2. Remove the transmission from the engine.
3. Remove the clutch from the flywheel.
4. Remove the flywheel from the crankshaft.
5. Remove the rear main bearing cap together with the bearing cap side seals.
6. Remove the rear main oil seal from around the crankshaft.
7. Apply lithium grease around the sealing lip of the oil seal and install the seal around the crankshaft using a suitable tool.

8. Apply sealer to the rear main bearing cap as indicated, install the rear main bearing cap, and tighten the cap bolts to 33–40 ft lbs.
9. Apply sealant to the rear main bearing cap side seals and install the side seals, driving the seals into place with a suitable drift.
10. Assemble the engine and install it in the vehicle in the reverse order of removal.

OIL PUMP

Removal and Installation

The oil pump is mounted externally on the engine, thus, eliminating the need to remove the oil pan in order to remove the oil pump. The A-series oil pump is in unit with oil filter mounting flange. The L-series oil pump is mounted in the timing chain cover.

1. Remove the distributor on L16, L18, L20B, and L24 engines.
2. Drain the engine oil.
3. Remove the front stabilizer bar.
4. Remove the splash shield.
5. Remove the oil pump body with the drive spindle assembly.

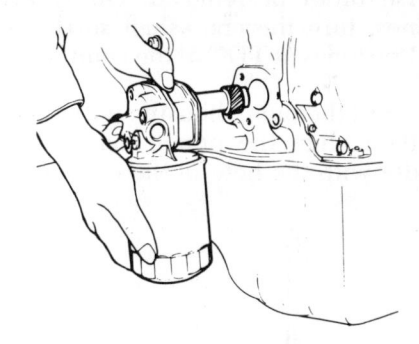

Removing A-series engine oil pump

Removing L-series engine oil pump

ENGINE AND ENGINE REBUILDING

Outer rotor

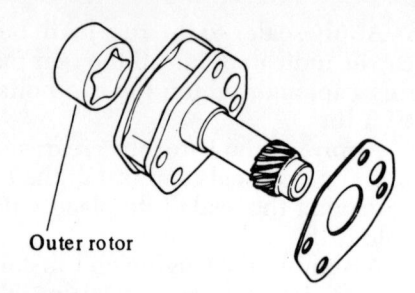

Exploded view of A-series engine oil pump

1. Oil pump body
2. Inner rotor and shaft
3. Outer rotor
4. Oil pump cover
5. Regulator valve
6. Regulator spring
7. Washer
8. Regulator cap
9. Cover gasket

Exploded view of L-series engine oil pump

6. Install the A-series oil pump in the reverse order or removal. On L-series engines, turn the crankshaft so that the No. 1 piston is at TDC of the compression stroke.

7. Fill the pump housing with engine oil, then align the punch mark on the spindle with the hole in the oil pump.

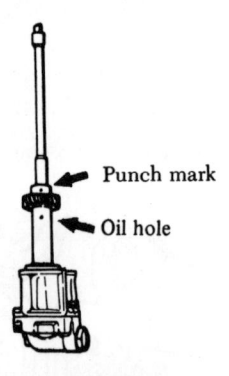

Punch mark
Oil hole

L-series engine oil pump alignment

8. With a new gasket placed over the drive spindle, install the oil pump and drive spindle assembly so that the projection on the top of the drive spindle is located in the 11:25 o'clock position.

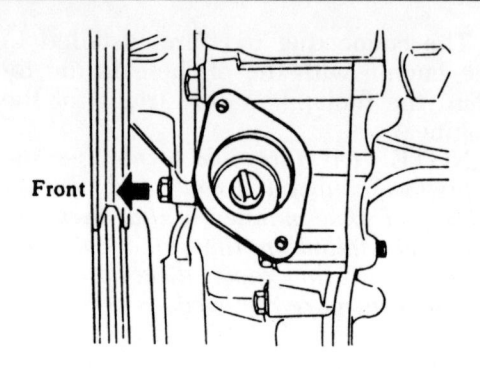

Front

Position of distributor drive spindle—L-series engines

9. Install the distributor with the metal tip of the rotor pointing toward the No. 1 spark plug tower of the distributor cap.

10. Assemble the remaining components in the reverse order of removal.

Engine Cooling

RADIATOR

Removal and Installation

1. Drain the engine coolant into a clean container.
2. Remove the front grille.
3. Disconnect the upper and lower radiator hoses. On cars with an automatic transmission, disconnect the oil cooler inlet and outlet lines from the radiator. Plug the lines to prevent the loss of transmission fluid and the entrance of dirt.

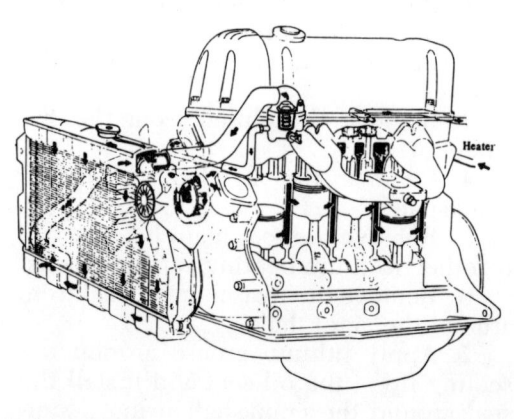

Cooling system

ENGINE AND ENGINE REBUILDING

4. Remove the bolts retaining the radiator from the radiator side supports and remove the radiator upward.
5. Install the radiator in the reverse order of removal.

WATER PUMP
Removal and Installation
ALL ENGINES

1. Drain the engine coolant into a clean container.
2. Loosen the four bolts retaining the fan shroud to the radiator and remove the shroud.
3. Loosen the belt, then remove the fan and pulley from the water pump hub.
4. Remove the five bolts retaining the pump and remove the pump together with the gasket from the front cover.
5. Remove all traces of gasket material and install the water pump in the reverse order with a new gasket and sealer. Tighten the bolts uniformly.

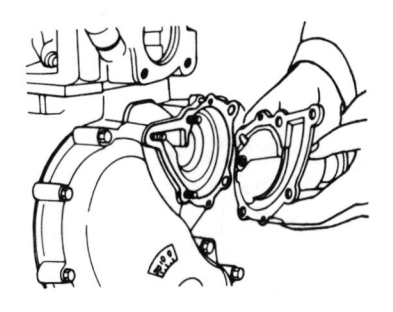

A-series engine water pump removal

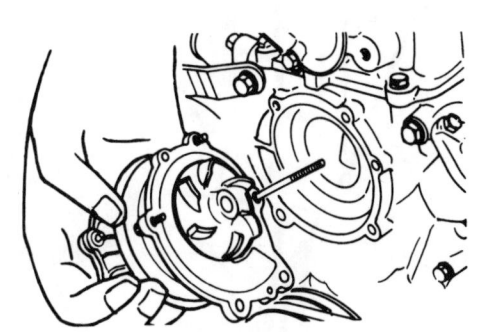

L-series engine water pump removal

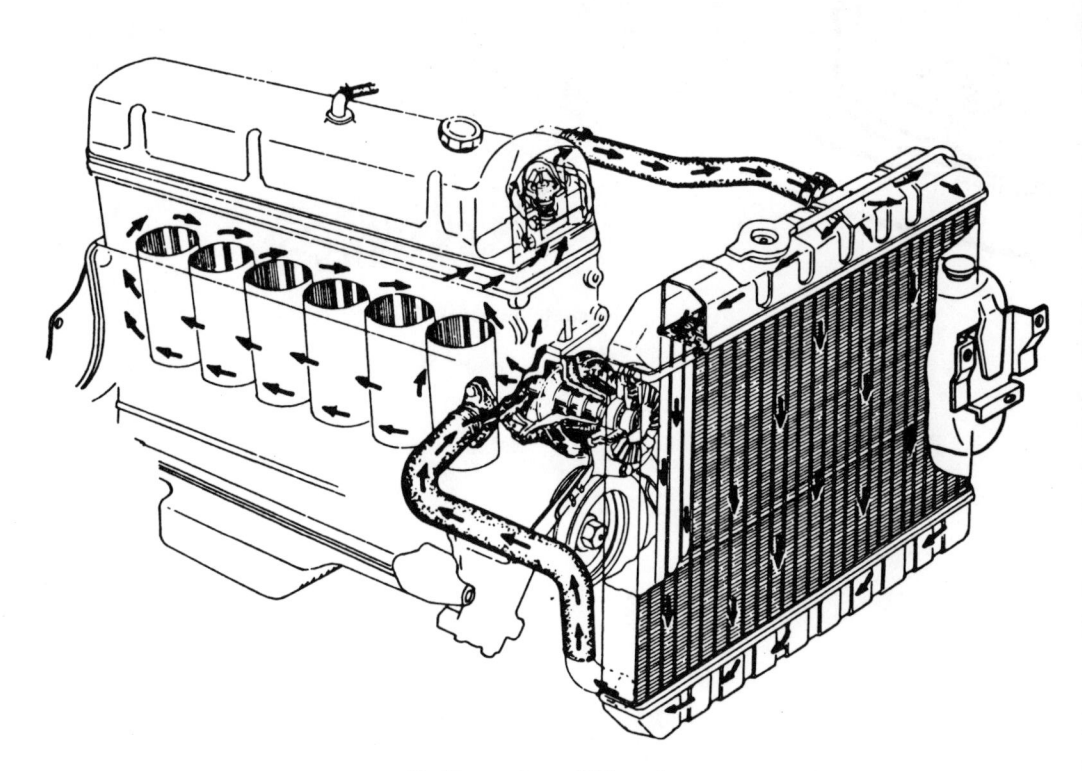

Cooling system—L24 engine

ENGINE AND ENGINE REBUILDING

THERMOSTAT

Removal and Installation

ALL ENGINES

1. Drain the engine coolant into a clean container so that the level is below the thermostat housing.
2. Disconnect the upper radiator hose at the water outlet.
3. Loosen the two securing nuts and remove the water outlet, gasket, and the thermostat from the thermostat housing.
4. Install the thermostat in the reverse order of removal, using a new gasket with sealer and with the thermostat spring toward the inside of the engine.

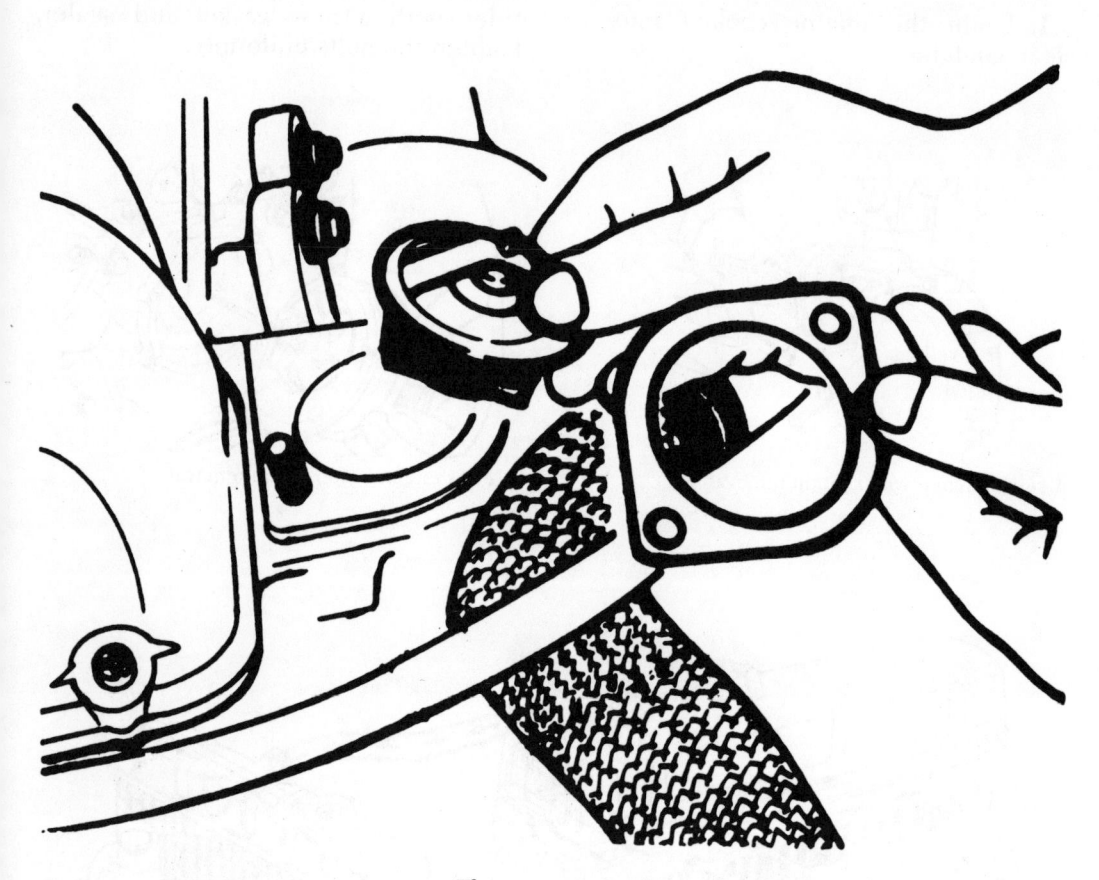

Thermostat removal

Engine Rebuilding

This section describes, in detail, the procedures involved in rebuilding a typical engine. The procedures specifically refer to an inline engine, however, they are basically identical to those used in rebuilding engines of nearly all design and configurations. Procedures for servicing atypical engines (i.e., horizontally opposed) are described in the appropriate section, although in most cases, cylinder head reconditioning procedures described in this chapter will apply.

The section is divided into two sections. The first, Cylinder Head Reconditioning, assumes that the cylinder head is removed from the engine, all manifolds are removed, and the cylinder head is on a workbench. The camshaft should be removed from overhead cam cylinder heads. The second section, Cylinder Block Reconditioning, covers the block, pistons, connecting rods and crankshaft. It is assumed that the engine is mounted on a work stand, and the cylinder head and all accessories are removed.

Procedures are identified as follows:

Unmarked—Basic procedures that must be performed in order to successfully complete the rebuilding process.

Starred (*)—Procedures that should be performed to ensure maximum performance and engine life.

Double starred (**)—Procedures that may be performed to increase engine performance and reliability. These procedures are usually reserved for extremely heavy-duty or competition usage.

In many cases, a choice of methods is also provided. Methods are identified in the same manner as procedures. The choice of method for a procedure is at the discretion of the user.

The tools required for the basic rebuilding procedure should, with minor exceptions, be those

TORQUE (ft. lbs.)*

U.S.

Bolt Diameter (inches)	Bolt Grade (SAE) 1 and 2	5	6	8	Wrench Size (inches) Bolt	Nut
1/4	5	7	10	10.5	3/8	7/16
5/16	9	14	19	22	1/2	9/16
3/8	15	25	34	37	9/16	5/8
7/16	24	40	55	60	5/8	3/4
1/2	37	60	85	92	3/4	13/16
9/16	53	88	120	132	7/8	7/8
5/8	74	120	167	180	15/16	1
3/4	120	200	280	296	1-1/8	1-1/8
7/8	190	302	440	473	1-5/16	1-5/16
1	282	466	660	714	1-1/2	1-1/2

Metric

Bolt Diameter (mm)	Bolt Grade 5D	8G	10K	12K	Wrench Size (mm) Bolt and Nut
6	5	6	8	10	10
8	10	16	22	27	14
10	19	31	40	49	17
12	34	54	70	86	19
14	55	89	117	137	22
16	83	132	175	208	24
18	111	182	236	283	27
22	182	284	394	464	32
24	261	419	570	689	36

*—Torque values are for lightly oiled bolts. CAUTION: Bolts threaded into aluminum require much less torque.

ENGINE AND ENGINE REBUILDING

Heli-Coil installation
(© Chrysler Corp.)

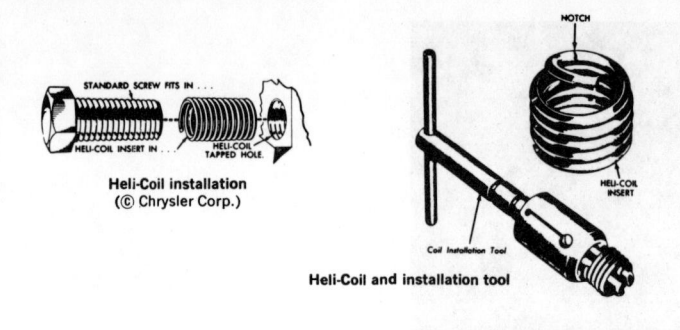

Heli-Coil and installation tool

Heli-Coil Specifications

Heli-Coil Insert		Insert Length (In.)	Drill Size	Tap	Insert Tool	Extracting Tool
Thread Size	Part No.			Part No.	Part No.	Part No.
1/2 -20	1185-4	3/8	17/64(.266)	4 CPB	528-4N	1227-6
5/16-18	1185-5	15/32	Q(.332)	5 CPB	528-5N	1227-6
3/8 -16	1185-6	9/16	X(.397)	6 CPB	528-6N	1227-6
7/16-14	1185-7	21/32	29/64(.453)	7 CPB	528-7N	1227-16
1/2 -13	1185-8	3/4	33/64(.516)	8 CPB	528-8N	1227-16

included in a mechanic's tool kit. An accurate torque wrench, and a dial indicator (reading in thousandths) mounted on a universal base should be available. Bolts and nuts with no torque specification should be tightened according to size (see chart). Special tools, where required, all are readily available from the major tool suppliers (i.e., Craftsman, Snap-On, K-D). The services of a competent automotive machine shop must also be readily available.

When assembling the engine, any parts that will be in frictional contact must be pre-lubricated, to provide protection on initial start-up. Vortex Pre-Lube, STP, or any product specifically formulated for this purpose may be used. NOTE: *Do not use engine oil.* Where semi-permanent (locked but removable) installation of bolts or nuts is desired, threads should be cleaned and coated with Loctite. Studs may be permanently installed using Loctite Stud and Bearing Mount.

Aluminum has become increasingly popular for use in engines, due to its low weight and excellent heat transfer characteristics. The following precautions must be observed when handling aluminum engine parts:

—Never hot-tank aluminum parts.

—Remove all aluminum parts (identification tags, etc.) from engine parts before hot-tanking (otherwise they will be removed during the process).

—Always coat threads lightly with engine oil or anti-seize compounds before installation, to prevent seizure.

—Never over-torque bolts or spark plugs in aluminum threads. Should stripping occur, threads can be restored according to the following procedure, using Heli-Coil thread inserts:

Tap drill the hole with the stripped threads to the specified size (see chart). Using the specified tap (NOTE: *Heli-Coil tap sizes refer to the size thread being replaced, rather than the actual tap size*), tap the hole for the Heli-Coil. Place the insert on the proper installation tool (see chart). Apply pressure on the insert while winding it clockwise into the hole, until the top of the insert is one turn below the surface. Remove the installation tool, and break the installation tang from the bottom of the insert by moving it up and down. If the Heli-Coil must be removed, tap the removal tool firmly into the hole, so that it engages the top thread, and turn the tool counter-clockwise to extract the insert.

Snapped bolts or studs may be removed, using a stud extractor (unthreaded) or Vise-Grip pliers (threaded). Penetrating oil (e.g., Liquid Wrench) will often aid in breaking frozen threads. In cases where the stud or bolt is flush with, or below the surface, proceed as follows:

Drill a hole in the broken stud or bolt, approximately 1/2 its diameter. Select a screw extractor (e.g., Easy-Out) of the proper size, and tap it into the stud or bolt. Turn the extractor counter-clockwise to remove the stud or bolt.

Magnaflux and Zyglo are inspection techniques used to locate material flaws, such as stress cracks. Magnafluxing coats the part with fine magnetic particles, and subjects the part to a magnetic field. Cracks cause breaks

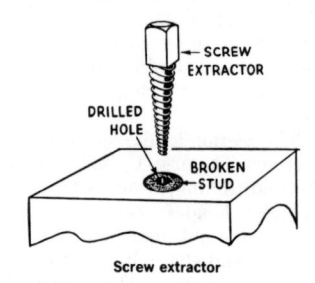

Screw extractor

in the magnetic field, which are outlined by the particles. Since Magnaflux is a magnetic process, it is applicable only to ferrous materials. The Zyglo process coats the material with a fluorescent dye penetrant, and then subjects it to blacklight inspection, under which cracks glow bright-

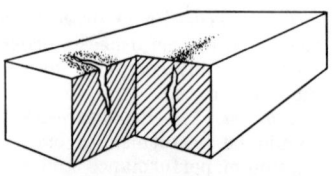

Magnaflux indication of cracks

ENGINE AND ENGINE REBUILDING

ly. Parts made of any material may be tested using Zyglo. While Magnaflux and Zyglo are excellent for general inspection, and locating hidden defects, specific checks of suspected cracks may be made at lower cost and more readily using spot check dye. The dye is sprayed onto the suspected area, wiped off, and the area is then sprayed with a developer. Cracks then will show up brightly. Spot check dyes will only indicate surface cracks; therefore, structural cracks below the surface may escape detection. When questionable, the part should be tested using Magnaflux or Zyglo.

CYLINDER HEAD RECONDITIONING

NOTE: *This engine rebuilding section is a guide to accpeted engine rebuilding procedures. Every effort is made to illustrate the engine(s) used by this manufacturer; but, occasionally, typical examples of standard engine rebuilding practices are illustrated.*

Procedure	*Method*
Identify the valves: 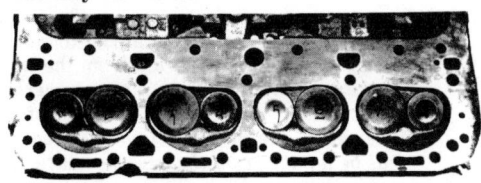 Valve identification	Invert the cylinder head, and number the valve faces front to rear, using a permanent felt-tip marker.
Remove the rocker arms: 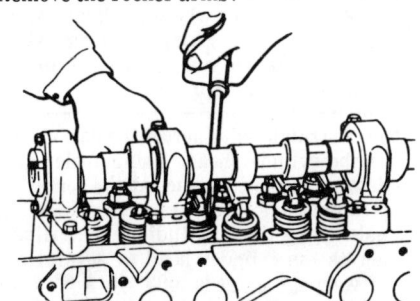	Remove the rocker arms with shaft(s) or balls and nuts. Wire the sets of rockers, balls and nuts together, and identify according to the corresponding valve.
Remove the valves and springs: 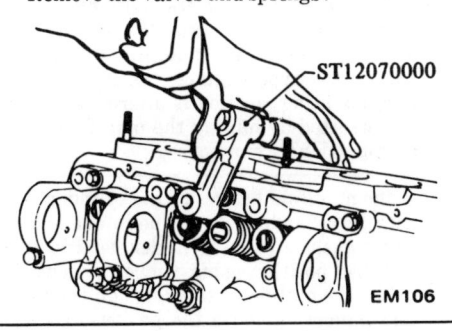 ST12070000 EM106	Using an appropriate valve spring compressor (depending on the configuration of the cylinder head), compress the valve springs. Lift out the keepers with needlenose pliers, release the compressor, and remove the valve, spring, and spring retainer.
Check the valve stem-to-guide clearance:  Checking the valve stem-to-guide clearance	Clean the valve stem with lacquer thinner or a similar solvent to remove all gum and varnish. Clean the valve guides using solvent and an expanding wire-type valve guide cleaner. Mount a dial indicator so that the stem is at 90° to the valve stem, as close to the valve guide as possible. Move the valve off its seat, and measure the valve guide-to-stem clearance by moving the stem back and forth to actuate the dial indicator. Measure the valve stems using a micrometer, and compare to specifications, to determine whether stem or guide wear is responsible for excessive clearance.

ENGINE AND ENGINE REBUILDING

Procedure	Method
De-carbon the cylinder head and valves: *Removing carbon from the cylinder head*	Chip carbon away from the valve heads, combustion chambers, and ports, using a chisel made of hardwood. Remove the remaining deposits with a stiff wire brush. NOTE: *Ensure that the deposits are actually removed, rather than burnished.*
Hot-tank the cylinder head:	Have the cylinder head hot-tanked to remove grease, corrosion, and scale from the water passages. NOTE: *In the case of overhead cam cylinder heads, consult the operator to determine whether the camshaft bearings will be damaged by the caustic solution.*
Degrease the remaining cylinder head parts:	Using solvent (i.e., Gunk), clean the rockers, rocker shaft(s) (where applicable), rocker balls and nuts, springs, spring retainers, and keepers. Do not remove the protective coating from the springs.
Check the cylinder head for warpage: *Checking the cylinder head for warpage* 1 & 3 CHECK DIAGONALLY 2 CHECK ACROSS CENTER	Place a straight-edge across the gasket surface of the cylinder head. Using feeler gauges, determine the clearance at the center of the straight-edge. Measure across both diagonals, along the longitudinal centerline, and across the cylinder head at several points. If warpage exceeds .003″ in a 6″ span, or .006″ over the total length, the cylinder head must be resurfaced. NOTE: *If warpage exceeds the manufacturers maximum tolerance for material removal, the cylinder head must be replaced.* When milling the cylinder heads of V-type engines, the intake manifold mounting position is altered, and must be corrected by milling the manifold flange a proportionate amount.
** Porting and gasket matching: *Marking the cylinder head for gasket matching*	** Coat the manifold flanges of the cylinder head with Prussian blue dye. Glue intake and exhaust gaskets to the cylinder head in their installed position using rubber cement and scribe the outline of the ports on the manifold flanges. Remove the gaskets. Using a small cutter in a hand-held power tool (i.e., Dremel Moto-Tool), gradually taper the walls of the port out to the scribed outline of the gasket. Further enlargement of the ports should include the removal of sharp edges and radiusing of sharp corners. Do not alter the valve guides. NOTE: *The most efficient port configuration is determined only by extensive testing. Therefore, it is best to consult someone experienced with the head in question to determine the optimum alterations.*

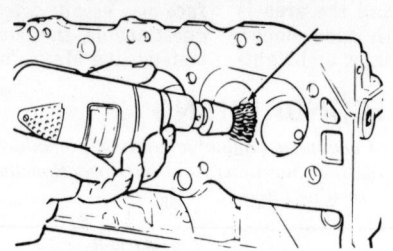

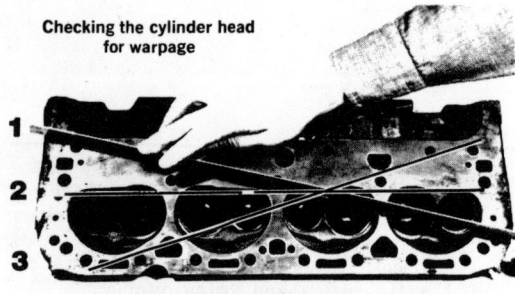

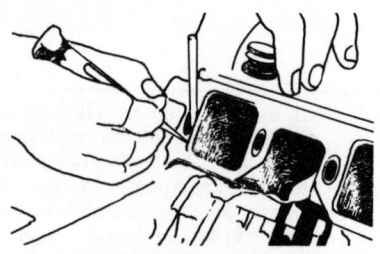

ENGINE AND ENGINE REBUILDING

Procedure	Method
Port configuration before and after gasket matching	
** Polish the ports: *Relieved and polished ports*	** Using a grinding stone with the above mentioned tool, polish the walls of the intake and exhaust ports, and combustion chamber. Use progressively finer stones until all surface imperfections are removed. NOTE: *Through testing, it has been determined that a smooth surface is more effective than a mirror polished surface in intake ports, and vice-versa in exhaust ports.*
* Knurling the valve guides: *Cut-away view of a knurled valve guide*	* Valve guides which are not excessively worn or distorted may, in some cases, be knurled rather than replaced. Knurling is a process in which metal is displaced and raised, thereby reducing clearance. Knurling also provides excellent oil control. The possibility of knurling rather than replacing valve guides should be discussed with a machinist.
Replacing the valve guides: NOTE: *Valve guides should only be replaced if damaged or if an oversize valve stem is not available.* A - VALVE GUIDE I.D. B - SLIGHTLY SMALLER THAN VALVE GUIDE O.D. Valve guide removal tool WASHERS A - VALVE GUIDE I.D. B - LARGER THAN THE VALVE GUIDE O.D. Valve guide installation tool (with washers used during installation)	Depending on the type of cylinder head, valve guides may be pressed, hammered, or shrunk in. In cases where the guides are shrunk into the head, replacement should be left to an equipped machine shop. In other cases, the guides are replaced as follows: Press or tap the valve guides out of the head using a stepped drift (see illustration). Determine the height above the boss that the guide must extend, and obtain a stack of washers, their I.D. similar to the guide's O.D., of that height. Place the stack of washers on the guide, and insert the guide into the boss. NOTE: *Valve guides are often tapered or beveled for installation.* Using the stepped installation tool (see illustration), press or tap the guides into position. Ream the guides according to the size of the valve stem.

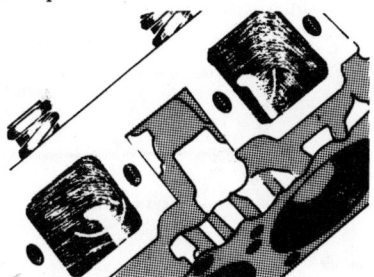

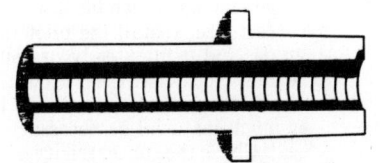

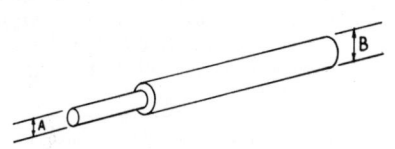

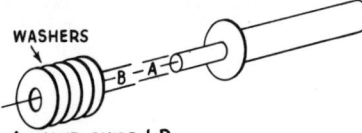

ENGINE AND ENGINE REBUILDING

Procedure	Method
Replacing valve seat inserts:	Replacement of valve seat inserts which are worn beyond resurfacing or broken, if feasible, must be done by a machine shop.
Resurfacing (grinding) the valve face: Grinding a valve Critical valve dimensions	Using a valve grinder, resurface the valves according to specifications. CAUTION: *Valve face angle is not always identical to valve seat angle.* A minimum margin of 1/32" should remain after grinding the valve. The valve stem tip should also be squared and resurfaced, by placing the stem in the V-block of the grinder, and turning it while pressing lightly against the grinding wheel.
Resurfacing the valve seats using reamers: Valve seat width and centering Reaming the valve seat	Select a reamer of the correct seat angle, slightly larger than the diameter of the valve seat, and assemble it with a pilot of the correct size. Install the pilot into the valve guide, and using steady pressure, turn the reamer clockwise. CAUTION: *Do not turn the reamer counter-clockwise.* Remove only as much material as necessary to clean the seat. Check the concentricity of the seat (see below). If the dye method is not used, coat the valve face with Prussian blue dye, install and rotate it on the valve seat. Using the dye marked area as a centering guide, center and narrow the valve seat to specifications with correction cutters. NOTE: *When no specifications are available, minimum seat width for exhaust valves should be 5/64", intake valves 1/16".* After making correction cuts, check the position of the valve seat on the valve face using Prussian blue dye.
* Resurfacing the valve seats using a grinder: Grinding a valve seat	Select a pilot of the correct size, and a coarse stone of the correct seat angle. Lubricate the pilot if necessary, and install the tool in the valve guide. Move the stone on and off the seat at approximately two cycles per second, until all flaws are removed from the seat. Install a fine stone, and finish the seat. Center and narrow the seat using correction stones, as described above.

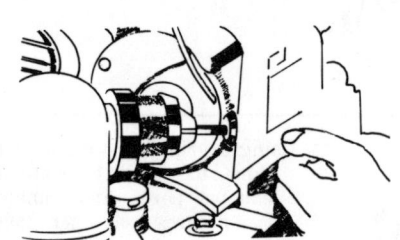

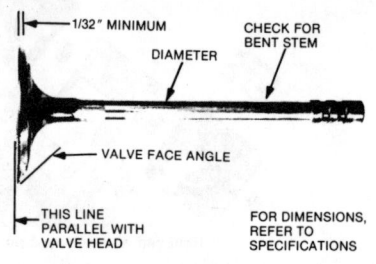

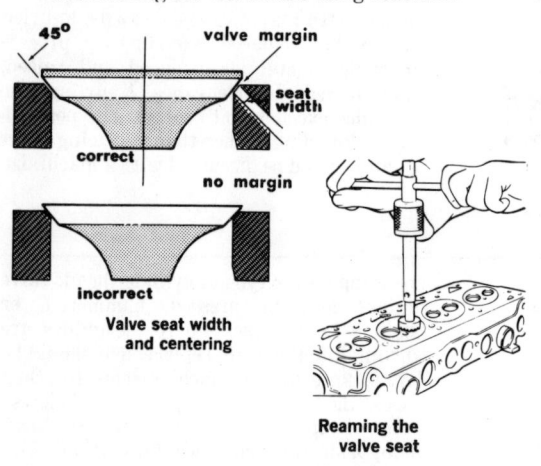

ENGINE AND ENGINE REBUILDING 89

Procedure	Method
Checking the valve seat concentricity:	Coat the valve face with Prussian blue dye, install the valve, and rotate it on the valve seat. If the entire seat becomes coated, and the valve is known to be concentric, the seat is concentric.
Checking the valve seat concentricity using a dial gauge	* Install the dial gauge pilot into the guide, and rest the arm on the valve seat. Zero the gauge, and rotate the arm around the seat. Run-out should not exceed .002".
* Lapping the valves: NOTE: *Valve lapping is done to ensure efficient sealing of resurfaced valves and seats. Valve lapping alone is not recommended for use as a resurfacing procedure.*	* Invert the cylinder head, lightly lubricate the valve stems, and install the valves in the head as numbered. Coat valve seats with fine grinding compound, and attach the lapping tool suction cup to a valve head (NOTE: *Moisten the suction cup*). Rotate the tool between the palms, changing position and lifting the tool often to prevent grooving. Lap the valve until a smooth, polished seat is evident. Remove the valve and tool, and rinse away all traces of grinding compound.
Hand lapping the valves **Home made mechanical valve lapping tool**	** Fasten a suction cup to a piece of drill rod, and mount the rod in a hand drill. Proceed as above, using the hand drill as a lapping tool. CAUTION: *Due to the higher speeds involved when using the hand drill, care must be exercised to avoid grooving the seat.* Lift the tool and change direction of rotation often.
Check the valve springs: **Checking the valve spring free length and squareness** **Checking the valve spring tension**	Place the spring on a flat surface next to a square. Measure the height of the spring, and rotate it against the edge of the square to measure distortion. If spring height varies (by comparison) by more than 1/16" or if distortion exceeds 1/16", replace the spring.
	** In addition to evaluating the spring as above, test the spring pressure at the installed and compressed (installed height minus valve lift) height using a valve spring tester. Springs used on small displacement engines (up to 3 liters) should be ± 1 lb. of all other springs in either position. A tolerance of ± 5 lbs. is permissible on larger engines.

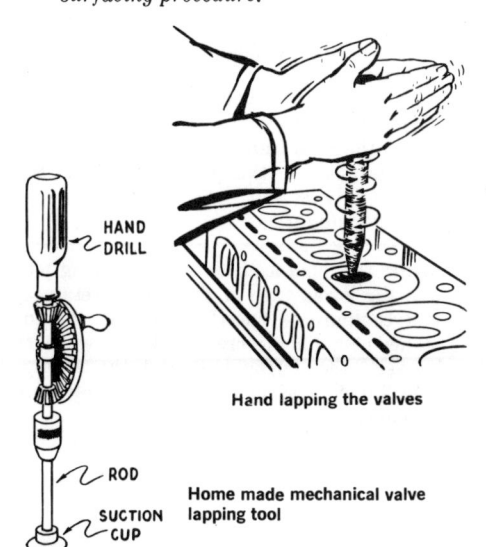

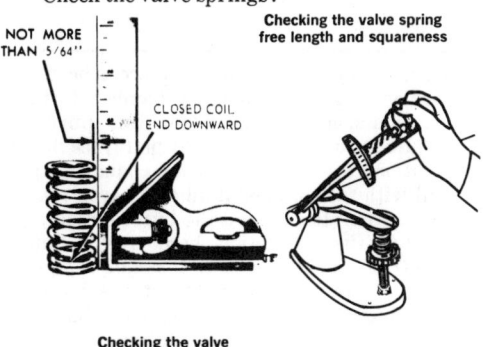

ENGINE AND ENGINE REBUILDING

Procedure	Method
* Install valve stem seals: *Valve stem seal installation*	* Due to the pressure differential that exists at the ends of the intake valve guides (atmospheric pressure above, manifold vacuum below), oil is drawn through the valve guides into the intake port. This has been alleviated somewhat since the addition of positive crankcase ventilation, which lowers the pressure above the guides. Several types of valve stem seals are available to reduce blow-by. Certain seals simply slip over the stem and guide boss, while others require that the boss be machined. Recently, Teflon guide seals have become popular. Consult a parts supplier or machinist concerning availability and suggested usages. NOTE: *When installing seals, ensure that a small amount of oil is able to pass the seal to lubricate the valve guides; otherwise, excessive wear may result.*
Install the valves:	Lubricate the valve stems, and install the valves in the cylinder head as numbered. Lubricate and position the seals (if used, see above) and the valve springs. Install the spring retainers, compress the springs, and insert the keys using needlenose pliers or a tool designed for this purpose. NOTE: *Retain the keys with wheel bearing grease during installation.*
Checking valve spring installed height: *Valve spring installed height dimension* *Measuring valve spring installed height*	Measure the distance between the spring pad and the lower edge of the spring retainer, and compare to specifications. If the installed height is incorrect, add shim washers between the spring pad and the spring. CAUTION: *Use only washers designed for this purpose.*
** CC'ing the combustion chambers:	** Invert the cylinder head and place a bead of sealer around a combustion chamber. Install an apparatus designed for this purpose (burette mounted on a clear plate; see illustration) over the combustion chamber, and fill with the specified fluid to an even mark on the burette. Record the burette reading, and fill the combustion chamber with fluid. (NOTE: *A hole drilled in the plate will permit air to escape*). Subtract the burette reading, with the combustion chamber filled, from the previous reading, to determine combustion chamber volume in cc's. Duplicate this procedure in all combustion

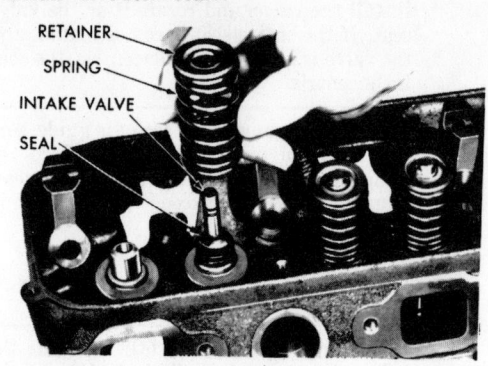

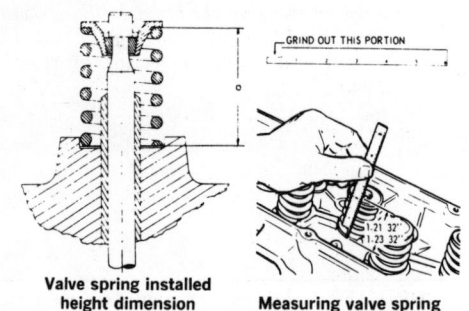

ENGINE AND ENGINE REBUILDING 91

Procedure	Method

CC'ing the combustion chamber

chambers on the cylinder head, and compare the readings. The volume of all combustion chambers should be made equal to that of the largest. Combustion chamber volume may be increased in two ways. When only a small change is required (usually), a small cutter or coarse stone may be used to remove material from the combustion chamber. NOTE: *Check volume frequently.* Remove material over a wide area, so as not to change the configuration of the combustion chamber. When a larger change is required, the valve seat may be sunk (lowered into the head). NOTE: *When altering valve seat, remember to compensate for the change in spring installed height.*

Inspect the rocker arms, balls, studs, and nuts (where applicable):

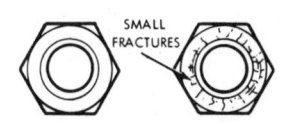

Stress cracks in rocker nuts (SMALL FRACTURES)

Visually inspect the rocker arms, balls, studs, and nuts for cracks, galling, burning, scoring, or wear. If all parts are intact, liberally lubricate the rocker arms and balls, and install them on the cylinder head. If wear is noted on a rocker arm at the point of valve contact, grind it smooth and square, removing as little material as possible. Replace the rocker arm if excessively worn. If a rocker stud shows signs of wear, it must be replaced (see below). If a rocker nut shows stress cracks, replace it. If an exhaust ball is galled or burned, substitute the intake ball from the same cylinder (if it is intact), and install a new intake ball. NOTE: *Avoid using new rocker balls on exhaust valves.*

Replacing rocker studs:

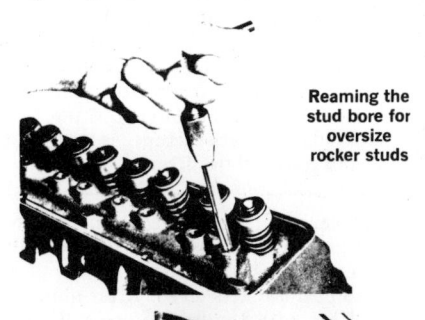

Reaming the stud bore for oversize rocker studs

Extracting a pressed in rocker stud (FLAT WASHERS — AS STUD BEGINS TO PULL UP, IT WILL BE NECESSARY TO REMOVE THE NUT AND ADD MORE WASHERS.)

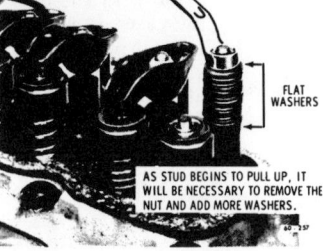

In order to remove a threaded stud, lock two nuts on the stud, and unscrew the stud using the lower nut. Coat the lower threads of the new stud with Loctite, and install.

Two alternative methods are available for replacing pressed in studs. Remove the damaged stud using a stack of washers and a nut (see illustration). In the first, the boss is reamed .005-.006" oversize, and an oversize stud pressed in. Control the stud extension over the boss using washers, in the same manner as valve guides. Before installing the stud, coat it with white lead and grease. To retain the stud more positively, drill a hole through the stud and boss, and install a roll pin. In the second method, the boss is tapped, and a threaded stud installed. Retain the stud using Loctite Stud and Bearing Mount.

ENGINE AND ENGINE REBUILDING

Procedure	Method
Inspect the rocker shaft(s) and rocker arms (where applicable):	Remove rocker arms, springs and washers from rocker shaft. NOTE: *Lay out parts in the order they are removed.* Inspect rocker arms for pitting or wear on the valve contact point, or excessive bushing wear. Bushings need only be replaced if wear is excessive, because the rocker arm normally contacts the shaft at one point only. Grind the valve contact point of rocker arm smooth if necessary, removing as little material as possible. If excessive material must be removed to smooth and square the arm, it should be replaced. Clean out all oil holes and passages in rocker shaft. If shaft is grooved or worn, replace it. Lubricate and assemble the rocker shaft.
Inspect the camshaft bushings and the camshaft (overhead cam engines):	See next section.
Inspect the pushrods:	Remove the pushrods, and, if hollow, clean out the oil passages using fine wire. Roll each pushrod over a piece of clean glass. If a distinct clicking sound is heard as the pushrod rolls, the rod is bent, and must be replaced.
	* The length of all pushrods must be equal. Measure the length of the pushrods, compare to specifications, and replace as necessary.
Inspect the valve lifters:	Remove lifters from their bores, and remove gum and varnish, using solvent. Clean walls of lifter bores. Check lifters for concave wear as illustrated. If face is worn concave, replace lifter, and carefully inspect the camshaft. Lightly lubricate lifter and insert it into its bore. If play is excessive, an oversize lifter must be installed (where possible). Consult a machinist concerning feasibility. If play is satisfactory, remove, lubricate, and reinstall the lifter.
* Testing hydraulic lifter leak down:	Submerge lifter in a container of kerosene. Chuck a used pushrod or its equivalent into a drill press. Position container of kerosene so pushrod acts on the lifter plunger. Pump lifter with the drill press, until resistance increases. Pump several more times to bleed any air out of lifter. Apply very firm, constant pressure to the lifter, and observe rate at which fluid bleeds out of lifter. If the fluid bleeds very quickly (less than 15 seconds), lifter is defective. If the time exceeds 60 seconds, lifter is sticking. In either case, recondition or replace lifter. If lifter is operating properly (leak down time 15-60 seconds), lubricate and install it.

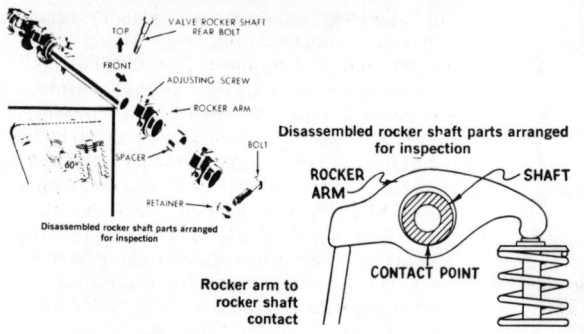

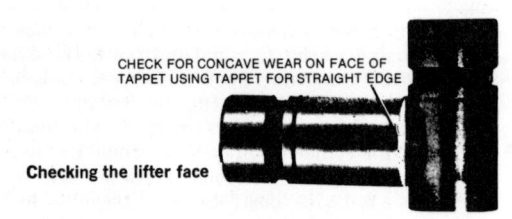

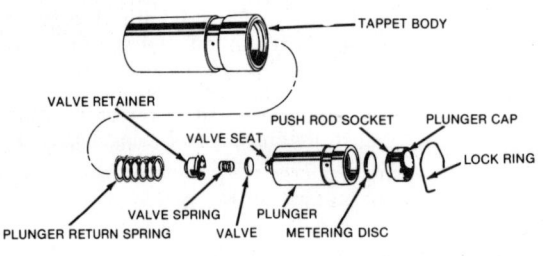

ENGINE AND ENGINE REBUILDING

CYLINDER BLOCK RECONDITIONING

Procedure	Method
Checking the main bearing clearance: *Installing Plastigage on lower bearing shell* *Measuring Plastigage to determine bearing clearance* *Causes of bearing failure*	Invert engine, and remove cap from the bearing to be checked. Using a clean, dry rag, thoroughly clean all oil from crankshaft journal and bearing insert. NOTE: *Plastigage is soluble in oil; therefore, oil on the journal or bearing could result in erroneous readings.* Place a piece of Plastigage along the full length of journal, reinstall cap, and torque to specifications. Remove bearing cap, and determine bearing clearance by comparing width of Plastigage to the scale on Plastigage envelope. Journal taper is determined by comparing width of the Plastigage strip near its ends. Rotate crankshaft 90° and retest, to determine journal eccentricity. NOTE: *Do not rotate crankshaft with Plastigage installed.* If bearing insert and journal appear intact, and are within tolerances, no further main bearing service is required. If bearing or journal appear defective, cause of failure should be determined before replacement. * Remove crankshaft from block (see below). Measure the main bearing journals at each end twice (90° apart) using a micrometer, to determine diameter, journal taper and eccentricity. If journals are within tolerances, reinstall bearing caps at their specified torque. Using a telescope gauge and micrometer, measure bearing I.D. parallel to piston axis and at 30° on each side of piston axis. Subtract journal O.D. from bearing I.D. to determine oil clearance. If crankshaft journals appear defective, or do not meet tolerances, there is no need to measure bearings; for the crankshaft will require grinding and/or undersize bearings will be required. If bearing appears defective, cause for failure should be determined prior to replacement.
Checking the connecting rod bearing clearance:	Connecting rod bearing clearance is checked in the same manner as main bearing clearance, using Plastigage. Before removing the crankshaft, connecting rod side clearance also should be measured and recorded. * Checking connecting rod bearing clearance, using a micrometer, is identical to checking main bearing clearance. If no other service

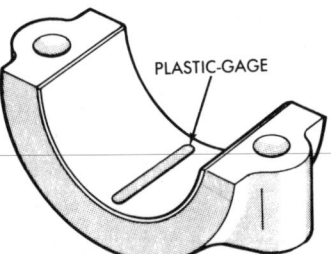

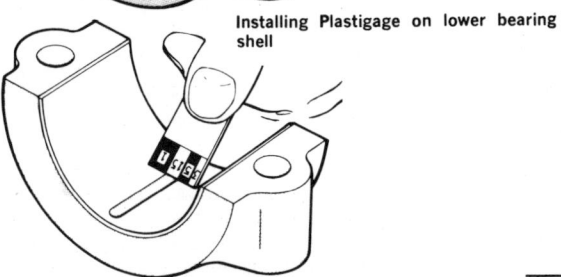

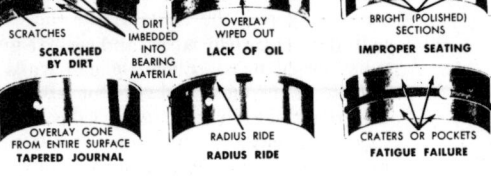

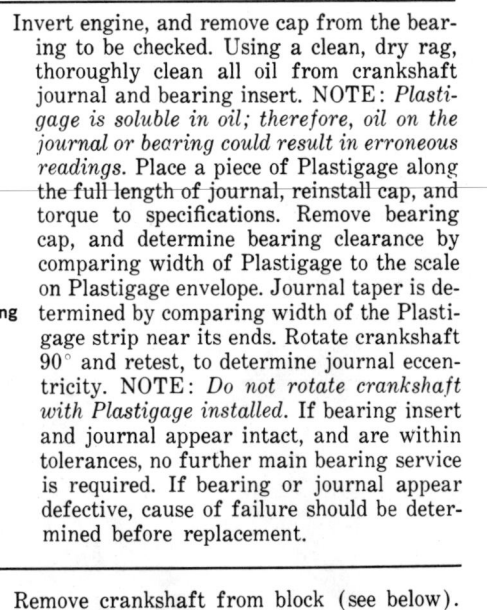

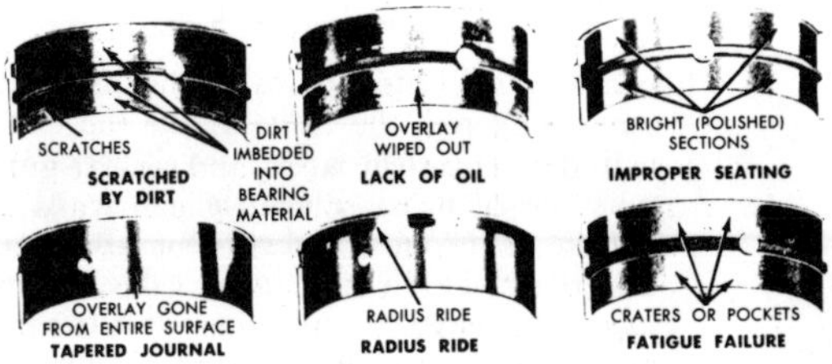

ENGINE AND ENGINE REBUILDING

Procedure	Method
	is required, the piston and rod assemblies need not be removed.
Removing the crankshaft:	Using a punch, mark the corresponding main bearing caps and saddles according to position (i.e., one punch on the front main cap and saddle, two on the second, three on the third, etc.). Using number stamps, identify the corresponding connecting rods and caps, according to cylinder (if no numbers are present). Remove the main and connecting rod caps, and place sleeves of plastic tubing over the connecting rod bolts, to protect the journals as the crankshaft is removed. Lift the crankshaft out of the block.

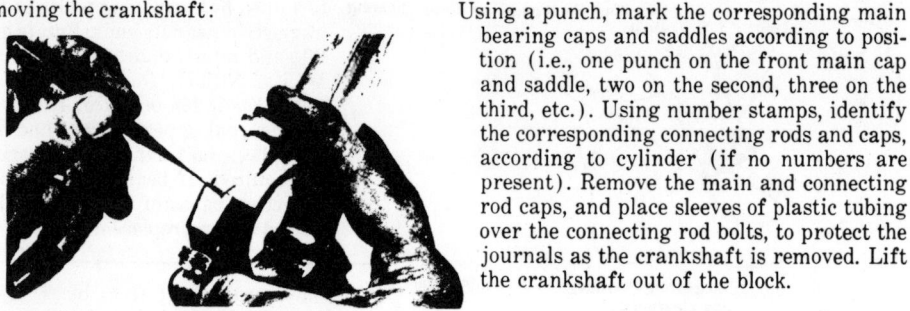

Connecting rod matching marks

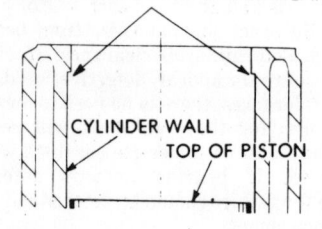 Remove the ridge from the top of the cylinder:	In order to facilitate removal of the piston and connecting rod, the ridge at the top of the cylinder (unworn area; see illustration) must be removed. Place the piston at the bottom of the bore, and cover it with a rag. Cut the ridge away using a ridge reamer, exercising extreme care to avoid cutting too deeply. Remove the rag, and remove cuttings that remain on the piston. CAUTION: *If the ridge is not removed, and new rings are installed, damage to rings will result.*

RIDGE CAUSED BY CYLINDER WEAR
CYLINDER WALL
TOP OF PISTON
Cylinder bore ridge

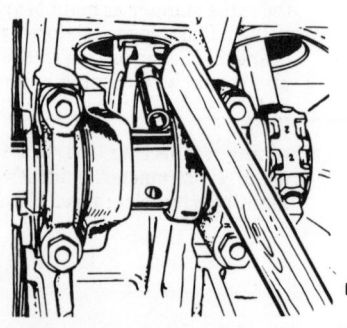 Removing the piston and connecting rod:	Invert the engine, and push the pistons and connecting rods out of the cylinders. If necessary, tap the connecting rod boss with a wooden hammer handle, to force the piston out. CAUTION: *Do not attempt to force the piston past the cylinder ridge* (see above).

Removing the piston

ENGINE AND ENGINE REBUILDING

Procedure	Method
Service the crankshaft:	Ensure that all oil holes and passages in the crankshaft are open and free of sludge. If necessary, have the crankshaft ground to the largest possible undersize.
	** Have the crankshaft Magnafluxed, to locate stress cracks. Consult a machinist concerning additional service procedures, such as surface hardening (e.g., nitriding, Tuftriding) to improve wear characteristics, cross drilling and chamfering the oil holes to improve lubrication, and balancing.
Removing freeze plugs:	Drill a small hole in the center of the freeze plugs. Thread a large sheet metal screw into the hole and remove the plug with a slide hammer.
Remove the oil gallery plugs:	Threaded plugs should be removed using an appropriate (usually square) wrench. To remove soft, pressed in plugs, drill a hole in the plug, and thread in a sheet metal screw. Pull the plug out by the screw using a slide hammer.
Hot-tank the block:	Have the block hot-tanked to remove grease, corrosion, and scale from the water jackets. NOTE: *Consult the operator to determine whether the camshaft bearings will be damaged during the hot-tank process.*
Check the block for cracks:	Visually inspect the block for cracks or chips. The most common locations are as follows: Adjacent to freeze plugs. Between the cylinders and water jackets. Adjacent to the main bearing saddles. At the extreme bottom of the cylinders. Check only suspected cracks using spot check dye (see introduction). If a crack is located, consult a machinist concerning possible repairs.
	** Magnaflux the block to locate hidden cracks. If cracks are located, consult a machinist about feasibility of repair.
Install the oil gallery plugs and freeze plugs:	Coat freeze plugs with sealer and tap into position using a piece of pipe, slightly smaller than the plug, as a driver. To ensure retention, stake the edges of the plugs. Coat threaded oil gallery plugs with sealer and install. Drive replacement soft plugs into block using a large drift as a driver.
	* Rather than reinstalling lead plugs, drill and tap the holes, and install threaded plugs.

ENGINE AND ENGINE REBUILDING

Procedure	Method

Check the bore diameter and surface:

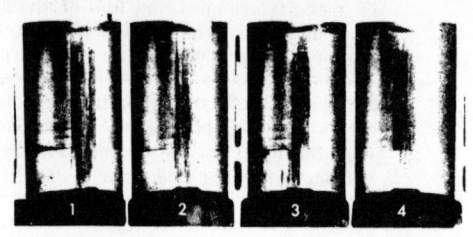

1, 2, 3 Piston skirt seizure resulted in this pattern. Engine must be rebored

4. Piston skirt and oil ring seizure caused this damage. Engine must be rebored

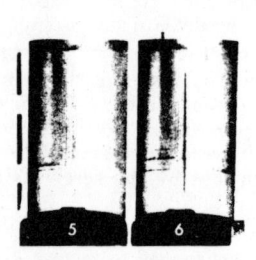

5, 6 Score marks caused by a split piston skirt. Damage is not serious enough to warrant reboring

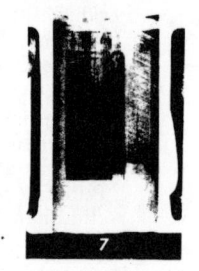

7. Ring seized longitudinally, causing a score mark 1 3/16" wide, on the land side of the piston groove. The honing pattern is destroyed and the cylinder must be rebored

Cylinder wall damage

8. Result of oil ring seizure. Engine must be rebored

9. Oil ring seizure here was not serious enough to warrant reboring. The honing marks are still visible

Visually inspect the cylinder bores for roughness, scoring, or scuffing. If evident, the cylinder bore must be bored or honed oversize to eliminate imperfections, and the smallest possible oversize piston used. The new pistons should be given to the machinist with the block, so that the cylinders can be bored or honed exactly to the piston size (plus clearance). If no flaws are evident, measure the bore diameter using a telescope gauge and micrometer, or dial gauge, parallel and perpendicular to the engine centerline, at the top (below the ridge) and bottom of the bore. Subtract the bottom measurements from the top to determine taper, and the parallel to the centerline measurements from the perpendicular measurements to determine eccentricity. If the measurements are not within specifications, the cylinder must be bored or honed, and an oversize piston installed. If the measurements are within specifications the cylinder may be used as is, with only finish honing (see below). NOTE: *Prior to submitting the block for boring, perform the following operation(s)*.

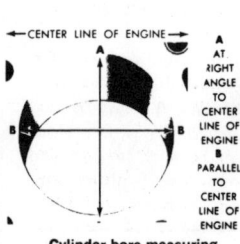

Cylinder bore measuring positions

Measuring the cylinder bore with a telescope gauge

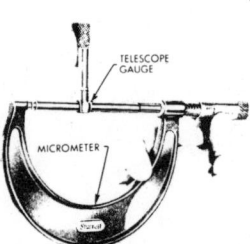

Determining the cylinder bore by measuring the telescope gauge with a micrometer

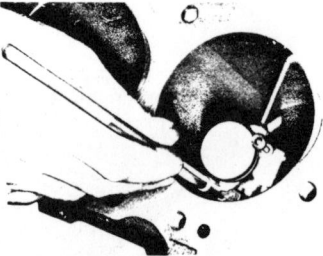

Measuring the cylinder bore with a dial gauge

ENGINE AND ENGINE REBUILDING 97

Procedure	Method
Check the block deck for warpage: 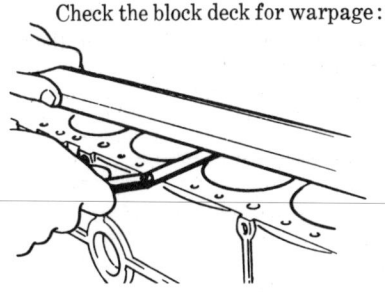	Using a straightedge and feeler gauges, check the block deck for warpage in the same manner that the cylinder head is checked (see Cylinder Head Reconditioning). If warpage exceeds specifications, have the deck resurfaced. NOTE: *In certain cases a specification for total material removal (Cylinder head and block deck) is provided. This specification must not be exceeded.*
* Check the deck height:	The deck height is the distance from the crankshaft centerline to the block deck. To measure, invert the engine, and install the crankshaft, retaining it with the center main cap. Measure the distance from the crankshaft journal to the block deck, parallel to the cylinder centerline. Measure the diameter of the end (front and rear) main journals, parallel to the centerline of the cylinders, divide the diameter in half, and subtract it from the previous measurement. The results of the front and rear measurements should be identical. If the difference exceeds .005″, the deck height should be corrected. NOTE: *Block deck height and warpage should be corrected concurrently.*
Check the cylinder block bearing alignment: 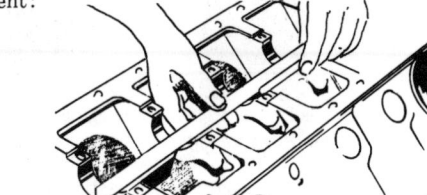 Checking main bearing saddle alignment	Remove the upper bearing inserts. Place a straightedge in the bearing saddles along the centerline of the crankshaft. If clearance exists between the straightedge and the center saddle, the block must be align-bored.
Clean and inspect the pistons and connecting rods:  RING EXPANDER Removing the piston rings	Using a ring expander, remove the rings from the piston. Remove the retaining rings (if so equipped) and remove piston pin. NOTE: *If the piston pin must be pressed out, determine the proper method and use the proper tools; otherwise the piston will distort.* Clean the ring grooves using an appropriate tool, exercising care to avoid cutting too deeply. Thoroughly clean all carbon and varnish from the piston with solvent. CAUTION: *Do not use a wire brush or caustic solvent on pistons.* Inspect the pistons for scuffing, scoring, cracks, pitting, or excessive ring groove wear. If wear is evident, the piston must be replaced. Check the connecting rod length by measuring the rod from the inside of the large end to the inside of the small end using calipers (see

ENGINE AND ENGINE REBUILDING

Procedure	Method
Cleaning the piston ring grooves (Ring Groove Cleaner) / *Connecting rod length checking dimension*	illustration). All connecting rods should be equal length. Replace any rod that differs from the others in the engine. * Have the connecting rod alignment checked in an alignment fixture by a machinist. Replace any twisted or bent rods. * Magnaflux the connecting rods to locate stress cracks. If cracks are found, replace the connecting rod.
Fit the pistons to the cylinders: *Measuring the piston for fitting* (90°)	Using a telescope gauge and micrometer, or a dial gauge, measure the cylinder bore diameter perpendicular to the piston pin, $2\frac{1}{2}''$ below the deck. Measure the piston perpendicular to its pin on the skirt. The difference between the two measurements is the piston clearance. If the clearance is within specifications or slightly below (after boring or honing), finish honing is all that is required. If the clearance is excessive, try to obtain a slightly larger piston to bring clearance within specifications. Where this is not possible, obtain the first oversize piston, and hone (or if necessary, bore) the cylinder to size.
Assemble the pistons and connecting rods: *Installing piston pin lock rings*	Inspect piston pin, connecting rod small end bushing, and piston bore for galling, scoring, or excessive wear. If evident, replace defective part(s). Measure the I.D. of the piston boss and connecting rod small end, and the O.D. of the piston pin. If within specifications, assemble piston pin and rod. CAUTION: *If piston pin must be pressed in, determine the proper method and use the proper tools; otherwise the piston will distort.* Install the lock rings; ensure that they seat properly. If the parts are not within specifications, determine the service method for the type of engine. In some cases, piston and pin are serviced as an assembly when either is defective. Others specify reaming the piston and connecting rods for an oversize pin. If the connecting rod bushing is worn, it may in many cases be replaced. Reaming the piston and replacing the rod bushing are machine shop operations.

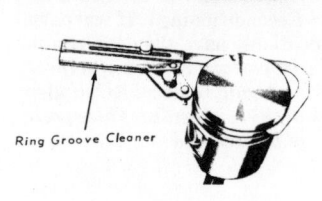

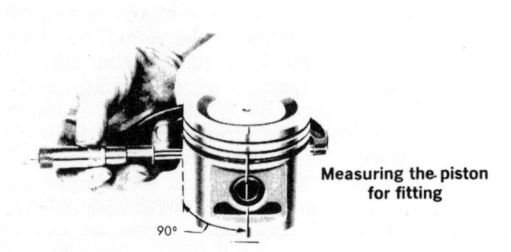

ENGINE AND ENGINE REBUILDING

Procedure	Method
Clean and inspect the camshaft: *Checking the camshaft for straightness* *Camshaft lobe measurement*	Degrease the camshaft, using solvent, and clean out all oil holes. Visually inspect cam lobes and bearing journals for excessive wear. If a lobe is questionable, check all lobes as indicated below. If a journal or lobe is worn, the camshaft must be reground or replaced. NOTE: *If a journal is worn, there is a good chance that the bushings are worn.* If lobes and journals appear intact, place the front and rear journals in V-blocks, and rest a dial indicator on the center journal. Rotate the camshaft to check straightness. If deviation exceeds .001", replace the camshaft. * Check the camshaft lobes with a micrometer, by measuring the lobes from the nose to base and again at 90° (see illustration). The lift is determined by subtracting the second measurement from the first. If all exhaust lobes and all intake lobes are not identical, the camshaft must be reground or replaced.
Replace the camshaft bearings: *Camshaft removal and installation tool (typical)*	If excessive wear is indicated, or if the engine is being completely rebuilt, camshaft bearings should be replaced as follows: Drive the camshaft rear plug from the block. Assemble the removal puller with its shoulder on the bearing to be removed. Gradually tighten the puller nut until bearing is removed. Remove remaining bearings, leaving the front and rear for last. To remove front and rear bearings, reverse position of the tool, so as to pull the bearings in toward the center of the block. Leave the tool in this position, pilot the new front and rear bearings on the installer, and pull them into position. Return the tool to its original position and pull remaining bearings into position. NOTE: *Ensure that oil holes align when installing bearings.* Replace camshaft rear plug, and stake it into position to aid retention.
Finish hone the cylinders: *Finish honed cylinder*	Chuck a flexible drive hone into a power drill, and insert it into the cylinder. Start the hone, and move it up and down in the cylinder at a rate which will produce approximately a 60° cross-hatch pattern (see illustration). NOTE: *Do not extend the hone below the cylinder bore.* After developing the pattern, remove the hone and recheck piston fit. Wash the cylinders with a detergent and water solution to remove abrasive dust, dry, and wipe several times with a rag soaked in engine oil.

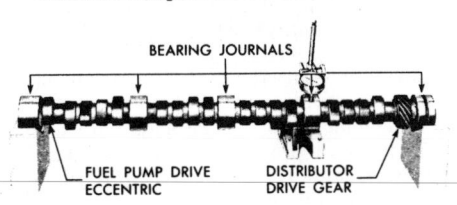

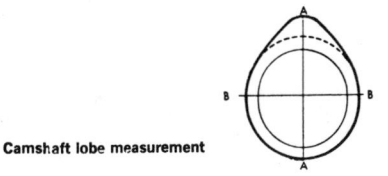

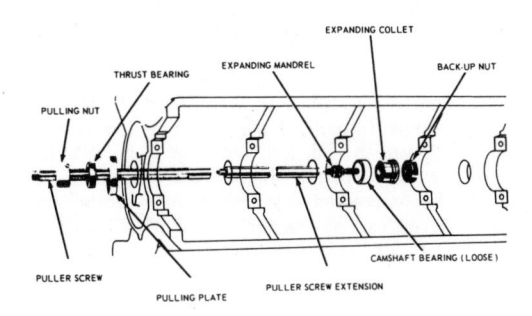

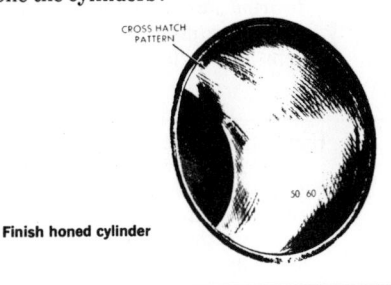

ENGINE AND ENGINE REBUILDING

Procedure	Method
Check piston ring end-gap: **Checking ring end-gap**	Compress the piston rings to be used in a cylinder, one at a time, into that cylinder, and press them approximately 1″ below the deck with an inverted piston. Using feeler gauges, measure the ring end-gap, and compare to specifications. Pull the ring out of the cylinder and file the ends with a fine file to obtain proper clearance. CAUTION: *If inadequate ring end-gap is utilized, ring breakage will result.*
Install the piston rings: **Checking ring side clearance** CORRECT INCORRECT **Piston groove depth** **Correct ring spacer installation**	Inspect the ring grooves in the piston for excessive wear or taper. If necessary, recut the groove(s) for use with an overwidth ring or a standard ring and spacer. If the groove is worn uniformly, overwidth rings, or standard rings and spacers may be installed without recutting. Roll the outside of the ring around the groove to check for burrs or deposits. If any are found, remove with a fine file. Hold the ring in the groove, and measure side clearance. If necessary, correct as indicated above. NOTE: *Always install any additional spacers above the piston ring.* The ring groove must be deep enough to allow the ring to seat below the lands (see illustration). In many cases, a "go-no-go" depth gauge will be provided with the piston rings. Shallow grooves may be corrected by recutting, while deep grooves require some type of filler or expander behind the piston. Consult the piston ring supplier concerning the suggested method. Install the rings on the piston, lowest ring first, using a ring expander. NOTE: *Position the ring markings as specified by the manufacturer (see car section).*
Install the camshaft:	Liberally lubricate the camshaft lobes and journals, and slide the camshaft into the block. CAUTION: *Exercise extreme care to avoid damaging the bearings when inserting the camshaft.* Install and tighten the camshaft thrust plate retaining bolts.
Check camshaft end-play: **Checking camshaft end-play with a feeler gauge** 0.0025″–0.0075″	Using feeler gauges, determine whether the clearance between the camshaft boss (or gear) and backing plate is within specifications. Install shims behind the thrust plate, or reposition the camshaft gear and retest end-play.

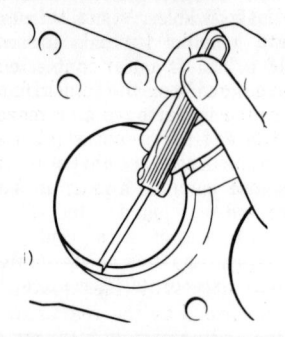

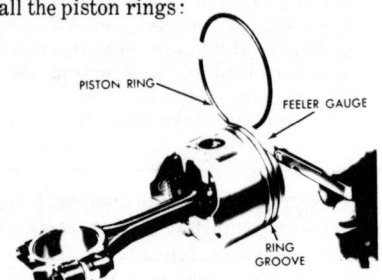

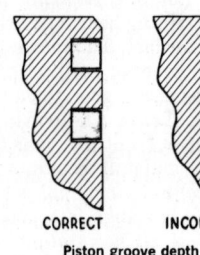

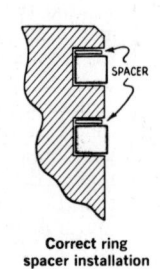

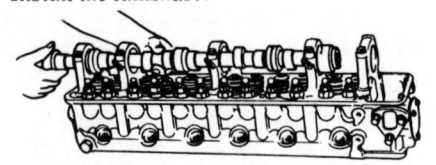

ENGINE AND ENGINE REBUILDING 101

Procedure	Method

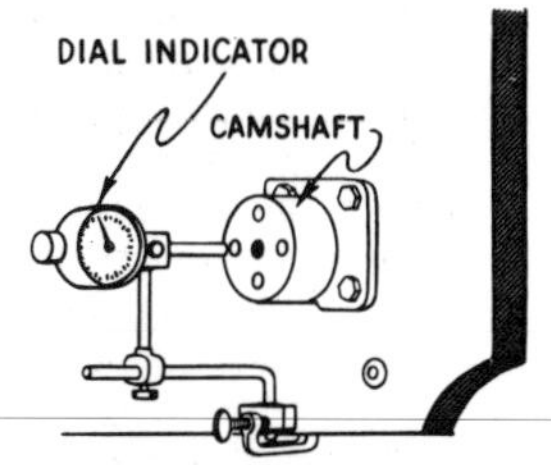

Checking camshaft end-play with a dial indicator

* Mount a dial indicator stand so that the stem of the dial indicator rests on the nose of the camshaft, parallel to the camshaft axis. Push the camshaft as far in as possible and zero the gauge. Move the camshaft outward to determine the amount of camshaft end-play. If the end-play is not within tolerance, install shims behind the thrust plate, or reposition the camshaft gear and retest.

Install the rear main seal (where applicable):

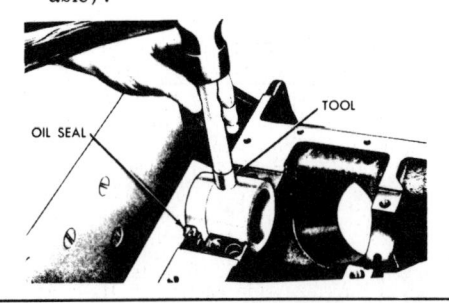

Position the block with the bearing saddles facing upward. Lay the rear main seal in its groove and press it lightly into its seat. Place a piece of pipe the same diameter as the crankshaft journal into the saddle, and firmly seat the seal. Hold the pipe in position, and trim the ends of the seal flush if required.

Seating the rear main seal

Install the crankshaft:

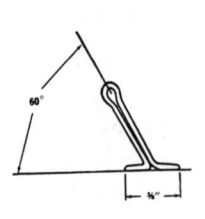

Home made bearing roll-out pin

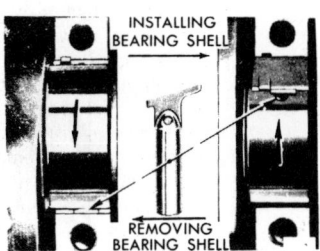

Removal and installation of upper bearing insert using a roll-out pin

Thoroughly clean the main bearing saddles and caps. Place the upper halves of the bearing inserts on the saddles and press into position. NOTE: *Ensure that the oil holes align.* Press the corresponding bearing inserts into the main bearing caps. Lubricate the upper main bearings, and lay the crankshaft in position. Place a strip of Plastigage on each of the crankshaft journals, install the main caps, and torque to specifications. Remove the main caps, and compare the Plastigage to the scale on the Plastigage envelope. If clearances are within tolerances, remove the Plastigage, turn the crankshaft 90°, wipe off all oil and retest. If all clearances are correct, remove all Plastigage, thoroughly

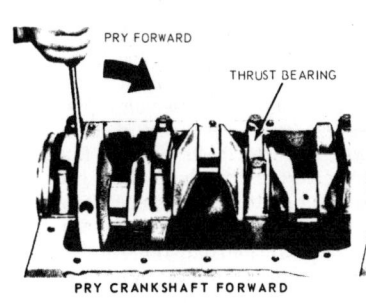

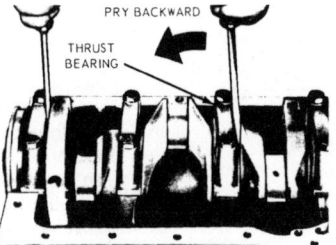

Aligning the thrust bearing
PRY CRANKSHAFT FORWARD — PRY CAP BACKWARD — TIGHTEN CAP

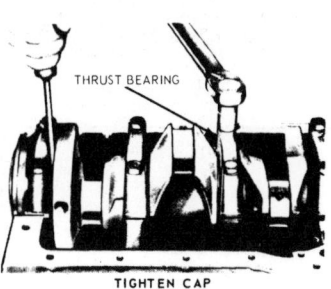

Procedure	Method
	lubricate the main caps and bearing journals, and install the main caps. If clearances are not within tolerance, the upper bearing inserts may be removed, without removing the crankshaft, using a bearing roll out pin (see illustration). Roll in a bearing that will provide proper clearance, and retest. Torque all main caps, excluding the thrust bearing cap, to specifications. Tighten the thrust bearing cap finger tight. To properly align the thrust bearing, pry the crankshaft the extent of its axial travel several times, the last movement held toward the front of the engine, and torque the thrust bearing cap to specifications. Determine the crankshaft end-play (see below), and bring within tolerance with thrust washers.
Measure crankshaft end-play:	Mount a dial indicator stand on the front of the block, with the dial indicator stem resting on the nose of the crankshaft, parallel to the crankshaft axis. Pry the crankshaft the extent of its travel rearward, and zero the indicator. Pry the crankshaft forward and record crankshaft end-play. NOTE: *Crankshaft end-play also may be measured at the thrust bearing, using feeler gauges* (see illustration).

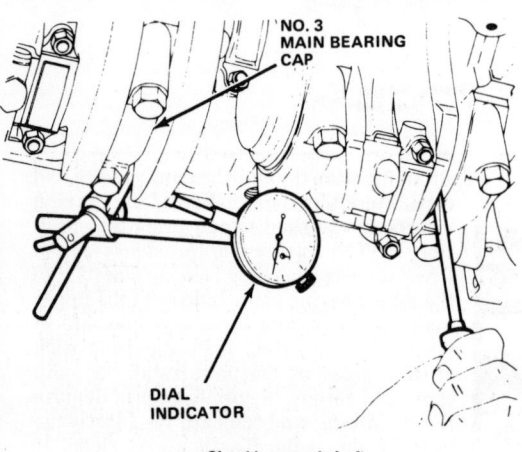

Checking crankshaft end-play with a dial indicator

Checking crankshaft end-play with a feeler gauge

| Install the pistons: | Press the upper connecting rod bearing halves into the connecting rods, and the lower halves into the connecting rod caps. Position the piston ring gaps according to specifications (see car section), and lubricate the pistons. Install a ring compresser on a piston, and press two long (8") pieces of plastic tubing over the rod bolts. Using the plastic tubes as a guide, press the pistons into the bores and onto the crankshaft with a wooden hammer handle. After seating the rod on the crankshaft journal, remove the tubes and install the cap finger tight. Install the remaining pistons in the same man- |

ENGINE AND ENGINE REBUILDING 103

Procedure	Method

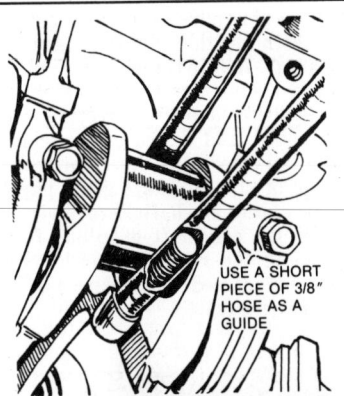

Tubing used as guide when installing a piston (USE A SHORT PIECE OF 3/8" HOSE AS A GUIDE)

ner. Invert the engine and check the bearing clearance at two points (90° apart) on each journal with Plastigage. NOTE: *Do not turn the crankshaft with Plastigage installed.* If clearance is within tolerances, remove *all* Plastigage, thoroughly lubricate the journals, and torque the rod caps to specifications. If clearance is not within specifications, install different thickness bearing inserts and recheck. CAUTION: *Never shim or file the connecting rods or caps.* Always install plastic tube sleeves over the rod bolts when the caps are not installed, to protect the crankshaft journals.

Installing a piston

Check connecting rod side clearance:

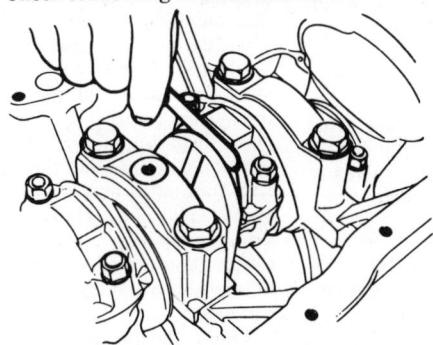

Determine the clearance between the sides of the connecting rods and the crankshaft, using feeler gauges. If clearance is below the minimum tolerance, the rod may be machined to provide adequate clearance. If clearance is excessive, substitute an unworn rod, and recheck. If clearance is still outside specifications, the crankshaft must be welded and reground, or replaced.

Checking connecting rod side clearance

Inspect the timing chain:

Visually inspect the timing chain for broken or loose links, and replace the chain if any are found. If the chain will flex sideways, it must be replaced. Install the timing chain as specified. NOTE: *If the original timing chain is to be reused, install it in its original position.*

Procedure	Method
Check timing gear backlash and runout:	Mount a dial indicator with its stem resting on a tooth of the camshaft gear (as illustrated). Rotate the gear until all slack is removed, and zero the indicator. Rotate the gear in the opposite direction until slack is removed, and record gear backlash. Mount the indicator with its stem resting on the edge of the camshaft gear, parallel to the axis of the camshaft. Zero the indicator, and turn the camshaft gear one full turn, recording the runout. If either backlash or runout exceed specifications, replace the worn gear(s).

Checking camshaft gear backlash

Checking camshaft gear runout

Completing the Rebuilding Process

Following the above procedures, complete the rebuilding process as follows:

Fill the oil pump with oil, to prevent cavitating (sucking air) on initial engine start up. Install the oil pump and the pickup tube on the engine. Coat the oil pan gasket as necessary, and install the gasket and the oil pan. Mount the flywheel and the crankshaft vibrational damper or pulley on the crankshaft. NOTE: *Always use new bolts when installing the flywheel.* Inspect the clutch shaft pilot bushing in the crankshaft. If the bushing is excessively worn, remove it with an expanding puller and a slide hammer, and tap a new bushing into place.

Position the engine, cylinder head side up. Lubricate the lifters, and install them into their bores. Install the cylinder head, and torque it as specified in the car section. Insert the pushrods (where applicable), and install the rocker shaft(s) (if so equipped) or position the rocker arms on the pushrods. If solid lifters are utilized, adjust the valves to the "cold" specifications.

Mount the intake and exhaust manifolds, the carburetor(s), the distributor and spark plugs. Adjust the point gap and the static ignition timing. Mount all accessories and install the engine in the car. Fill the radiator with coolant, and the crankcase with high quality engine oil.

Break-in Procedure

Start the engine, and allow it to run at low speed for a few minutes, while checking for leaks. Stop the engine, check the oil level, and fill as necessary. Restart the engine, and fill the cooling system to capacity. Check the point dwell angle and adjust the ignition timing and the valves. Run the engine at low to medium speed (800-2500 rpm) for approximately ½ hour, and re-torque the cylinder head bolts. Road test the car, and check again for leaks.

Follow the manufacturer's recommended engine break-in procedure and maintenance schedule for new engines.

Chapter Four

Emission Controls and Fuel System

Emission Controls

There are three types of automotive pollutants; crankcase fumes, exhaust gases and gasoline evaporation. The equipment that is used to limit these pollutants is commonly called emission control equipment.

CRANKCASE EMISSION CONTROLS

The crankcase emission control equipment consists of a positive crankcase ventilation valve (PCV), a closed or open oil filler cap and hoses to connect this equipment.

When the engine is running, a small portion of the gases which are formed in the combustion chamber during combustion leak by the piston rings and enter the crankcase. Since these gases are under pressure they tend to escape from the crankcase and enter into the atmosphere. If these gases were allowed to remain in the crankcase for any length of time, they would contaminate the engine oil and cause sludge to build up. If the gases are allowed to escape into the atmosphere, they would pollute the air, as they contain unburned hydrocarbons. The crankcase emission control equipment recycles these gases back into the engine combustion chamber where they are burned.

Crankcase gases are recycled in the following manner: while the engine is running, clean filtered air is drawn into the crankcase through the carburetor into the crankcase through the carburetor air filter and then through a hose leading to the rocket cover. As the air passes through the crankcase it picks up the combustion gases and carries them out of the crankcase, up through the PCV valve and into the intake manifold. After they enter the intake manifold they are drawn into the combustion chamber and burned.

The most critical component in the system is the PCV valve. This vacuum controlled valve regulates the amount of gases which are recycled into the combustion chamber. At low engine speeds the valve is partially closed, limiting the flow of gases into the intake manifold. As engine speed increases, the valve opens to admit greater quantities of the gases into the intake manifold. If the valve should become blocked or plugged, the gases will be prevented from escaping from the crankcases by the normal route.

106 EMISSION CONTROLS AND FUEL SYSTEM

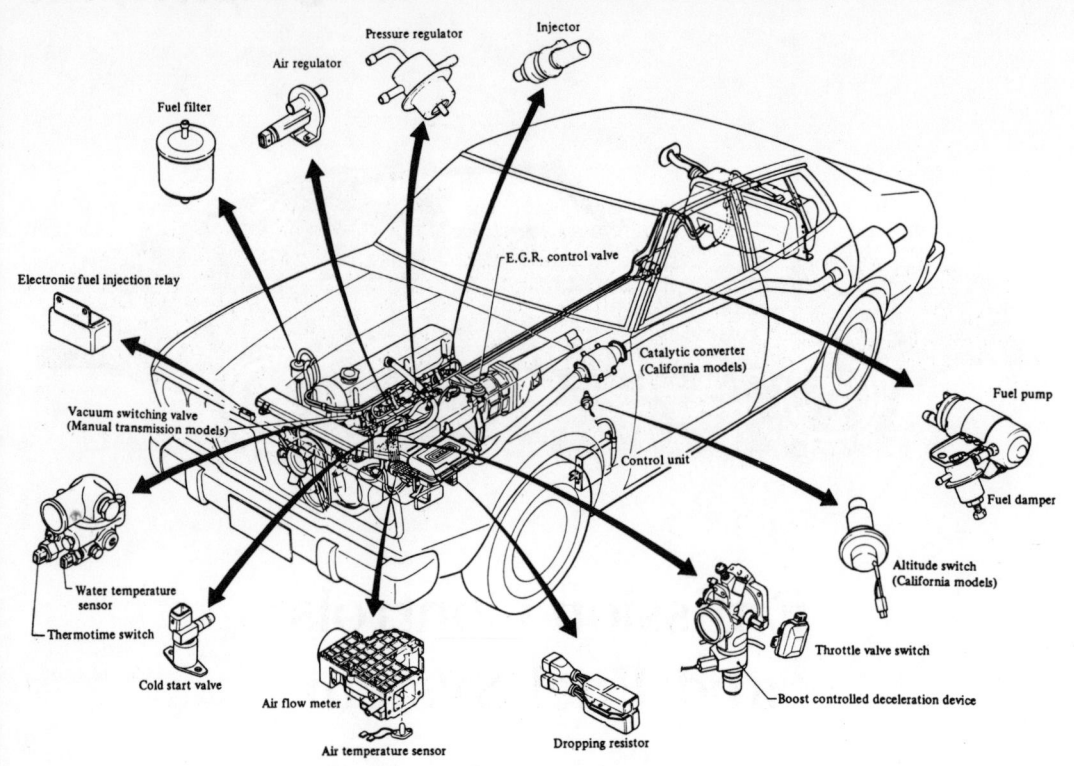

Overall view of 810 emissions control system

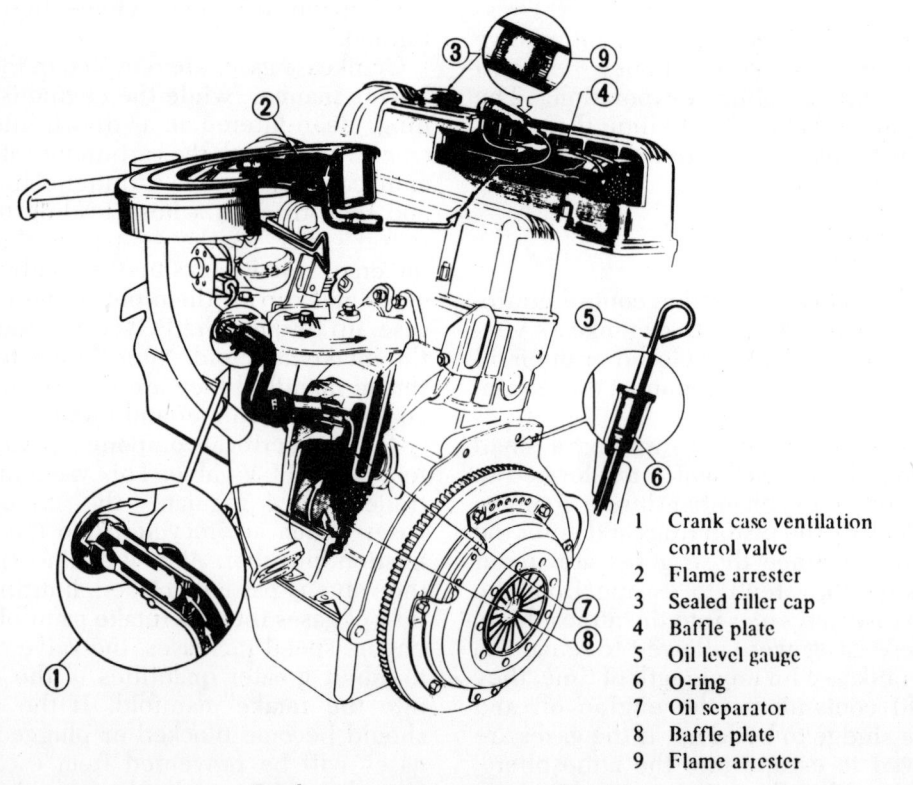

1. Crank case ventilation control valve
2. Flame arrester
3. Sealed filler cap
4. Baffle plate
5. Oil level gauge
6. O-ring
7. Oil separator
8. Baffle plate
9. Flame arrester

Crankcase ventilation system schematic

EMISSION CONTROLS AND FUEL SYSTEM

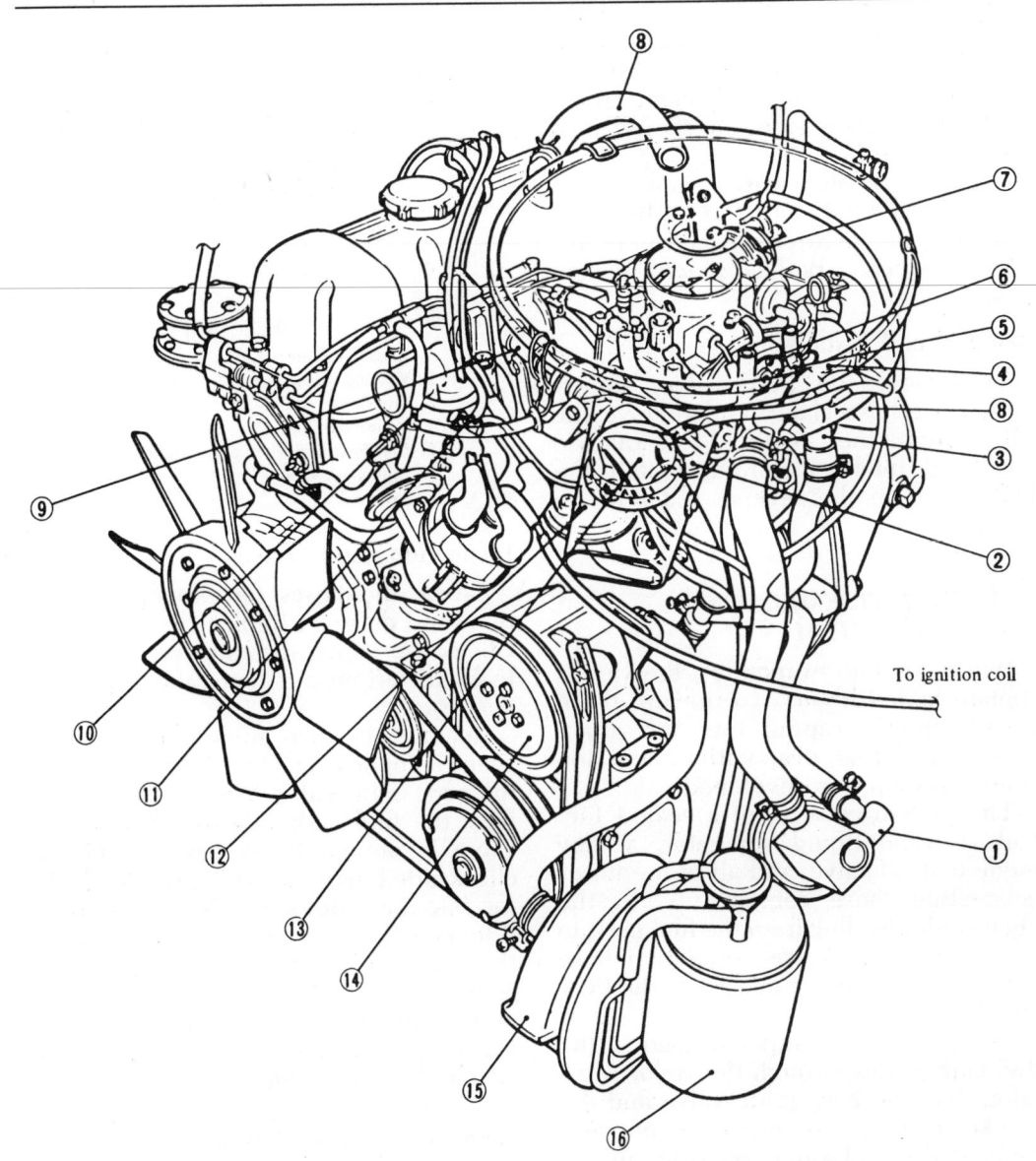

Overall view of 1978 510 emission controls system—others similar

1. Air control valve
2. E.G.R. control valve
3. Air relief valve
4. A.B. valve
5. B.C.D.D. solenoid valve
6. B.C.D.D.
7. Auto-choke
8. P.C.V. hose
9. Check valve
10. 3-way connector (M/T only)
11. Thermal vacuum valve
12. B.P.T. valve
13. A.T.C. air cleaner
14. Air pump for A.I.S.
15. Air pump air cleaner
16. Canister

Since these gases are under pressure, they will find their own way out of the crankcase. This alternate route is usually a weak oil seal or gasket in the engine. As the gas escapes by the gasket, it also creates an oil leak. Besides causing oil leaks, a clogged PCV valve also allows these gases to remain in the crankcase for an extended period of time, promoting the formation of sludge in the engine.

The above explanation and the troubleshooting procedure which follows applies to all engines with PCV systems.

Testing

Check the PCV system hoses and connections, to see that there are no leaks; then replace or tighten, as necessary.

To check the valve, remove it and blow through both of its ends. When blowing

EMISSION CONTROLS AND FUEL SYSTEM

from the side which goes toward the intake manifold, very little air should pass through it. When blowing from the crankcase (valve cover) side, air should pass through freely.

Replace the valve with a new one, if the valve fails to function as outlined.

NOTE: *Do not attempt to clean or adjust the valve; replace it with a new one.*

Removal and Installation

To remove the PCV valve, simply loosen the hose clamp and remove the valve from the manifold-to-crankcase hose and intake manifold. Install the PCV valve in the reverse order of removal.

EVAPORATIVE EMISSION CONTROL SYSTEM

When raw fuel evaporates, the vapors contain hydrocarbons. To prevent these nasties from escaping into the atmosphere, the fuel evaporative emission control system was developed.

The system consists of a sealed fuel tank, a vapor-liquid separator, a flow guide (check) valve, and all of the hoses connecting these components, in the above order leading from the fuel tank, to the positive crankcase ventilation hose which connects the crankcase to the PCV valve.

In operation, the vapor formed in the fuel tank passes through the vapor separator, onto the flow guide valve and the crankcase. When the engine is not running, if the fuel vapor pressure in the vapor separator goes above 0.4 in. Hg, the flow guide valve opens and allows the vapor to enter the engine crankcase. Otherwise the flow guide valve is closed to the vapor separator while the engine is not running. When the engine is running, and a vacuum is developed in the fuel tank or in the engine crankcase and the difference of pressure between the relief side and the fuel tank or crankcase becomes 2 in. Hg, the relief valve opens and allows ambient air from the air cleaner into the fuel tank or the engine crankcase. This ambient air replaces the vapor within the fuel tank or crankcase, bringing the fuel tank or crankcase back into a neutral or positive pressure range.

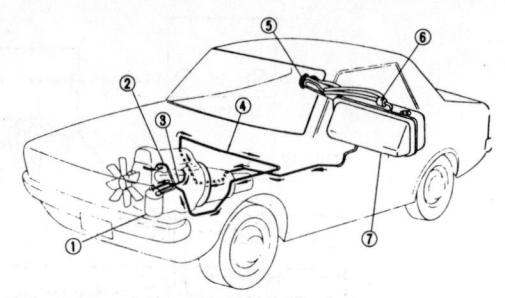

Evaporative emission control system schematic

1. Carbon canister
2. Vacuum signal line
3. Canister vent line
4. Vapor vent line
5. Fuel filler cap with vacuum relief valve
6. Fuel check valve
7. Fuel tank

Inspection and Service

Check the hoses for proper connections and damage. Replace as necessary. Check the vapor separator tank for fuel leaks, distortion and dents, and replace as necessary.

Remove the flow guide valve and inspect it for leakage by blowing air into the ports in the valve. When air is applied from the fuel tank side, the flow guide valve is normal if air passes into the check side (crankcase side), but not leaking into the relief side (air cleaner side). When air is applied from the check side, the valve is normal if the passage of air is restricted. When air is applied from the relief side (air cleaner side), the valve is normal if air passes into the fuel tank side or into the check side.

Removal and Installation

Removal and installation of the various evaporative emission control system components consists of disconnecting the hoses, loosening retaining screws, and removing the part which is to be replaced or checked. Install in the reverse order. When replacing hose, make sure that it is fuel and vapor resistant.

SPARK TIMING CONTROL SYSTEM DUAL POINT DISTRIBUTOR

The 1973 510 and 610 are equipped with this system. The dual point distributor has two sets of breaker points which operate independently of each other and are positioned with a relative phase angle of 7° apart. This makes one set the ad-

EMISSION CONTROLS AND FUEL SYSTEM

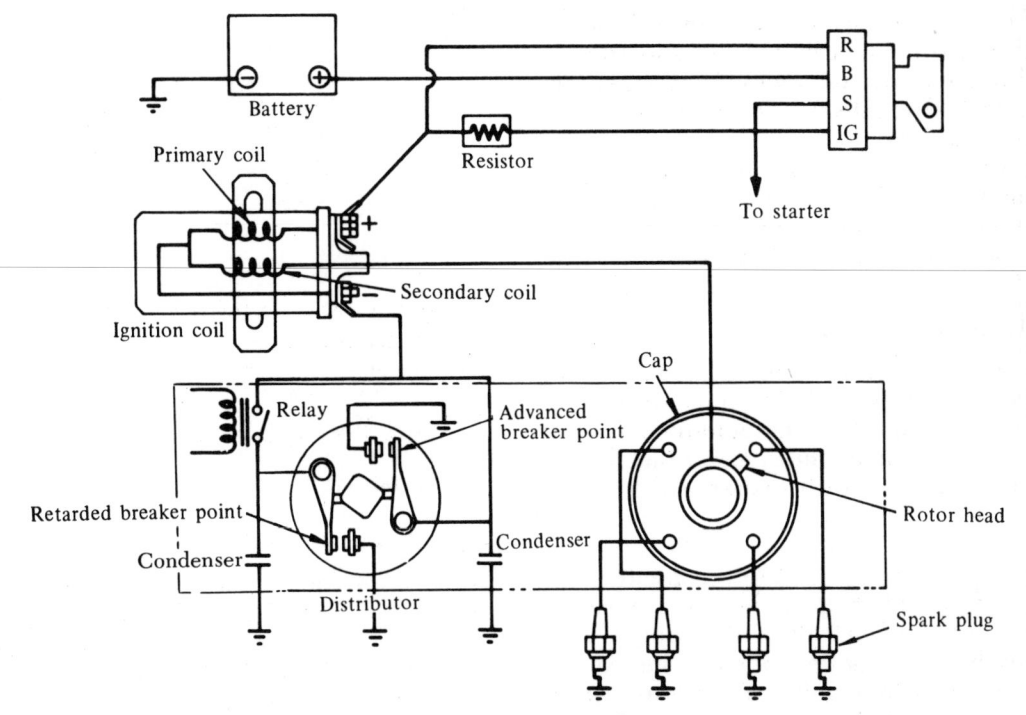

Dual point ignition system schematic

vanced points and the other set the retarded points.

The two sets of points, which mechanically operate continuously, are connected in parallel to the primary side of the ignition circuit. One set of points controls the firing of the spark plugs and hence, the ignition timing, depending on whether or not the retarded set of points is energized.

When both sets of points are electrically energized, the first set to open (the advanced set, 7° sooner) has no control over breaking the ignition coil primary circuit because the retarded set is still closed and maintaining a complete circuit to ground. When the retarded set of points opens, the advanced set is still open, and the primary circuit is broken causing the electromagnetic field in the coil to collapse and the ignition spark is produced.

When the retarded set of points is removed from the primary ignition circuit through the operation of a distributor relay inserted into the retarded points circuit, the advanced set of points controls the primary circuit. The retarded set of points is activated as follows:

The retarded set of points is activated only while the throttle is partially open, the temperature is above 50° F and the transmission is in any gear but Fourth gear.

NOTE: *When the ambient temperature is below 30° F, the retarded set of points is removed from the ignition circuit no matter what switch is On.*

In the case of an automatic transmission, the retarded set of points is activated at all times except under heavy acceleration and high-speed cruising (wide open throttle) with the ambient temperature above 50° F.

There are three switches which control the operation of the distributor relay. All of the switches must be On in order to energize the distributor relay, thus energizing the retarded set of points.

The switches and their operation are as follows:

A transmission switch located in the transmission closes an electrical circuit when the transmission is in all gears except Fourth gear.

A throttle switch located on the throttle linkage at the carburetor is On when the throttle valve is moved within a 45° angle.

The temperature sensing switch is located near the hood release lever inside the passenger compartment. The temper-

EMISSION CONTROLS AND FUEL SYSTEM

ature sensing switch comes on between 41° F and 55° F when the temperature is rising and goes Off above 34° F when the temperature falls.

The distributor vacuum advance mechanism produces a spark advance based on the amount of vacuum in the intake manifold. With a high vacuum, less air/fuel mixture enters the engine cylinders and the mixture is therefore less highly compressed. Consequently, this mixture burns more slowly and the advance mechanism gives it more time to burn. This longer burning time results in higher combustion temperatures at peak pressure and hence, more time for nitrogen to react with oxygen and form nitrogen oxides (NO_x). At the same time, this advance timing results in less complete combustion due to the greater area of cylinder wall (quench area) exposed at the instant of ignition. This "cooled" fuel will not burn as readily and hence, results in higher unburned hydrocarbons (HC). The production of NO_x and HC resulting from vacuum advance is highest during idle and moderate acceleration in lower gears.

Retardation of the ignition timing is necessary to reduce NO_x and HC emissions. Various ways of retarding the ignition spark have been used in automobiles, all of which remove vacuum to the distributor vacuum advance mechanism at different times under certain conditions. Another way of accomplishing the same goal is the dual point distributor system.

Inspection and Adjustments

PHASE DIFFERENCE

1. Disconnect the wiring harness of the distributor from the engine harness.
2. Connect the black wire of the engine harness to the black wire of the distributor harness with a jumper wire. This connects the advanced set of points.
3. With the engine idling, adjust the ignition timing by rotating the distributor.
4. Disconnect the jumper wire from the black wire of the distributor harness and connect it to the yellow wire of the distributor harness. The retarded set of points is now activated.
5. With the engine idling, check the

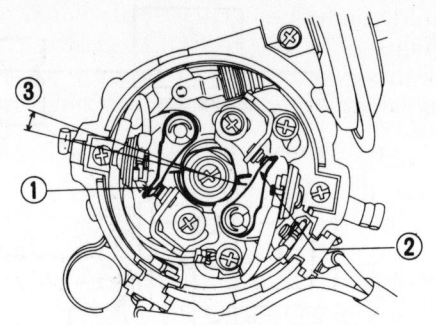

(1) Advance point set (2) Retarded point set (3) Phase difference

ignition timing. The timing should be retarded from the advanced setting 7°.

6. To adjust the out-of-phase angle of the ignition timing, loosen the adjuster plate set screws on the same side as the retarded set of points.

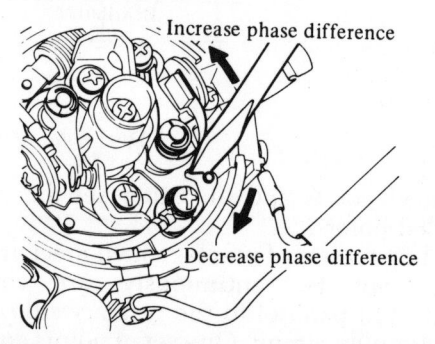

Adjusting phase difference

7. Place the blade of a screwdriver in the adjusting notch of the adjuster plate and turn the adjuster plate as required to obtain the correct retarded ignition timing specification. The ignition timing is retarded when the adjuster plate is turned counterclockwise. There are graduations on the adjuster plate to make the adjustment easier; one graduation is equal to 4° of crankshaft rotation.
8. Replace the distributor cap, start the engine and check the ignition timing with the retarded set of points activated (yellow wire of the distributor wiring harness connected to the black wire of the engine wiring harness).
9. Repeat the steps above as necessary to gain the proper retarded ignition timing.

TRANSMISSION SWITCH

Disconnect the electrical leads at the switch and connect a self-powered test light to the electrical leads. The switch

EMISSION CONTROLS AND FUEL SYSTEM 111

should conduct electricity only when the gearshift is moved to Fourth gear.

If the switch fails to perform in the above manner, replace it with a new one.

THROTTLE SWITCH

The throttle switch located on the throttle linkage at the carburetor is checked with a self-powered test light. Disconnect the electrical leads of the switch and connect the test light. The switch should not conduct current when the throttle valve is closed or opened, up to 45°. When the throttle is fully opened, the switch should conduct current.

TEMPERATURE SENSING SWITCH

The temperature sensing switch mounted in the passenger compartment near the hood release lever should not conduct current when the temperature is above 55° F when connected to a self-powered test light as previously outlined for the throttle switch.

EARLY FUEL EVAPORATION SYSTEM

The Early Fuel Evaporation System is used on the A-series engines. Essentially, it is an improvement on the old style exhaust manifold heat riser. Its function is simply to provide a quicker warm-up time. The only adjustment necessary is to occasionally lubricate the counterweight. Other than that, the system should be trouble-free.

BOOST CONTROL DECELERATION DEVICE (BCDD)

Used on the L-series engines, the BCDD reduces hydrocarbon emissions during coasting conditions.

High manifold vacuum during coasting prevents the complete combustion of the air/fuel mixture because of the reduced amount of air. This condition will result in a large amount of HC emission. Enriching the air/fuel mixture for a short time (during the high vacuum condition) will reduce the emission of HC.

However, enriching the air/fuel mixture with only the mixture adjusting screw will cause poor engine idle or invite an increase in the carbon monoxide (CO) content of the exhaust gases.

The BCDD consists of an independent operative auxiliary fuel system. This system functions when the engine is coasting, to enrich the air/fuel mixture, which reduces the hydrocarbon content of the exhaust gases through more efficient combustion. This is accomplished without adversely affecting engine idle and the carbon monoxide content of the exhaust gases.

When intake manifold vacuum exceeds a predetermined value, a vacuum-actuated diaphragm opens an air passage allowing additional air to enter the intake manifold. When the additional air passage is opened, vacuum is brought to bear on another diaphragm which opens a fuel passage allowing additional fuel to enter the intake manifold.

When the engine goes from a coasting condition to that of idling, the transmission speed sensor closes an electrical circuit, energizing the vacuum control solenoid valve. When energized, the vacuum control solenoid valve vents the intake manifold vacuum to the atmosphere, thus causing the two diaphragms to return to their normal positions, closing off the additional air and fuel mixture.

Adjustment

Normally, the BCDD never needs adjustment. However, if the need should arise because of suspected malfunction of the system, proceed as follows:

1. Connect a tachometer to the engine.

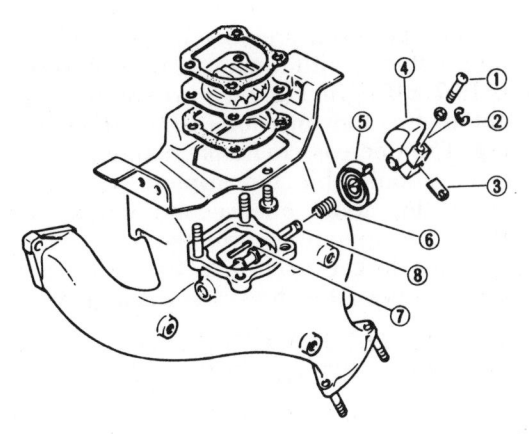

Exploded view—E.F.E. system

1. Snap-ring
2. Lock bolt
3. Key
4. Counterweight
5. Thermostat spring
6. Coil spring
7. Heat control valve
8. Valve shaft

EMISSION CONTROLS AND FUEL SYSTEM

2. Connect a quick-response vacuum gauge to the intake manifold.

3. Disconnect the solenoid valve electrical leads.

4. Start and warm up the engine until it reaches normal operating temperature.

5. Adjust the idle speed to the proper specification.

6. Raise the engine speed to 3,000–3,500 rpm under no-lead (transmission in Neutral or Park), then allow the throttle to close quickly. Take notice as to whether or not the engine rpm returns to idle speed and if it does, how long the fall in rpm is interrupted before it reaches idle speed.

At the moment the throttle is snapped closed at high engine rpm, the vacuum in the intake manifold reaches −27.7 in. Hg and then gradually falls to about −16.5 in. Hg at idle speed. The process of the fall of intake manifold vacuum and engine rpm will take one of the following three forms:

a. When the operating pressure of the BCDD is too high, the system remains inoperative, and the vacuum in the intake manifold decreases without interruption just like that of an engine without a BCDD;

b. When the operating pressure is lower than that of the case given above, but still higher than the proper set pressure, the fall of vacuum in the intake manifold is interrupted and kept constant at a certain level (operating pressure) for about one second and then gradually falls down to the normal vacuum at idle speed;

c. When the set operating pressure of the BCDD is lower than the intake manifold vacuum when the throttle is suddenly released, the engine speed will not lower to idle speed.

To adjust the set operating pressure of the BCDD, remove the adjusting screw cover from the BCDD mechanism mounted on the side of the carburetor. On 810 models, the BCDD system is installed under the throttle chamber.

The adjusting screw is a left-hand threaded screw. Late models may have an adjusting nut instead of a screw. Turning the screw 1/8 of a turn in either direction will change the operation pressure about 0.79 in. Hg. Turning the screw counterclockwise will increase the amount of vacuum needed to operate the mechanism. Turning the screw clockwise will decrease the amount of vacuum needed to operate the mechanism.

Adjusting B.C.D.D. pressure—810

The operating pressure for the BCDD on a vehicle with a manual transmission is 19.7 ± 0.79 in. Hg; for a vehicle with an automatic transmission 18.9 ± 0.79 in. Hg. The decrease in intake manifold vacuum should be interrupted at these levels for about one second when the BCDD is operating correctly.

Don't forget to install the adjusting screw cover after the system is adjusted.

AUTOMATIC TEMPERATURE CONTROLLED AIR CLEANER

This system is used on all Datsun models covered in this guide except the 810.

The rate of fuel atomization varies with the temperature of the air that the fuel is being mixed with. The air/fuel ratio cannot be held constant for efficient fuel combustion with a wide range of air temperatures. Cold air being drawn into the engine causes a denser and richer air/fuel

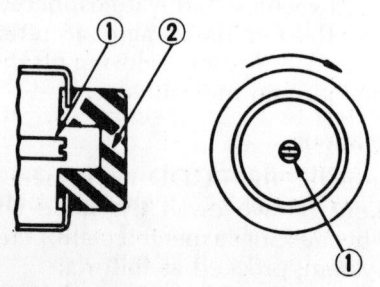

(1) BCDD adjusting screw (2) Cover

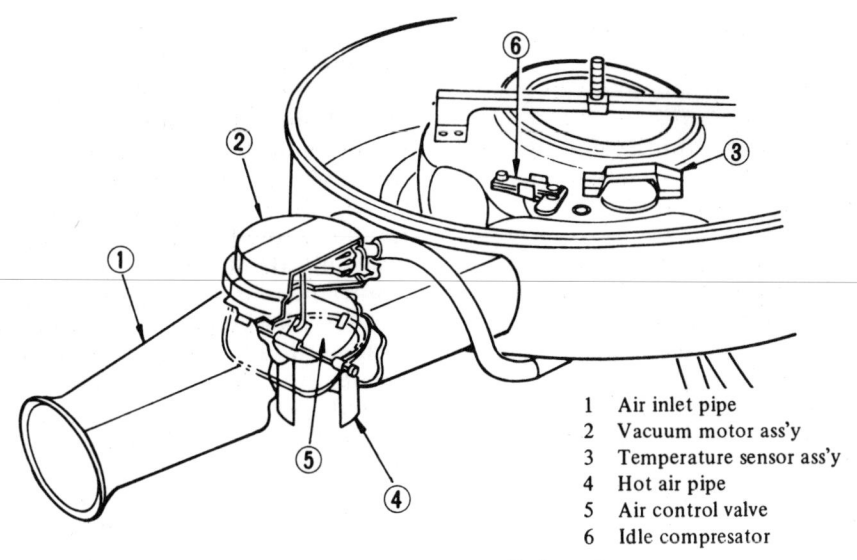

EMISSION CONTROLS AND FUEL SYSTEM

1. Air inlet pipe
2. Vacuum motor ass'y
3. Temperature sensor ass'y
4. Hot air pipe
5. Air control valve
6. Idle compresator

Automatic temperature controlled air cleaner

mixture, inefficient fuel atomization, and thus, more hydrocarbons in the exhaust gas. Hot air being drawn into the engine causes a leaner air/fuel mixture and more efficient atomization and combustion for less hydrocarbons in the exhaust gases.

The automatic temperature controlled air cleaner is designed so that the temperature of the ambient air being drawn into the engine is automatically controlled, to hold the temperature of the air and, consequently, the fuel/air ratio at a constant rate for efficient fuel combustion.

A temperature sensing vacuum switch controls vacuum applied to a vacuum motor operating a valve in the intake snorkle of the air cleaner. When the engine is cold or the air being drawn into the engine is cold, the vacuum motor opens the valve, allowing air heated by the exhaust manifold to be drawn into the engine. As the engine warms up, the temperature sensing unit shuts off the vacuum applied to the vacuum motor which allows the valve to close, shutting off the heated air and allowing cooler, outside (under hood) air to be drawn into the engine.

Testing

When the air around the temperature sensor of the unit mounted inside the air cleaner housing reaches 100° F, the sensor should block the flow of vacuum to the air control valve vacuum motor.

When the temperature around the temperature sensor is below 100° F, the sensor should allow vacuum to pass onto the air valve vacuum motor thus blocking off the air cleaner snorkle to underhood (unheated) air.

When the temperature around the sensor is above 118° F, the air control valve should be completely open to under hood air.

If the air cleaner fails to operate correctly, check for loose or broken vacuum hoses. If the hoses are not the cause, replace the vacuum motor in the air cleaner.

EXHAUST GAS RECIRCULATION (EGR)

This system is used on all 1974 and later models. Exhaust gas recirculation is used to reduce combustion temperatures in the engine, thereby reducing the oxides of nitrogen emissions.

An EGR valve is mounted on the center of the intake manifold. The recycled exhaust gas is drawn into the bottom of the intake manifold riser portion through the exhaust manifold heat stove and EGR valve. A vacuum diaphragm is connected to a timed signal port at the carburetor flange.

As the throttle valve is opened, vacuum is applied to the EGR valve vacuum diaphragm. When the vacuum reaches about 2 in. Hg, the diaphragm moves against spring pressure and is in a fully up posi-

EMISSION CONTROLS AND FUEL SYSTEM

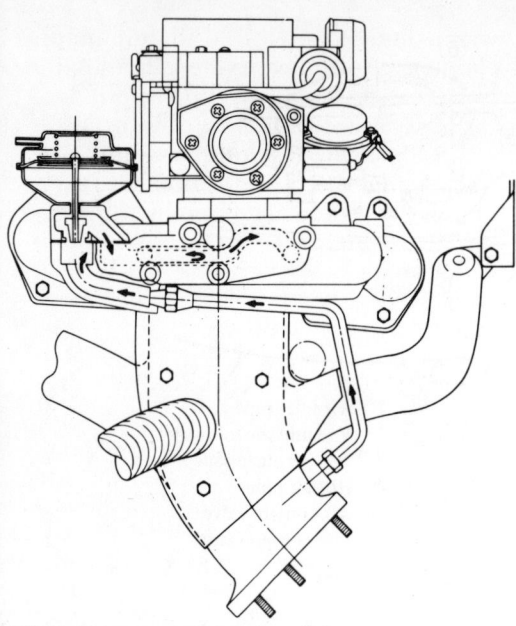

EGR system—carbureted models

tion at 8 in. Hg of vacuum. As the diaphragm moves up, it opens the exhaust gas metering valve which allows exhaust gas to be pulled into the engine intake manifold. The system does not operate when the engine is idling because the exhaust gas recirculation would cause a rough idle.

An electrically-operated solenoid vacuum control valve is inserted in the vacuum line between the EGR valve and the carburetor. The operation of the solenoid is controlled by a temperature sensing switch mounted in the coolant outlet housing. When the temperature of the coolant is below normal operating temperature, the solenoid is electrically-activated and blocks the vacuum line leading to the EGR valve, thus preventing exhaust gas recirculation. When the temperature of the engine coolant reaches operating temperature, the solenoid is deactivated and vacuum is allowed to act upon the EGR valve diaphragm and exhaust gas recirculation takes place.

Testing

Check the operation of the EGR system as follows:

1. Visually inspect the entire EGR control system. Clean the mechanism free of oil and dirt. Replace any rubber hoses found to be cracked or broken.
2. Make sure that the EGR solenoid valve is properly wired.

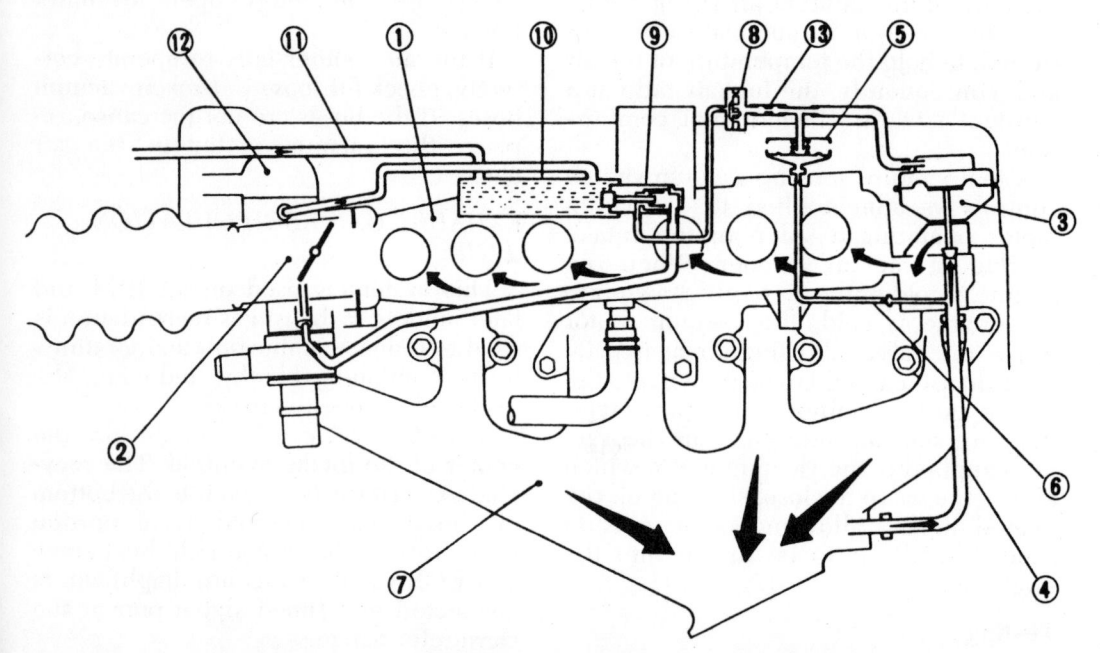

810 E.G.R. system schematic

1. Intake manifold
2. Throttle chamber
3. E.G.R. control valve
4. E.G.R. tube
5. B.P.T. valve
6. B.P.T. valve control tube
7. Exhaust manifold
8. Vacuum delay valve (California automatic transmission models only)
9. Thermal vacuum valve
10. Heater housing
11. Water return tube
12. Thermostat housing
13. Vacuum orifice

EMISSION CONTROLS AND FUEL SYSTEM

3. Increase the engine speed from idling to 3,000–3,500 rpm. The plate of the EGR control valve diaphragm and the valve shaft should move upward as the engine speed is increased.

4. Disconnect the EGR solenoid valve electrical leads and connect them directly to the vehicle's 12-volt electrical supply (battery). Race the engine again with the EGR solenoid valve connected to a 12-volt power source. The EGR control valve should remain stationary.

5. With the engine running at idle, push up on the EGR control valve diaphragm with your finger. When this is done, the engine idle should become rough and uneven.

Inspect the two components of the EGR system as necessary in the following manner:

EGR valve removal

    a. Remove the EGR control valve from the intake manifold;
    b. Apply 4.7–5.1 in. Hg of vacuum to the EGR control valve by sucking on a tube attached to the outlet on top of the valve. The valve should move to the full up position. The valve should remain open for more than 30 seconds after the application of vacuum is discontinued and the vacuum hose is blocked;
    c. Inspect the EGR valve for any signs of warpage or damage;
    d. Clean the EGR valve seat with a brush and compressed air to prevent clogging;
    e. Connect the EGR solenoid valve to a 12-volt DC power source and notice if the valve clicks when intermittently electrified. If the valve clicks, it is considered to be working properly;
    f. Check the EGR temperature sensing switch by removing it from the engine and placing it in a container of water together with a thermometer. Connect a self-powered test light to the two electrical leads of the switch;
    g. Heat the container of water;
    h. The switch should conduct current when the water temperature is below 77° F and stop conducting current when the water reaches a temperature somewhere between 88°–106° F. Replace the switch if it functions otherwise.

TRANSMISSION CONTROLLED SPARK SYSTEM

The Transmission Controlled Spark System (TCS) was introduced on the 1972 A12 engine and is now used on most models.

The TCS system consists of a thermal vacuum valve, a vacuum switching valve, a high gear detecting switch, and a number of vacuum hoses.

Basically, the system is designed to retard full spark advance except when the car is in high gear and the engine is at normal operating temperature. At all other times, the spark advance is retarded to one degree or another.

Inspection and Adjustments

Normally, the TCS system should be trouble-free. However, if you suspect a problem in the system, first check to make sure all wiring connections are clean and tight, and that all the vacuum hoses are properly connected. Also check to make sure the distributor vacuum advance is working properly. If everything appears all right, connect a timing light to the engine and make sure initial timing is correct. Run the engine until it reaches normal operating temperature, and then have an assistant sit in the car and shift the transmission through all the gears slowly. If the system is functioning properly, the timing will be 10 to 15 degrees advanced in high gear (compared to the other gear positions). If the system is still not operating correctly, you will have to check for continuity at all the connections with a test light.

AIR INJECTION REACTOR SYSTEM

This system is used on 1974 and later models. In gasoline engines, it is difficult

EMISSION CONTROLS AND FUEL SYSTEM

to completely burn the air/fuel mixture through normal combustion in the combustion chambers. Under certain operating conditions, unburned fuel is exhausted into the atmosphere.

The air injection reactor system is designed so that ambient air, pressurized by the air pump, is injected through the injection nozzles into the exhaust ports near each exhaust valve. The exhaust gases are at high temperatures and ignite when brought into contact with the oxygen. Unburned fuel is then burned in the exhaust ports and manifold.

Testing

AIR PUMP

If the air pump makes an abnormal noise and cannot be corrected without removing the pump from the vehicle, check the following in sequence:

1. Turn the pulley ¾ of a turn in the clockwise direction and ¼ of a turn in the counterclockwise direction. If the pulley is binding and if rotation is not smooth, a defective bearing is indicated.
2. Check the inner wall of the pump body, vanes and rotor for wear. If the rotor has abnormal wear, replace the air pump.
3. Check the needle roller bearing for wear and damage. If the bearings are defective, the air pump should be replaced.
4. Check and replace the rear side seal if abnormal wear or damage is noticed.
5. Check and replace the carbon shoes holding the vanes if they are found to be worn or damaged.
6. A deposit of carbon particles on the inner wall of the pump body and vanes is normal, but should be removed with compressed air before reassembling the air pump.

CHECK VALVE

Remove the check valve from the air pump discharge line. Test it for leakage by blowing air into the valve from the air pump side and from the air manifold side. Air should only pass through the valve from the air pump side if the valve is functioning normally. A small amount of air leakage from the manifold side can be overlooked. Replace the check valve if it is found to be defective.

ANTI-BACKFIRE VALVE

Disconnect the rubber hose connecting the mixture control valve with the intake manifold and plug the hose. If the mixture control valve is operating cor-

Air pump (arrow)

EMISSION CONTROLS AND FUEL SYSTEM 117

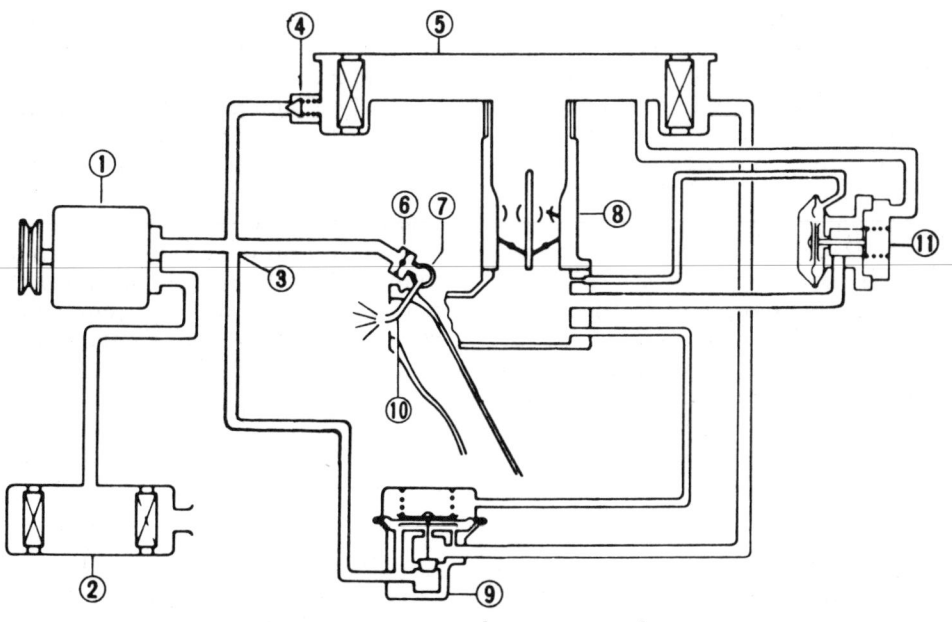

Air injection system schematic—typical

1. Air pump
2. Air pump air cleaner
3. 4-way connector
4. Air relief valve
5. Air cleaner
6. Check valve
7. Air gallery pipe
8. Carburetor
9. Air control valve
10. Injection nozzle
11. A.B. valve

rectly, air will continue to blow out the mixture control valve for a few seconds after the accelerator pedal is fully depressed (engine running) and released quickly. If air continues to blow out for more than five seconds, replace the mixture control valve.

Air Pump Relief Valve

Disconnect the air pump discharge hose leading to the exhaust manifold. With the engine running, restrict the airflow coming from the pump. The air pump relief valve should vent the pressurized air to the atmosphere if it is working properly.

NOTE: *When performing this test do not completely block the discharge line of the air pump as damage may result if the relief valve fails to function properly.*

Air Injection Nozzles

Check around the air manifold for air leakage with the engine running at 2,000 rpm. If air is leaking from the eye joint bolt, retighten or replace the gasket. Check the air nozzles for restrictions by blowing air into the nozzles.

Hoses

Check and replace hoses if they are found to be weakened or cracked. Check all hose connections and clips. Be sure that the hoses are not in contact with other parts of the engine.

ELECTRIC CHOKE

The purpose of the electric choke, used on all models, except the 810, covered in this guide is to shorten the time the

Electric choke (arrow)

EMISSION CONTROLS AND FUEL SYSTEM

choke is in operation after the engine is started, thus shortening the time of high HC output.

An electric heater warms the bimetal spring which controls the opening and closing of the choke valve. The heater starts to heat as soon as the engine starts.

CATALYTIC CONVERTER

This system is used on all 1975 and later models delivered in California in addition to the air injection system, EGR and the engine modifications, the catalyst further reduces pollutants. Through catalytic action, it changes residual hydrocarbons and carbon monoxide in the exhaust gas into carbon dioxide and water before the exhaust gas is discharged into the atmosphere.

NOTE: *Only unleaded fuel must be used with catalytic converters; lead in fuel will quickly pollute the catalyst and render it useless.*

The emergency air relief valve is used as a catalyst protection device. When the temperature of the catalyst goes above maximum operating temperature, the temperature sensor signals the switching module to activate the emergency air relief valve. This stops air injection into the exhaust manifold and lowers the temperature of the catalyst.

1. Fuel pump cap
2. Cap gasket
3. Valve packing assembly
4. Fuel pump valve assembly
5. Valve retainer
6. Diaphragm assembly
7. Diaphragm spring
8. Pull rod
9. Lower body seal washer
10. Lower body seal
11. Inlet connector
12. Outlet connector
13. Rocker arm spring
14. Rocker arm
15. Rocker arm side pin
16. Fuel pump packing
17. Spacer-fuel pump to cylinder block

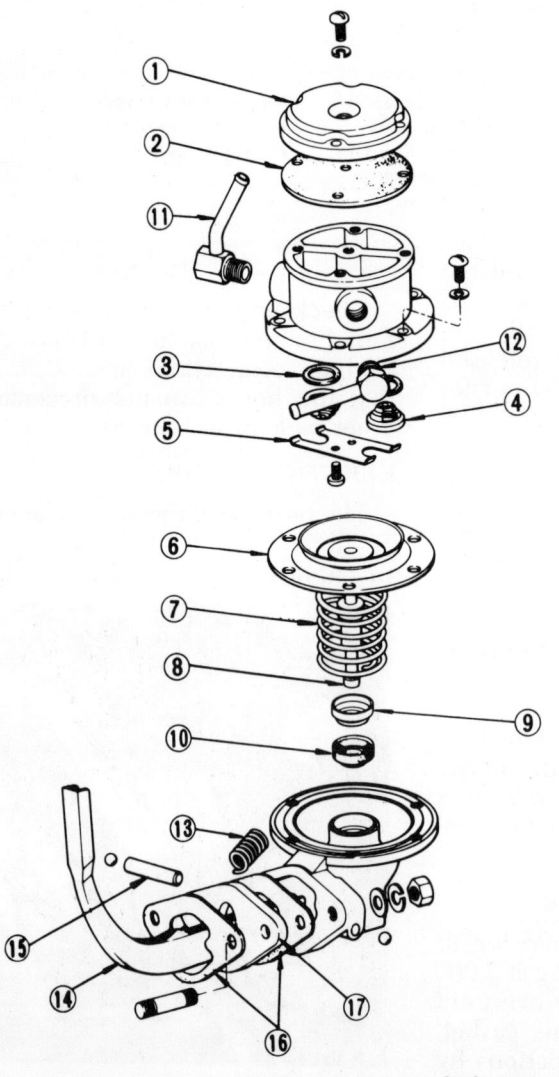

L-series engine fuel pump

EMISSION CONTROLS AND FUEL SYSTEM

Fuel System

FUEL PUMP—ALL EXCEPT 810

The fuel pump is a mechanically-operated, diaphragm-type driven by the fuel pump eccentric on the camshaft.

Design of the fuel pump permits disassembly, cleaning, and repair or replacement of defective parts.

Removal and Installation

1. Disconnect the two fuel lines from the fuel pump. Be sure to keep the line leading from the fuel tank up high to prevent the excess loss of fuel.
2. Remove the two fuel pump mounting nuts and remove the fuel pump assembly from the side of the engine.
3. Install the fuel pump in the reverse order of removal, using a new gasket and sealer on the mating surface.

FUEL PUMP—810

The 810, since it is fuel-injected, utilizes an electric fuel pump mounted near

Fuel pump location—L-series fours

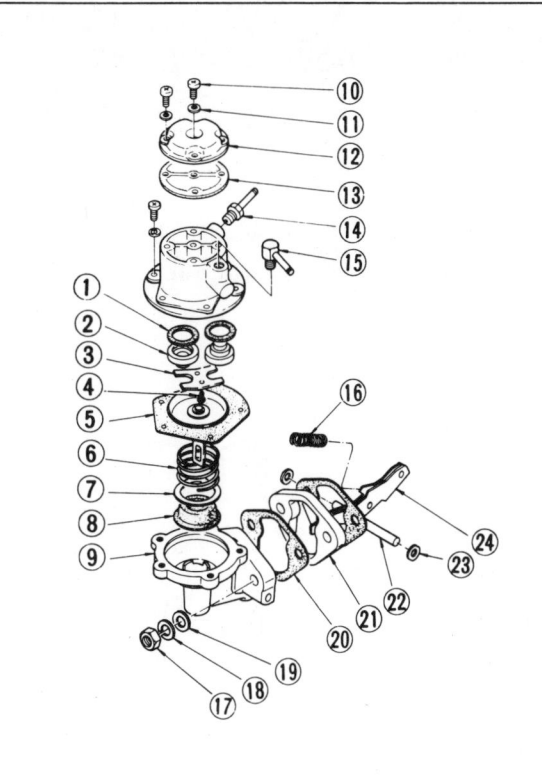

1	Packing
2	Valve assembly
3	Retainer
4	Screw
5	Diaphragm assembly
6	Diaphragm spring
7	Retainer
8	Diaphragm assembly
9	Complete-body lower
10	Screw
11	Washer-spring
12	Fuel pump cap
13	Cap gasket
14	Connector-inlet
15	Connector-outlet
16	Rocker arm spring
17	Nut
18	Washer-spring
19	Washer-plain
20	Gasket
21	Spacer
22	Rocker pin
23	Spacer
24	Rocker arm

A-series engine fuel pump

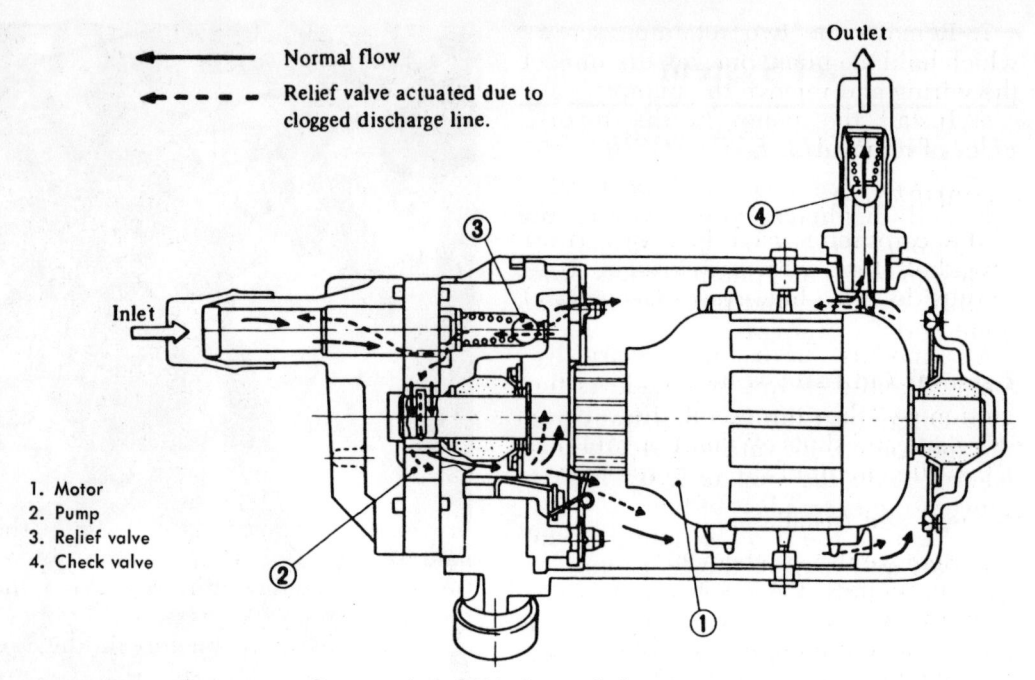

← Normal flow
◄--- Relief valve actuated due to clogged discharge line.

1. Motor
2. Pump
3. Relief valve
4. Check valve

Cross-section of 810 electric fuel pump

the fuel tank and right rear wheel. The pump is of wet type construction. A vane pump and roller are directly coupled to a motor filled with fuel. A relief valve in the pump is designed to open when the pressure in the fuel line rises over 64 psi. Normal operating pressure is 36–43 psi. The pump is automatically activated when the ignition switch is turned to the "start" position. If the engine stalls for some reason, the fuel pump is cut off even though the ignition switch remains in the "on" position.

Fuel Pump Removal and Installation— 810

1. Disconnect the negative battery cable.
2. Locate and disconnect the cold start valve harness connector. See the illustration for the location.
3. Using two jumper wires from the battery, energize the cold start valve for two or three seconds to relieve pressure in the fuel system.
4. Jack up the rear of the car and support it with jackstands. Have a can and a rag handy to catch any spilled fuel.
5. Clamp the hose between the fuel tank and the pump.
6. Loosen the hose clamps on the fuel lines at both ends of the pump and remove the lines from the pump.

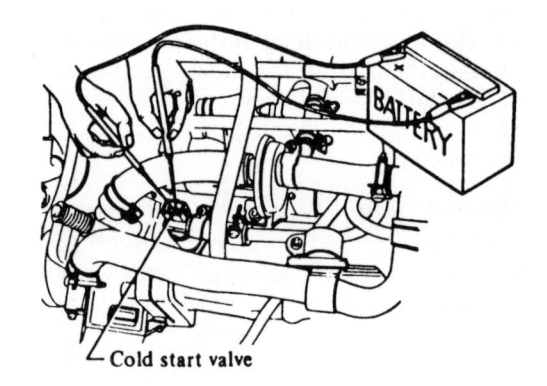

Releasing pressure at the cold-start valve

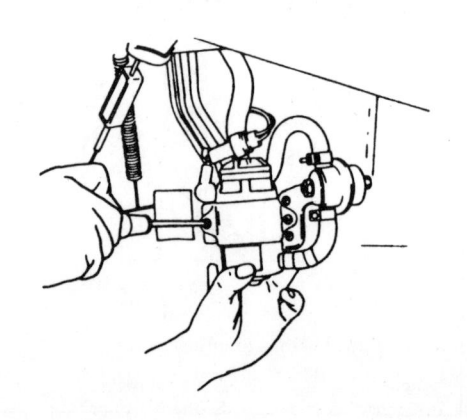

Fuel pump removal

EMISSION CONTROLS AND FUEL SYSTEM

7. Remove the two retaining screws which hold the pump bracket, disconnect the wiring and remove the pump.

8. Install the pump in the reverse order of removal.

CARBURETOR

The carburetor used is a two-barrel downdraft type with a low-speed (primary) side and a high-speed (secondary) side.

All models have an electrically-operated anti-dieseling solenoid. As the ignition switch is turned off, the valve is energized and shuts off the supply of fuel to the idle circuit of the carburetor.

Removal and Installation

1. Remove the air cleaner.
2. Disconnect the fuel and vacuum lines from the carburetor.
3. Remove the throttle lever.
4. Remove the four nuts and washers retaining the carburetor to the manifold.
5. Lift the carburetor from the manifold.
6. Remove and discard the gasket used between the carburetor and the manifold.
7. Install the carburetor in the reverse order of removal, using a new carburetor base gasket.

Secondary Throttle Linkage Adjustment

All Datsun carburetors discussed in this book are two stage type carburetors. On this type of carburetor, the engine runs on the primary barrel most of the time, with the secondary barrel being used for acceleration purposes. When the throttle valve on the primary side opens to an angle of approximately 50 degrees (from its fully closed position), the secondary throttle valve is pulled open by the connecting linkage. The fifty degree angle of throttle valve opening works out to a clearance measurement of somewhere between 0.26–0.32 in. between the throttle valve and the carburetor body. The easiest way to measure this is to use a drill bit. Drill bits from size H to size P (standard letter size drill bits) should fit. Check the appendix in the back of the book for the exact size of the various drill bits. If an adjustment is necessary, bend the connecting link between the two linkage assemblies.

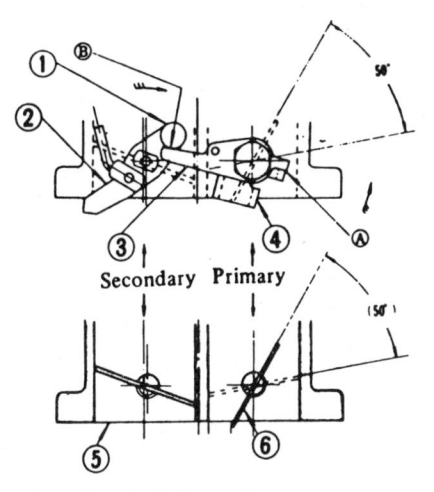

Float Level Adjustment

The fuel level is normal if it is within the lines on the window glass of the float

Carburetor used on later L-series engines

Secondary throttle linkage adjustment

1. Roller
2. Connecting lever
3. Return plate
4. Adjust plate
5. Throttle chamber
6. Throttle valve

Close-up of float level sight window

122 EMISSION CONTROLS AND FUEL SYSTEM

chamber (or the sight glass) when the vehicle is resting on level ground and the engine is off.

If the fuel level is outside the lines, remove the float housing cover. Have an absorbent cloth under the cover to catch the fuel from the fuel bowl. Adjust the float level by bending the needle seat on the float.

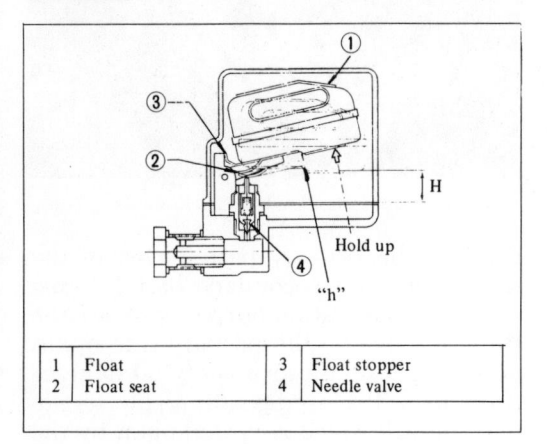

| 1 | Float | 3 | Float stopper |
| 2 | Float seat | 4 | Needle valve |

1200 and B210 float level adjustment

The needle valve should have an effective stroke of about 0.0591 in. When necessary, the needle valve stroke can be adjusted by bending the float stopper.

NOTE: *Be careful not to bend the needle valve rod when installing the float and baffle plate, if removed.*

Fast Idle Adjustment

1. With the carburetor removed from the vehicle, place the upper side of the fast idle screw on the second step of the fast idle cam and measure the clearance between the throttle valve and the wall of the throttle valve chamber at the center of the throttle valve. The clearance should be 0.0374 in. with a manual transmission and 0.0461 in. with an automatic transmission.
2. Install the carburetor on the engine.
3. Start the engine and measure the fast idle rpm with the engine at operating temperature. This should be about 2,000 rpm with a manual transmission and 2,400 rpm with an automatic transmission.
4. To adjust the fast idle speed, turn the fast idle adjusting screw; counterclockwise to increase the fast idle speed and clockwise to decrease the fast idle speed.

NOTE: *The first step of the fast idle adjustment procedure is not absolutely necessary.*

Choke Unloader Adjustment

1. Close the choke valve completely.
2. Hold the choke valve closed by stretching a rubber band between the choke piston lever and a stationary part of the carburetor.
3. Open the throttle lever fully.
4. With the throttle lever fully open, adjust the clearance between the choke valve and the carburetor body to 0.173 in. on L-series engines, or 0.079 in. on A-series engines, by bending the unloader tongue.

NOTE: *Make sure that the throttle valve opens completely when the carburetor is mounted on the engine.*

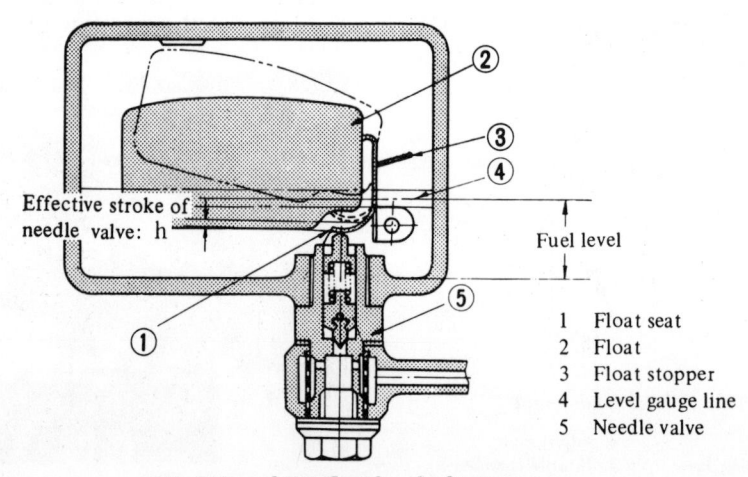

1	Float seat
2	Float
3	Float stopper
4	Level gauge line
5	Needle valve

510, 610, and 710 float level adjustment

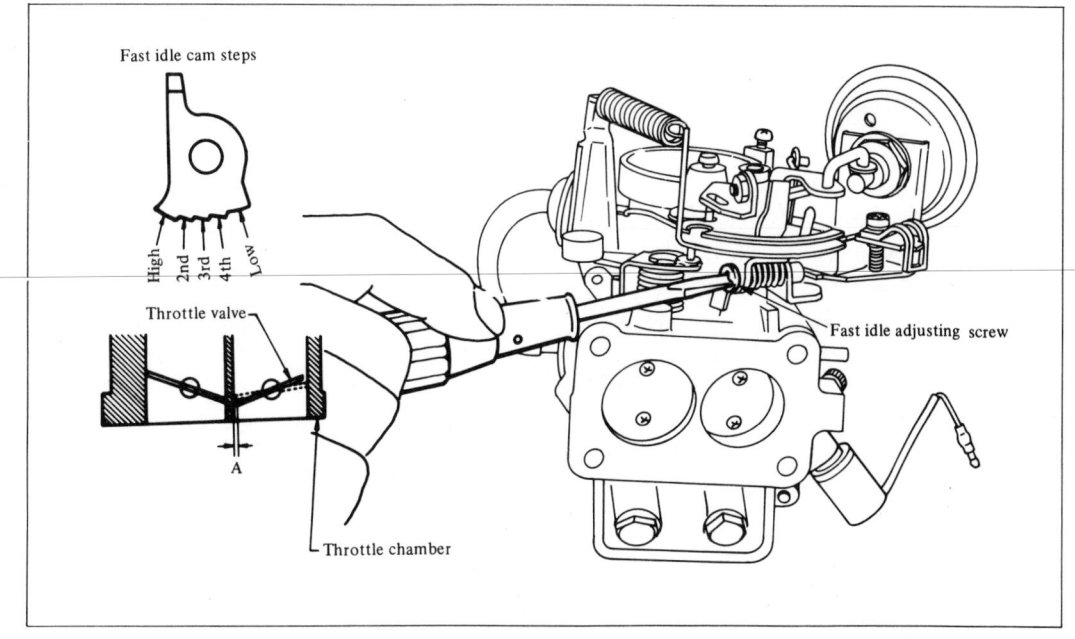

Fast idle adjustment

Overhaul

Efficient carburetion depends greatly on careful cleaning and inspection during overhaul, since dirt, gum, water, or varnish in or on the carburetor parts are often responsible for poor performance.

Overhaul your carburetor in a clean, dust-free area. Carefully disassemble the carburetor, referring often to the exploded views. Keep all similar and look-alike parts segregated during disassembly and cleaning to avoid accidental interchange during assembly. Make a note of all jet sizes.

When the carburetor is disassembled, wash all parts (except diaphragms, electric choke units, pump plunger, and any other plastic, leather, fiber, or rubber parts) in clean carburetor solvent. Do not leave parts in the solvent any longer than is necessary to sufficiently loosen the deposits. Excessive cleaning may remove the special finish from the float bowl and choke valve bodies, leaving these parts unfit for service. Rinse all parts in clean solvent and blow them dry with compressed air to allow them to air dry. Wipe clean all cork, plastic, leather, and fiber parts with a clean, lint-free cloth.

Blow out all passages and jets with compressed air and be sure that there are no restrictions or blockages. Never use wire or similar tools to clean jets, fuel passages, or air bleeds. Clean all jets and valves separately to avoid accidental interchange.

Check all parts for wear or damage. If wear or damage is found, replace the defective parts. Especially check the following:

1. Check the float needle and seat for wear. If wear is found, replace the complete assembly.

2. Check the float hinge pin for wear and the float(s) for dents or distortion. Replace the float if fuel has leaked into it.

3. Check the throttle and choke shaft bores for wear or an out-of-round condition. Damage or wear to the throttle arm, shaft, or shaft bore will often require replacement of the throttle body. These parts require a close tolerance of fit; wear may allow air leakage, which could affect starting and idling.

NOTE: *Throttle shafts and bushings are not included in overhaul kits. They can be purchased separately.*

4. Inspect the idle mixture adjusting needles for burrs or grooves. Any such condition requires replacement of the needle, since you will not be able to obtain a satisfactory idle.

5. Test the accelerator pump check valves. They should pass air one way but

124 EMISSION CONTROLS AND FUEL SYSTEM

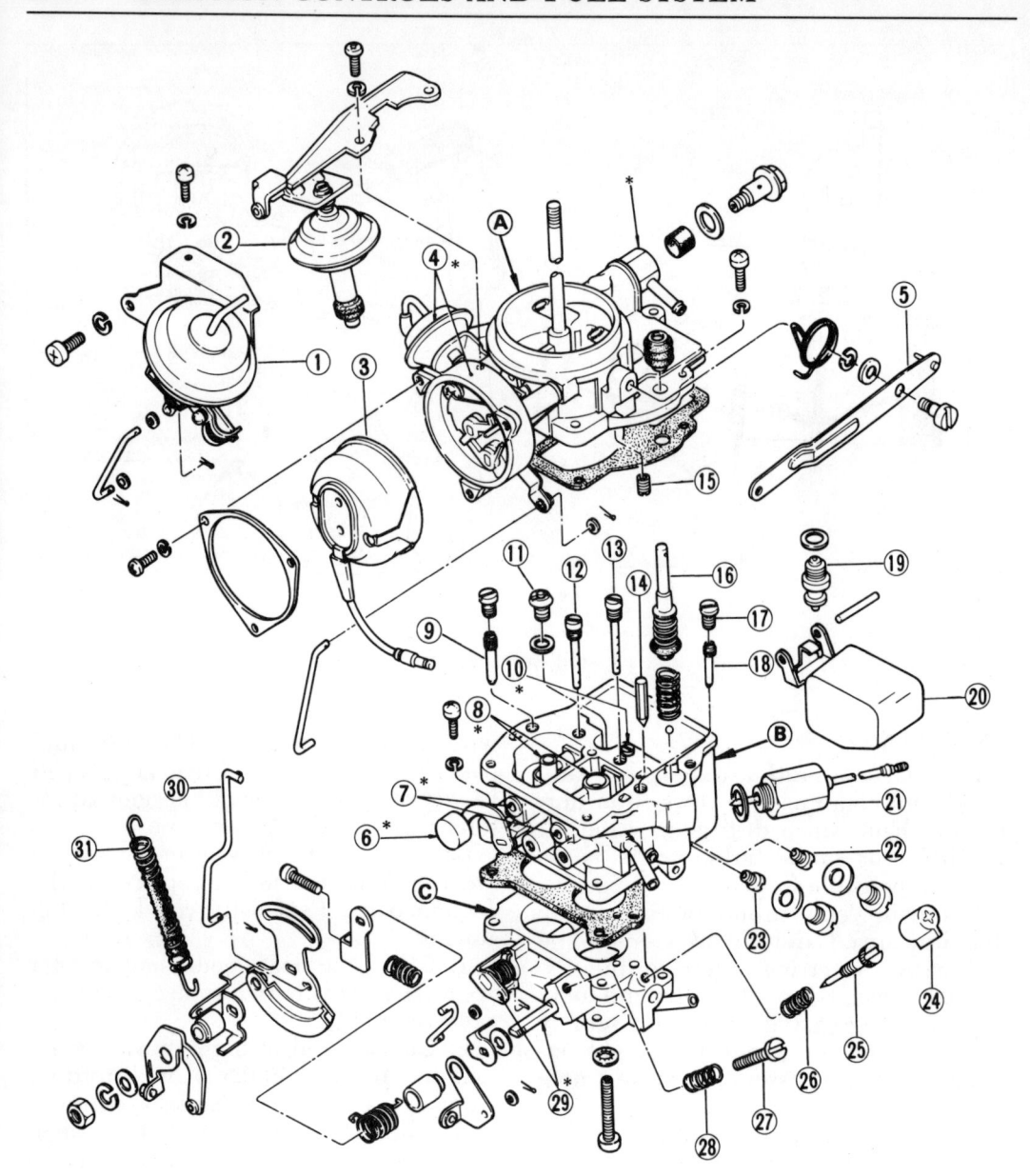

- Ⓐ Choke chamber
- Ⓑ Center body
- Ⓒ Throttle chamber
1. Servo diaphragm of throttle opener
2. Dash pot
3. Automatic choke cover
4.* Automatic choke body and diaphragm chamber
5. Accelerating pump lever
6.* Auxiliary valve
7.* Venturi stopper screw
8.* Primary and secondary small venturi
9. Secondary slow jet
10.* Safe orifice
11. Power valve
12. Secondary main air bleed
13. Primary main air bleed
14. Injector weight
15. Primary slow air bleed
16. Accelerating pump
17. Plug
18. Primary slow jet
19. Needle valve
20. Float
21. Anti-dieseling solenoid valve
22. Primary main jet
23. Secondary main jet
24. Idle limiter cap
25. Idle adjust screw
26. Spring
27. Throttle adjust screw
28. Spring
29.* Primary and secondary throttle valve
30. Accelerating pump rod
31. Throttle return spring

Note: Do not remove the parts marked with an asterisk "*"

Exploded view of 1975 B210 carburetor—earlier models and 1200 similar

EMISSION CONTROLS AND FUEL SYSTEM 125

A Choke chamber
B Center body
C Throttle chamber

1. Lock lever
2. Filter set screw
3. Fuel filter
4. Fuel nipple
5. Needle valve body
6. Needle valve
7. Fuel chamber parts
8. Accelerating pump parts
9. Altitude compensator pipe (for California)
10* Coasting air bleed adjusting screw
11* High speed enricher air bleed
12* Choke valve
13. Accelerating pump lever
14. Throttle return spring
15. Accelerating pump rod
16. Automatic choke cover
17* Automatic choke body and diaphragm chamber
18* Richer jet
19* Coasting air bleed I
20. Primary main jet
21. Secondary main jet
22. Secondary slow air bleed
23. Secondary slow jet
24. Plug
25* Safe orifice
26. Coasting jet
27. Secondary main air bleed
28. Power valve
29. Primary main air bleed
30. Plug
31. Primary slow jet
32. No. 2 primary slow air bleed
33* Primary and secondary small venturi
34* Venturi stopper screw
35. Choke connecting rod
36. Anti-dieseling solenoid valve
37. Fast idle cam
38. Diaphragm chamber parts
39. Idle limiter cap
40. Idle adjust screw
41. Idle adjust screw spring
42. Throttle adjust screw
43. Throttle adjust screw spring
44* Primary and secondary throttle valve
45. B.C.D.D. (for California)
46. Vacuum control solenoid valve
47. B.C.D.D. (except California)

Note: Do not remove the parts marked with an asterisk "*."

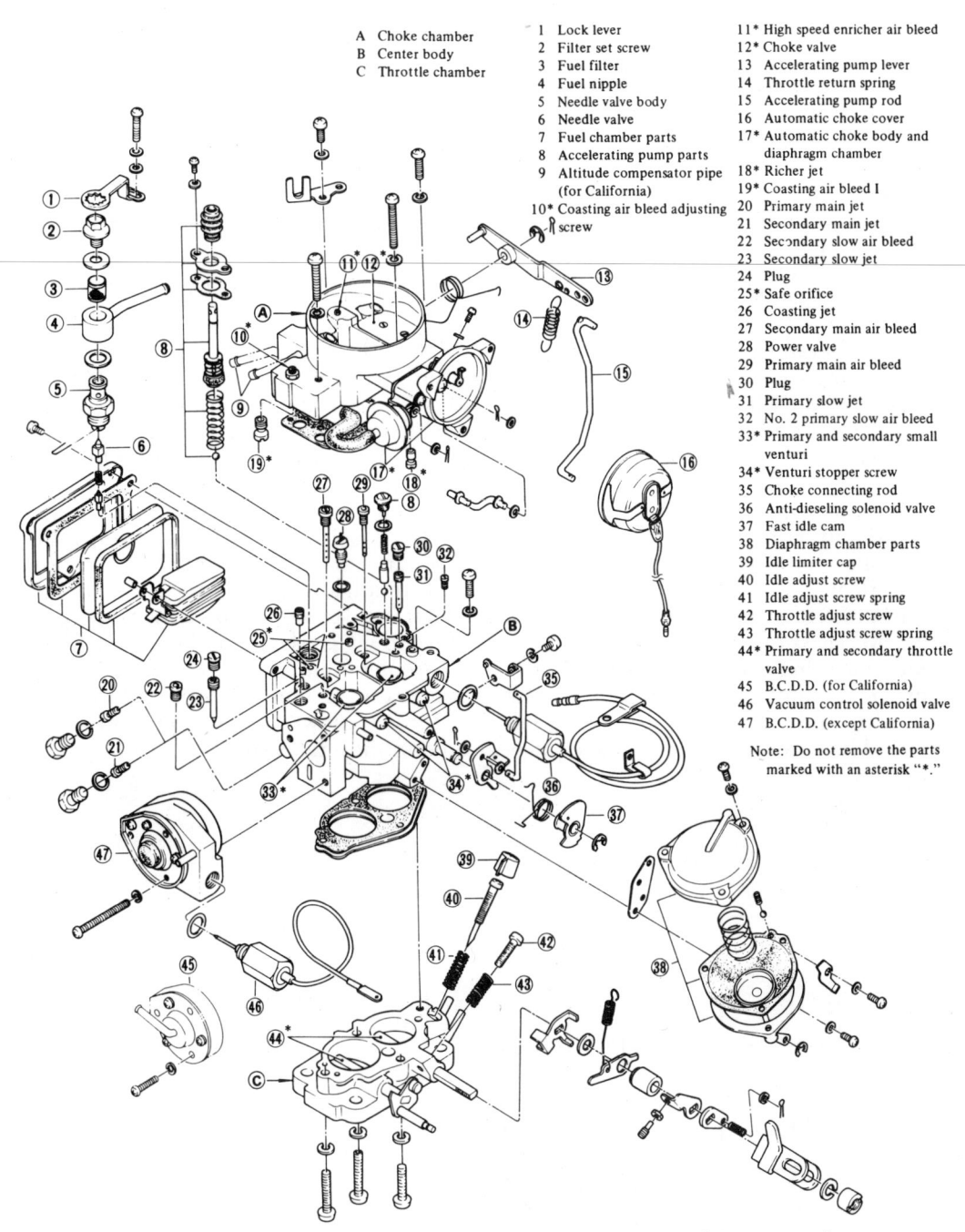

Exploded view of 1975 710 carburetor—earlier models, 610, and 510 are similar

not the other. Test for proper seating by blowing and sucking on the valve. Replace the valve if necessary. If the valve is satisfactory, wash the valve again to remove breath moisture.

6. Check the bowl cover for warped surfaces with a straightedge.

7. Closely inspect the valves and seats for wear and damage, replacing as necessary.

8. After the carburetor is assembled, check the choke valve for freedom of operation.

Carburetor overhaul kits are recommended for each overhaul. These kits contain all gaskets and new parts to re-

EMISSION CONTROLS AND FUEL SYSTEM

place those that deteriorate most rapidly. Failure to replace all parts supplied with the kit (especially gaskets) can result in poor performance later.

Some carburetor manufacturers supply overhaul kits of three basic types: minor repair; major repair; and gasket kits. Basically, they contain the following:

Minor Repair Kits:
    All gaskets
    Float needle valve
    Volume control screw
    All diaphragms
    Spring for the pump diaphragm

Major Repair Kits:
    All jets and gaskets
    All diaphragms
    Float needle valve
    Volume control screw
    Pump ball valve
    Main jet carrier
    Float

Gasket Kits:
    All gaskets

After cleaning and checking all components, reassemble the carburetor, using new parts and referring to the exploded view. When reassembling, make sure that all screws and jets are tight in their seats, but do not overtighten as the tips will be distorted. Tighten all screws gradually in rotation. Do not tighten needle valves into their seats; uneven jetting will result. Always use new gaskets. Be sure to adjust the float level when reassembling.

ELECTRONIC FUEL INJECTION SYSTEM

The electronic fuel injection system used on the L24 engine in the 810 is a Bosch L-Jetronic unit built under license in Japan. The Bosch L-Jetronic system precisely controls fuel injection to match engine requirements, reducing emissions and increasing driveability.

The electric fuel pump pumps fuel through a damper and filter to the pressure regulator. The six fuel injectors are electric solenoid valves which open and close by signals from the control unit. The control unit receives input from six sensors (seven on California models).

1. Air flow meter—measures the amount of intake air.

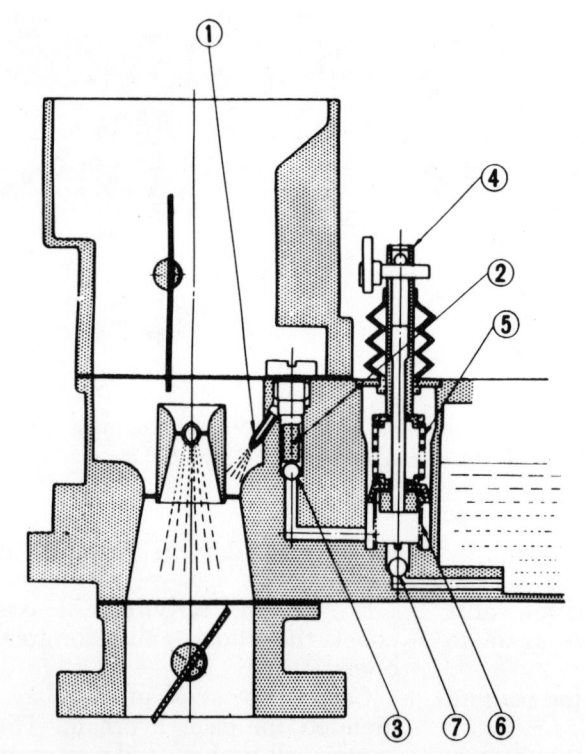

1 Pump injector
2 Weight
3 Outlet valve
4 Piston
5 Damper spring
6 Piston return spring
7 Inlet valve

L-series carburetor acceleration circuit

EMISSION CONTROLS AND FUEL SYSTEM

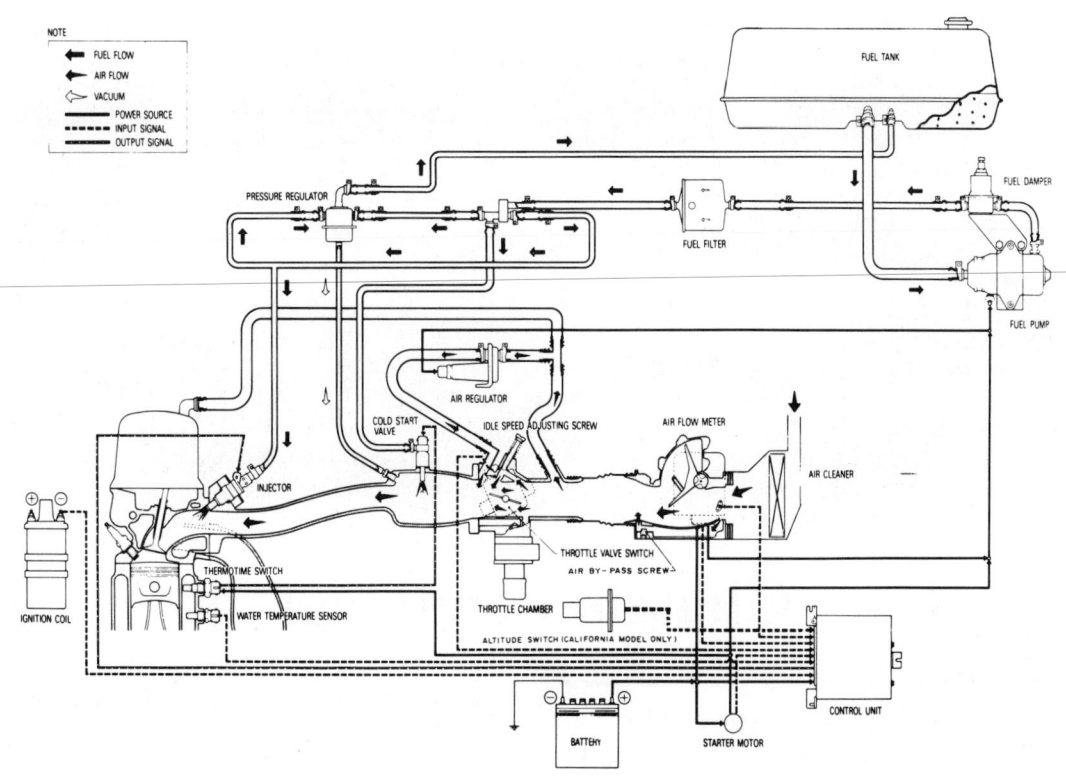

Electronic fuel injection schematic

2. Ignition coil—engine rpm.
3. Throttle valve switch—amount of throttle opening.
4. Water temperature sensor—temperature of coolant.
5. Air temperature sensor—temperature of intake air.
6. Starting switch—signals that starter is operating.
7. Altitude switch—used on California cars to signal changes in atmospheric pressure.

The sensors provide the input to the control unit, which determines the amount of fuel to be injected by its preset program.

The L-Jetronic fuel injection system is a highly complex unit. All repair or adjustment should be left to an expert Datsun technician.

Chapter Five

Chassis Electrical

Understanding and Troubleshooting Electrical Systems

For any electrical system to operate, it must make a complete circuit. This simply means that the power flow from the battery must make a complete circle. When an electrical component is operating, power flows from the battery to the component, passes through the component causing it to perform its function (lighting a light bulb), and then returns to the battery through the ground of the circuit. This ground is usually (but not always) the metal part of the car on which the electrical component is mounted.

Perhaps the easiest way to visualize this is to think of connecting a light bulb with two wires attached to it to your car battery. The battery in your car has two posts (negative and positive). If one of the two wires attached to the light bulb was attached to the negative post of the battery and the other wire was attached to the positive post of the battery, you would have a complete circuit. Current from the battery would flow out one post, through the wire attached to it and then to the light bulb, where it would pass through causing it to light. It would then leave the light bulb, travel through the other wire, and return to the other post of the battery.

The normal automotive circuit differs from this simple example in two ways. First, instead of having a return wire from the bulb to the battery, the light bulb returns the current to the battery through the chassis of the vehicle. Since the negative battery cable is attached to the chassis and the chassis is made of electrically conductive metal, the chassis of the vehicle can serve as a ground wire to complete the circuit. Secondly, most automotive circuits contain switches to turn components on and off as required.

There are many types of switches, but the most common simply serves to prevent the passage of current when it is turned off. Since the switch is a part of the circle necessary for a complete circuit, it operates to leave an opening in the circuit, and thus an incomplete or open circuit, when it is turned off.

Some electrical components which require a large amount of current to operate also have a relay in their circuit. Since these circuits carry a large amount of current, the thickness of the wire in the circuit (gauge size) is also greater. If this large wire were connected from the component to the control switch on the instrument panel, and then back to the component, a voltage drop would occur in the circuit. To prevent this potential drop in voltage, an electromagnetic switch (relay) is used. The large wires in the circuit are connected from the car battery to one side of the relay, and from the opposite side of the relay to the component. The relay is normally open, preventing current from passing through the circuit. An additional, smaller, wire is connected from the relay to the control switch for the circuit. When the control switch is turned on, it grounds the smaller wire from the relay and completes the circuit. This closes the relay and allows current to flow from the battery to the component. The horn, headlight, and starter circuits are three which use relays.

Did you ever notice how your instrument panel lights get brighter the faster your car goes? This happens because your alternator (which supplies the battery) puts out more current at speeds above idle. This is normal. However, it is possible for larger surges of current to pass through the electrical system of your car. If this surge of current were to reach an electrical component, it could burn it out. To prevent this from happening, fuses are connected into the current supply wires of most of the major electrical systems of your car. The fuse serves to head off the surge at the pass. When an electrical current of excessive power passes through the component's fuse, the fuse blows out and breaks the circuit, saving it from destruction.

The fuse also protects the component from damage if the power supply wire to the component is grounded before the current reaches the component.

Let us here interject another rule to the complete circle circuit. *Every complete circuit from a power source must include a component which is using the power from the power source.* If you were to disconnect the light bulb (from the previous example of a lightbulb being connected to the battery by two wires) from the wires and touch the two wires together (please take my word for this; don't try it), the result would be shocking. You probably haven't seen so many sparks since the Fourth of July. A similar thing happens (on a smaller scale) when the power supply wire to a component or the electrical component itself becomes grounded before the normal ground connection for the circuit. To prevent damage to the system, the fuse for the circuit blows to interrupt the circuit—protecting the components from damage. Because grounding a wire from a power source makes a complete circuit—less the required component to use the power—this phenomenon is called a short circuit. The most common causes of short circuits are: the rubber insulation on a wire breaking or rubbing through to expose the current carrying core of the wire to a metal part of the car, or a short switch.

Some electrical systems on the car are protected by a circuit breaker which is, basically, a self-repairing fuse. When either of the above-described events takes place in a system which is protected by a circuit breaker, the circuit breaker opens the circuit the same way a fuse does. However, when either the short is removed from the circuit or the surge subsides, the circuit breaker resets itself and does not have to be replaced as a fuse does.

The final protective device in the chassis electrical system is a fuse link. A fuse link is a wire that acts as a fuse. It is connected between the starter relay and the main wiring harness for the car. This connection is under the hood, very near a similar fuse link which protects all the chassis electrical components, it is the probable cause of trouble when none of the electrical components function, unless the battery is disconnected or dead. The procedure for replacing the fuse link is described in chapter three, in the "Engine Electrical" section.

Electrical problems generally fall into one of three areas:

1. The component that is not functioning is not receiving current.

2. The component itself is not functioning.

3. The component is not properly grounded.

Problems that fall into the first category are by far the most complicated. It is the current supply system to the component which contains all the switches, relays, fuses, etc.

The electrical system can be checked with a test light and a jumper wire. A test light is a device that looks like a pointed screwdriver with a wire attached to it. It has a light bulb in its handle. A jumper wire is a piece of insulated wire with an alligator clip attached to each end. To check the system you must follow the wiring diagrams found in this chapter. A wiring diagram is a road map of the car's electrical system.

If a light bulb is not working, you must follow a systematic plan to determine which of the three causes is the villain.

1. Turn on the switch that controls the inoperable bulb.
2. Disconnect the power supply wire from the bulb.
3. Attach the ground wire on the test light to a good metal ground.
4. Touch the probe end of the test light to the end of the power supply wire that was disconnected from the bulb. If the bulb is receiving current, the test light will go on.

NOTE: *If the bulb is one which works only when the ignition key is turned on (turn signal), make sure the key is turned on.*

If the test light does not go on, then the problem is in the circuit between the battery and the bulb. As mentioned before, this includes all the switches, fuses, and relays in the system. Turn to the wiring diagram and find the bulb on the diagram. Follow the wire that runs back to the battery. The problem is an open circuit between the battery and the bulb. If the fuse is blown and, when replaced, immediately blows again, there is a short circuit in the system which must be located and repaired. If there is a switch in the system, bypass it with a jumper wire. This is done by connecting one end of the jumper wire to the power supply wire into the switch and the other end of the jumper wire to the wire coming out of the switch. Again, consult the wiring diagram. If the test light lights with the jumper wire installed, the switch or whatever was bypassed is defective.

NOTE: *Never substitute the jumper wire for the bulb, as the bulb is the component required to use the power from the power source.*

5. If the bulb in the test light goes on, then the current is getting to the bulb that is not working in the car. This eliminates the first of the three possible causes. Connect the power supply wire and connect a jumper wire from the bulb to a good metal ground. Do this with the switch which controls the bulb turned on, and also the ignition switch turned on if it is required for the light to work. If the bulb works with the jumper wire installed, then it has a bad ground. This is usually caused by the metal area on which the bulb mounts to the car being coated with some type of foreign matter.

6. If neither test located the source of the trouble, then the light bulb itself is defective.

The above test procedure can be applied to any of the components of the chassis electrical system by substituting the component that is not working for the light bulb. Remember that for any electrical system to work, all connections must be clean and tight.

Heater

HEATER ASSEMBLY

Removal and Installation

1973 510

1. Drain the coolant.
2. Disconnect the water pipes to the engine.
3. Disconnect the blower motor electrical connector.
4. Remove the three heater control wires at the heater unit.
5. Remove the two bolts and ventilator.
6. Remove the four bolts and detach the heater unit.
7. Reverse the procedure for installation.

1973 1200

1. Remove the package tray and ashtray.
2. Disconnect the two hoses between the heater and engine.
3. Disconnect the cables from the heater unit and heater controls. Disconnect the wiring.
4. Disconnect the two control wires from the water cock and interior valve, and the control rod from the shut valve. Set the heater control upper lever to DEF and lower lever to OFF.
5. Pull off the right and left defroster hoses.

CHASSIS ELECTRICAL

6. Remove the four screws holding the heater unit to the firewall. Remove the control knob and remove the screws holding the control unit to the instrument panel. Remove the heater unit.

7. Reverse the procedure for installation.

1973–76 610, 1974–77 710, AND 1974–78 B210

1. Disconnect the battery ground cable.
2. Drain the coolant.
3. Detach the coolant inlet and outlet hoses.
4. Remove the center ventilator grille from the bottom of the instrument panel.
5. Remove the heater duct hose.
6. Detach the defroster hose from each side of the heater unit.
7. Disconnect the control cables.
8. Disconnect the wires at the connectors.
9. Remove the bolt at each side of the unit and the one on the top.
10. Remove the unit.
11. Reverse the procedure for installation. Run the engine for a few minutes with the heater on to make sure that the system is filled with coolant.

1977–78 200SX

1. Disconnect the battery cable.
2. Drain the engine coolant and remove the heater hoses from the engine side.
3. Inside the passenger compartment, disconnect the lead wires from the heater unit to the instrument harness.
4. At this point, the instrument panel must be removed in order to remove the heater assembly. To remove the panel, proceed as follows:
5. Remove the steering wheel cover.
6. Disconnect the speedometer cable and the radio antenna cable.
7. After noting their position, disconnect the following connectors: instrument harness to body, harness to engine room, transistor ignition unit, and the wiring to the console.
8. Remove the bolts securing column clamp and lower the steering column.
9. Remove the package tray.
10. Remove the bolts which attach the instrument panel to the mounting brackets on the left and right-hand sides.
11. Remove the trim on the right side windshield pillar, and remove the bolt attaching the instrument panel to the pillar.

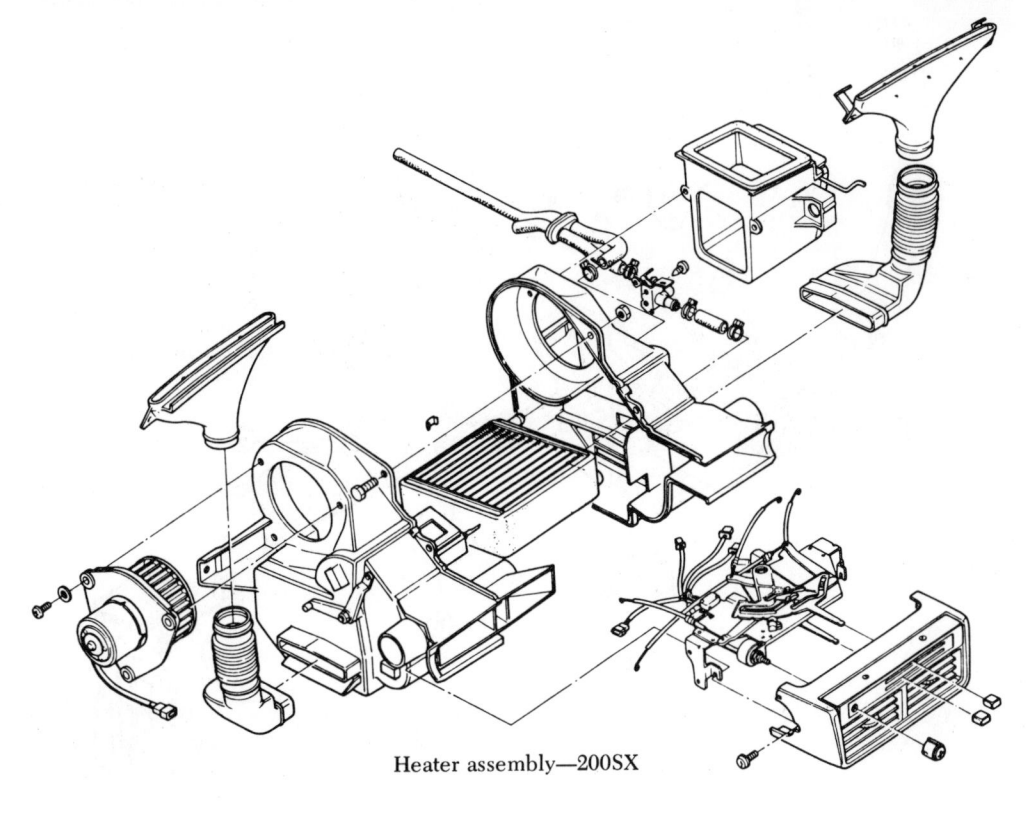

Heater assembly—200SX

12. Remove the trim on the top of the instrument panel. It is referred to as instrument garnish in the illustration.
13. Remove the bolts attaching the instrument panel.
14. Move the instrument panel to the right to remove it.
15. Remove the defroster hoses on both sides of the heater unit.
16. If the car is air-conditioned, disconnect the wires to the air-conditioner.
17. Remove the three heater retaining bolts and remove the heater assembly.
18. Installation is in the reverse order of removal.

1977-78 810

1. Disconnect the battery ground cable.
2. Drain the engine coolant.
3. Remove the console box and the console box bracket. Remove the front floor mat.
4. Loosen the screws and remove the rear heater duct.
5. Remove the hose clamps and remove the inlet and outlet hoses.
6. Remove the heater duct and remove the defroster hoses from the assembly.
7. Remove the air intake door control cable.
8. Disconnect the wiring harness to the heater.
9. Remove the retaining bolts and remove the heater unit.
10. Installation is in the reverse order of removal.

1977-78 F10

1. Disconnect the battery ground cable.
2. Drain the engine coolant and remove the heater hoses.
3. Remove the defroster hoses from each side of the heater assembly.
4. Remove the cable retaining clamps and remove the cables for the intake and floor doors.
5. Disconnect the three pole connector.
6. Remove the four heater retaining screws. Remove the heater.
7. Installation is in the reverse order of removal.

1978 510

1. Disconnect the battery ground cable.
2. Drain the engine coolant.

1. Heater unit
2. Defroster duct L/H
3. Defroster nozzle L/H
4. Heater hose
5. Defroster nozzle R/H
6. Heater duct
7. Intake box
8. Defroster duct R/H
9. Air guide plate

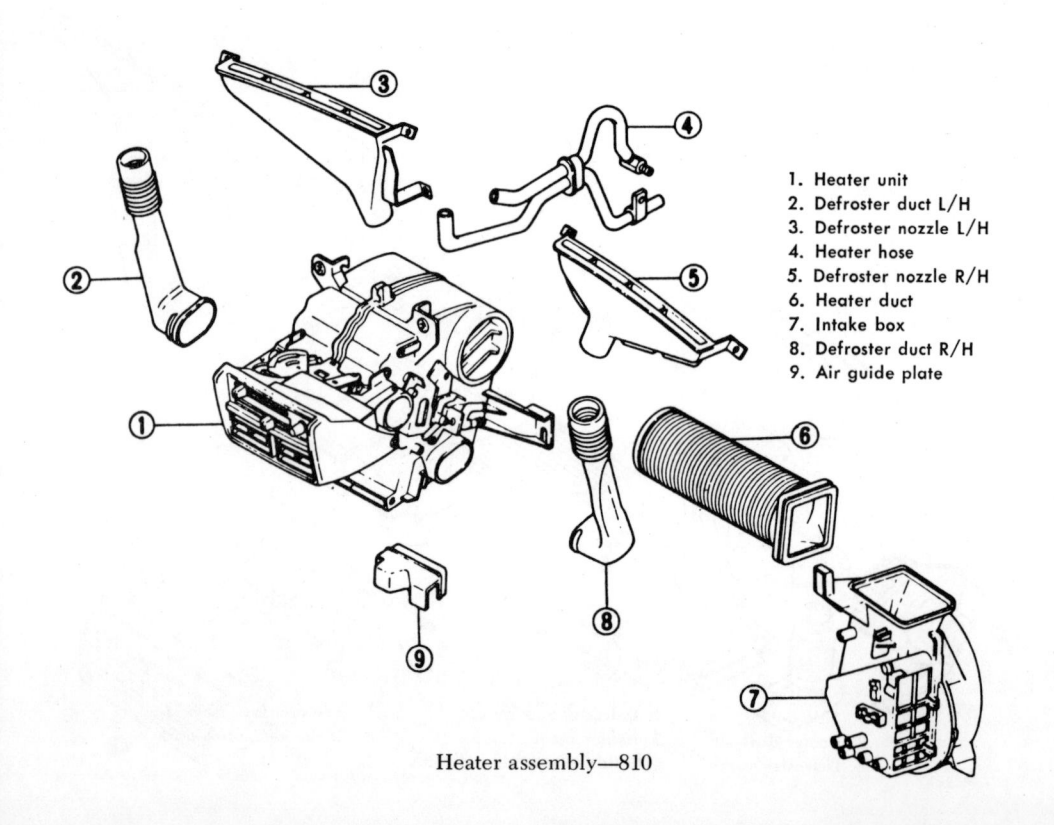

Heater assembly—810

CHASSIS ELECTRICAL 133

Heater assembly—F10

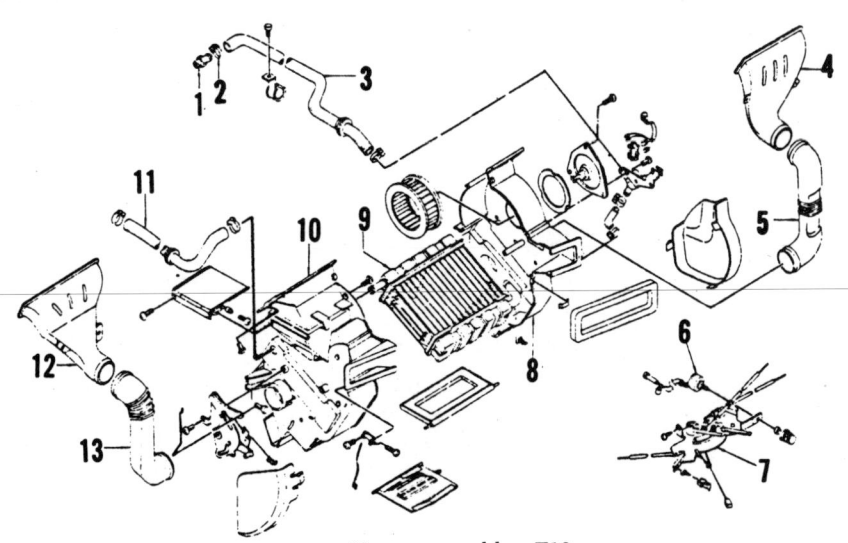

1. Connector
2. Clip
3. Heater hose (inlet)
4. Defroster nozzle (R.H.)
5. Defroster duct (R.H.)
6. Heater switch
7. Heater control
8. Heater case (R.H.)
9. Heater core
10. Heater case (L.H.)
11. Heater hose (outlet)
12. Defroster nozzle (L.H.)
13. Defroster duct (L.H.)

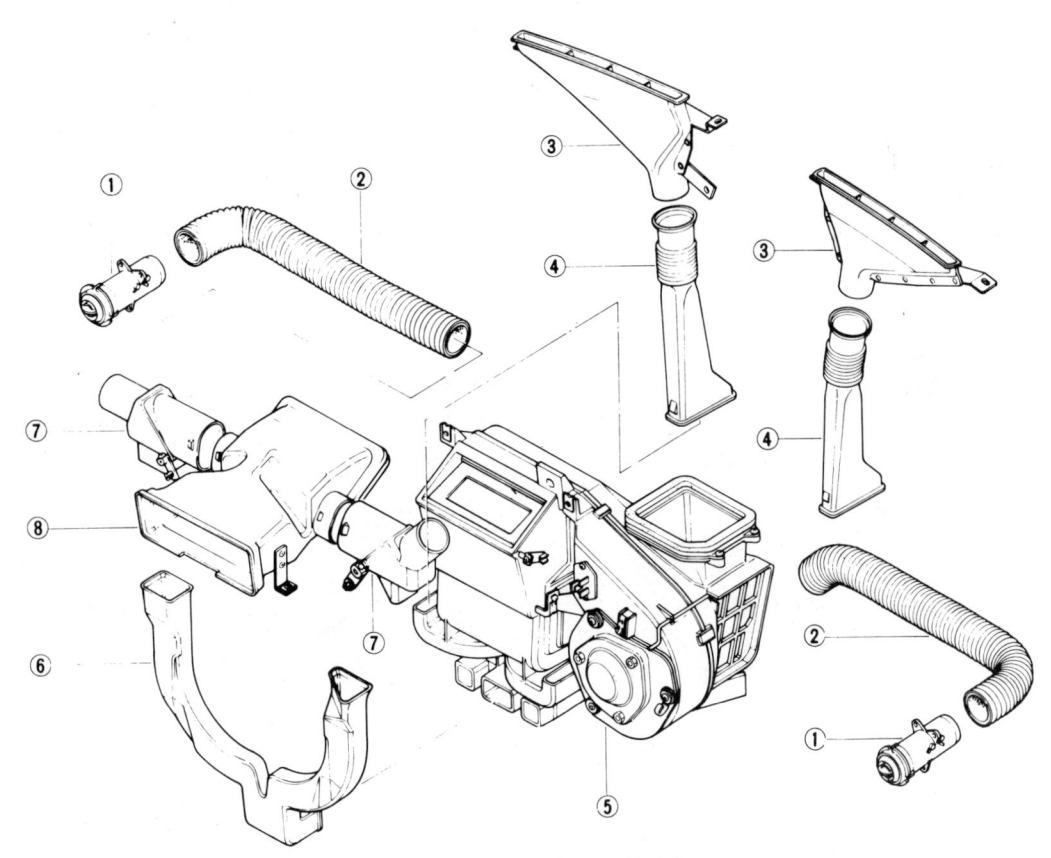

Heater assembly—1978 510

1. Side outlet
2. Cooler duct
3. Defroster nozzle
4. Defroster duct
5. Heater unit
6. Side defroster center duct
7. Side defroster connector
8. Center ventilation duct

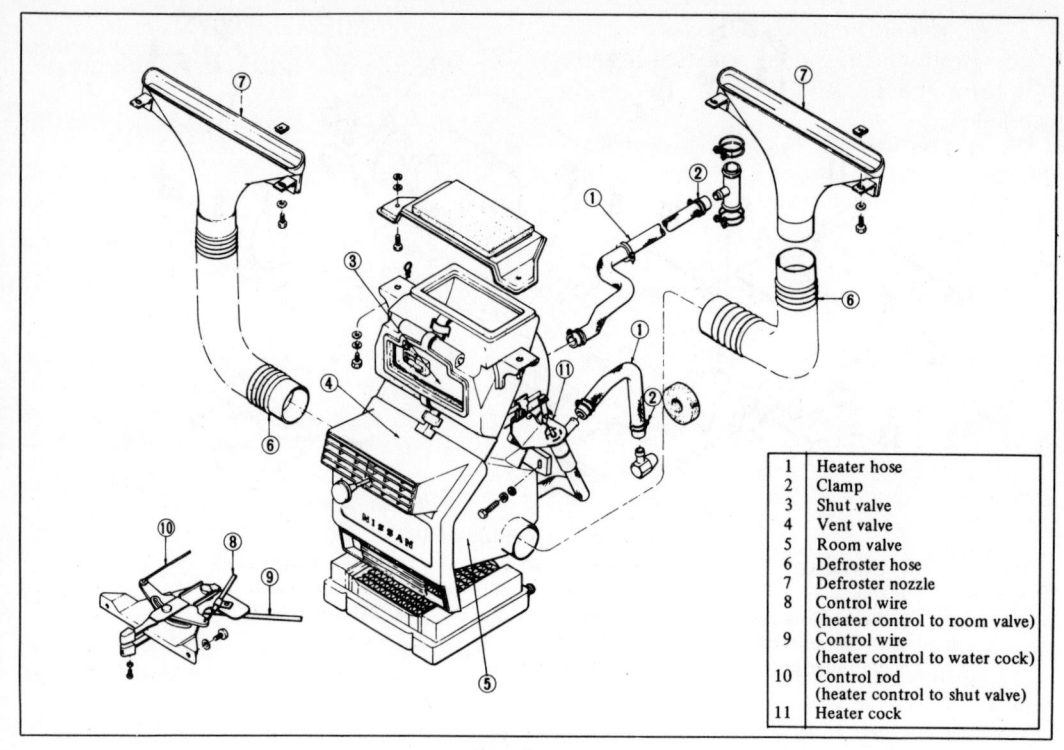

134 CHASSIS ELECTRICAL

1	Heater hose
2	Clamp
3	Shut valve
4	Vent valve
5	Room valve
6	Defroster hose
7	Defroster nozzle
8	Control wire (heater control to room valve)
9	Control wire (heater control to water cock)
10	Control rod (heater control to shut valve)
11	Heater cock

1200 heater

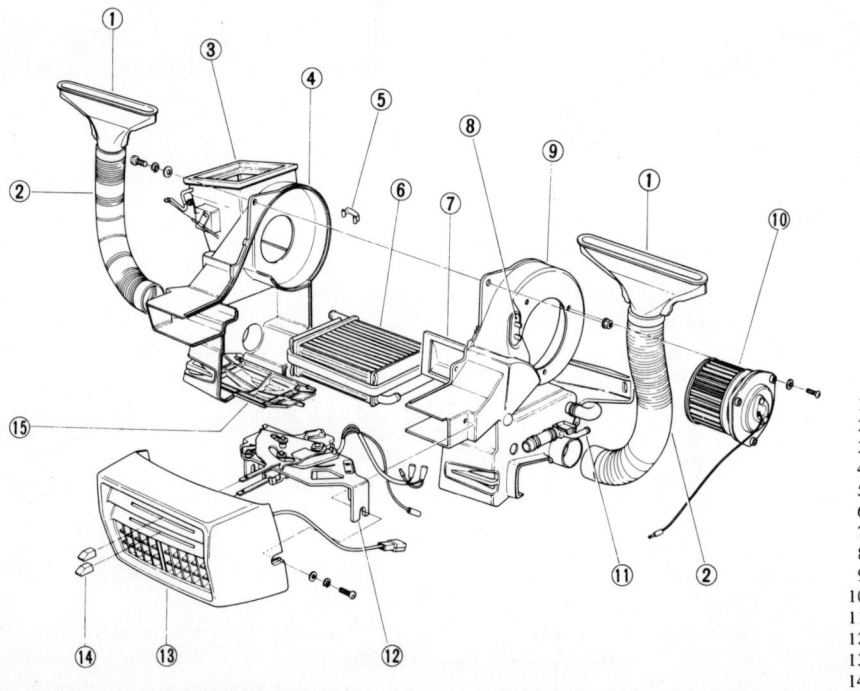

1	Defroster nozzle
2	Defroster hose
3	Air intake box
4	Heater box (L.H.)
5	Clip
6	Heater core
7	Ventilator valve
8	Resistor
9	Heater box (R.H.)
10	Fan and fan motor
11	Heater cock
12	Heater control
13	Center ventilator
14	Knob
15	Heat valve

B210 heater

CHASSIS ELECTRICAL 135

3. Remove the console box.
4. Remove the heater control assembly from the heater. Remove the radio receiver.
5. Disconnect the cooler ducts. These are the vent ducts which supply fresh air.
6. Remove the defroster ducts. Remove the center ventilator ducts.
7. Disconnect the blower motor wiring harness from the heater.
8. Loosen the hose clamps and disconnect the inlet and outlet hoses.
9. Remove the retaining bolts and remove the heater assembly.
10. Installation is in the reverse order of removal.

HEATER CORE
Removal and Installation
1973 510

1. Remove the four clips and separate the lower cover.
2. Unbolt and remove the heater core.
3. Installation is the reverse of removal.

1973-76 610, 1974-77 710, AND 1974-78 B210

The heater unit need not be removed to remove the heater core. It must be removed to remove the blower motor.
1. Drain the coolant.
2. Detach the coolant hoses.
3. Disconnect the control cables on the sides of the heater unit.
4. Remove the clips and the cover from the front of the heater unit.
5. Pull out the core.
6. Reverse the procedure for installation. Run the engine with the heater on for a few minutes to make sure that the system fills with coolant.

1977-78 F10

1. Remove the heater assembly as described earlier.
2. Remove the sealing sponges. Unfasten the seven clips that hold the heater case together.
3. Remove the heater core from the cases.
4. Installation is the reverse of removal.

1977-78 200SX

1. Remove the heater assembly as described earlier.
2. Remove the heater controls from the heater body.
3. Remove the connecting rod from the air mix door.
4. Unclip the five clips and separate the heater box into two pieces. The heater core can now be taken out.
5. Installation is in the reverse order of removal.

1977-78 810

1. Remove the heater assembly as outlined earlier.
2. Loosen the clips and screws and remove the center ventilation cover and heater control assembly.
3. Remove the screws securing the door shafts.
4. Remove the clips securing the left and right heater cases, and then separate the cases.
5. Remove the heater core.
6. Installation is in the reverse order of removal.

1978 510

1. Remove the heater unit as outlined earlier.
2. Loosen the hose clamps and disconnect the inlet and outlet hoses.
3. Remove the clips securing the case halves and separate the cases.
4. Remove the heater core.
5. Installation is in the reverse order of removal.

Radio

Removal and Installation
1973 510

1. Detach all electrical connections.
2. Remove the radio knobs and retaining nuts.
3. Remove the mounting screws, tip the radio down at the rear, and remove.
4. Reverse the procedure for installation.

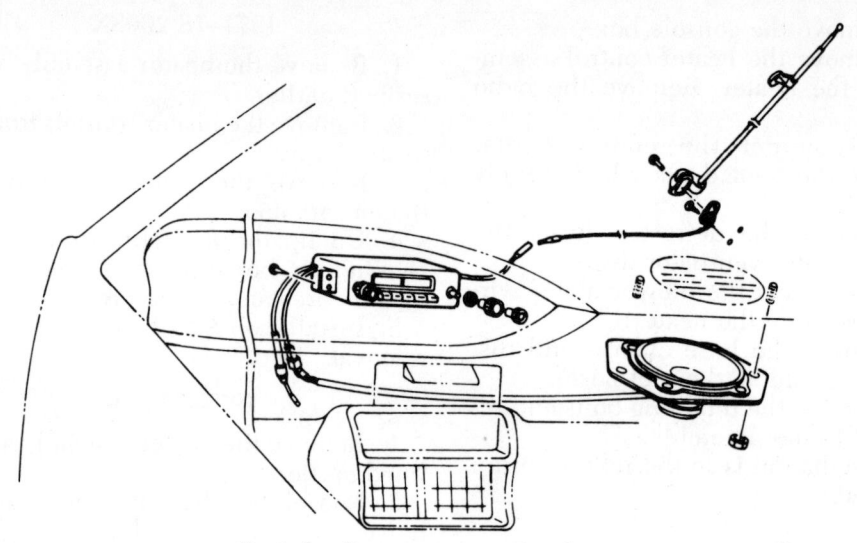

CHASSIS ELECTRICAL

Typical radio components—710 shown

1200, B210, 610, 710, F10

1. Remove the instrument cluster.
2. Detach all electrical connections.
3. Remove the radio knobs and retaining nuts.
4. Remove the rear support bracket.
5. Remove the radio.
6. Reverse the procedure for installation.

200SX

1. The instrument panel must be removed in order to remove the radio. The instrument panel is referred to as the cluster lid in the illustrations.
2. Pull out the radio switch knobs.
3. In order to remove the instrument panel, first remove the steering wheel and cover.
4. Remove the control knobs on the instrument panel by pushing in on them and turning them counterclockwise. Once the knobs are removed, remove the nuts.
5. Remove the instrument panel screws. See the illustration for their location.
6. Disconnect the switch wires (after noting their location) and remove the panel.
7. Loosen the screws and remove the radio from its bracket. Disconnect the wires and pull the radio free.

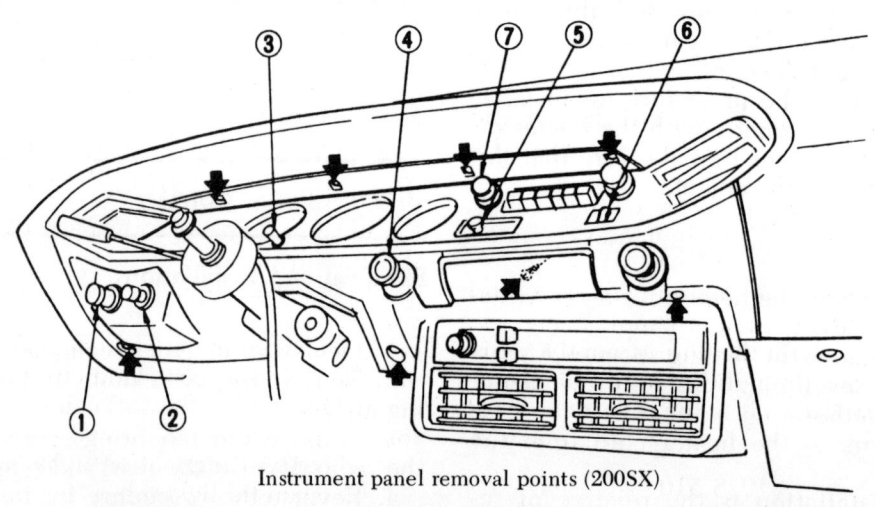

Instrument panel removal points (200SX)

1. Light switch
2. Illumination control knob
3. Trip meter knob
4. Windshield wiper and washer switch knob
5. Hazard switch
6. Rear defogger switch
7. Radio knob

CHASSIS ELECTRICAL 137

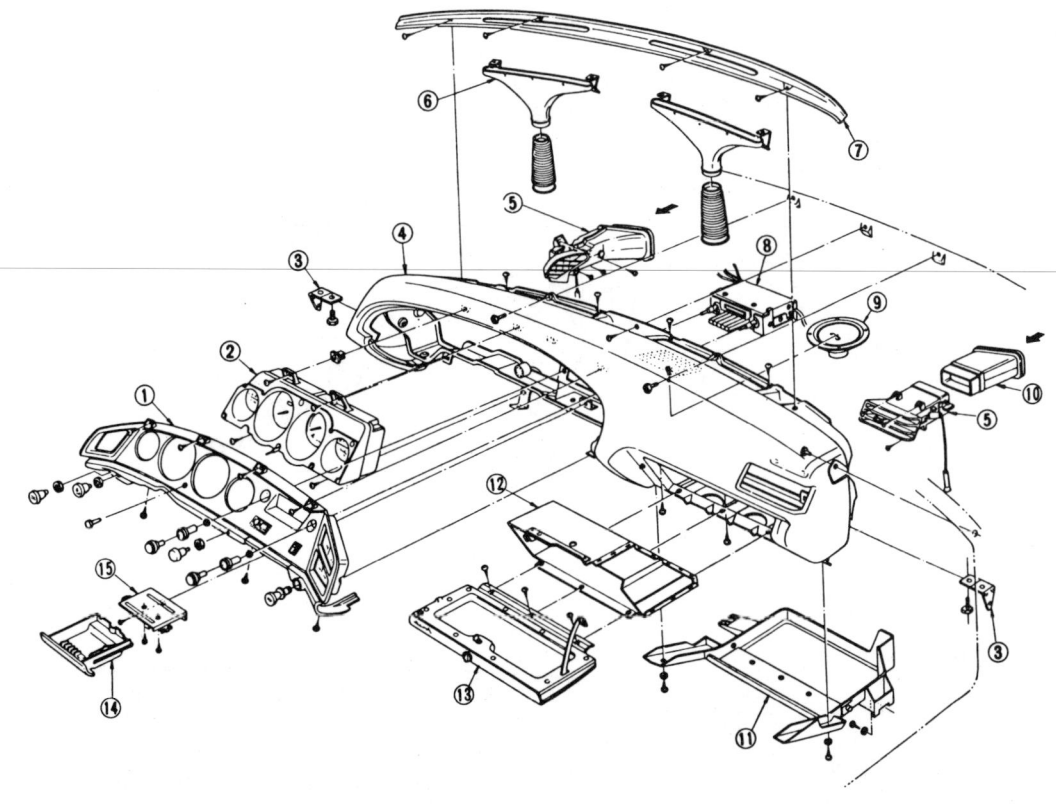

200SX instrument panel

1. Cluster lid
2. Meter assembly
3. Instrument mounting lower bracket
4. Instrument pad
5. Ventilation grille
6. Defroster nozzle
7. Instrument garnish
8. Radio
9. Speaker
10. Ventilation duct
11. Package tray
12. Glove box
13. Glove box lid
14. Ash tray
15. Outer case

8. Installation is in the reverse order of removal.

810

1. Disconnect the battery ground cable.
2. Remove the knobs and nuts on the radio and the choke control wire. Remove the ash tray.
3. Remove the steering column cover, and disconnect the main harness connectors.
4. Remove the retaining screws and remove the instrument panel cover.
5. Disconnect the wires from the radio and remove the radio from the bracket.
6. Installation is in the reverse order of removal.

1978 510

1. Disconnect the battery ground cable.
2. Remove the steering column covers and disconnect the hazard warning switch connector.
3. Loosen the wiper switch attaching screws and remove the wiper switch.
4. Pull out the ash try and the heater control knobs.
5. Remove the heater control finisher. See the illustration. Insert a screwdriver into the FAN lever slit to remove the finisher. Remove finisher A. (See the illustration.
6. Remove the radio knobs, nuts and washers.
7. Remove the manual choke knob and the defroster control knob.
8. Disconnect the following connectors:
   a. center illumination light
   b. cigarette lighter
   c. clock
   d. turn signal switch

138 CHASSIS ELECTRICAL

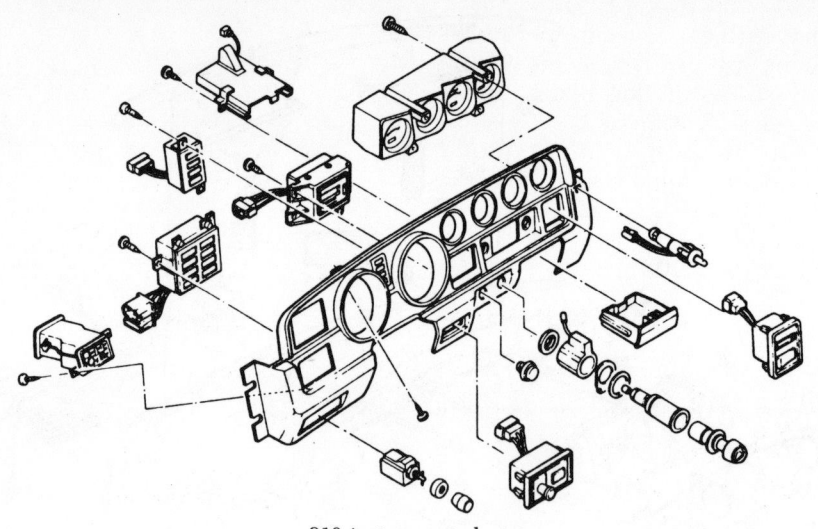

810 instrument cluster

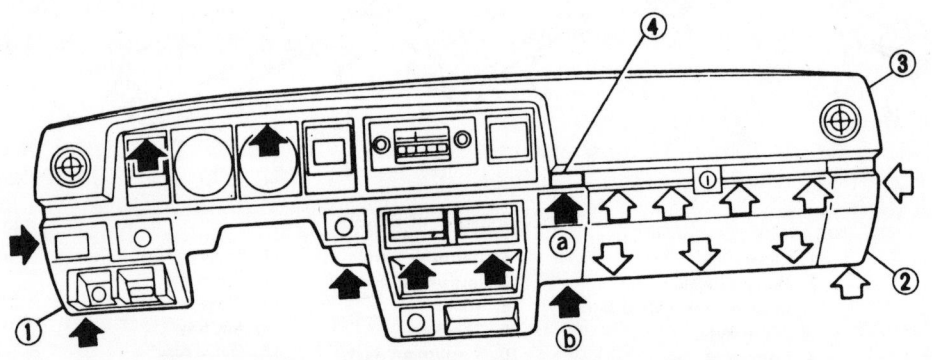

1978 510 instrument panel removal points

1. Cluster lid A
2. Cluster lid B
3. Instrument panel
4. Finisher A
◀ Cluster lid A securing screw positions
◁ Cluster lid B securing screw positions

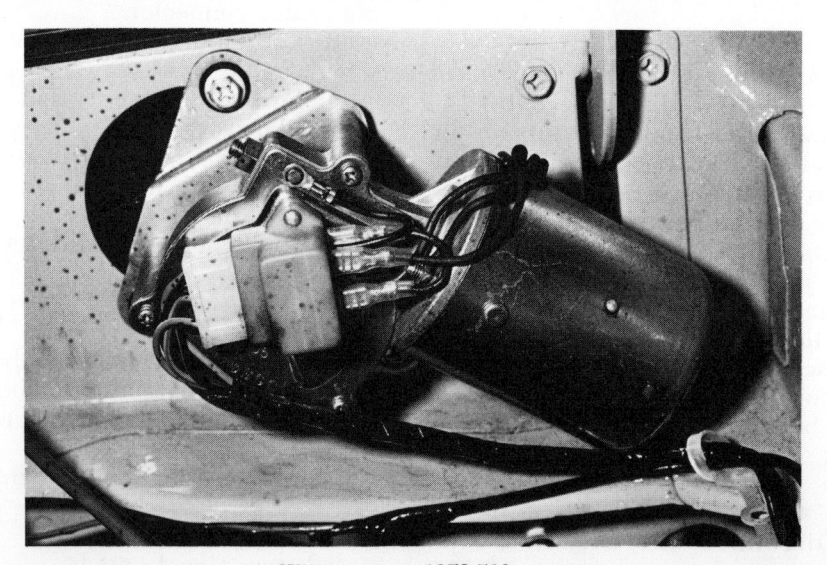

Wiper motor—1978 510

CHASSIS ELECTRICAL 139

9. Remove the screws from the instrument panel (referred to as cluster lid A in the illustration). The black arrows mark the screws locations.
10. Remove the instrument panel cover. Remove the connections from the radio and remove the radio from its bracket.
11. Installation is in the reverse order of removal.

Windshield Wiper Motor and Linkage

Windshield wiper motor and linkage—710

Removal and Installation

ALL EXCEPT 1200, B210, AND F10

The wiper motor and operating linkage is on the firewall under the hood.
1. Lift the wiper arms. Remove the securing nuts and detach the arms.
2. Remove the nuts holding the wiper pivots to the body. Remove the air intake grille for access.
3. Open the hood and unscrew the motor from the firewall.
4. Disconnect the wiring connector and remove the wiper motor with the linkage.
5. Reverse the procedure for installation.

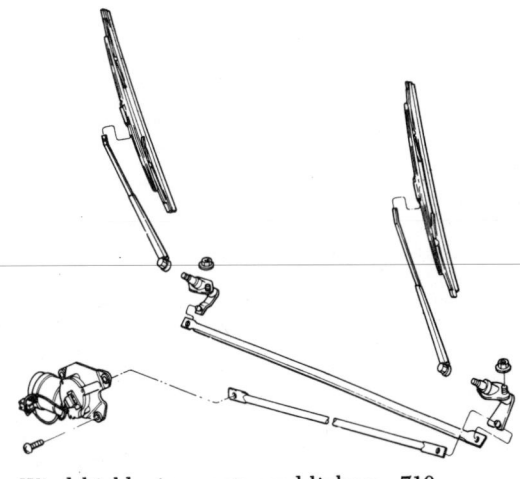

NOTE: *If the wipers do not park correctly, adjust the position of the automatic stop cover on the wiper motor.*

1200, B210, AND F10

The wiper motor is on the firewall under the hood. The operating linkage is on the firewall inside the car.
1. Detach the motor wiring plug.
2. Inside the car, remove the nut connecting the linkage to the wiper shaft.
3. Unbolt and remove the wiper motor from the firewall.
4. Reverse the procedure for installation.

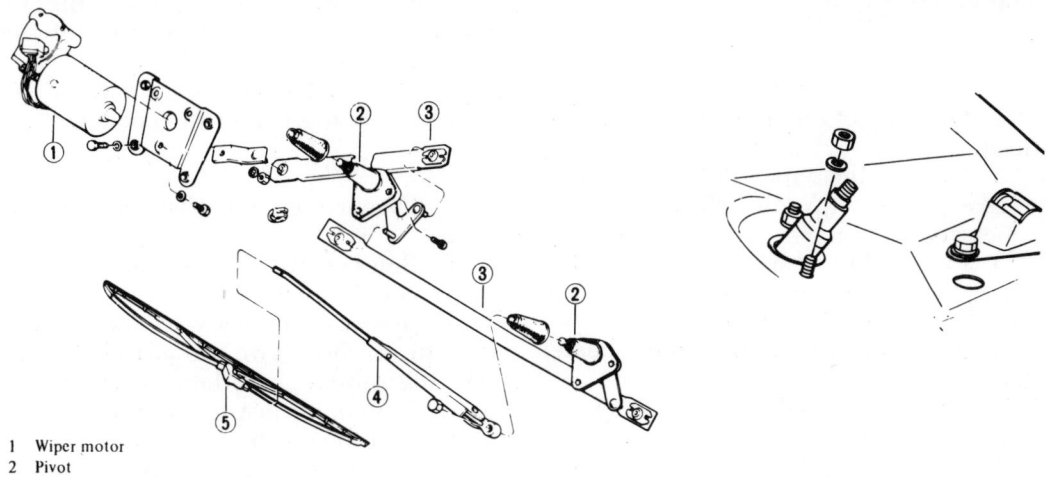

1 Wiper motor
2 Pivot
3 Linkage
4 Wiper arm
5 Wiper blade

Windshield wiper motor and linkage—B210

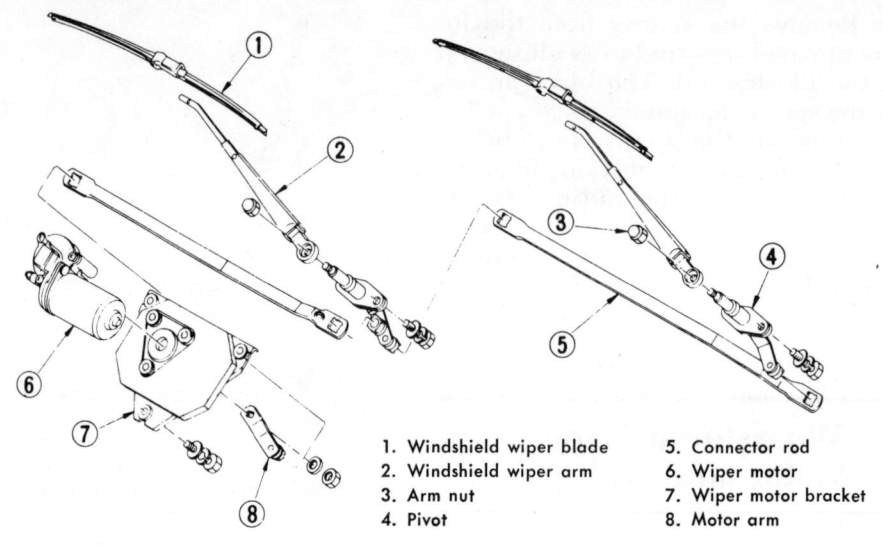

CHASSIS ELECTRICAL

1. Windshield wiper blade
2. Windshield wiper arm
3. Arm nut
4. Pivot
5. Connector rod
6. Wiper motor
7. Wiper motor bracket
8. Motor arm

F10 wiper motor and linkage

Instrument Cluster

Removal and Installation

510

1. Disconnect the speedometer cable by unscrewing the nut at the back of the speedometer.
2. Remove the screws holding the instrument cluster to the instrument panel.
3. Pull out the instrument cluster enough to detach the wiring.
4. Remove the cluster. Individual instrument units can be removed from the rear of the cluster.

1200

1. Disconnect the battery negative lead.
2. Depress the wiper, light switch, and choke knobs, turning them counterclockwise to remove.
3. From the rear, disconnect the lighter wire. Turn and remove the lighter outer case.
4. Remove the radio and heater knobs.
5. Remove the shell cover from the steering column.
6. Remove the screws which hold the instrument cluster to the instrument panel. Pull out the cluster.
7. Disconnect the wiring connector.

1200 instrument cluster removal

Disconnect the speedometer cable by unscrewing the nut at the back of the speedometer.

8. Individual instruments may be removed from the rear of the cluster.

610, 710, AND B210

1. Disconnect the battery ground cable.
2. Remove the four screws and the steering column cover.
3. Remove the screws which attach the cluster face. Two are just above the steering column, and there is one inside each of the outer instrument recesses.
4. Pull the cluster lid forward.
5. Disconnect the multiple connector.
6. Disconnect the speedometer cable.

CHASSIS ELECTRICAL 141

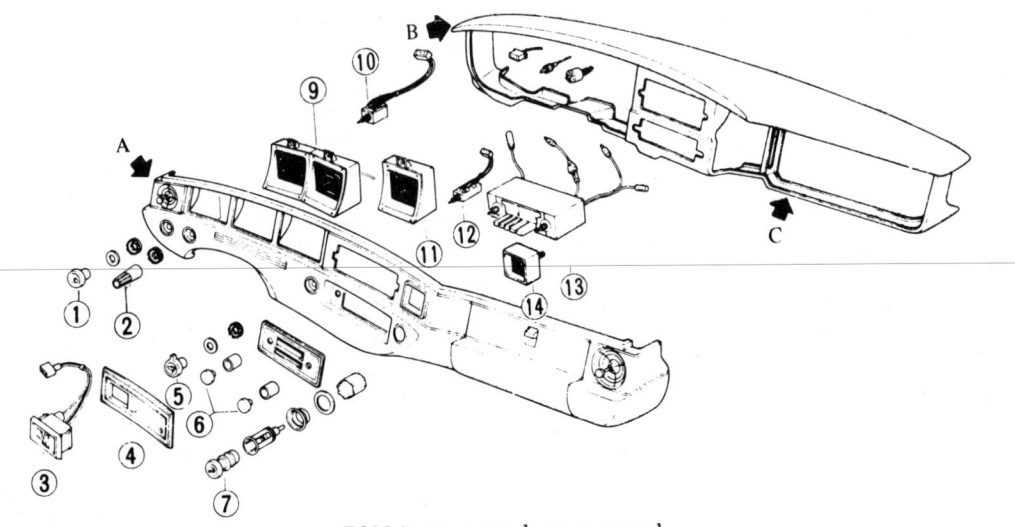

B210 instrument cluster removal

A. Cluster cover
B. Instrument pad
C. Instrument panel
1. Light switch knob
2. Light control knob
3. Rear window defogger switch
4. Escutcheon
5. Wiper switch knob
6. Radio knob
7. Cigarette lighter
8. Gauges
9. Light switch
10. Tachometer
11. Wiper switch
12. Radio
13. Clock

7. Disconnect any other wiring.
8. Remove the cluster face.
9. Remove the odometer knob if the vehicle has one.
10. Remove the six screws and the cluster.
11. Instruments may now be readily replaced.
12. Reverse the procedure for installation.

F10

1. Disconnect the battery ground cable.
2. Disconnect the speedometer cable from the back of the speedometer.
3. Remove the package tray and disconnect the heater control cables from the heater.
4. Disconnect all wire harness con-

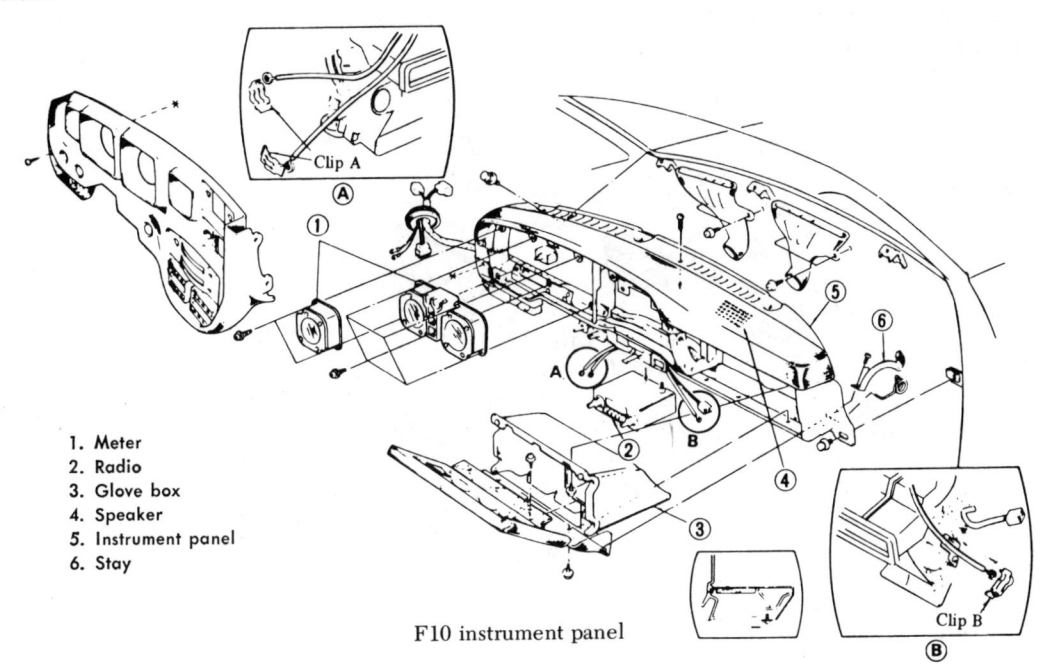

1. Meter
2. Radio
3. Glove box
4. Speaker
5. Instrument panel
6. Stay

F10 instrument panel

CHASSIS ELECTRICAL

nectors from the back of the instrument panel after noting their locations and tagging them.

5. Remove the choke knob and nut.
6. Remove the steering column bracket installation bolts.
7. Loosen the instrument panel upper attaching screws.
8. Remove the bolts securing the sides of the instrument panel.
9. Remove the bolts attaching the instrument panel to the pedal bracket.
10. Remove the instrument panel.
11. Installation is in the reverse order of removal.

810

1. Disconnect the battery ground cable.
2. Remove the knobs and nuts on the radio and the knob on the choke control wire. Remove the ash tray.
3. Remove the steering column covers.
4. Disconnect the harness connectors after noting their location and marking them.
5. Remove the retaining screws and remove the instrument panel.
6. Installation is in the reverse order of removal.

200SX

1. Disconnect the battery ground cable.
2. Remove the steering column covers.
3. Disconnect the speedometer cable and the radio antenna.
4. Disconnect all the wires from the back of the panel after noting their location and marking them.
5. Remove the bolts which secure the steering column clamp. Remove the package tray.
6. Unbolt the panel from the brackets on the left and right-hand sides.
7. Remove the right-side windshield pillar trim and remove the bolt which attaches the panel to the pillar.
8. Remove the instrument garnish (see the illustration).
9. Remove the retaining bolts and remove the panel.
10. Installation is in the reverse order of removal.

1978 510

1. Disconnect the battery ground cable.
2. Remove the instrument panel cover (see the radio removal procedure).
3. Disconnect the speedometer cable from the back of the speedometer. Remove the antenna.
4. Mark their location and remove the wiring connectors.
5. Disconnect the heater control cables. Disconnect the heater ground harness connector.
6. Remove the screws and remove the instrument panel.
7. Installation is in the reverse order of removal.

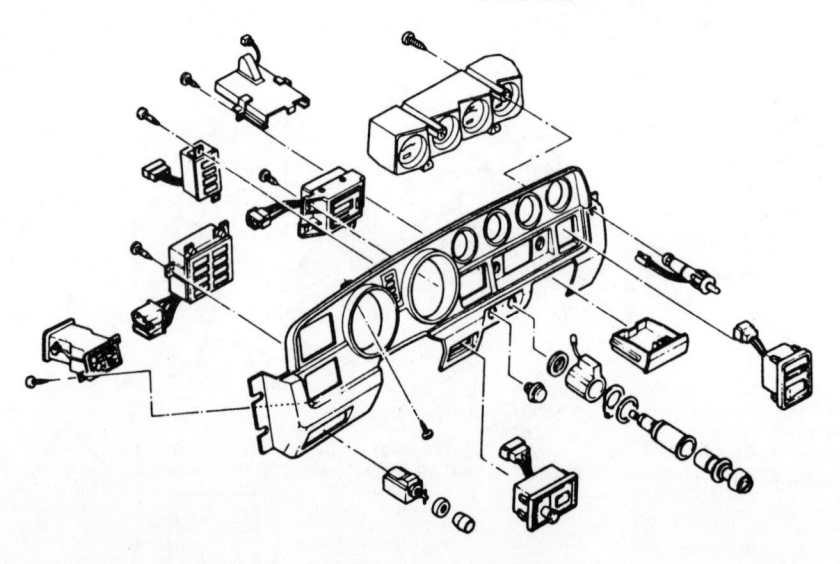

810 instrument panel

CHASSIS ELECTRICAL 143

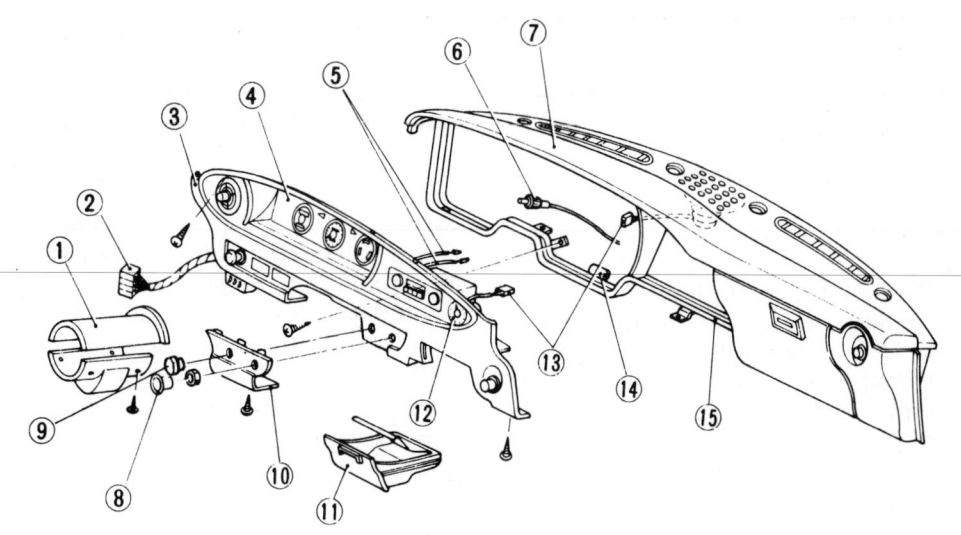

710 instrument cluster removal

1. Steering column covers
2. Instrument harness
3. Cluster cover
4. Gauges
5. Light monitor
6. Speedometer cable
7. Upper instrument pad
8. Wiper/washer switch knob
9. Light control switch
10. Cluster cover
11. Ash tray
12. Clock
13. Speaker harness
14. Illumination bulb
15. Instrument panel

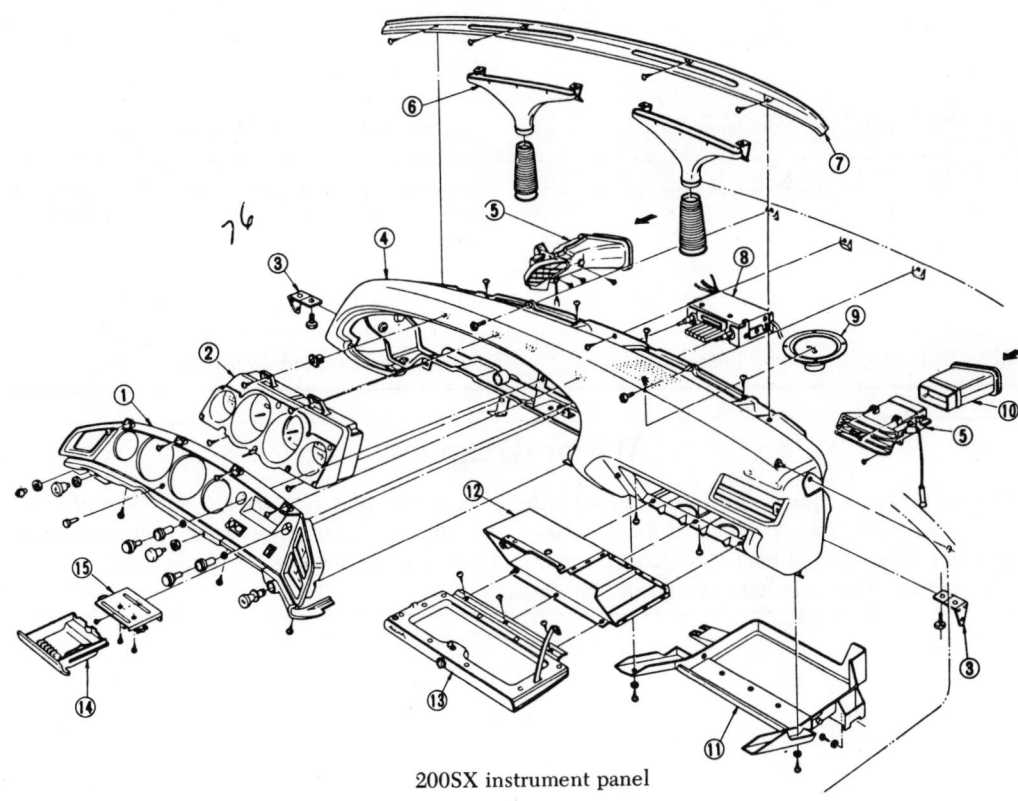

200SX instrument panel

1. Cluster lid
2. Meter assembly
3. Instrument mounting lower bracket
4. Instrument pad
5. Ventilation grille
6. Defroster nozzle
7. Instrument garnish
8. Radio
9. Speaker
10. Ventilation duct
11. Package tray
12. Glove box
13. Glove box lid
14. Ash tray
15. Outer case

CHASSIS ELECTRICAL

Headlights

Removal and Installation

NOTE: *On 610, 710, B210, and 1200 coupe models it is necessary to remove the grille to gain access to the headlights.*

1. Remove the grille if necessary.
2. Remove headlight retaining ring screws. These are the three short screws, do not tamper with the two longer adjusting screws or the headlight will have to be reaimed.
3. Remove the ring by rotating it clockwise.
4. Pull the headlight bulb from its socket and disconnect the electrical plug.
5. Connect the plug to the new bulb.
6. Position the headlight in the shell. Make sure that the word "TOP" is, indeed, at the top and that the knobs in the headlight lens engage the slots in the mounting shell.
7. Place the retaining ring over the bulb and install the screws.
8. Install the grille if it was removed from the car.

Fuses

Model		Fuse Box Location	Fuse Link Location
1973	510	Engine compartment right rear	
1973–78	1200	Under instrument panel right of steering column	Between battery and alternator
	610, 710	Under instrument panel	Between battery and alternator (behind windshield washer tank)
	B210, F10	Below hood release knob	Adjacent to battery positive terminal
	810	Kick panel right side	Engine compartment relay bracket(1) and at the battery positive terminal of the electronic fuel injection harness.(2)
	200SX	Underneath the glove box	Adjacent to battery positive terminal
1978	510	Under instrument panel	Between battery and alternator

Wiring Diagrams

Wiring diagrams have been left out of this book. As cars have become more complex, and available with longer and longer option lists, wiring diagrams have grown in size and complexity also. It has become virtually impossible to provide a readable reproduction in a reasonable number of pages.

Chapter Six

Clutch and Transmission

Manual Transmission

A four speed manual transmission is standard equipment on all models covered in this guide, with the exception of the 200SX, which is equipped with a five speed transmission as standard equipment. Five speeds are also available on the F10, the B210, and the new 510. With the exception of the F10, all models feature integral shift linkage, which requires no adjustment.

F10 Linkage Adjustment

Four-Speed Models

1. The adjustment is made at the shift rods on the transmission. Loosen the adjusting nuts marked 1 and 2 in the illustration.
2. Measure the clearance between the shift lever marked 3 in the illustration and the transmission case. Make sure the shift lever is pushed completely into the transmission case. The clearance is marked "A" in the illustration.
3. Place the transmission in fourth gear. Shift lever 3 should now be fully downward.
4. Increase the initial clearance "A" by 8 mm (0.31 in.).
5. Push lever 4 fully upward. Now tighten nut 1 until it makes contact with trunnion 7. Then back the nut off one full turn and tighten it with nut 2.

Five Speed Models

1. Loosen locknuts 1, 2, 3, and 4.
2. Make sure shift lever 5 is pushed completely into the transmission case, then move it back 8 mm (0.31 in.).
3. Place the car in third gear.
4. Push select lever 6 fully down. Turn nut 3 until it comes into contact with trunnion 9. Back the nut off one or two turns, and then tighten nut 3 with nut 4. Tighten nuts 1 and 2.

Removal and Installation

All Models Except F10

1. Raise and support the vehicle. Disconnect the battery. On the 510, disconnect the handbrake cable at the equalizer pivot. Disconnect the backup light switch on all models.
2. On the 510, loosen the muffler clamps and turn the muffler to one side to allow room for driveshaft removal. Disconnect the exhaust pipe from the manifold.
3. Unbolt the driveshaft at the rear and remove. If there is a center bearing, unbolt it from the crossmember. Seal the

146 CLUTCH AND TRANSMISSION

For 4-speed transmission

For 5-speed transmission

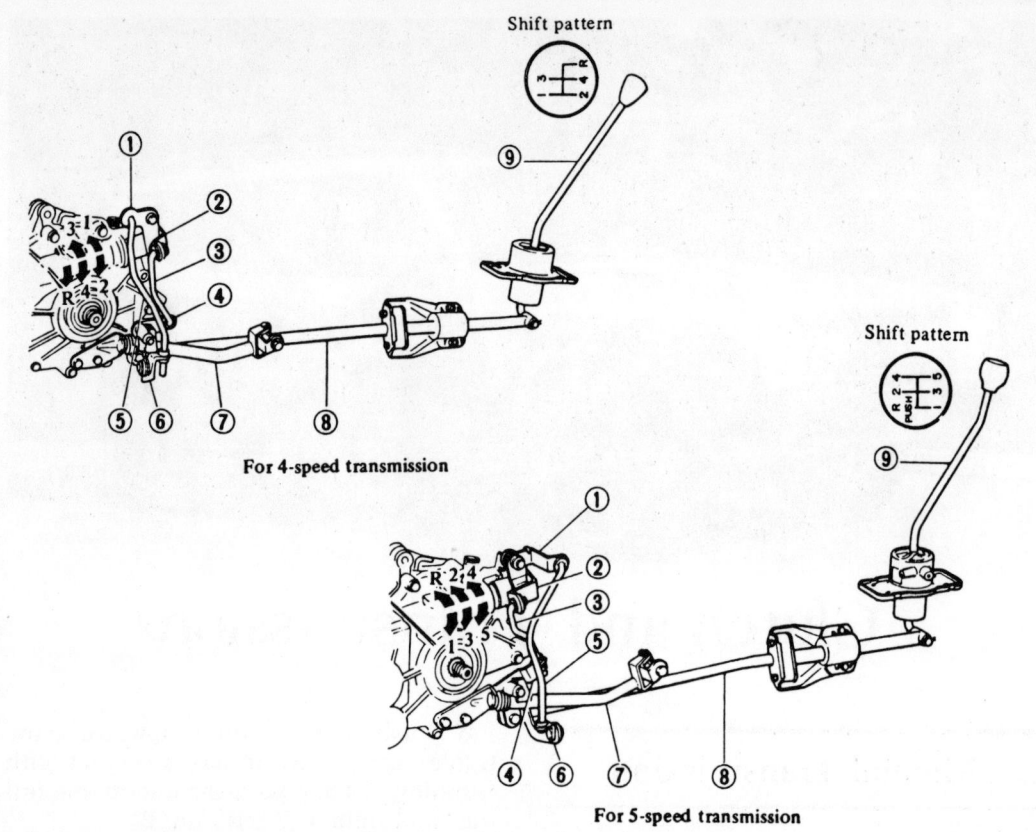

F10 shift linkage assemblies

1. Select lever E
2. Shift lever E
3. Shift rod
4. Shift lever
5. Select rod
6. Select lever
7. Radius link
8. Control rod
9. Hand lever

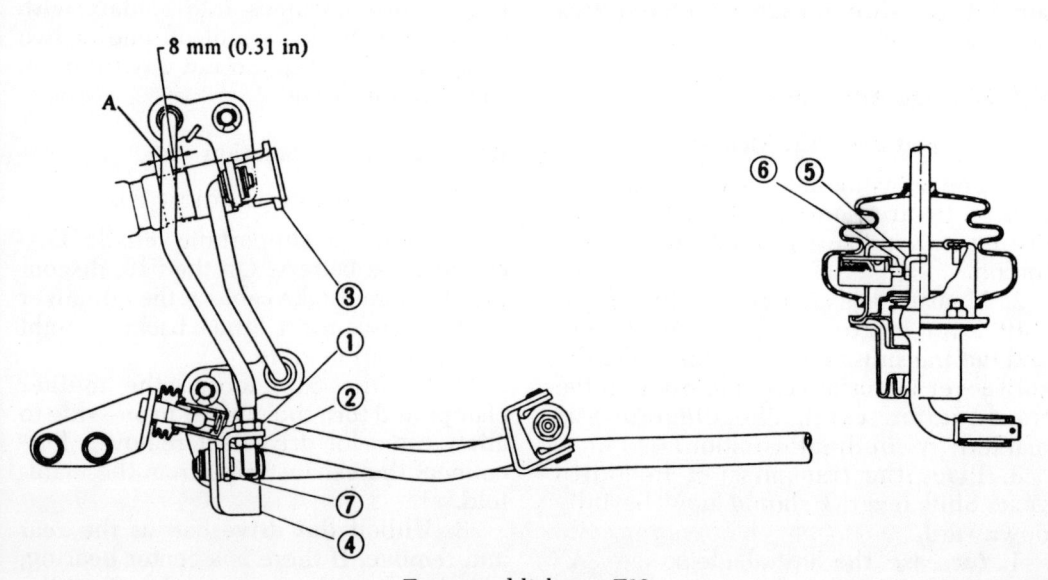

8 mm (0.31 in)

Four speed linkage—F10

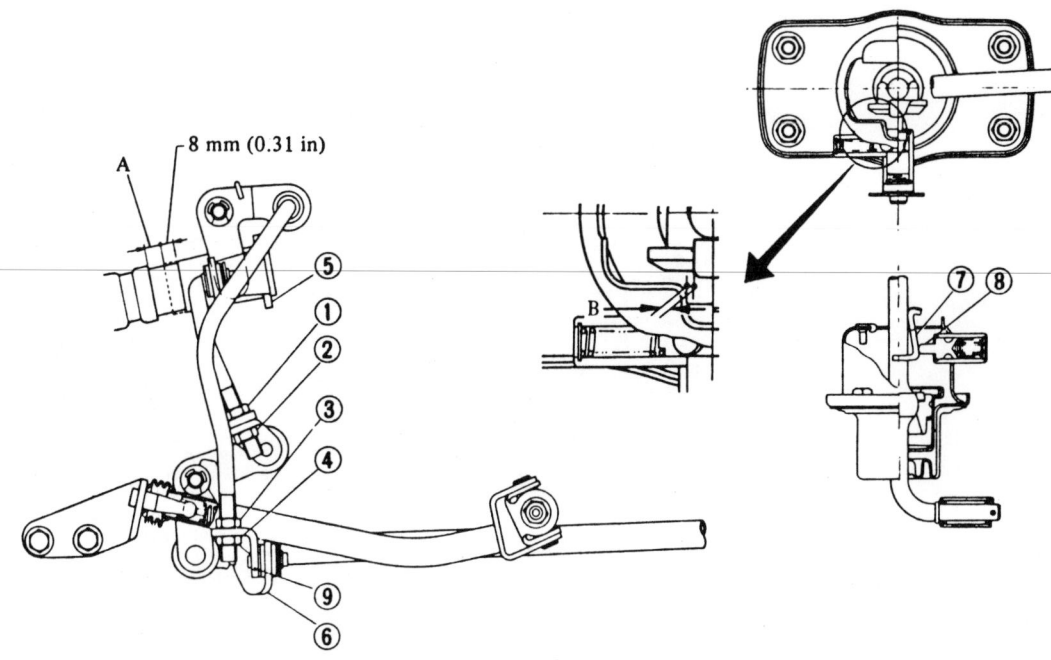

CLUTCH AND TRANSMISSION 147

Five speed linkage—F10

510, 610, and 710 shift lever removal

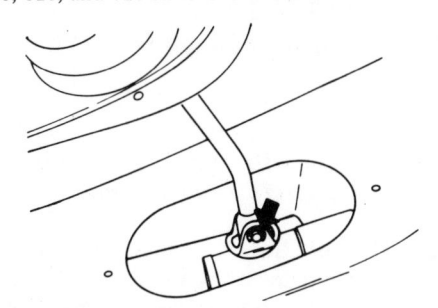

1200 and B210 shift lever removal

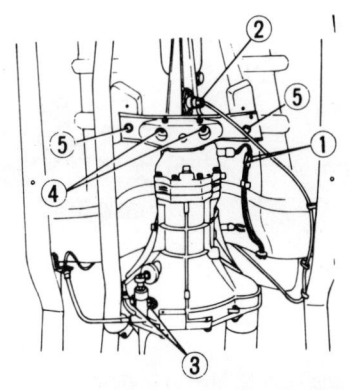

1200 and B210—disconnect the back-up light, switch (1), speedometer cable (2), clutch slave cylinder (3), rear engine mount bolts (4), crossmember bolts (5).

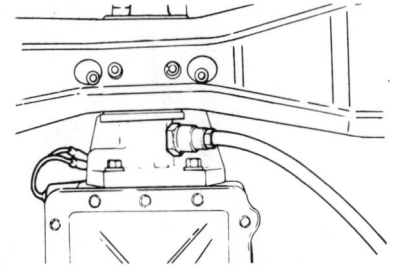

Disconnect speedometer and back-up light switch

end of the transmission extension housing to prevent leakage.

    4. Disconnect the speedometer drive cable from the transmission. Disconnect the backup light switch.

    5. Remove the shift lever.

    6. Remove the clutch operating cylinder from the clutch housing.

    7. Support the engine with a large wood block and a jack under the oil pan.

    8. Unbolt the transmission from the crossmember. Support the transmission with a jack. Remove the crossmember.

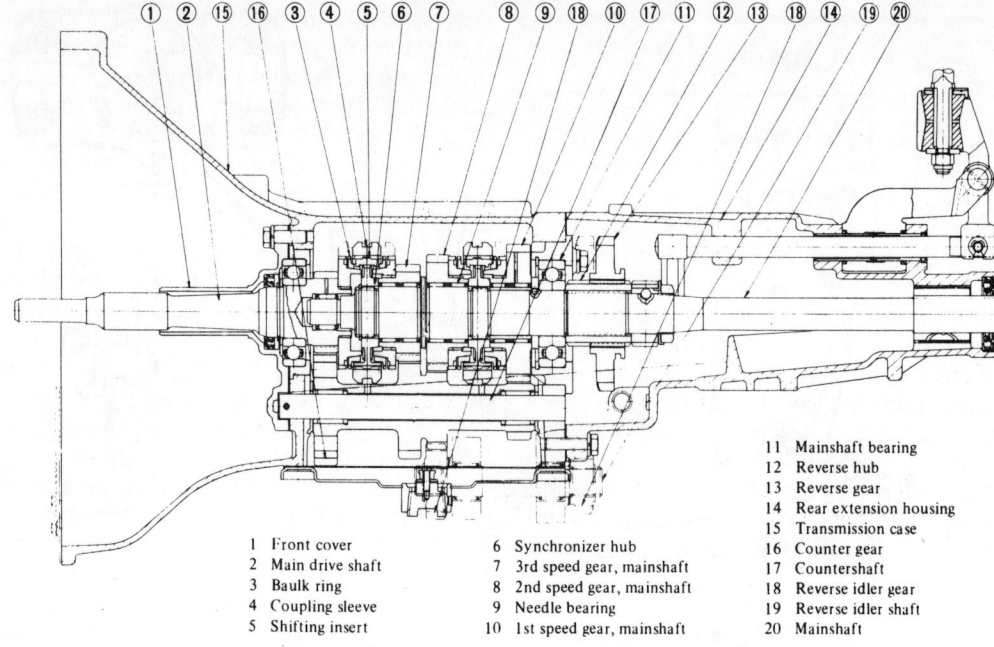

CLUTCH AND TRANSMISSION

Cutaway of four-speed transmission used in the 710

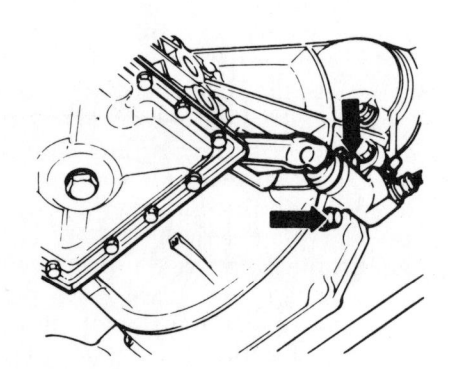

1. Front cover
2. Main drive shaft
3. Baulk ring
4. Coupling sleeve
5. Shifting insert
6. Synchronizer hub
7. 3rd speed gear, mainshaft
8. 2nd speed gear, mainshaft
9. Needle bearing
10. 1st speed gear, mainshaft
11. Mainshaft bearing
12. Reverse hub
13. Reverse gear
14. Rear extension housing
15. Transmission case
16. Counter gear
17. Countershaft
18. Reverse idler gear
19. Reverse idler shaft
20. Mainshaft

Remove the clutch slave cylinder

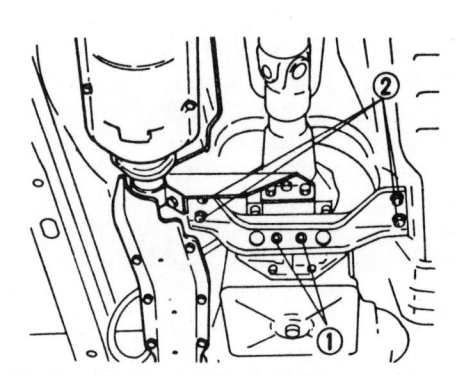

1978 510 crossmember removal

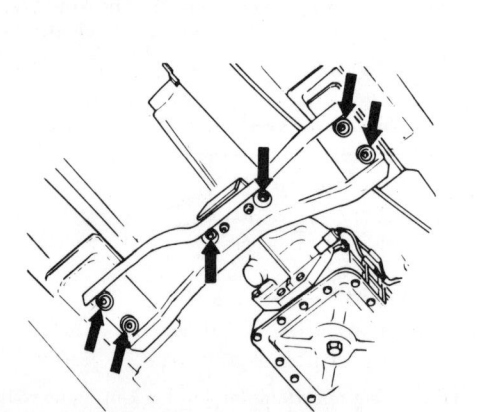

510, 610, and 710 crossmember bolts

9. Lower the rear of the engine to allow clearance.

10. Remove the starter.
NOTE: *On 610 and 710, unbolt the support gussets from the engine and transmission.*
11. Unbolt the transmission. Lower and remove it to the rear.
12. Reverse the procedure for reinstallation. Check the clutch linkage adjustment.

F10 Transmission Removal and Installation

According to Datsun, the engine and transmission must be removed as a unit and then separated. See Chapter 3 for information on removing the F10 engine and transmission.

Clutch

The purpose of the clutch is to disconnect and connect engine power from the transmission. A car at rest requires a lot of engine torque to get all that weight moving. An internal-combustion engine does not develop a high starting torque (unlike steam engines), so it must be allowed to operate without any load until it builds up enough torque to move the car. Torque increases with engine rpm. The clutch allows the engine to build up torque by physically disconnecting the engine from the transmission, relieving the engine of any load or resistance. The transfer of engine power to the transmission (the load) must be smooth and gradual; if it weren't, driveline components would wear out or break quickly. This gradual power transfer is made possible by gradually releasing the clutch pedal. The clutch disc and pressure plate are the connecting link between the engine and transmission. When the clutch pedal is released, the disc and plate contact each other (clutch engagement), physically joining the engine and transmission. When the pedal is pushed in, the disc and plate separate (the clutch is disengaged), disconnecting the engine from the transmission.

The clutch assembly consists of the flywheel, the clutch disc, the clutch pressure plate, the throwout bearing and fork, the clutch master cylinder, slave cylinder and connecting line, and the pedal. The flywheel and clutch pressure plate (driving members) are connected to the engine crankshaft and rotate with it. The clutch disc is located between the flywheel and pressure plate, and splined to the transmission shaft. A driving member is one that is attached to the engine and transfers engine power to a driven member (clutch disc) on the transmission shaft. A driving member (pressure plate) rotates (drives) a driven member (clutch disc) on contact and, in so doing, turns the transmission shaft. There is a circular diaphragm spring within the pressure plate cover (transmission side). In a relaxed state (when the clutch pedal is fully released), this spring is convex; that is, it is dished outward toward the transmission. Pushing in the clutch pedal actuates the slave cylinder. Connected to the other end of the slave cylinder rod is the throwout bearing fork. The throwout bearing is attached to the fork. When the clutch pedal is depressed, the slave cylinder pushes the fork and bearing forward to contact the diaphragm spring of the pressure plate. The outer edges of the spring are secured to the pressure plate and are pivoted on rings so that when the center of the spring is compressed by the throwout bearing, the outer edges bow outward and, by so doing, pull the pressure plate in the same direction—away from the clutch disc. This action separates the disc from the plate, disengaging the clutch and allowing the transmission to be shifted into another gear. Releasing the pedal allows the throwout bearing to pull away from the diaphragm spring resulting in a reversal of spring position. As bearing pressure is gradually released from the spring center, the outer edges of the spring bow inward, pushing the pressure plate into closer contact with the clutch disc. As the disc and plate move closer together, friction between the two increases and slippage is reduced until, when full spring pressure is applied (by fully releasing the pedal), the speed of the disc and plate are the same. This stops all slipping, creating a direct connection between the plate and disc which results in the transfer of power from the engine to the transmission. The clutch disc is now rotating with the pressure plate at engine speed and, because it is splined to the transmission shaft, the shaft now turns at the same engine speed.

All Datsun models included in this guide are equipped with hydraulic clutch control. This system consists of the clutch pedal and return spring, master cylinder, connecting hydraulic line, and slave (operating) cylinder.

Adjustment

Refer to the "Clutch Specifications" chart for clutch pedal height above the floor and pedal free-play.

Pedal height is adjusted at the pedal stopper locknut which limits upward travel of the pedal. Pedal free-play is adjusted at the master cylinder pushrod. Tighten the locknuts after adjusting pedal height and free-play.

150 CLUTCH AND TRANSMISSION

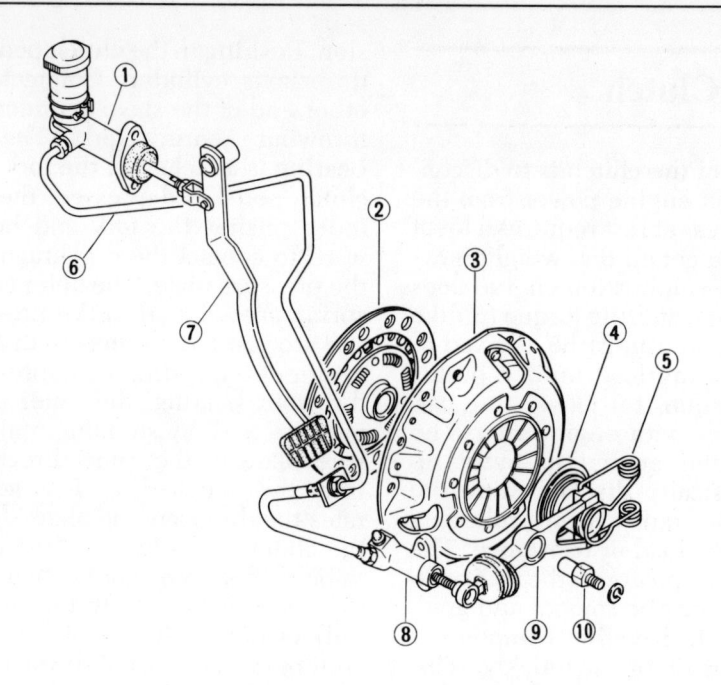

1200 and B210 clutch control system

1. Clutch master cylinder
2. Clutch disc assembly
3. Clutch cover assembly
4. Release bearing and sleeve assembly
5. Return spring
6. Clutch line
7. Clutch pedal
8. Operating cylinder
9. Withdrawal lever
10. Withdrawal lever ball pin

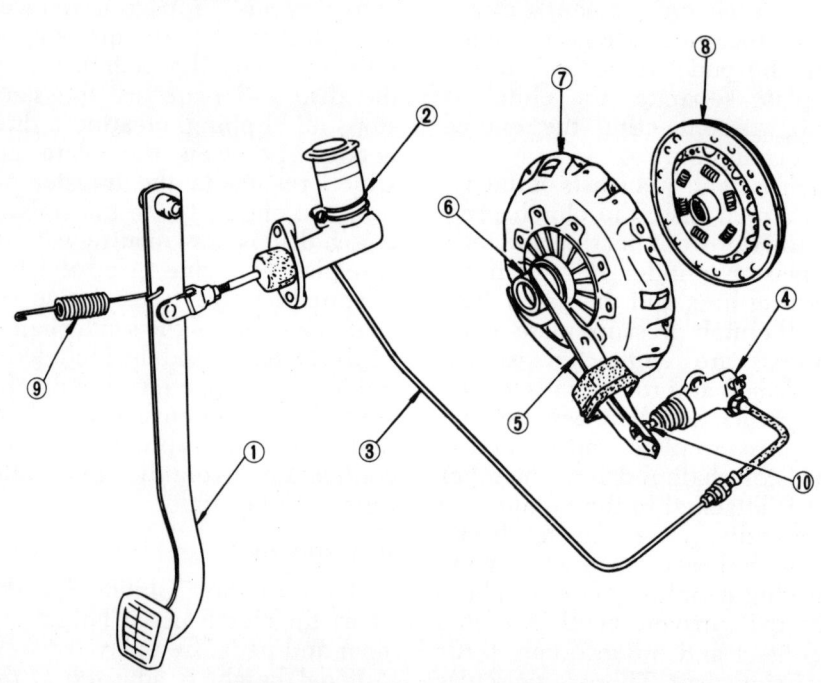

510, 610, and 710 clutch control system

1. Clutch pedal
2. Clutch master cylinder
3. Clutch piping
4. Operating cylinder
5. Withdrawal lever
6. Release bearing
7. Clutch cover
8. Clutch disc
9. Return spring
10. Push rod

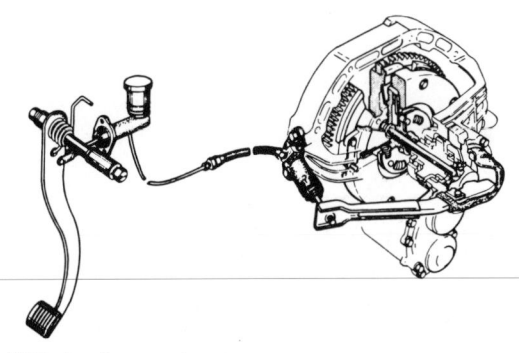

CLUTCH AND TRANSMISSION

Clutch Specifications

Model	Pedal Height Above Floor (in.)	Pedal Free-Play (in.)
510	5.3	0.10
1200	5.6	0.12
610	6.9	0.04–0.12
B210	6.02	0.04–0.12
710	7.09	0.04–0.20
F10	6.9	0.23–0.55
200SX	7.60	0.04–0.12
810	6.9	0.04–0.20
1978 510	6.5	0.04–0.20

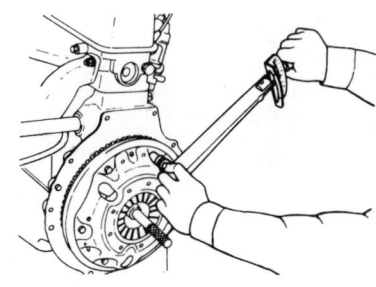

F10 clutch control system

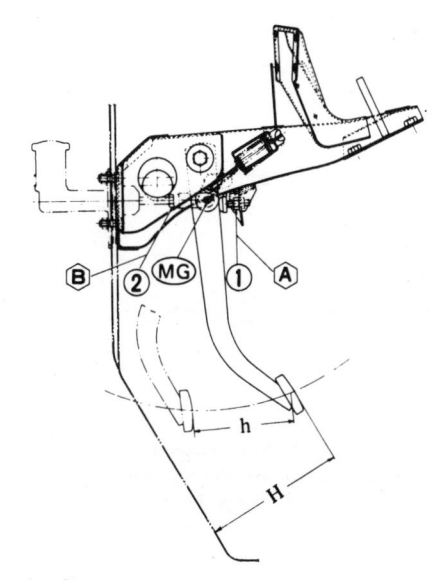

Clutch adjustment points
1. Adjust pedal height here
2. Adjust pedal free-play here
MG. Lubricate with multipurpose grease here
H. is pedal height
h. is free-play

Tightening the pressure plate bolts. The dummy shaft keeps the plate in alignment.

Removal and Installation

ALL MODELS EXCEPT F10

1. Remove the transmission from the engine.
2. Loosen the bolts in sequence, a turn at a time. Remove the bolts.
3. Remove the pressure plate and clutch disc.
4. On A12 and A13 engines, remove the release mechanism. Apply multipurpose grease to the bearing sleeve inside groove, the contact point of the withdrawal lever and bearing sleeve, the contact surface of the lever ball pin and lever. Replace the release mechanism.
5. Install the disc, aligning it with a splined dummy shaft.
6. Install the pressure plate and torque the bolts to 17–18 ft lbs on L16 engines, and 11–16 ft lbs on all other engines.
7. Remove the dummy shaft.
8. Replace the transmission.

F10

Because the F10 is a front wheel drive car, the engine and transmission must be removed as a unit. Therefore, Datsun has engineered the F10 so that it is possible to remove and replace the clutch without removing the engine or transmission from the car.

1. Disconnect the following cables, hoses, and wires:
   battery ground strap
   fresh air duct

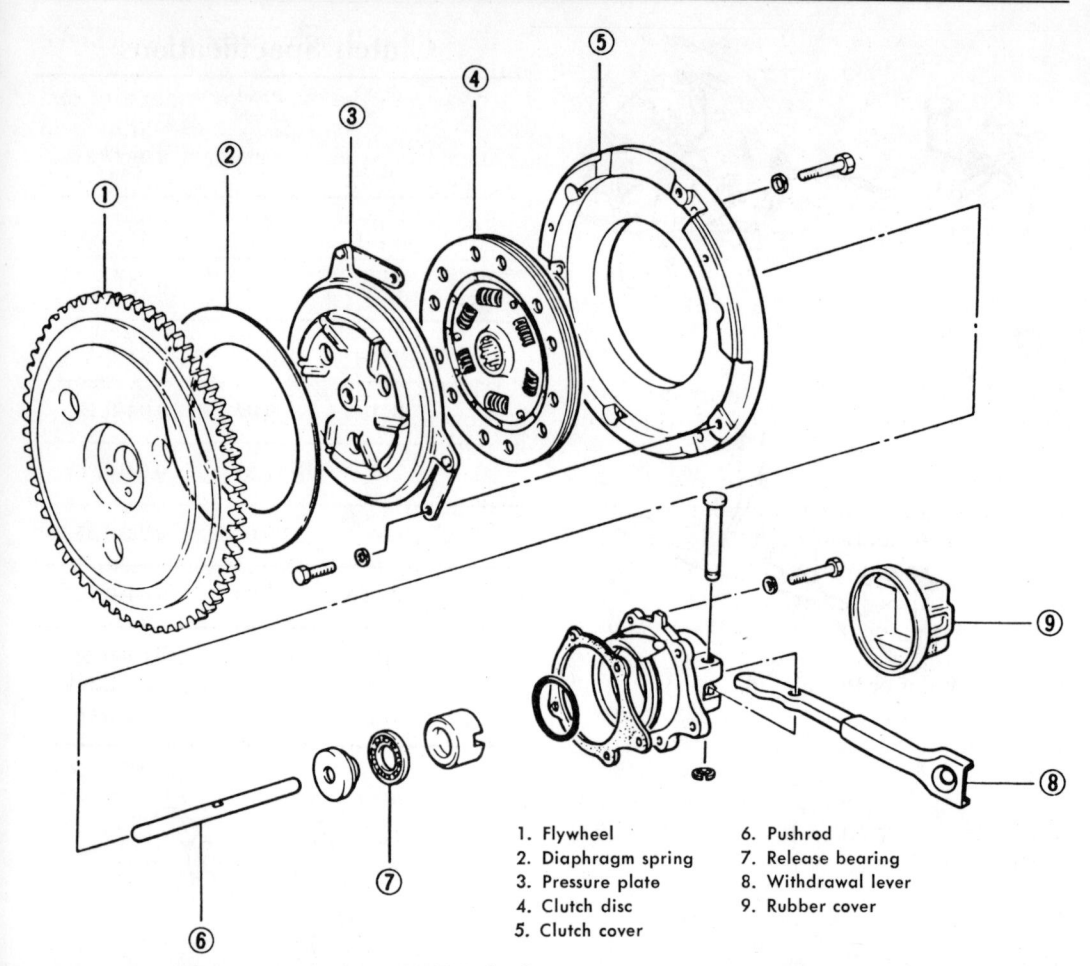

152 CLUTCH AND TRANSMISSION

1. Flywheel
2. Diaphragm spring
3. Pressure plate
4. Clutch disc
5. Clutch cover
6. Pushrod
7. Release bearing
8. Withdrawal lever
9. Rubber cover

F10 clutch components

engine harness connectors on the clutch housing
coil wire from the distributor
carbon canister hoses

2. Detach the inspection cover from the upper section of the clutch housing.

3. Remove the six bolts which secure the clutch cover. The easiest way to turn the engine over to reach all the bolts is to jack up the right front wheel, place the

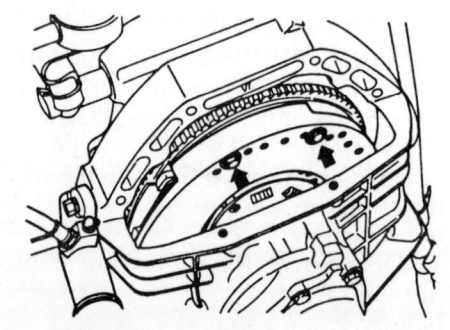

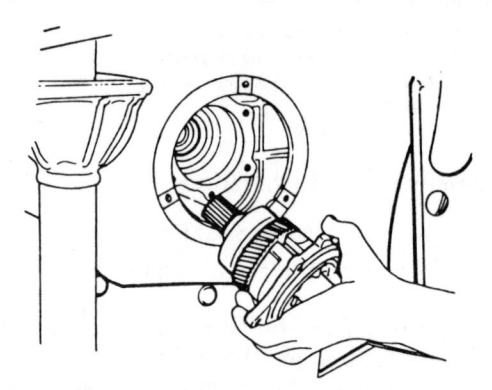

Removing primary drive gear

transmission in high gear, and rotate the wheel by hand.

4. Remove the inspection hole cover on the right side wheel housing.

5. Remove the throwout bearing lever. It is referred to as the withdrawal lever in the illustration.

6. Remove the six bolts on the bearing

Removing clutch cover bolts

CLUTCH AND TRANSMISSION

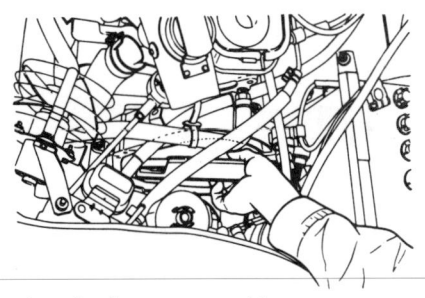

Removing clutch cover assembly

housing and take out the primary drive gear assembly through the inspection hole.

7. Lift out the clutch cover and disc assembly through the inspection opening in the upper section of the clutch housing. The diaphragm spring can also be removed at this time.

8. The clutch cover and pressure plate must be replaced as an assembly since they are balanced as an assembly. If you disassemble the plate and cover, be sure to mark them if you are going to use them over.

9. Installation is in the reverse order of removal. Adjust the clutch free play after installation.

CLUTCH MASTER CYLINDER

Removal and Installation

1. Disconnect the clutch pedal arm from the pushrod.
2. Disconnect the clutch hydraulic line from the master cylinder.

   NOTE: *Take precautions to keep brake fluid from coming in contact with any painted surfaces.*

3. Remove the nuts attaching the master cylinder and remove the master cylinder and pushrod toward the engine compartment side.
4. Install the master cylinder in the reverse order of removal and bleed the clutch hydraulic system.

Overhaul

1. Remove the master cylinder from the vehicle.
2. Drain the clutch fluid from the master cylinder reservoir.
3. Remove the boot and circlip and remove the pushrod.
4. Remove the stopper, piston, cup and return spring.
5. Clean all of the parts in clean brake fluid.
6. Check the master cylinder and piston for wear, corrosion and scores and replace the parts as necessary. Light scoring and glaze can be removed with crocus cloth soaked in brake fluid.
7. Generally, the cup seal should be replaced each time the master cylinder is disassembled. Check the cup and replace it if it is worn, fatigued, or damaged.
8. Check the clutch fluid reservoir, filler cap, dust cover and the pipe for distortion and damage and replace the parts as necessary.
9. Lubricate all new parts with clean brake fluid.
10. Reassemble the master cylinder parts in the reverse order of disassembly, taking note of the following:

   a. Reinstall the cup seal carefully to prevent damaging the lipped portions;
   b. Adjust the height of the clutch pedal after installing the master cylinder in position on the vehicle;
   c. Fill the master cylinder and clutch fluid reservoir and then bleed the clutch hydraulic system.

CLUTCH SLAVE CYLINDER

Removal and Installation

1. Remove the slave cylinder attaching bolts and the pushrod from the shift fork.
2. Disconnect the flexible fluid hose from the slave cylinder and remove the unit from the vehicle.
3. Install the slave cylinder in the reverse order of removal and bleed the clutch hydraulic system.

Overhaul

1. Remove the slave cylinder from the vehicle.
2. Remove the pushrod and boot.
3. Force out the piston by blowing compressed air into the slave cylinder at the hose connection.

   NOTE: *Be careful not to apply excess air pressure to avoid possible injury.*

4. Clean all of the parts in clean brake fluid.
5. Check and replace the slave cylinder bore and piston if wear or severe scoring exists. Light scoring and glaze can be removed with crocus cloth soaked in brake fluid.

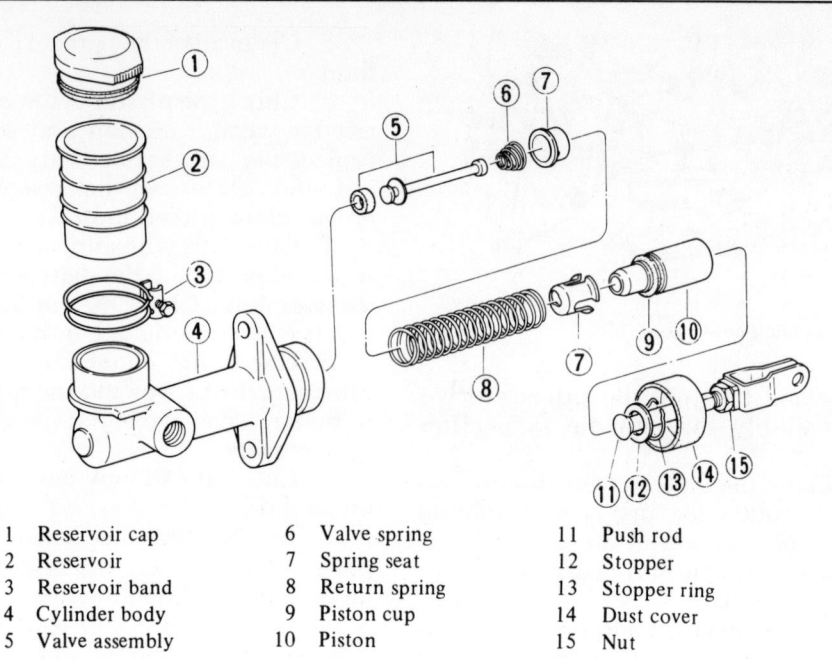

154 CLUTCH AND TRANSMISSION

1	Reservoir cap	6	Valve spring	11	Push rod
2	Reservoir	7	Spring seat	12	Stopper
3	Reservoir band	8	Return spring	13	Stopper ring
4	Cylinder body	9	Piston cup	14	Dust cover
5	Valve assembly	10	Piston	15	Nut

Exploded view of typical master cylinder

6. Normally the piston cup should be replaced when the slave cylinder is disassembled. Check the piston cup and replace it if it is found to be worn, fatigued or scored.

7. Replace the rubber boot if it is cracked or broken.

8. Lubricate all of the new parts in clean brake fluid and reassemble in the reverse order of disassembly, taking note of the following:

a. Use care when reassembling the piston cup to prevent damaging the lipped portion of the piston cup;

b. Fill the master cylinder with brake fluid and bleed the clutch hydraulic system;

c. Adjust the clearance between the pushrod and the shift fork to $5/64$ in.

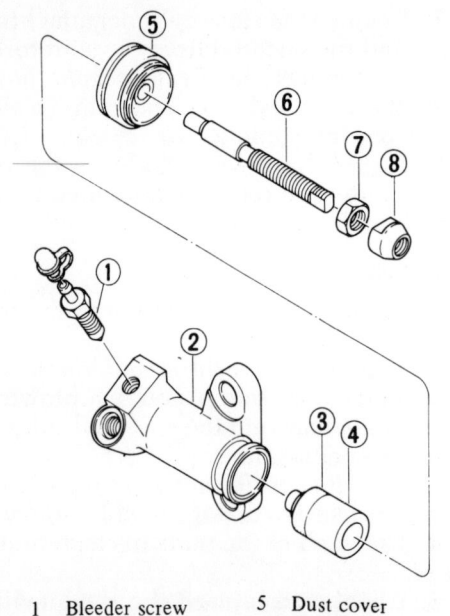

1	Bleeder screw	5	Dust cover
2	Cylinder body	6	Push rod
3	Piston cup	7	Lock nut
4	Piston	8	Push nut

Exploded view of 510, 610, and 710 slave cylinder

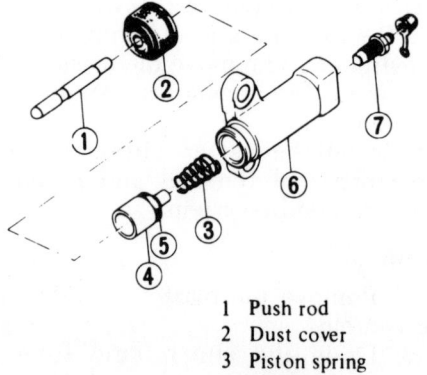

1 Push rod
2 Dust cover
3 Piston spring
4 Piston
5 Piston cup
6 Operating cylinder
7 Bleeder screw

Exploded view of 1200 and B210 slave cylinder

CLUTCH AND TRANSMISSION

BLEEDING THE CLUTCH HYDRAULIC SYSTEM

1. Check and fill the clutch fluid reservoir to the specified level as necessary. During the bleeding process, continue to check and replenish the reservoir to prevent the fluid level from getting lower than ½ the specified level.
2. Remove the dust cap from the bleeder screw on the clutch slave cylinder and connect a tube to the bleeder screw and insert the other end of the tube into a clean glass or metal container.

NOTE: *Take precautionary measures to prevent the brake fluid from getting on any painted surfaces.*

3. Pump the clutch pedal several times, hold it down and loosen the bleeder screw slowly.
4. Tighten the bleeder screw and release the clutch pedal gradually. Repeat this operation until air bubbles disappear from the brake fluid being expelled out through the bleeder screw.
5. Repeat until all evidence of air bubbles completely disappears from the brake fluid being pumped out through the tube.
6. When the air is completely removed, securely tighten the bleeder screw and replace the dust cap.
7. Check and refill the master cylinder reservoir as necessary.
8. Depress the clutch pedal several times to check the operation of the clutch and check for leaks.

Automatic Transmission

All Datsuns, except the F10, covered in this book can be optionally equipped with an automatic three-speed transmission. Except for the procedures outlined here, it is recommended that automatic transmission service be left to an authorized Datsun dealer who has the special tools and expertise to work on these units.

Pan Removal

1. Jack up the front of the car and support it safely on stands.
2. Slide a drain pan under the transmission. Loosen the rear oil pan bolts first, to allow most of the fluid to drain off without making a mess on your garage floor.
3. Remove the remaining bolts and drop the pan.
4. Discard the old gasket, clean the pan, and reinstall the pan with a new gasket.
5. Tighten the retaining bolts in a criss-cross pattern starting at the center.

CAUTION: *The transmission case is aluminum, so don't exert too much force on the bolts.*

6. Refill the transmission through the dipstick tube. Check the fluid level as described in Chapter 1.

Shift Linkage Adjustment

1. Loosen the trunnion locknuts at the lower end of the control lever. Remove the selector lever knob and console.
2. Place the selector lever in Neutral.
3. Place the transmission shift lever in the Neutral position by pushing it all the way back, then pulling it forward two stops.
4. Check the vertical clearance between the top of the shift lever pin and transmission control bracket. The clearance, should be 0.020–0.059 in. Adjust by turning the nut at the lower end of the selector lever compression rod.
5. Check the horizontal clearance, of the shift lever pin and transmission control bracket. This should be 0.020 in. Adjust with the trunnion locknuts.
6. Replace the console, making sure that the shift pointer is correctly aligned. Install the knob.

Downshift Solenoid Check

This solenoid is controlled by a downshift switch on the accelerator linkage inside the car. To test the switch and solenoid operation:

1. Turn the ignition on.
2. Push the accelerator all the way down to actuate the switch.
3. The solenoid should click when actuated. The transmission solenoid is screwed into the outside of the case. If there is no click, check the switch, wiring, and solenoid.

To remove the solenoid, first drain 2–3 pints of fluid, then unscrew the unit.

Neutral Safety and Backup Light Switch Adjustment

The switch unit is bolted to the left-side of the transmission case, behind the transmission shift lever. The switch prevents the engine from being started in any transmission position except Park or Neutral. It also controls the backup lights.

1. Remove the transmission shift lever retaining nut and the lever.
2. Remove the switch.
3. Remove the machine screw in the case under the switch.
4. Align the switch to the case by inserting a 0.059 in. (1.5 mm.) diameter pin through the hole in the switch into the screw hole. Mark the switch location.
5. Remove the pin, replace the machine screw, install the switch as marked, and replace the transmission shift lever and retaining nut.
6. Make sure while holding the brakes on, that the engine will start only in Park or Neutral. Check that the backup lights go on only in Reverse.

Removal and Installation

1. Disconnect the battery cable.
2. Remove the accelerator linkage.
3. Detach the shift linkage.
4. Disconnect the neutral safety switch and downshift solenoid wiring.
5. Remove the drain plug and drain the torque converter. If there is no converter drain plug, drain the transmission.

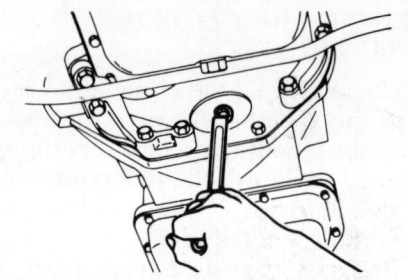

Disconnecting torque converter bolts through access hole

If there is no transmission drain plug, remove the pan to drain. Replace the pan to keep out dirt.

6. Remove the front exhaust pipe.
7. Remove the vacuum tube and speedometer cable.
8. Disconnect the fluid cooler tubes.
9. Remove the driveshaft and starter.
10. Support the transmission with a jack under the oil pan. Support the engine also.
11. Remove the rear crossmember.
12. Mark the relationship between the torque converter and the drive plate. Remove the four bolts holding the converter to the drive plate through the hole at the front, under the engine. Unbolt the transmission from the engine.
13. Reverse the procedure for installation. Make sure that the drive plate is warped no more than 0.020 in. Torque the drive plate-to-torque converter and converter housing-to-engine bolts to 29–36 ft lbs. Drive plate-to-crankshaft bolt torque is 101–116 ft lbs.
14. Refill the transmission and check the fluid level.

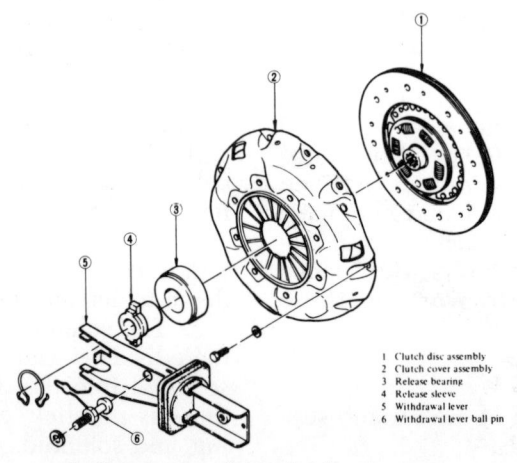

1 Clutch disc assembly
2 Clutch cover assembly
3 Release bearing
4 Release sleeve
5 Withdrawal lever
6 Withdrawal lever ball pin

Exploded view of 710 clutch components

Chapter Seven

Drive Train

Driveline

DRIVESHAFT AND UNIVERSAL JOINTS

The driveshaft transfers power from the engine and transmission to the differential and rear axles and then to the rear wheels to drive the car. All of the models covered in this book utilize a conventional driveshaft except for the F10, which of course does not, being a front wheel drive model. Except on the 610 wagon, the 810, and the 200SX manual transmission models, the driveshaft assembly has two universal joints—one at each end—and a slip yoke at the front of the assembly which fits into the back of the transmission. The 610, 810, and 200SX incorporate an additional universal joint at the center of the driveshaft with a support bearing. The F10 does not use a driveshaft in the conventional sense. Instead, power is transmitted to the front wheels through a pair of axle

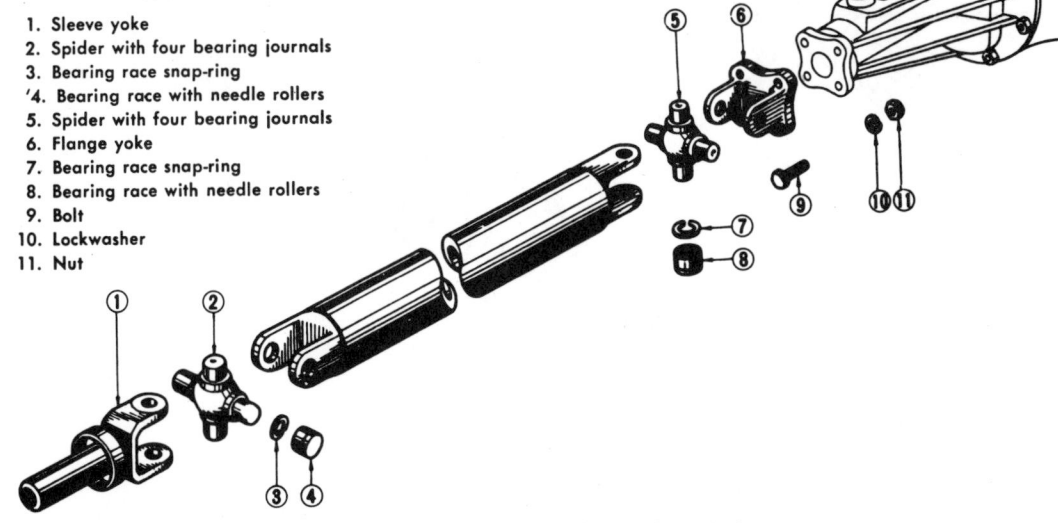

1. Sleeve yoke
2. Spider with four bearing journals
3. Bearing race snap-ring
'4. Bearing race with needle rollers
5. Spider with four bearing journals
6. Flange yoke
7. Bearing race snap-ring
8. Bearing race with needle rollers
9. Bolt
10. Lockwasher
11. Nut

Exploded view of 1200 and B210 driveshaft

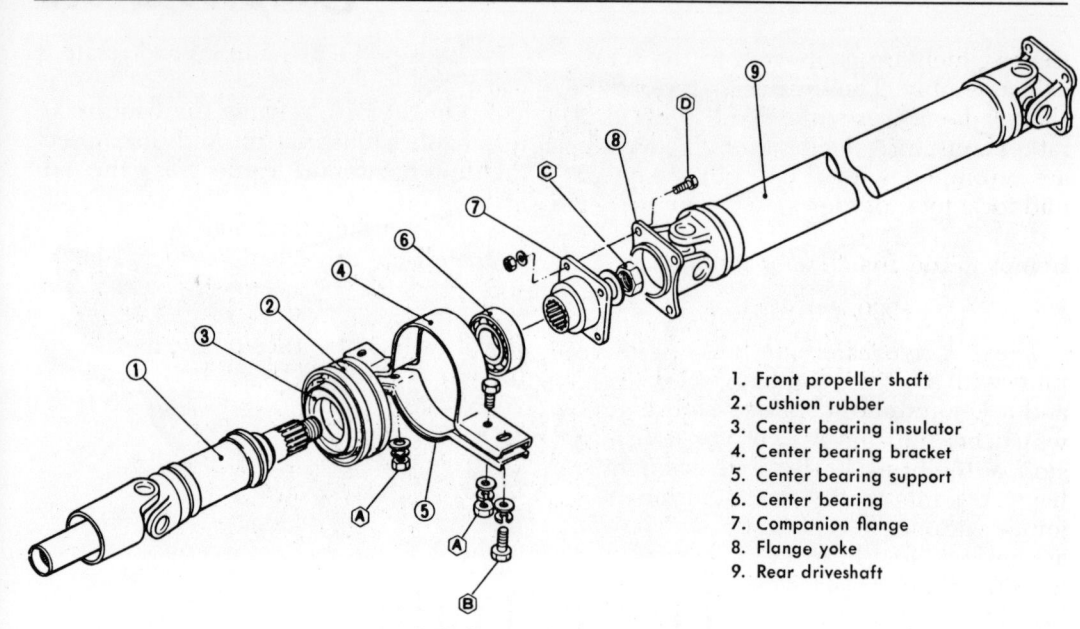

158 DRIVE TRAIN

1. Front propeller shaft
2. Cushion rubber
3. Center bearing insulator
4. Center bearing bracket
5. Center bearing support
6. Center bearing
7. Companion flange
8. Flange yoke
9. Rear driveshaft

Exploded view of 810 driveshaft

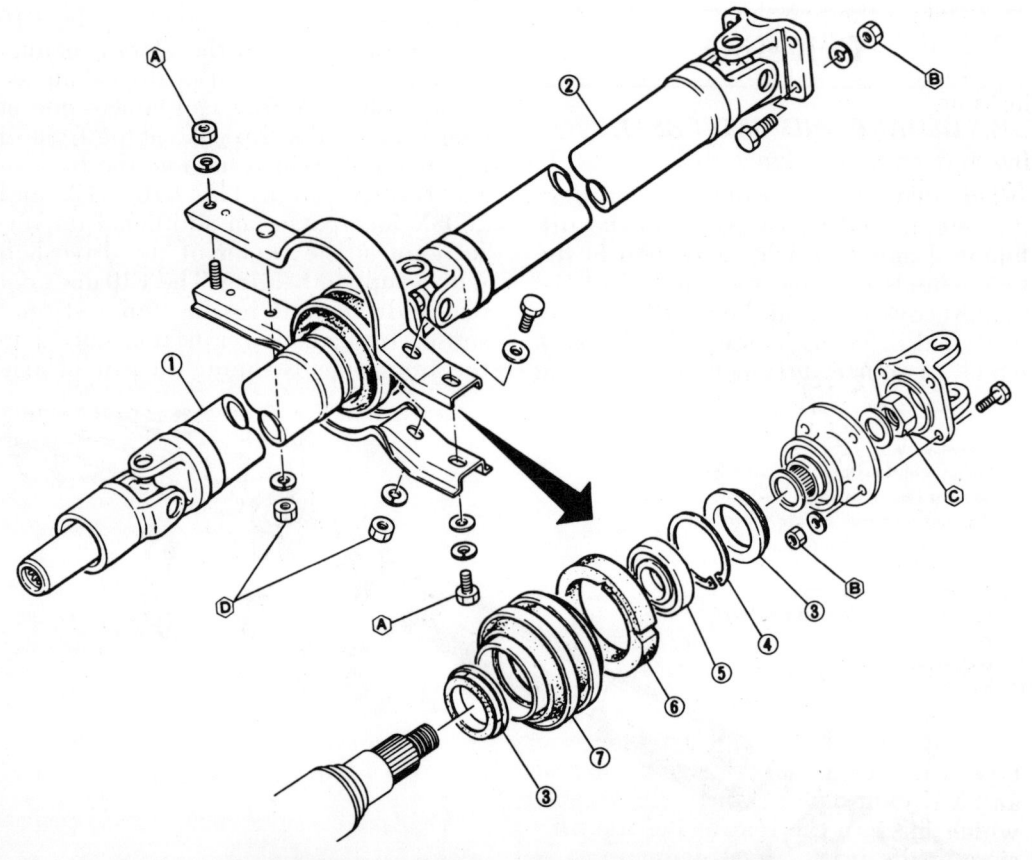

Exploded view of 200SX manual transmission driveshaft

1. Front driveshaft
2. Rear driveshaft
3. Dust seal
4. Snap-ring
5. Ball bearing
6. Cushion
7. Center bearing insulator

DRIVE TRAIN

shafts which are connected to the transaxle assembly. These driveshafts (or axle shafts) do not use universal joints, but rather constant velocity joints. The shafts are equipped with a CV joint at either end for a total of four.

Removal and Installation

1200 AND B210

These driveshafts are all one-piece units with a U-joint and flange at the rear, and a U-joint and a splined sleeve yoke which fits into the rear of the transmission, at the front. Early models generally have U-joints with grease fittings. U-joints without grease fittings must be disassembled for lubrication, usually at 24,000 mile intervals. The splines are lubricated by transmission oil.

1. Be ready to catch oil coming from the rear of the transmission and to plug the extension housing.
2. Unbolt the rear flange.
3. Pull the driveshaft down and back.
4. Plug the transmission extension housing.
5. Reverse the procedure to install, oiling the splines. Flange bolt torque is 15–20 ft lbs.

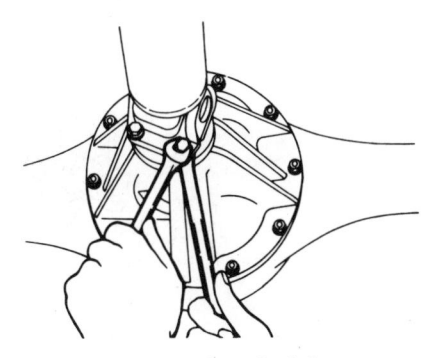

Disconnecting the rear driveshaft flange

510, 610 (EXCEPT STATION WAGON), AND 710

These driveshafts are the one-piece type with a U-joint and flange at the rear, and a U-joint and a splined sleeve yoke which fits into the rear of the transmission, at the front. The U-joints must be disassembled for lubrication at 24,000 mile intervals. The splines are lubricated by transmission oil.

1. Release the handbrake.
2. Loosen the 510 muffler and rotate it out of the way.
3. On the 510, remove the handbrake rear cable adjusting nut and disconnect the left handbrake cable from the adjuster.
4. Unbolt the rear flange.
5. Pull the driveshaft down and back.
6. Plug the transmission extension housing.
7. Reverse the procedure to install, oiling the splines. Flange bolt torque is 29–62 ft lbs on the 510, and 15–20 ft lbs on the 610.

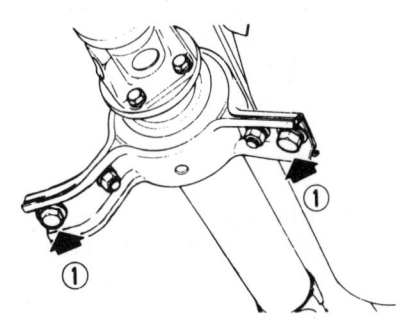

610 station wagon center bearing bracket

610 STATION WAGON, 810, 200SX (MANUAL TRANS.)

These models use a driveshaft with three U-joints and a center support bearing. The driveshaft is balanced as an assembly. It is not recommended that it be disassembled.

1. Mark the relationship of the driveshaft flange to the differential flange.
2. Unbolt the center bearing bracket.
3. Unbolt the driveshaft flange from the differential flange.
4. Pull the driveshaft back under the rear axle. Plug the rear of the transmission to prevent oil or fluid loss.
5. On installation, align the marks made in Step 1. Torque the flange bolts to 15–20 ft lbs. Center bearing bracket bolt torque is 26–35 ft lbs.

U-Joint Overhaul

DISASSEMBLY

1. Mark the relationship of all components for reassembly.
2. Remove the snap-rings. On early units, the snap-rings are seated in the yokes. On later units, the snap-rings seat in the needle bearing races.

DRIVE TRAIN

3. Tap the yoke with brass or rubber mallet to relase one bearing cap. Be careful not to lose the needle rollers.

4. Remove the other bearing caps. Remove the U-joint spiders from the yokes.

INSPECTION

1. Spline backlash should not exceed 0.0197 in. (0.5 mm).
2. Driveshaft run-out should not exceed 0.015 in. (0.4 mm).
3. On later models with snap-rings seated in the needle bearing races, different thicknesses of snap-rings are available for U-joint adjustment. Play should not exceed 0.0008 in. (0.02 mm).
4. U-joint spiders must be replaced if their bearing journals are worn more than 0.0059 in. (0.15 mm) from their original diameter.

ASSEMBLY

1. Place the needle rollers in the races and hold them in place with grease.
2. Put the spider into place in its yokes.
3. Replace all seals.
4. Tap the races into position and secure them with snap-rings.

F-10 Driveshaft Removal and Installation

The F-10 drive axles are variously called driveshafts or axles, or drive axles. Strictly speaking, they are not driveshafts, but drive axles. A special puller is necessary to remove the axles. The tool is illustrated here.

1. Jack up the car and support it with safety stands.
2. Remove the wheel and tire.
3. Pull out the cotter pin and then remove the wheel bearing nut. You'll have to hold the wheel hub still somehow while you do this.
4. Remove the bolts which secure the driveshaft to the transaxle assembly. The driveshaft is splined into the hub assembly and is removed from underneath the car.

F10 axle shaft removal tool

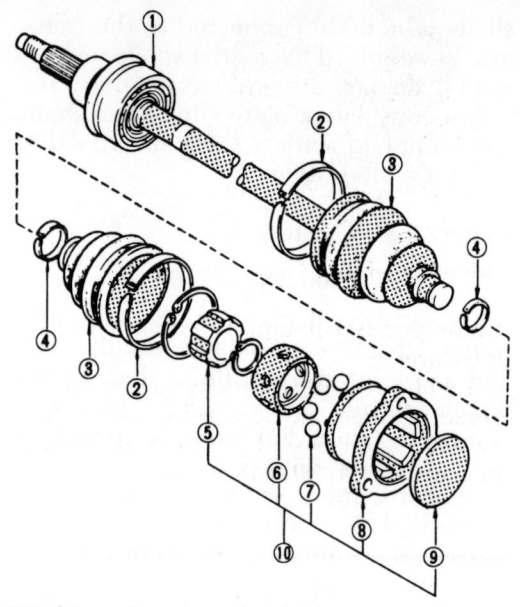

F10 drive axle components

1. Outside joint assembly (Birfield joint)
2. Band
3. Dust cover
4. Band
5. Inner ring
6. Cage
7. Ball
8. Outer ring
9. Plug
10. Inside joint assembly (Double offset joint)

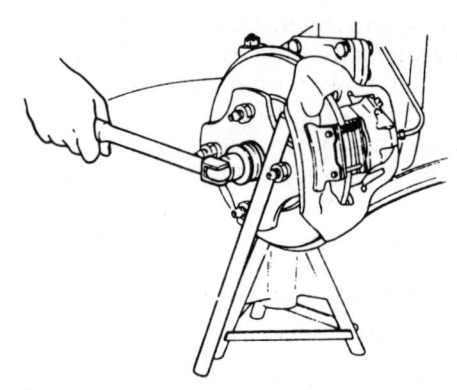

Hub nut removal

5. Install the puller on the hub and remove the driveshaft by screwing the tool inward. This will force the driveshaft out the back of the hub assembly.

6. The driveshaft is installed by lightly hammering it back into place in the hub assembly. Quite often, this is a difficult job since the splines are a tight fit. Unfortunately, there is no other way to do it unless you want to remove the steering knuckle and then press the shaft on.

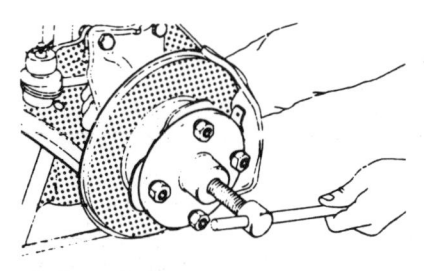

Driveshaft removal

Light persistent tapping should get the job done.

7. The rest of the procedure is the reverse of removal. Be careful not to damage the grease seal. Torque the wheel bearing nut to 90–145 ft lbs.

Rear Axle

There are several different types of rear axles used on the cars covered in this guide. A solid rear axle is used on 1200, B210, 200SX, 710, and all station wagon models. The 1978 510 uses a solid rear axle with either coil springs or leaf springs, depending on whether it is a sedan or a wagon. Independent rear suspension is used on the 1973 510, the 610 sedans, and the 810 sedan. In this design, separate axle driveshafts are used to transmit power from the differential to the wheels. The F10, being a front wheel drive car, utilizes a simple beam axle in the rear on wagon models, and trailing arms on the sedans.

AXLE SHAFT
Removal and Installation
SOLID REAR AXLE MODELS

NOTE: *Bearings must be pressed on and off the shaft with an arbor press. Unless you have access to one, it is in-* advisable *to attempt any repair work on the axle shaft and bearing assemblies.*

1. Remove the hub cap or wheel cover. Loosen the lug nuts.
2. Raise the rear of the car and support it safely on stands.
3. Remove the rear wheel. Remove the four brake backing plate retaining nuts. Detach the parking brake linkage from the brake backing plate.
4. Attach a slide hammer to the axle shaft and remove it. Use the slide hammer and a two-pronged puller to remove the oil seal from the housing.

NOTE: *If a slide hammer is not available, the axle can sometimes be pried out using pry bars on opposing sides of the hub.*

If end-play is found to be excessive, the bearing should be replaced. Shimming the bearing is not recommended as this ignores end-play of the bearing itself and could result in improper seating of the bearing.

5. Using a chisel, carefully nick the bearing retainer in three or four places. The retainer does not have to be cut, only collapsed enough to allow the bearing retainer to be slid off the shaft.
6. Pull or press the old bearing off and install the new one by pressing it into position.
7. Install the outer bearing retainer with its raised surface facing the wheel hub, and then install the bearing and the inner bearing retainer in that order on the axle shaft.
8. With the smaller chamfered side of the inner bearing retainer facing the bearing, press on the retainer. The edge of the retainer should fully touch the bearing.
9. Clean the oil seal seat in the rear axle housing. Apply a thin coat of chassis grease.
10. Using a seal installation tool, drive the oil seal into the rear axle housing. Wipe a thin coat of bearing grease on the lips of the seal.
11. Determine the number of retainer gaskets which will give the correct bearing-to-outer retainer clearance of 0.01 in.
12. Insert the axle shaft assembly into the axle housing, being careful not to damage the seal. Ensure that the shaft

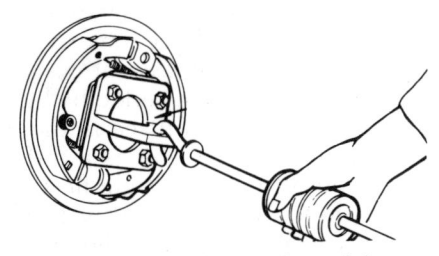

Removing axle on solid rear axle models

DRIVE TRAIN

splines engage those of the diferential pinion. Align the vent holes of the gasket and the outer bearing retainer. Install the retaining bolts.

13. Install the nuts on the bolts and tighten them evenly, and in a criss-cross pattern, to 20 ft lbs.

AXLE DRIVESHAFTS

Wheel Bearing, Seal, and Axle Shaft Service

INDEPENDENT REAR SUSPENSION MODELS

1. Jack up and support the rear of the car.
2. Remove the wheel and brake drum.
3. Disconnect the axle driveshaft from the axle shaft at the flange.
4. Remove the wheel bearing locknut while holding the axle shaft outer flange from turning.
5. Pull out the axle shaft with a slide hammer. Remove the distance piece and inner flange.
6. Drive the inner wheel bearing and oil seal out toward the center of the car.
7. Press or pull the outer wheel bearing from the axle shaft.
8. Pack the wheel bearings with grease. Coat the seal lip also.
9. Reinstall the wheel bearings. Install the outer bearing on the axle shaft so that the side with the seal will be toward the wheel. Always press or drive on the inner bearing race.
10. The distance piece may be reused if it is not collapsed or deformed. The distance piece must always carry the same mark, A, B, or C, as the bearing housing.
11. Fill the area illustrated with grease.
12. Replace the axle shaft and flange. Tighten the bearing locknut to the specified torque.
13. The torque required to start the axle shaft turning should be 3.9 in. lbs or less. This is a 28.7 oz or less pull at the

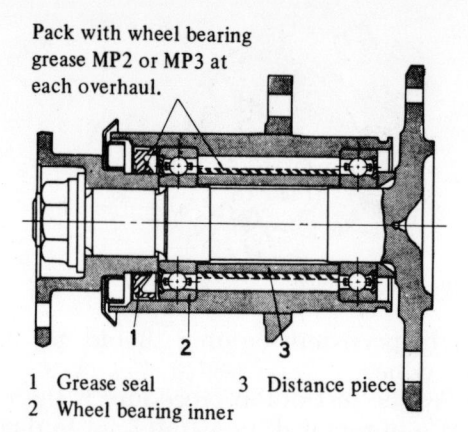

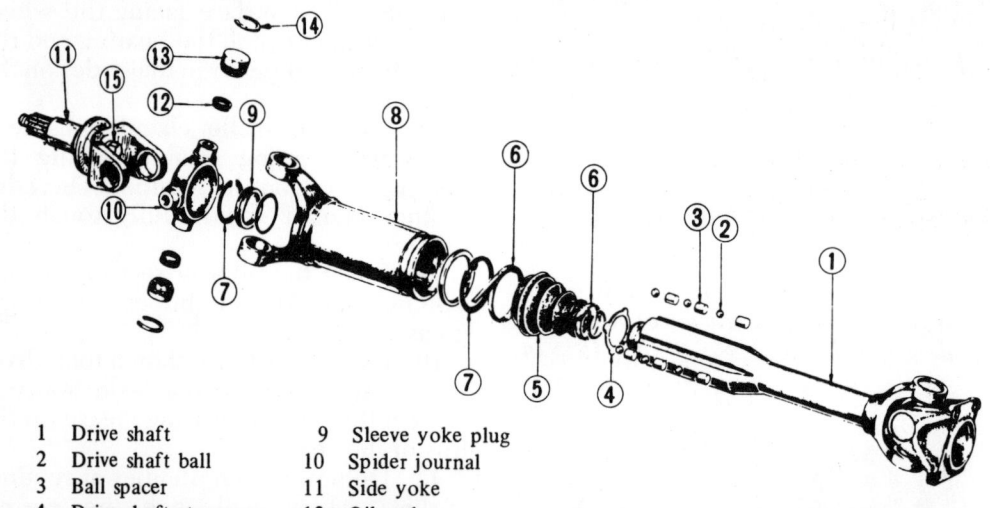

Pack with wheel bearing grease MP2 or MP3 at each overhaul.

1 Grease seal
2 Wheel bearing inner
3 Distance piece

Cutaway of wheel bearing

1	Drive shaft	9	Sleeve yoke plug
2	Drive shaft ball	10	Spider journal
3	Ball spacer	11	Side yoke
4	Drive shaft stopper	12	Oil seal
5	Rubber boot	13	Needle bearing
6	Boot band	14	Snap ring
7	Snap ring	15	Side yoke fitting bolt
8	Sleeve yoke		

Exploded view of axle driveshaft—1973 510
610 models similar

DRIVE TRAIN 163

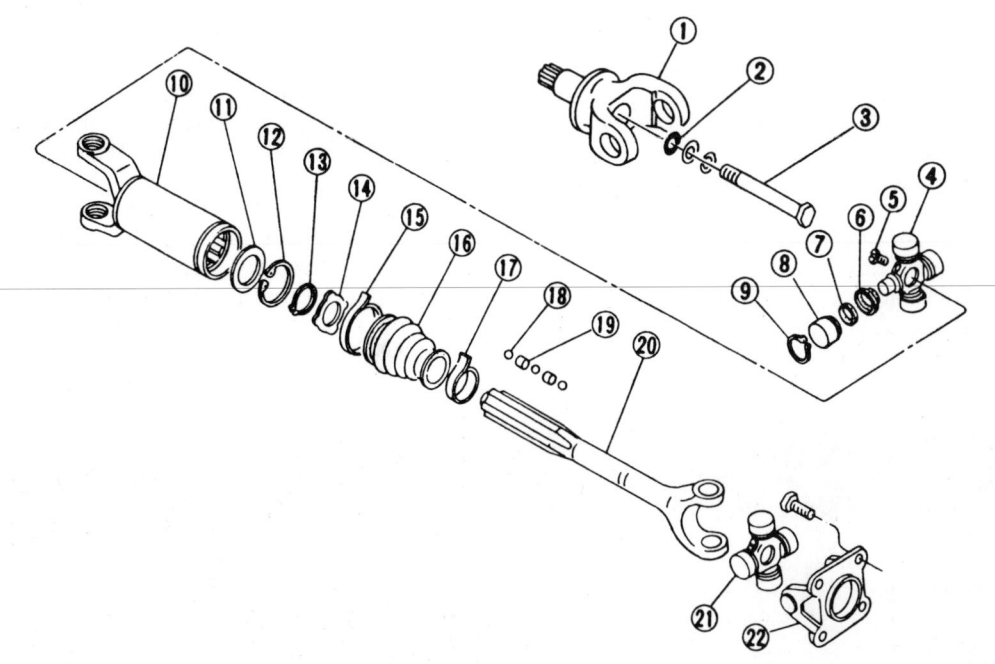

810 axle shaft—exploded view

1. Side yoke
2. O-ring
3. Side yoke bolt
4. Spider journal
5. Filler plug
6. Dust cover
7. Oil seal
8. Bearing race assembly
9. Bearing race snap ring
10. Sleeve yoke
11. Sleeve yoke stopper
12. Snap ring
13. Drive shaft snap ring
14. Drive shaft stopper
15. Boot band (long)
16. Rubber boot
17. Boot band (short)
18. Ball
19. Ball spacer
20. Driveshaft
21. Spider assembly
22. Flange yoke

hub bolt. Axle shaft end-play, checked with a dial indicator, should be 0–0.006 in.

14. If the turning torque or axle shaft play is incorrect, disassemble the unit and install a new distance piece.

The axle driveshafts must be removed and disassembled to lubricate the ball splines every 30,000 miles. Handle the driveshaft carefully; it is easily damaged. No repair parts for the driveshafts are available. If a driveshaft is defective in any way, it must be replaced as an assembly.

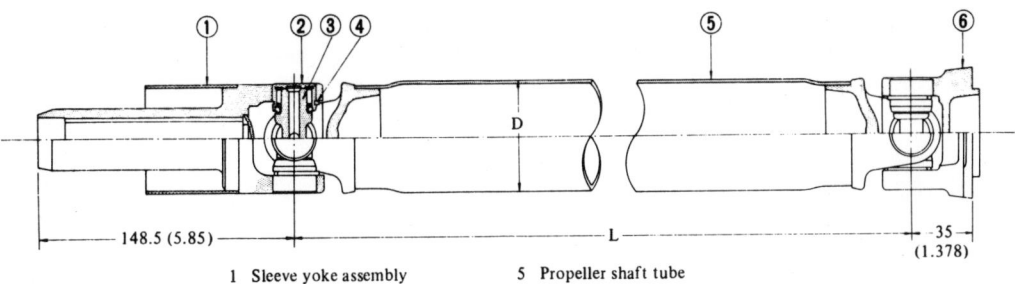

Fastener	Torque (ft lbs)
Wheel nut	58–65
Axle driveshaft flange nuts	36–43
Bearing locknut	181–239
Axle shaft inner flange mounting nut	14–19

1 Sleeve yoke assembly
2 Bearing race assembly
3 Journal assembly
4 Snap ring
5 Propeller shaft tube assembly
6 Flange yoke

Cutaway of 710 driveshaft

To disassemble:

1. Remove the U-joint spider from the differential end of the shaft.
2. Remove the snap-ring and sleeve yoke plug.
3. Compress the driveshaft and remove the snap-ring and stopper.
4. Disconnect the boot and separate the driveshaft carefully so as not to lose the balls and spacer.
5. Pack about 10 grams (0.35 oz) of grease into the ball grooves. Also pack about 35 grams (1.23 oz) of grease into the other area.
6. Twisting play between the two shaft halves should not exceed 0.004 in. Check play with the driveshaft completely compressed.
7. While reassembling, adjust the U-joint side play to 0.001 in. or less by selecting suitable snap-rings. Four different thicknesses are available for adjustment. Axle driveshaft flange nut torque is 36–43 ft lbs.

Chapter Eight

Suspension and Steering

Front Suspension

All the models covered in this book use MacPherson strut front suspension. In this type of suspension, each strut combines the function of coil spring and shock absorber. The spindle is mounted to the lower part of the strut through a single ball joint. No upper suspension arm is required in this design. The lower suspension arm is bolted to the front subframe assembly. Except on the F10, the spindle and lower control arm are located fore and aft by tension rods which attach to the chassis.

STRUT

Removal and Installation

1. Jack up the car and support it safely. Remove the wheel.
2. Disconnect and plug the brake hose. Remove the brake caliper as outlined in Chapter 9. Remove the disc and hub as described in this chapter.
3. Disconnect the tension rod and stabilizer bar from the transverse link.
4. Unbolt the steering arm. Pry the control arm down to detach it from the strut.
5. Place a jack under the bottom of the strut.

Strut mounting points (top)—1978 510 shown, others similar

6. Open the hood and remove the nuts holding the top of the strut.
7. Lower the jack slowly and cautiously until the strut assembly can be removed.

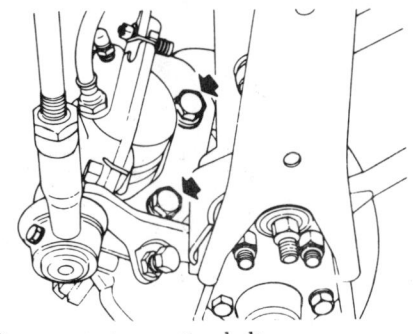

Caliper-to-strut mounting bolts

166 SUSPENSION AND STEERING

1. Strut mounting insulator
2. Coil spring
3. Strut assembly
4. Stabilizer
5. Suspension crossmember
6. Tension rod bracket
7. Tension rod
8. Transverse link
9. Lower ball joint

200SX front suspension

1. Strut mounting insulator
2. Strut mounting bearing
3. Upper spring seat
4. Bumper rubber
5. Dust cover
6. Piston rod
7. Front spring
8. Strut assembly
9. Hub assembly
10. Spindle
11. Ball joint
12. Transverse link
13. Tension rod
14. Stabilizer
15. Suspension member

1200 and B210 front suspension

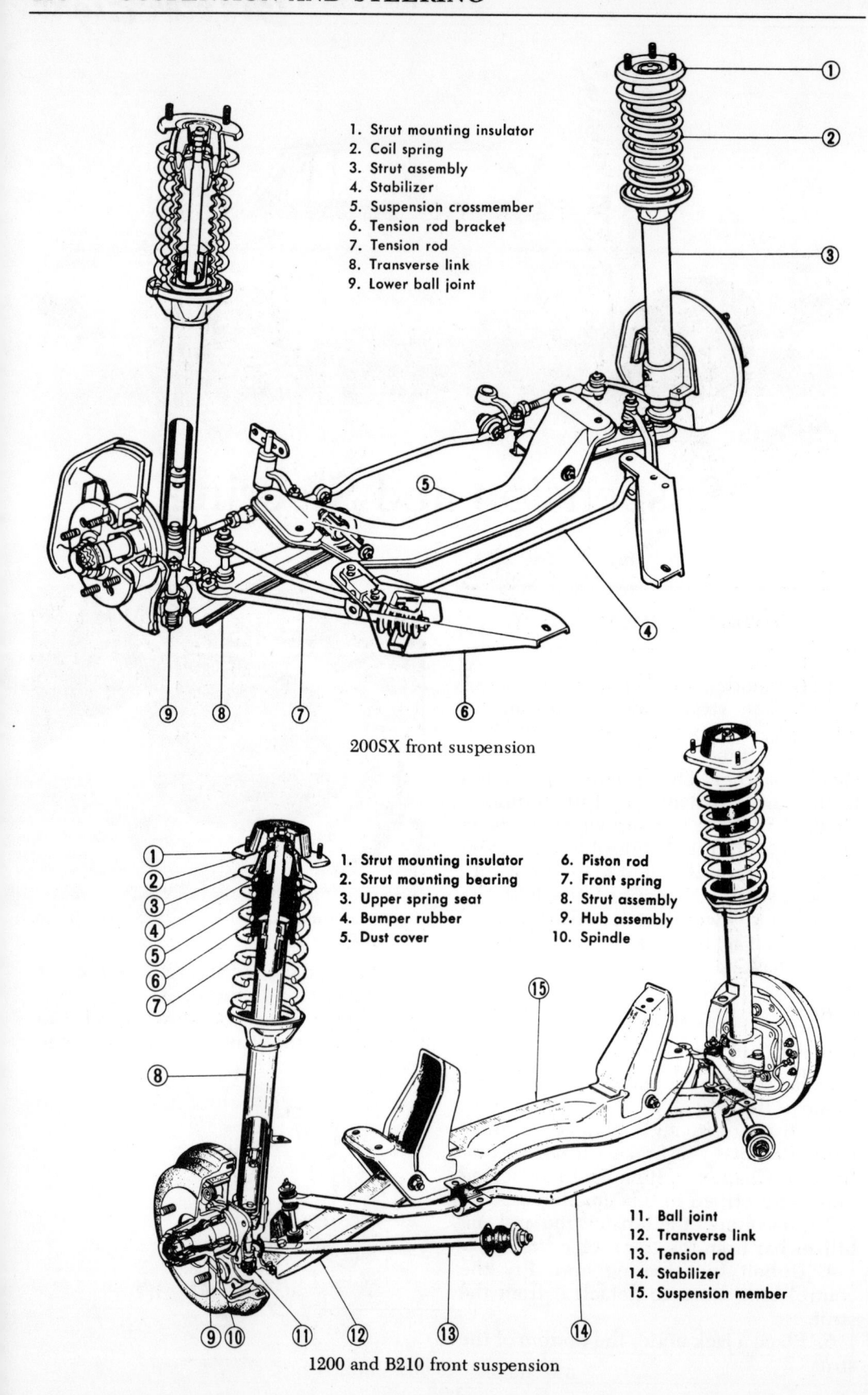

SUSPENSION AND STEERING 167

1. Strut assembly
2. Knuckle
3. Ball joint
4. Transverse link
5. Sub-frame
6. Driveshaft
7. Stabilizer

F10 front suspension

1.	Strut mounting insulator
2.	Coil spring
3.	Strut assembly
4.	Suspension cross member
5.	Stabilizer
6.	Tension rod
7.	Transverse link
8.	Steering knuckle arm

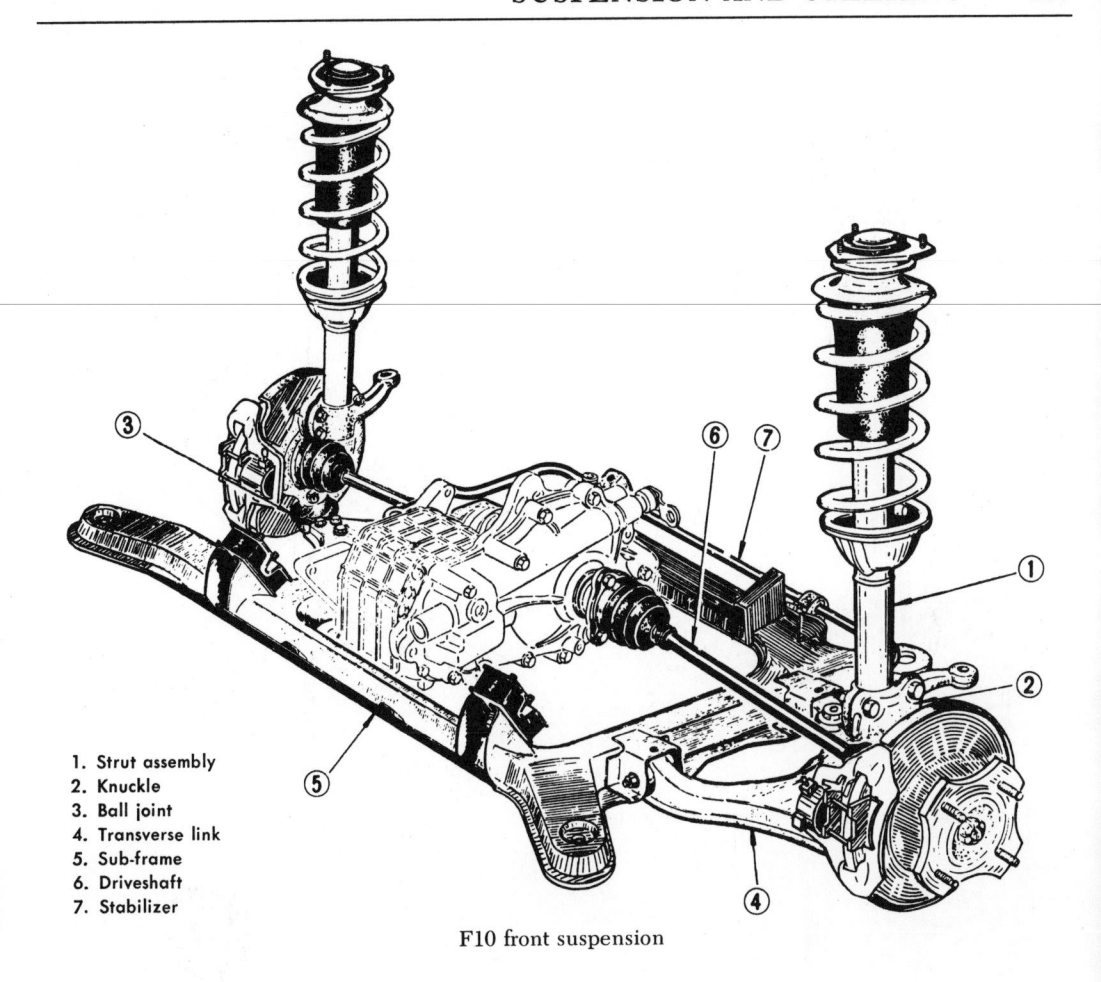

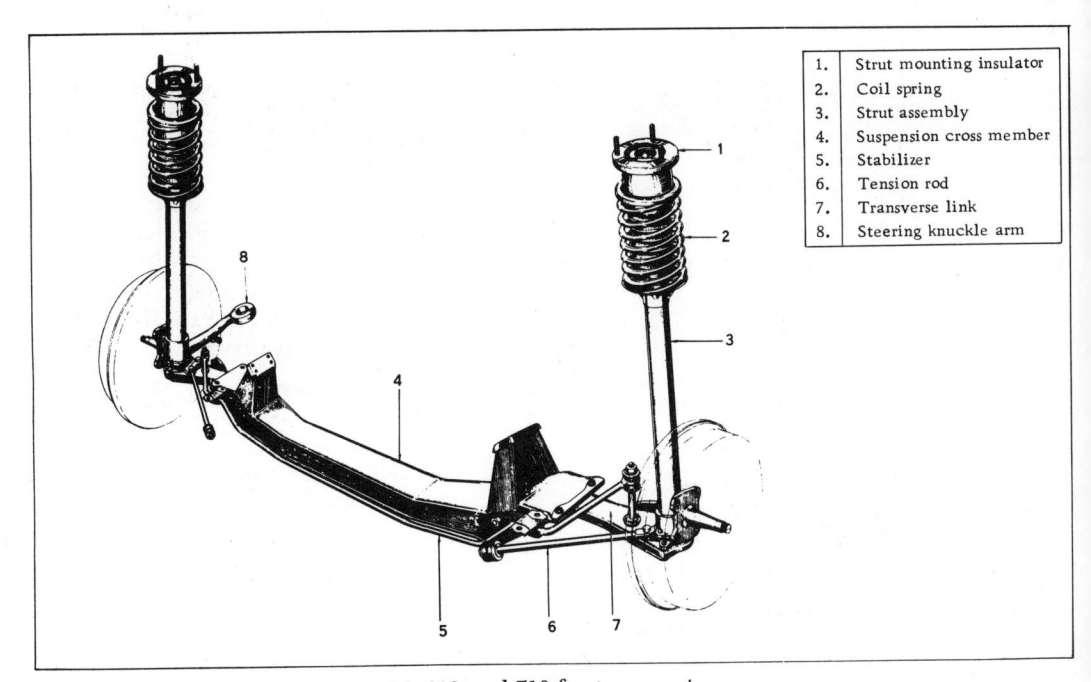

510, 610, and 710 front suspension

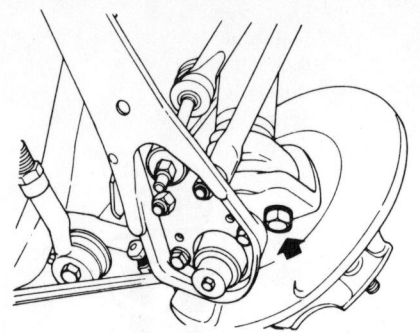

SUSPENSION AND STEERING

1200 and B210 strut-to-control arm/steering knuckle bolts

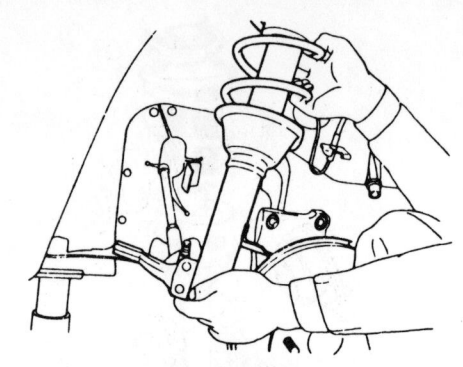

Removing the strut and spring—F10

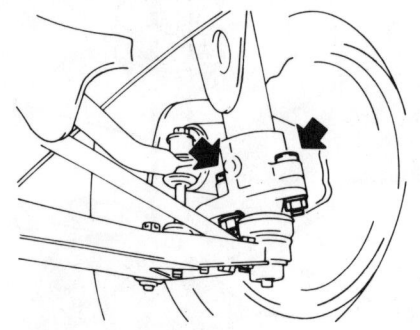

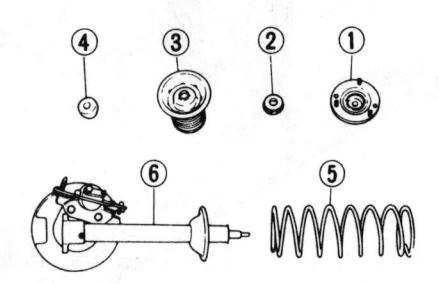

510, 610, and 710 strut-to-control arm/steering knuckle bolts

1 Strut mounting insulator
2 Bearing
3 Spring upper seat and dust cover
4 Damper rubber
5 Coil spring
6 Strut assembly

Exploded view of 1200 and B210 strut

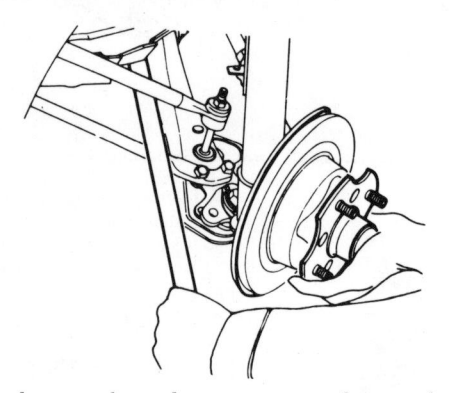

Pry the control arm down to separate the strut from the knuckle

8. Reverse the procedure to install. The self-locking nuts holding the top of the strut must be replaced. Bleed the brakes.

NOTE: *The shock absorber within the strut can be replaced by disassembling the strut. As this requires compressing the coil spring, we recommend removing the strut yourself and then having either a dealer or spring shop replace the shock absorber insert.*

BALL JOINT

Inspection

The lower ball joint should be replaced when play becomes excessive. Datsun does not publish specifications on just what constitutes excessive play, relying instead on a method of determining the force (in inch pounds) required to keep the ball joint turning. This method is not very helpful to the backyard mechanic since it involves removing the ball joint, which is what we are trying to avoid in

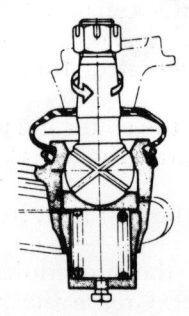

Ball joint cross-section

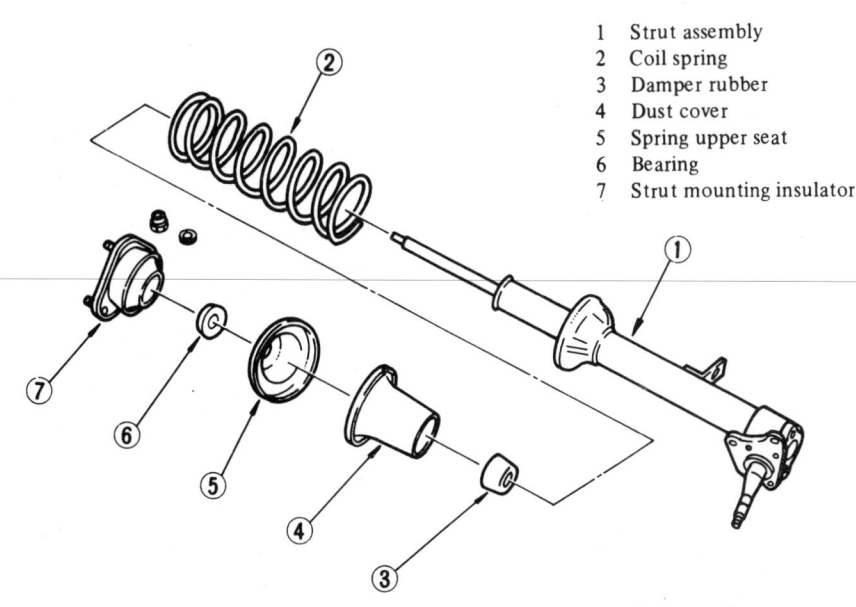

SUSPENSION AND STEERING

1 Strut assembly
2 Coil spring
3 Damper rubber
4 Dust cover
5 Spring upper seat
6 Bearing
7 Strut mounting insulator

Exploded view of 510, 610, and 710 strut—others similar

the first place. An effective way to determine ball joint play is to jack up the car until the wheel is just a couple of inches off the ground and the ball joint is unloaded (meaning you can't jack directly underneath the ball joint). Place a long bar under the tire and move the wheel and tire assembly up and down. Keep one hand on top of the tire while you are doing this. If there is over ¼ inch of play at the top of the tire, the ball joint is probably bad. This is assuming that the wheel bearings are in good shape and properly adjusted. As a double check on this, have someone watch the ball joint while you move the tire up and down with the bar. If you can see considerable play, besides feeling play at the top of the wheel, the ball joint needs replacing.

Removal and Installation

1. Raise and support the car so that the wheels hang free. Remove the wheel.
2. Unbolt the tension rod and stabilizer bar from transverse link.
3. Unbolt the strut from the steering arm.
4. Remove the cotter pin and ball joint stud nut. Separate the ball joint and steering arm.
5. Unbolt the ball joint from the transverse link.
6. Reverse the procedure to install a new ball joint. Grease the joint after installation.

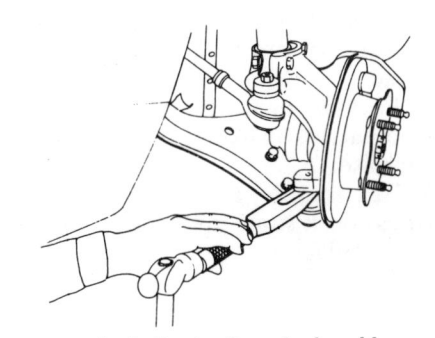

Separating the ball joint from the knuckle

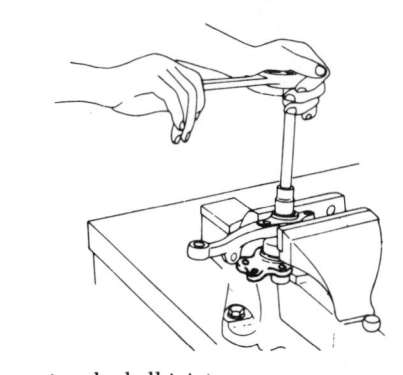

Removing the ball joint

HUB ASSEMBLY

Removal and Installation—All Except F10

1. Jack up the vehicle, remove the wheel, and disconnect the brake hose.

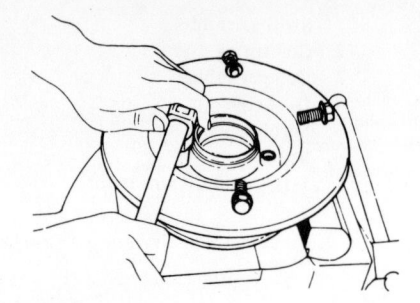

SUSPENSION AND STEERING

Separating the disc from the hub

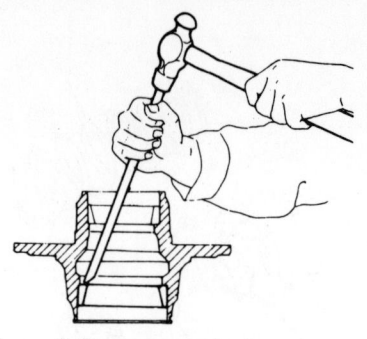

Use a brass drift to remove the bearing races

2. Unbolt and remove the brake caliper assembly.

3. Remove the hubcap, cotter pin, and spindle nut.

4. Remove the wheel hub with bearing washer, bearing, and brake rotor.

5. Remove the screws and brake splash shield.

6. Disassemble the hub. Use a drift in the two grooves inside the hub to drive out the bearing outer race.

7. Drive or press back in the bearing outer race.

8. Pack the bearings, the hub, and the grease seal lip pocket (use a new seal) with grease.

9. Reassemble, and adjust the wheel bearings. Pack some grease into the hubcap and replace it.

10. Replace the caliper, brake hose, and wheel. Lower the vehicle.

F10 Hub Assembly Removal and Installation

1. Jack up the car and support it with jackstands.

2. Remove the wheel and tire assembly. Detach the brake line and plug it to prevent fluid loss.

3. Remove the caliper assembly.

4. Remove the cotter pin and remove the hub nut. You'll have to hold the hub assembly still while you do this.

5. Datsun recommends the use of a special tool (illustrated here) to remove the hub assembly. Attach this tool to the

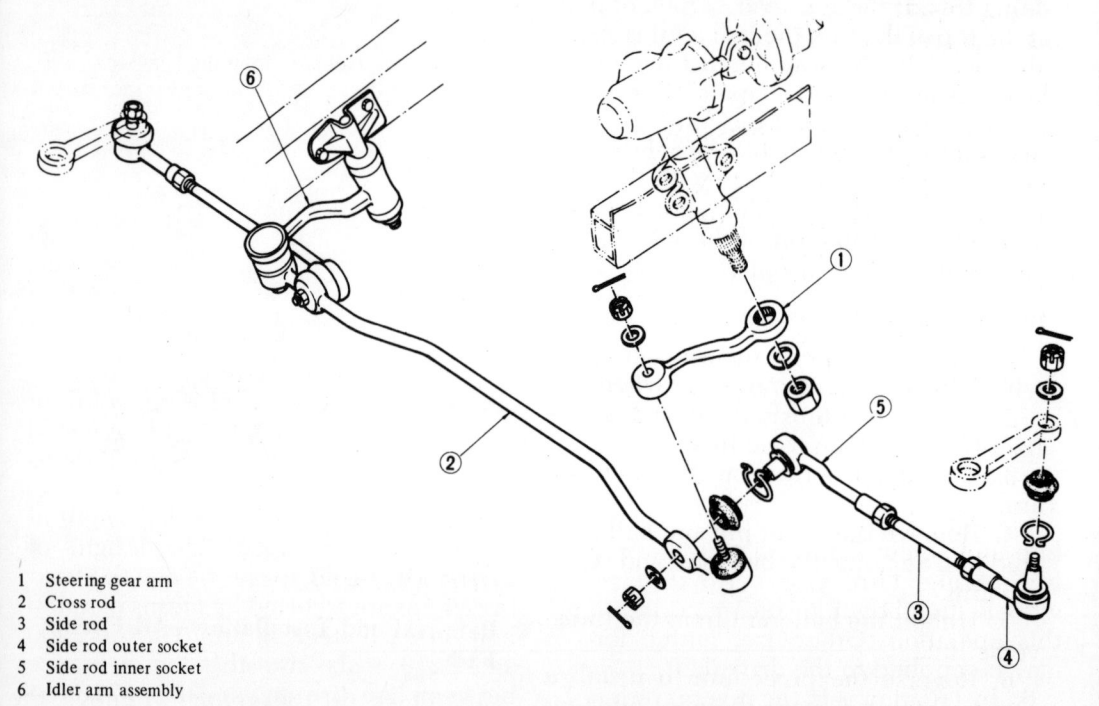

1 Steering gear arm
2 Cross rod
3 Side rod
4 Side rod outer socket
5 Side rod inner socket
6 Idler arm assembly

Steering linkage—toe-in adjustment is made at the side rod (tie-rod)

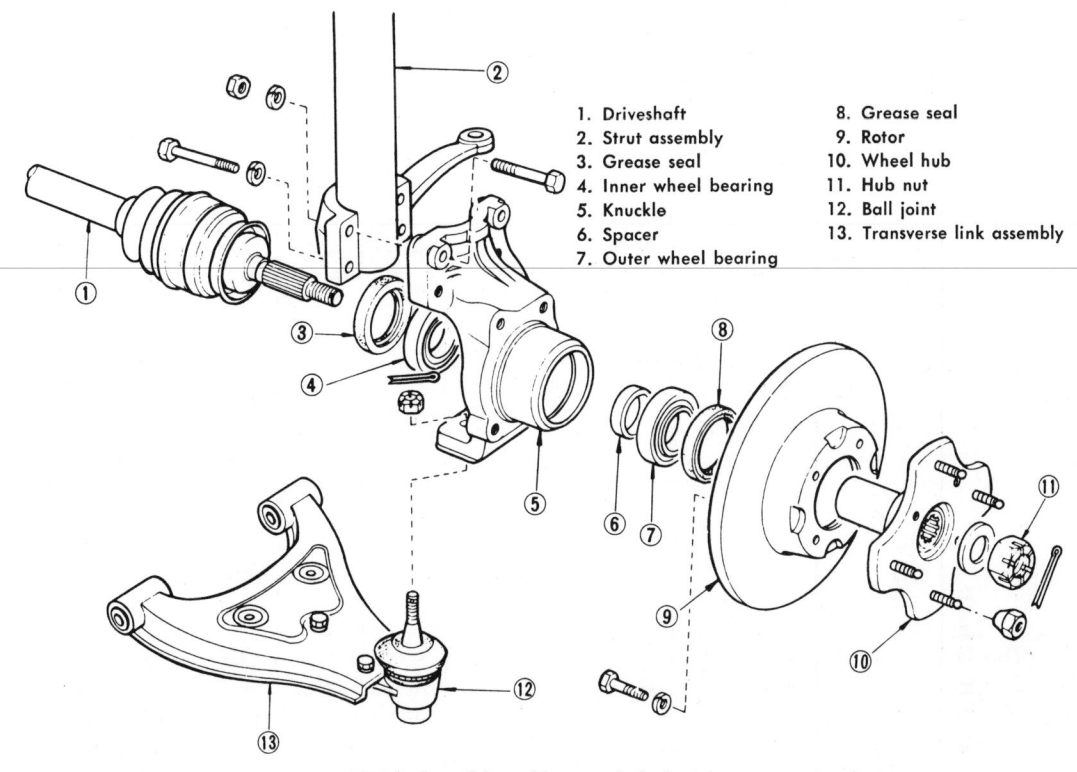

SUSPENSION AND STEERING

1. Driveshaft
2. Strut assembly
3. Grease seal
4. Inner wheel bearing
5. Knuckle
6. Spacer
7. Outer wheel bearing
8. Grease seal
9. Rotor
10. Wheel hub
11. Hub nut
12. Ball joint
13. Transverse link assembly

F10 hub and knuckle—exploded view

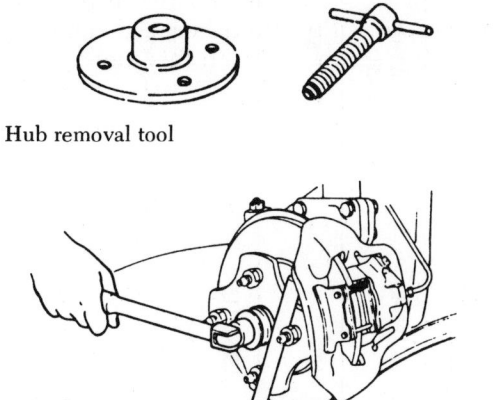

Hub removal tool

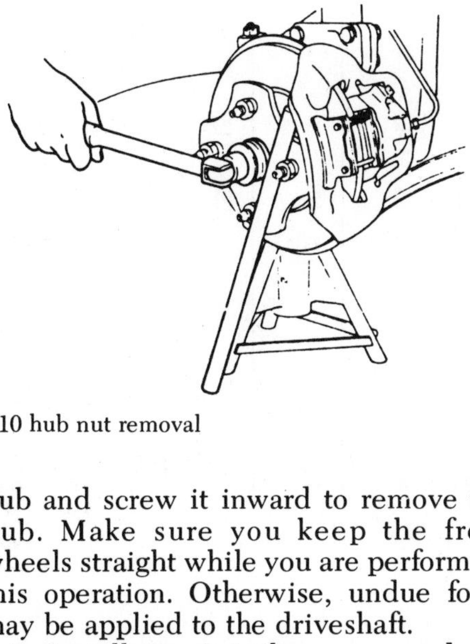

Hub removal

F10 hub nut removal

hub and screw it inward to remove the hub. Make sure you keep the front wheels straight while you are performing this operation. Otherwise, undue force may be applied to the driveshaft.

6. Installation is in the reverse order of removal.

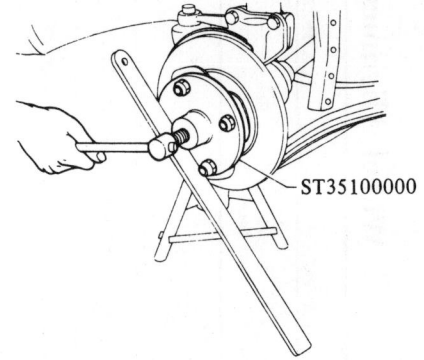

FRONT END ALIGNMENT

Caster and camber angles cannot be adjusted except by replacing worn or bent parts. Suspension height is adjusted by replacing the front springs. Various springs are available for adjustment. Toe-in is adjusted by changing the length of the steering side-rods. The length of these rods should always be equal. Steering angles are adjusted by means of a stop bolt on each steering arm. On the 1200 and B210, make sure that the clearance between the tire and tension rod is at least 1.181 in.

SUSPENSION AND STEERING

Wheel Alignment Specifications

Model	CASTER Range (deg)	CASTER Preferred Setting (deg)	CAMBER Range (deg)	CAMBER Preferred Setting (deg)	Toe-In (in.)	Steering Axis Inclination (deg)	WHEEL PIVOT RATIO (deg) Inner Wheel	WHEEL PIVOT RATIO (deg) Outer Wheel
510	—	1° 40'	—	1	0.35–0.47	8	38–39	22° 30'–33° 30'
1200	40'–1° 40'	1° 10'	35'–1° 35'	1° 05'	0.16–0.24	7° 55'	42–44	35–37
610	0° 45'–2° 15'	—	1°–2° 30'	—	0.24–0.35	7° 05'	37–38	30° 40'–32° 40'
610 Station Wagon	0° 55'–2° 25'	—	1° 10'–2° 40'	—	0.32–0.43	6° 55'	37–38	30° 40'–32° 40'
B210	1° 15'–2° 15'	—	40'–1° 40'	—	0.079–0.157	7° 47'–8° 47'	37°–39°	31°–33°
610	1° 15'–2° 45'	—	1° 15'–2° 45' 1° 30'–3°	—	0.430–0.550	5° 55'–7° 25' 5° 45'–7° 15'	37°	30° 42'–32° 42'
710	1° 10'–2° 40'	—	1° 25'–2° 55'	—	0.550–0.670	6° 25'	37°–38°	30° 42'–32° 42'
610 1975 and later	1° 15'–2° 15'	1° 50'	1° 15'–2° 45'	2°	0.43–0.55	5° 55'–7° 25'	32–33	29° 30'–31° 30'
610 Station Wagon 1975 and later	1° 15'–2° 15'	1° 50'	1° 30'–3° 00'	2° 15'	0.43–0.55	5° 45'–7° 15'	32–33	29° 30'–31° 30'
710 1975 and later	1° 10'–2° 40'	1° 55'	1° 25'–2° 55'	2° 10'	0.32–0.43	6° 25'	32–33	29° 30'–31° 30'

SUSPENSION AND STEERING

B210 1975 and later	1°00'–2°30'	1°45'	0°25'–1°55'	1°10'	0.08–0.16	7°32'–9°02'	37–39	31–33
200SX All	1°05'–2°35'	—	20'–1°50'	—	0.08–0.16	7°20'–8°20'	34°–36°	29°–31°
810 All	1°10'–2°40'	—	0°–1°30'	—	0.0–0.08	7°10'–8°40'	38°	30°
510 Sedan, Hatchback 1978	1°05'–2°35'	—	–15' to 1°15'	—	0.04–0.12	8°05'–9°35'	40°–42°	33°30'–35°30'
510 Station Wagon 1978	55'–2°25'	—	5'–1°35'	—	0.04–0.12	7°45'–9°15'	40°–42°	33°30'–35°30'
F10 All	20'–1°50'	—	50'–2°20'	—	0.20–0.28 (bias ply tire) 0–0.79 (radial ply tire)	9°15'–10°45'	36°30'–39°30'	31°–34°

—— Information not applicable

174 SUSPENSION AND STEERING

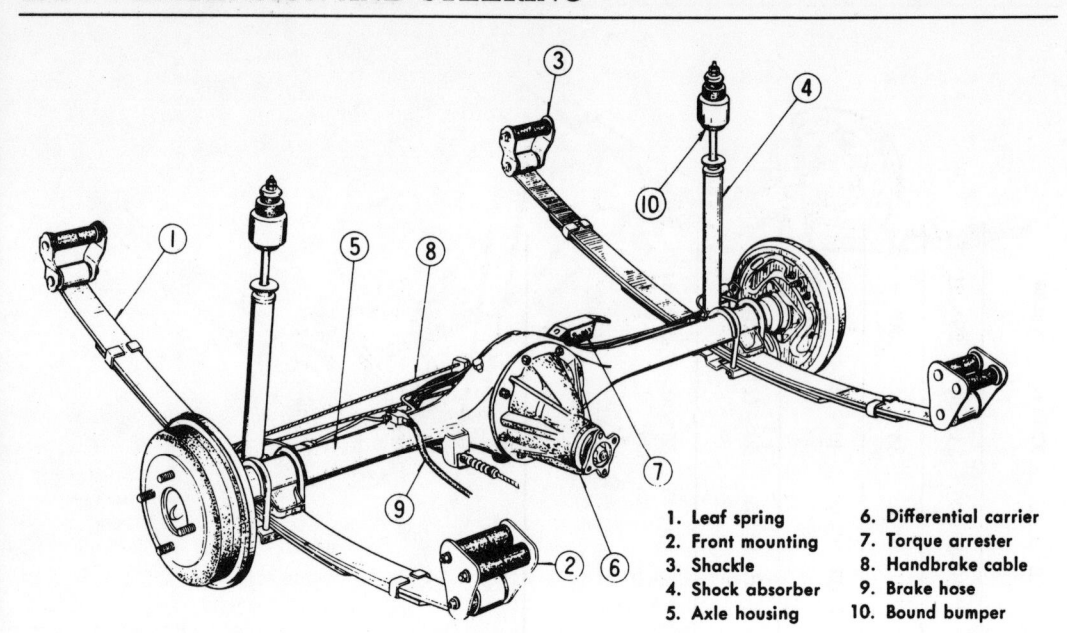

1. Leaf spring
2. Front mounting
3. Shackle
4. Shock absorber
5. Axle housing
6. Differential carrier
7. Torque arrester
8. Handbrake cable
9. Brake hose
10. Bound bumper

1200 and B210 rear suspension

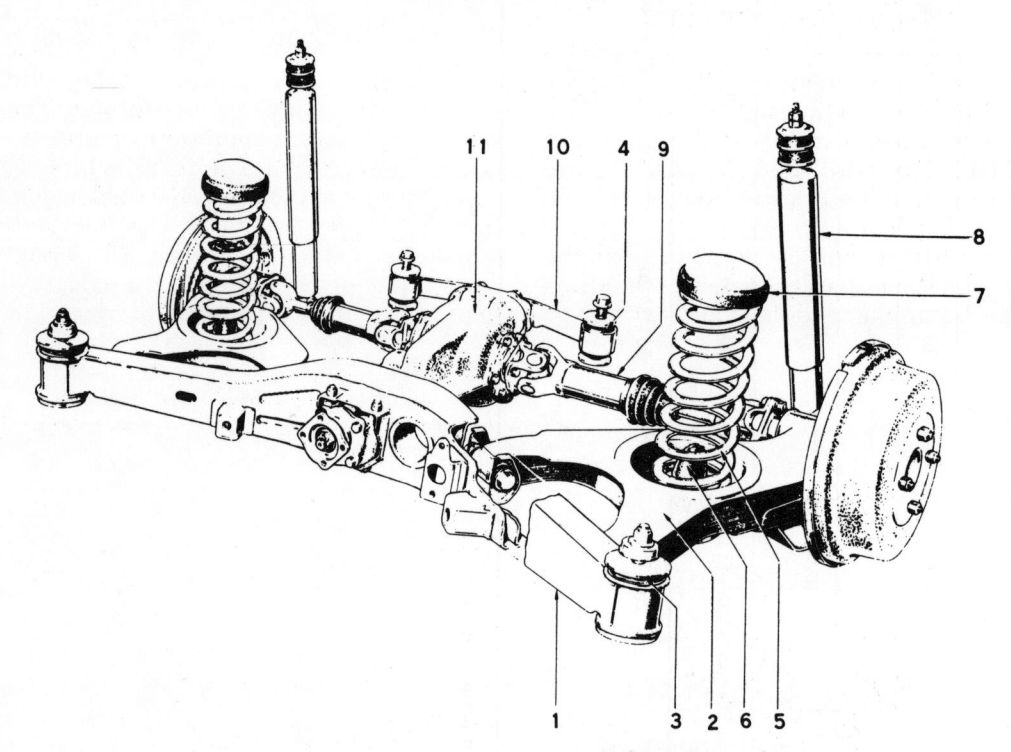

1. Suspension member
2. Suspension arm
3. Member mounting insulator
4. Differential mounting insulator
5. Coil spring
6. Bumper rubber
7. Spring seat
8. Shock absorber
9. Drive shaft
10. Differential mounting member
11. Differential carrier

510 and 610 rear suspension (except station wagon)

SUSPENSION AND STEERING 175

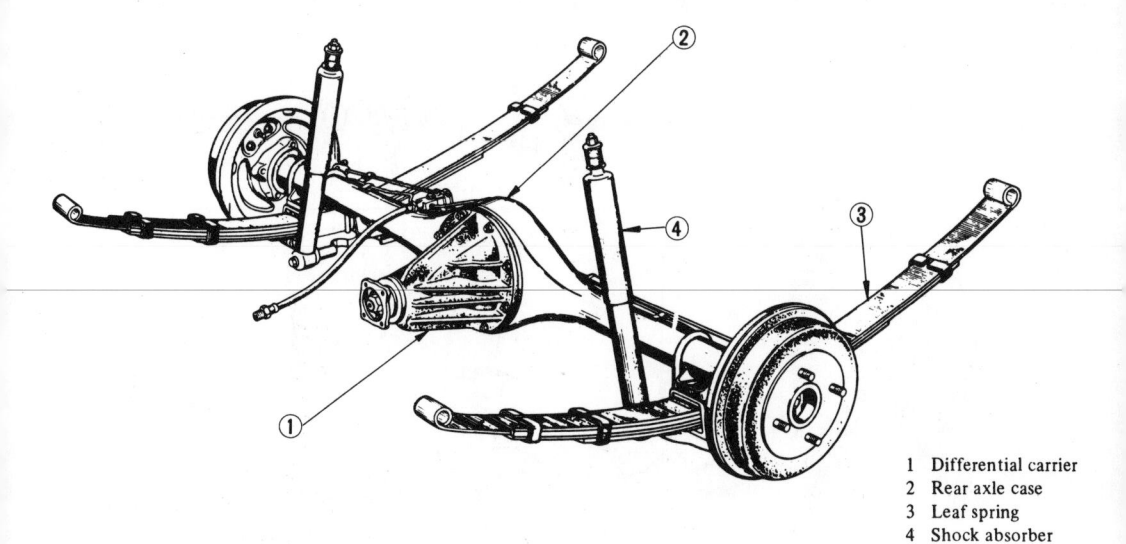

Rear suspension—610 station wagon and all 710 models

1 Differential carrier
2 Rear axle case
3 Leaf spring
4 Shock absorber

Rear Suspension

There are a number of different types of rear suspension used on the various models covered in this guide. All 1200, B210, 710, and 200SX models are equipped with a solid rear axle suspended by leaf springs. The 1973 510 and all the 610 sedans are equipped with an independent rear suspension. Trailing arms locate the wheels, which are driven by separate axle shafts. Coil springs are used along with hydraulic shock absorbers. The 1978 510 sedans and hatchbacks are equipped with a four-link type solid rear axle which utilizes coil springs. The 810 sedans use a semi-trailing arm independent rear suspension which is quite similar to the early 510 suspension. The F10 sedan and hatchback use trailing arms and coil springs. All station wagon models use a solid rear axle supported by semi-elliptic leaf springs.

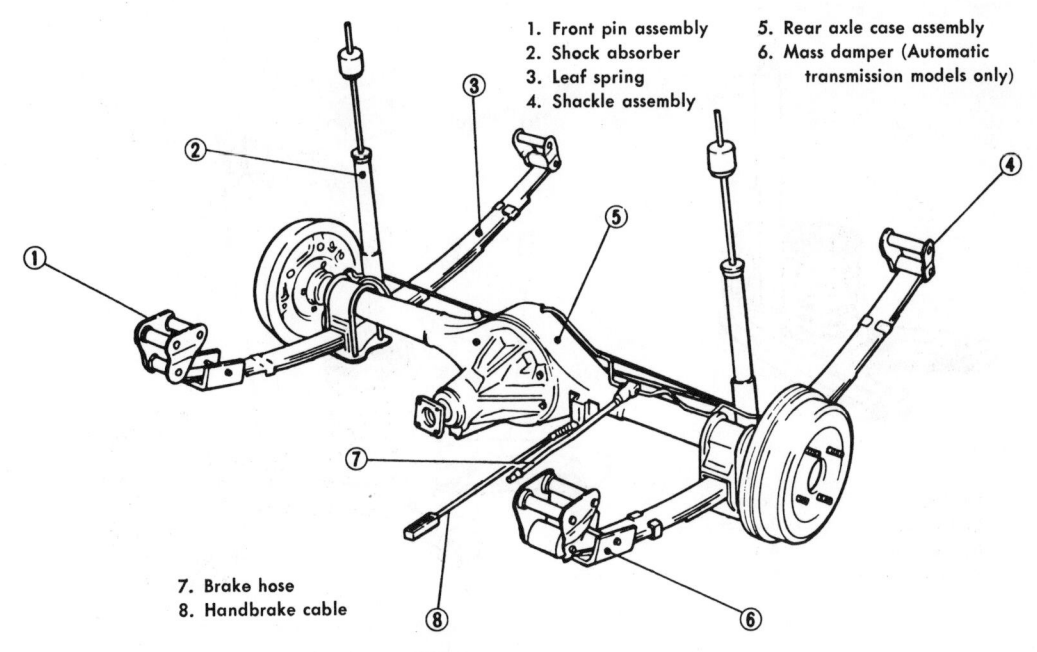

1. Front pin assembly
2. Shock absorber
3. Leaf spring
4. Shackle assembly
5. Rear axle case assembly
6. Mass damper (Automatic transmission models only)
7. Brake hose
8. Handbrake cable

200SX rear suspension

176 SUSPENSION AND STEERING

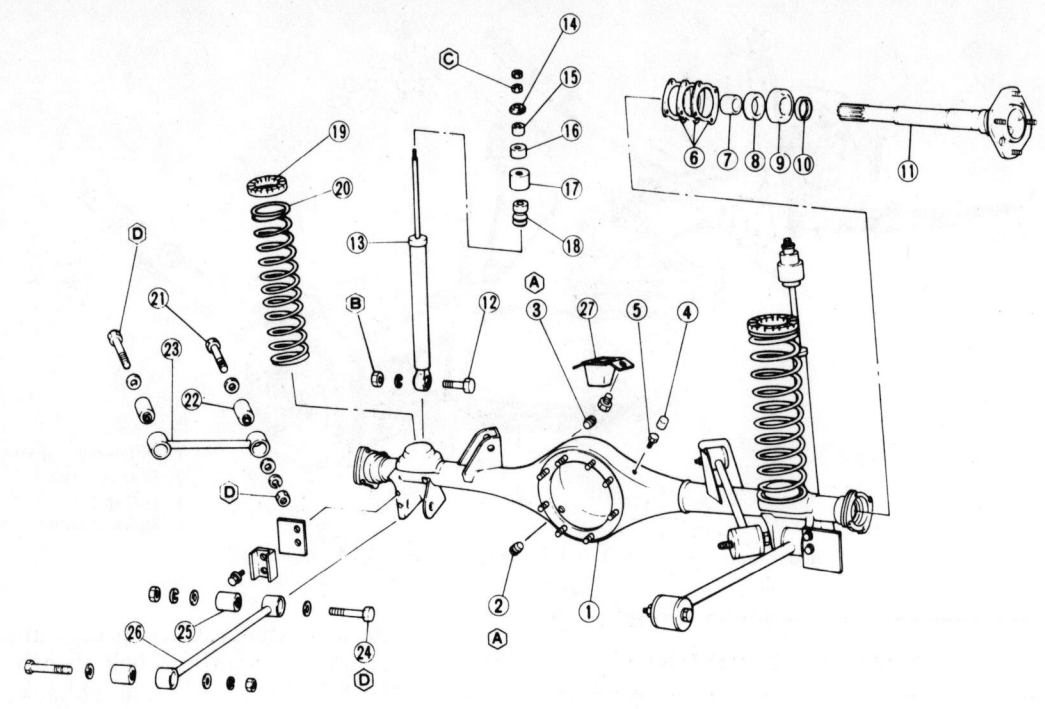

1978 510 sedan rear suspension

1. Rear axle case
2. Drain plug
3. Filler plug
4. Breather cap
5. Breather
6. Rear axle case end shim
7. Bearing collar
8. Oil seal
9. Rear axle bearing
10. Bearing spacer
11. Rear axle shaft
12. Shock absorber lower end bolt
13. Shock absorber assembly
14. Special washer
15. Shock absorber mounting bushing A
16. Shock absorber mounting bushing B
17. Bound bumper cover
18. Bound bumper rubber
19. Shock absorber mounting insulator
20. Coil spring
21. Upper link bushing bolt
22. Upper link bushing

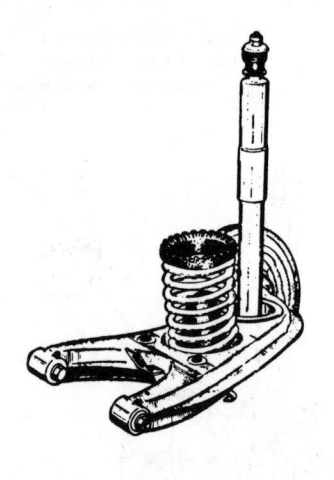

1. Rear arm
2. Coil spring
3. Rubber seat
4. Shock absorber
5. Drum
6. Bumper
7. Bushing
8. Rear arm bolt

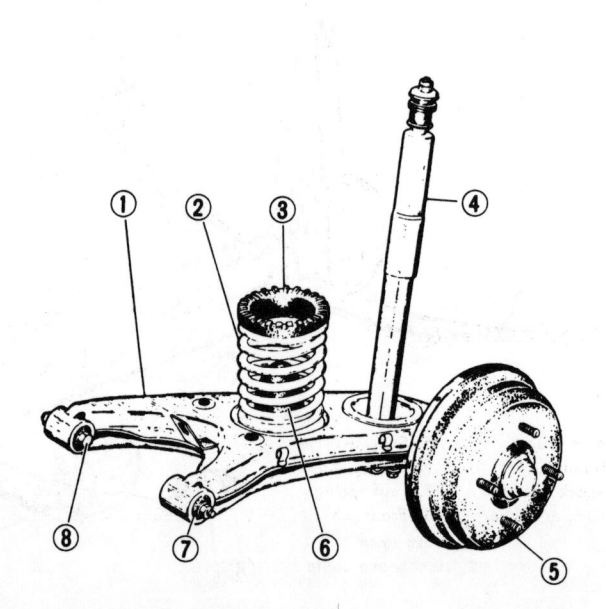

F10 sedan and hatchback rear suspension

SUSPENSION AND STEERING 177

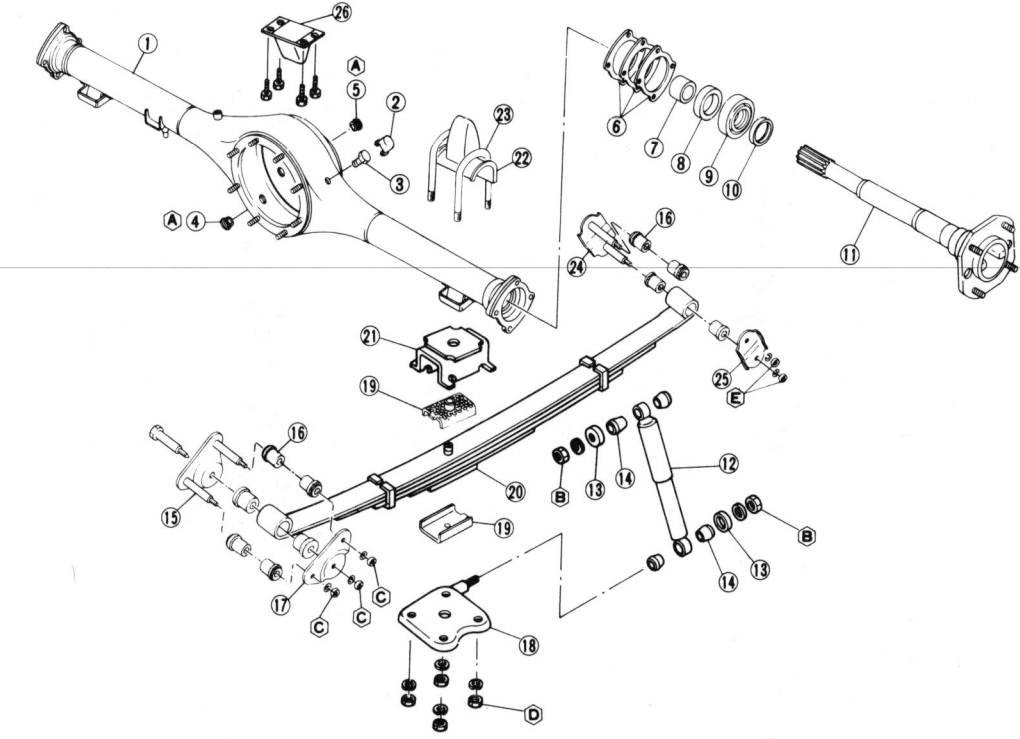

1978 510 wagon rear suspension—other wagons similar

1. Rear axle case
2. Breather cap
3. Breather
4. Drain plug
5. Filler plug
6. Rear axle case end shim
7. Bearing collar
8. Oil seal
9. Rear axle bearing
10. Bearing spacer
11. Rear axle shaft
12. Shock absorber assembly
13. Special washer
14. Shock absorber bushing
15. Front pin assembly
16. Spring bushing
17. Front pin outer plate
18. Lower spring seat
19. Spring seating pad
20. Rear spring assembly
21. Location plate
22. Rear axle bumper
23. U-bolt (Spring clip)
24. Shackle pin assembly
25. Shackle
26. Torque arrester

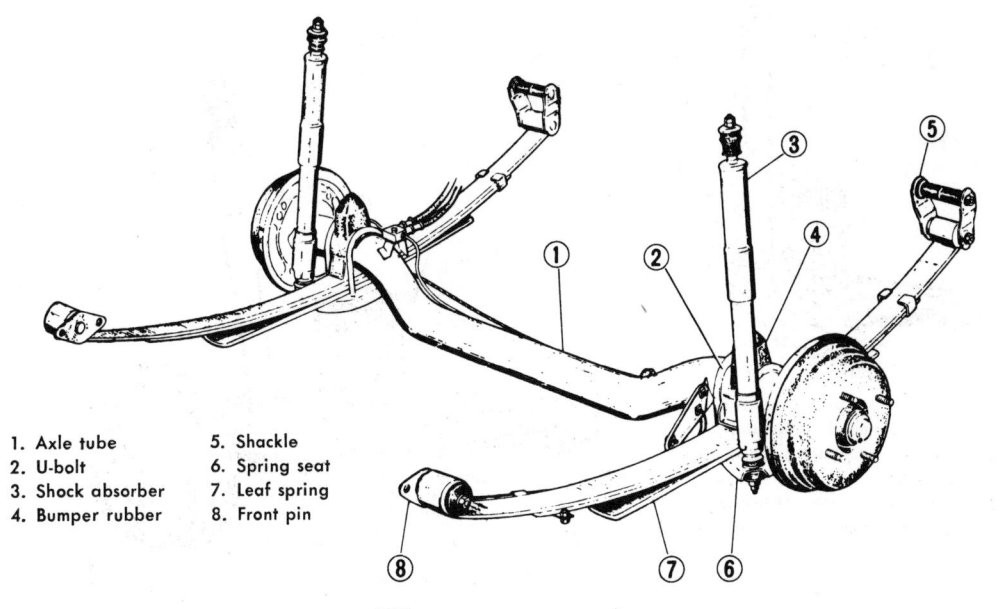

1. Axle tube
2. U-bolt
3. Shock absorber
4. Bumper rubber
5. Shackle
6. Spring seat
7. Leaf spring
8. Front pin

F10 wagon rear suspension

178 SUSPENSION AND STEERING

Exploded view—810 sedan rear suspension

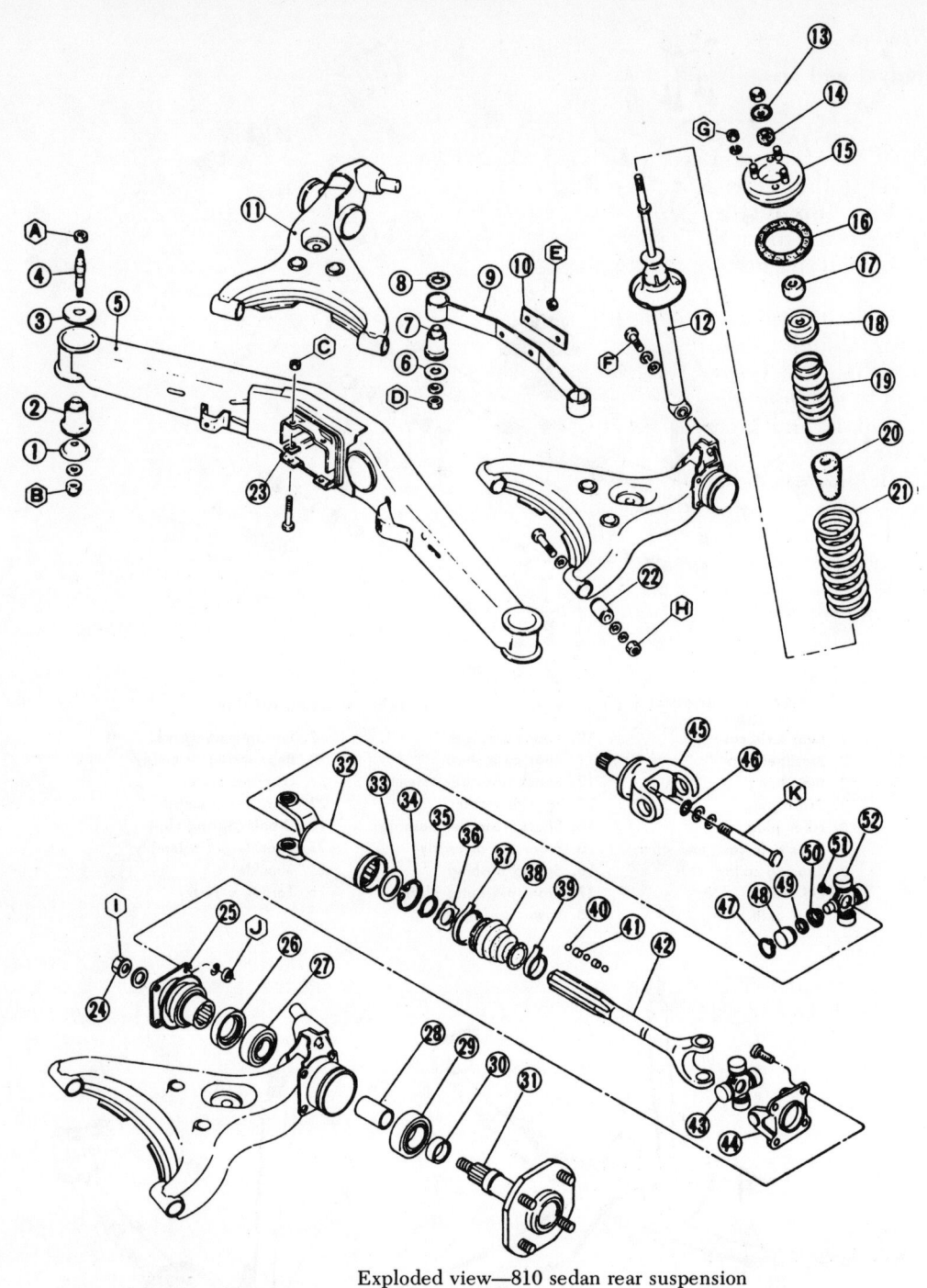

1. Member mounting lower stopper
2. Member mounting insulator
3. Member mounting upper stopper
4. Suspension mounting bolt
5. Suspension member assembly
6. Differential mounting lower stopper
7. Differential mounting insulator
8. Differential mounting upper stopper
9. Differential mounting member
10. Differential mounting plate
11. Suspension arm assembly
12. Shock absorber
13. Special washer
14. Shock absorber mounting bushing A
15. Shock absorber mounting
16. Spring seat rubber
17. Shock absorber mounting bushing B
18. Bumper cover
19. Dust cover
20. Bumper
21. Coil spring
22. Suspension arm bushing
23. Differential mounting spacer
24. Wheel bearing locknut
25. Companion flange
26. Grease seal
27. Inner wheel bearing
28. Spacer

SUSPENSION AND STEERING 179

SPRINGS
Removal and Installation
LEAF SPRING TYPE

1200 and B210

1. Raise the rear axle until the wheels hang free. Support the car on stands. Support the rear axle with a jack.
2. Unbolt the bottom end of shock absorber.
3. Unbolt the axle from the spring leaves. Unbolt and remove the front spring bracket. Lower the front of the spring to the floor.
4. Unbolt and remove the spring rear shackle.
5. Before reinstallation, coat the front bracket pin, bushing, shackle pin, and shackle bushing with a soap solution.
6. Reverse the procedure to install. The front pin nut and the shock absorber mounting should be tightened before the vehicle is lowered to the floor.

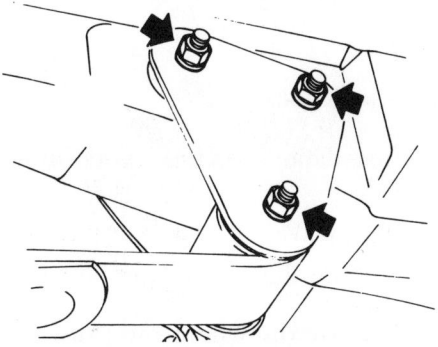

1200 and B210 front spring bracket

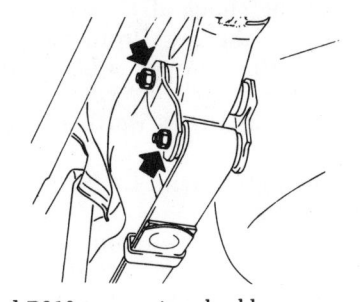

1200 and B210 rear spring shackle

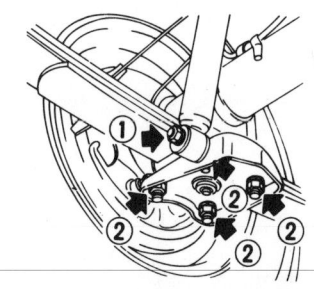

Detach lower shock absorber mount (1) and spring U-bolts (2)—1200 and B210 coupe shown

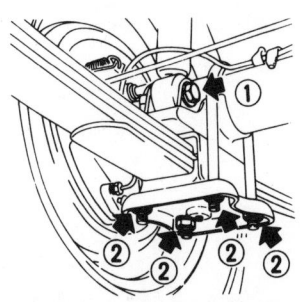

Detach lower shock absorber mount (1) and spring U-bolts (2)—1200 and B210 sedan shown

610 Station Wagon and All 710 and 200SX Models

1. Raise the rear axle until the wheels hang free. Support the car on stands. Support the rear axle with a floor jack.
2. Remove the spare tire.
3. Unbolt the bottom end of the shock absorber.
4. Unbolt the axle from the spring leaves.
5. Unbolt the front spring bracket from the body. Lower the spring end and bracket to the floor.
6. Unbolt and remove the rear shackle.
7. Unbolt the bracket from the spring.
8. Before reinstallation, coat the front bracket pin and bushing, and the shackle pin and bushing with a soap solution.
9. Reverse the procedure to install. The front pin nut and the shock absorber mounting should be tightened after the vehicle is lower to the floor. Make sure

29. Outer wheel bearing	37. Boot band (Long)	45. Side yoke
30. Bearing spacer	38. Rubber boot	46. O-ring
31. Rear axle shaft assembly	39. Boot band (Short)	47. Bearing race snap-ring
32. Sleeve yoke	40. Ball	48. Bearing race assembly
33. Sleeve yoke stopper	41. Ball spacer	49. Oil seal
34. Snap-ring	42. Driveshaft	50. Dust cover
35. Driveshaft snap-ring	43. Spider assembly	51. Filler plug
36. Driveshaft stopper	44. Flange yoke	52. Spider journal

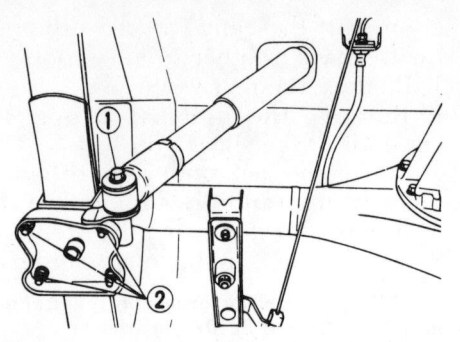

SUSPENSION AND STEERING

Detach lower shock absorber mount (1) and spring U-bolts (2)—610 station wagon and all 710 models

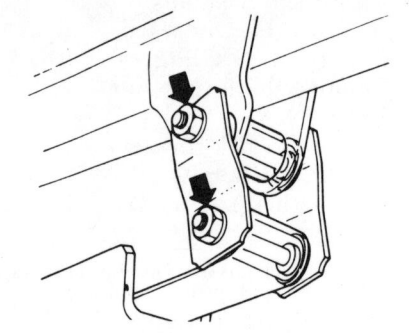

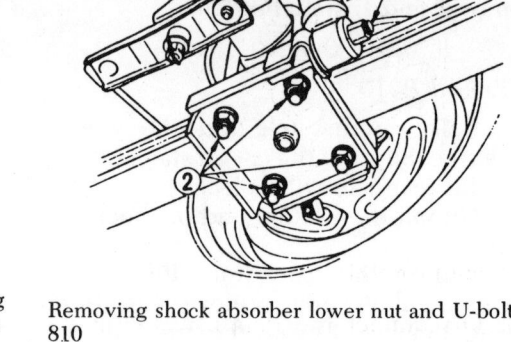

Removing shock absorber lower nut and U-bolts—810

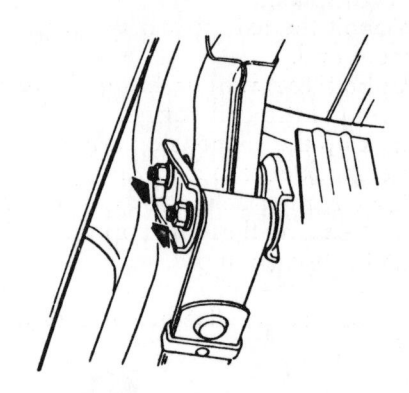

Remove spring shackle

Spring shackle bolts

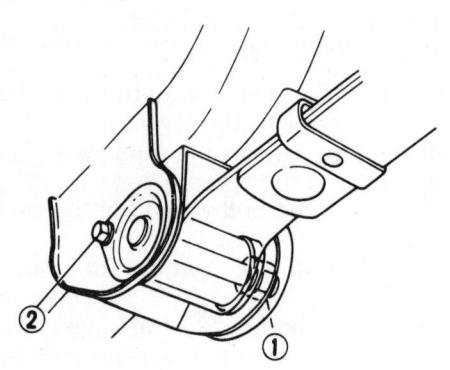

Remove spring pin by removing nuts (1) and (2)—610 station wagon and all 710 models

that the elongated flange of the rubber bumper is to the rear.

510, and 810 Station Wagons

1. Raise the rear of the car and support it with jackstands.
2. Remove the wheels and tires.
3. Disconnect the lower end of the shock absorber and remove the U-bolt nuts.
4. Place a jack under the rear axle.
5. Disconnect the spring shackle bolts at the front and rear of the spring.
6. Lower the jack slowly and remove the spring.
7. Installation is in the reverse order of removal.

F10 Station Wagon

1. Jack up the car and support it with safety stands.
2. Remove the wheel and tire.
3. Remove the nuts from the lower portion of the shock absorber.
4. Remove the nuts from the U-bolts, and detach the bumper rubbers and the spring seat.
5. Jack up the axle until it clears the leaf spring.
6. Remove the hand brake clamp from the leaf spring.
7. Remove the front pin and shackle, and detach the spring from the body.
8. Installation is in the reverse order of removal.

COIL SPRING TYPE

1973 510 and 610 Models
(except station wagon)

1. Raise the rear of the vehicle and support it on stands.
2. Remove the wheels.

SUSPENSION AND STEERING

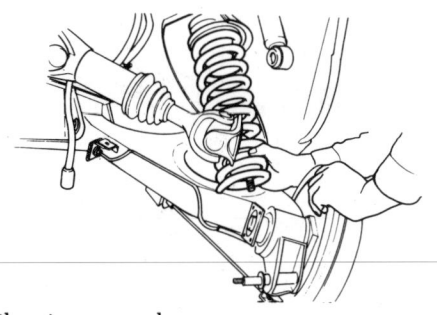

Coil spring removal

3. Disconnect the handbrake linkage and return spring.
4. Unbolt the axle driveshaft flange at the wheel end.
5. Unbolt the rubber bumper inside the bottom of the coil spring.
6. Jack up the suspension arm and unbolt the shock absorber lower mounting.
7. Lower the jack slowly and cautiously. Remove the coil spring, spring seat, and rubber bumper.
8. Reverse the procedure to install, making sure that the flat face of the spring is at the top.

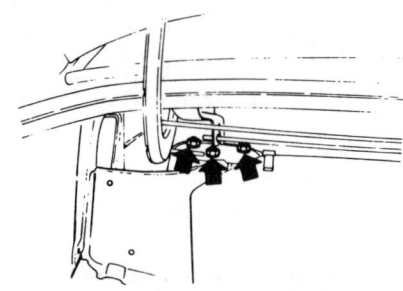

Top mounting point—810 rear shock

810 Sedan Models

1. The coil spring and shock absorber are removed as a unit. Disassembly of the unit requires a spring compressor.
2. Raise the rear of the car and support it with jackstands.
3. Open the trunk and remove the three nuts which secure the top of the shock to the body.
4. Disconnect the shock absorber at the bottom by removing the bolt at the suspension arm.
5. Installation is in the reverse order of removal.

1978 510 Sedan and Hatchback Models

1. Raise the car and support it with jackstands.

2. Support the center of the differential with a jack or other suitable tool.
3. Remove the rear wheels.
4. Remove the bolts securing the lower ends of the shock absorbers.
5. Lower the jack under the differential slowly and carefully and remove the coil springs after they are fully extended.
6. Installation is in the reverse order of removal.

F10 Sedan and Hatchback

1. Jack up the rear of the car and support it with safety stands.
2. Remove the wheels and tires.
3. Support the trailing arm with a jack.
4. Remove the upper and lower shock absorber nuts.
5. Lower the jack slowly and carefully. Remove the coil spring.
6. Installation is in the reverse order of removal.

SHOCK ABSORBER

Removal and Installation

1200 AND B210

1. Jack up the rear of the car and support the rear axle on two stands.
2. Disconnect the lower shock mounting bolt at the spring plate.
3. From inside the car, remove the rear

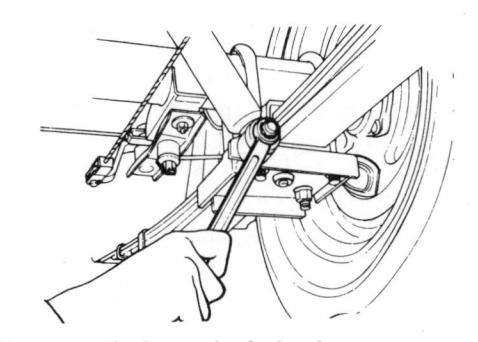

Removing the lower shock absorber nut

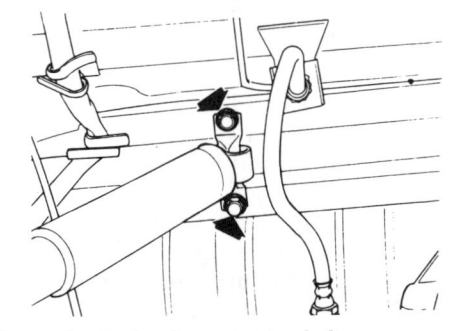

Upper shock absorber retaining bolts

SUSPENSION AND STEERING

seat back and disconnect the upper mounting nut.

4. Remove the shock absorber.

5. Install the replacement shock in the reverse of the removal procedure.

510 AND ALL 610 MODELS (EXCEPT STATION WAGON)

1. Open the trunk and remove the cover panel.

2. Remove the two nuts holding the top of the shock absorber. Unbolt the bottom of the shock absorber.

3. The shock absorbers can not be repaired. Replace them if defective.

4. Reverse the procedure to install.

610 STATION WAGON

1. Jack up the rear of the car and support the axle on stands.

2. Remove the lower retaining nut on the spring seat.

3. Remove the two upper retaining bolts.

4. Remove the shock from under the car.

5. Remove the retaining strap from the old shock and install it on the replacement shock.

6. Install the new shock in the reverse order of removal.

810 SEDAN MODELS

The shock absorber and coil spring are removed as a unit on these models. See "Spring Removal" in this chapter. Disassembly of the spring/shock unit requires a spring compressor. It is recommended that you leave this job to a professional.

ALL LEAF SPRING MODELS

1. Raise the rear of the car and support it with jackstands.

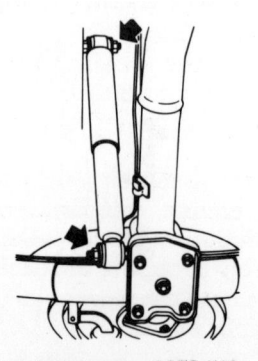

Rear shock retaining nuts—1978 510

2. Disconnect the lower end of the shock absorber by removing the nut at the spring seat. It is a good idea to spray the nut with penetrating oil first, since they have a tendency to be stubborn.

3. Remove the upper attaching nuts and remove the shock.

4. Installation is in the reverse order of removal.

Steering

STEERING WHEEL

Removal and Installation

First remove the horn button or ring. On the 1200 and B210, the horn ring is retained by two screws which can be removed from the rear of the wheel spokes. To remove the pad on the other models, press in and turn to the left. Some can be simply pulled off. Next remove the rest of the horn switching mechanism, noting the relative location of the parts. Hold the steering wheel and remove the nut. Using a puller, remove the steering wheel. Do not attempt to pry or hammer

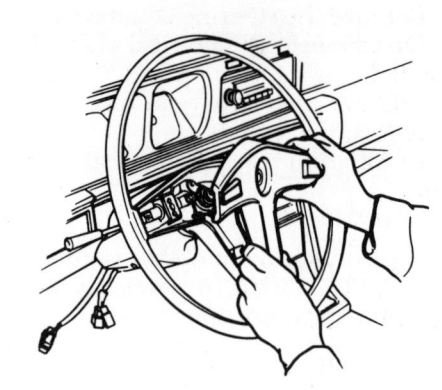

610 horn pad removal

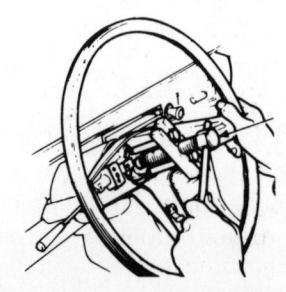

Using puller to remove the steering wheel

SUSPENSION AND STEERING

off the wheel. This is particularly important because of collapsible steering columns. When replacing the wheel, make sure that it is correctly aligned when the wheels are straight ahead. Do not drive or hammer the wheel into place. Tighten the nut while holding the wheel. Specified wheel nut torque is 22–25 ft lbs for the 1200 and B210 and 29–36 ft lbs for all other models. Reinstall the horn button, pad, or ring.

TURN SIGNAL SWITCH

Removal and Installation

1. Disconnect the battery ground cable.
2. Remove the steering wheel as previously outlined.

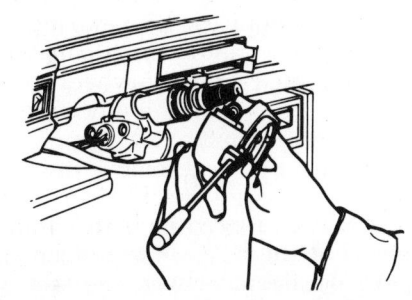

Removing the turn signal switch—610 shown

3. Remove the steering column covers.
4. Disconnect the electrical plugs from the switch.
5. Remove the two retaining screws and remove the switch.
6. Installation is the reverse of removal.

STEERING LOCK

Removal and Installation

The steering lock/ignition switch/warning buzzer assembly is attached to the steering column by special screws whose heads shear off on installation. The screws must be drilled out to remove the assembly. The ignition switch or warning switch can be replaced without removing the assembly. The ignition switch is on the back of the assembly, and the warning switch on the side. The warning buzzer, which sounds when the driver's door is opened with the steering unlocked, is located behind the instrument panel.

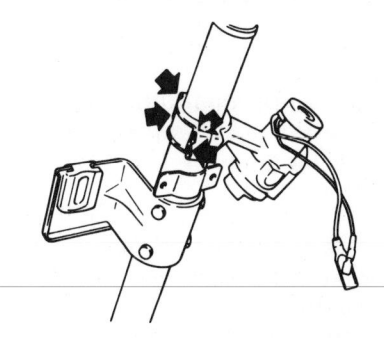

Steering lock securing screws—200SX, others similar

STEERING GEAR

Removal and Installation

510, 610, 710

1. Remove the steering shaft U-joint clamp bolt.
2. Remove the stud nut and pull the steering rod ball joint from the steering arm.
3. Unbolt the steering gear box from the frame and remove. If necessary, remove the horn button and pull the steering wheel and shaft up slightly.
4. Reverse the procedure to install. Torque the U-joint clamp bolt to 22 ft lbs or 29–36 ft lbs for the 610 and 710. If the upper and lower shaft sections of the collapsible column have been separated, the slit of the universal joint must align with the punch mark on the upper end of the upper steering shaft.

1200 AND B210

1. Remove the steering wheel.
2. Separate and remove the upper steering column shell.
3. Remove the turn signal and light switch assembly. Disconnect the automatic transmission linkage.
4. Unbolt the steering column from the instrument panel.
5. Remove the steering column hole cover from the floorboards.
6. Unbolt the steering box from the body.
7. Pull the assembly out of the car toward the engine compartment. Be extremely cautious with the collapsible column. Merely dropping or leaning on the assembly could cause enough damage to require replacement.
8. Reverse the procedure to install.

SUSPENSION AND STEERING

200SX

1. Disconnect the front exhaust pipe from the exhaust manifold.
2. Remove the bolt which secures the front exhaust pipe to the transmission mounting insulator.
3. Remove the bolt securing the worm shaft to the rubber coupling.
4. Remove the nut and lock washer which secure the gear arm to the sector shaft. Using a puller, remove the arm from the shaft.
5. Remove the three bolts securing the gear housing to the frame member and remove the gearbox.
6. Installation is in the reverse order of removal.

810

1. Remove the bolt securing the worm shaft to the rubber coupling.
2. Remove the nut and the lock washer securing the gear arm to the sector shaft.
3. Using a puller, remove the steering gear arm from the sector shaft.
4. Remove the bolts securing the gearbox to the frame member and remove the gearbox.
5. Installation is in the reverse of removal. Be sure to align the gear arm

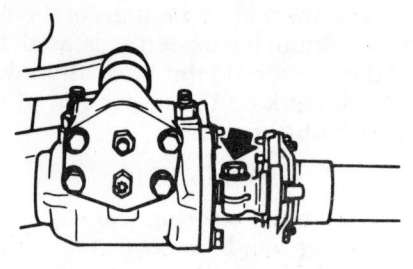

Removing the worm shaft from the rubber coupling

grooves with the serrations on the sector shaft.

1978 510

1. Remove the bolt securing the worm shaft to the rubber coupling.
2. Remove the nut and the lock washer which secure the gear arm to the sector shaft.

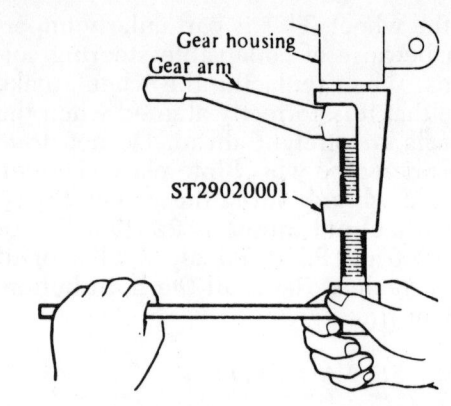

Removing the steering gear arm with a puller

3. Using a puller, remove the steering gear arm from the sector shaft.
4. Unbolt the front exhaust pipe from the exhaust manifold.
5. Remove the bolts securing the gearbox to the frame and remove the gearbox.
6. Installation is in the reverse order of removal.

F10

Since it is equipped with rack and pinion steering, the F10 has no steering gear box. An occasional check to make sure the rack bolts are tight is all that is necessary.

Adjustment—All Except F10

The adjusting screw is adjacent to the filler plug on the steering gear box cover.
1. Disconnect the steering gear arm from the steering linkage.
2. Adjust the backlash at the steering center point so that play at the end of the steering gear arm is 0–0.004 in.
3. Tighten the adjusting screw 1/8–1/6 turn more and tighten the locknut.
4. Reconnect the steering linkage. Specified linkage stud nut torque is 22–36 ft lbs for the 1200 and B210, and 40–55 ft lbs for the 510, 610, 710.
5. Maximum free-play at the steering wheel rim should be 0.79–0.98 in. for the 1200 and B210, 0.98–1.18 in. for the 510, and 1–1.4 in for all other models.

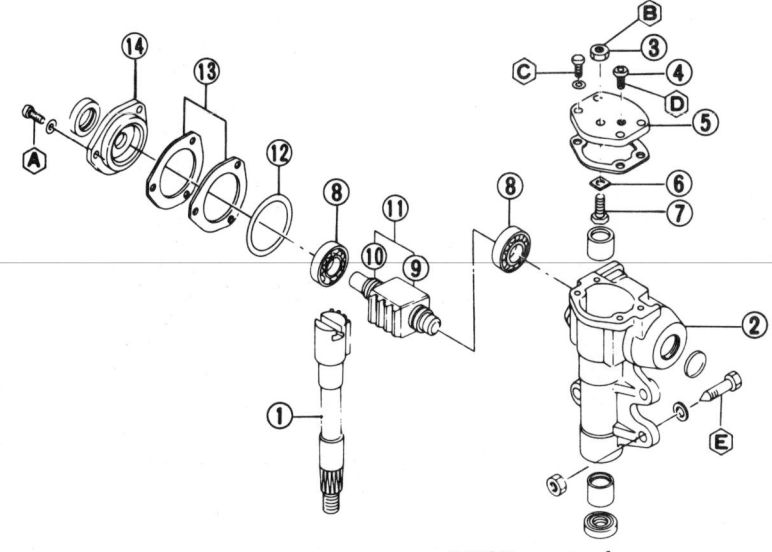

SUSPENSION AND STEERING 185

1. Sector shaft
2. Steering gear housing
3. Locknut
4. Filler plug
5. Sector shaft cover
6. Sector shaft adjusting shim
7. Sector shaft adjusting screw
8. Worm bearing
9. Ball nut
10. Worm shaft
11. Steering worm assembly
12. O-ring
13. Worm bearing shim
14. Rear cover

200SX steering box

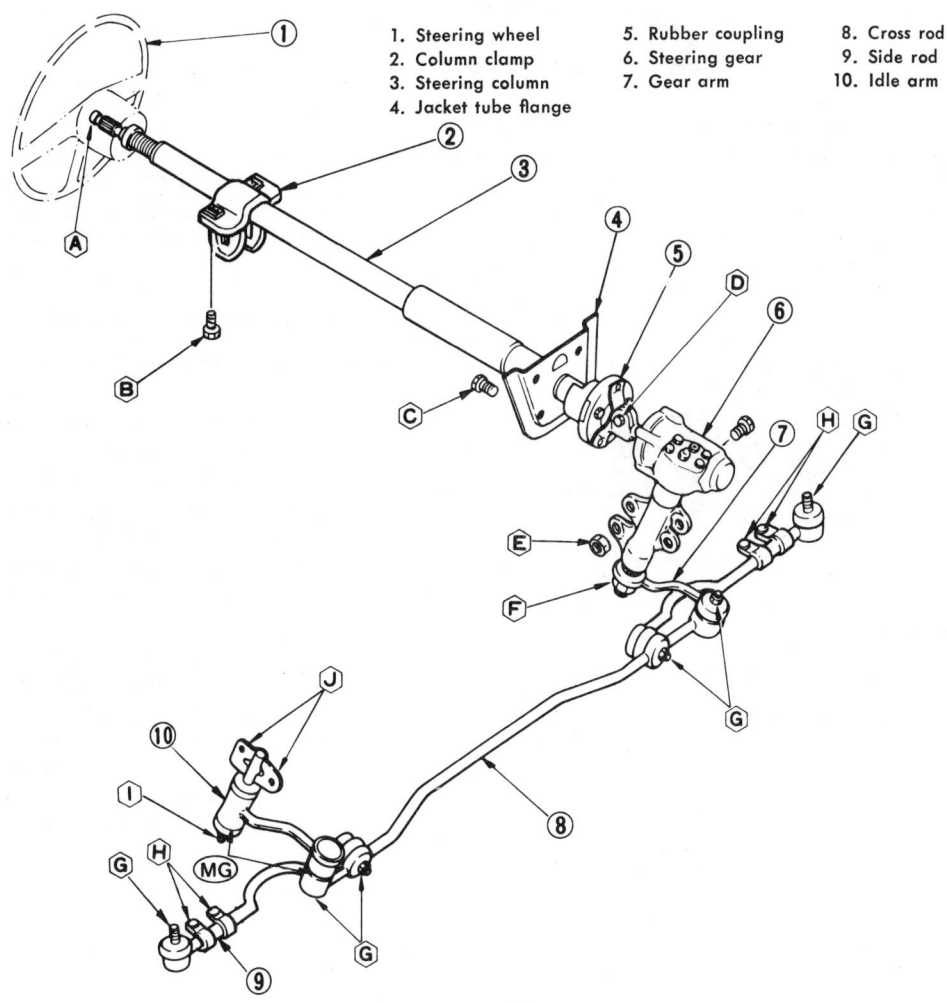

1. Steering wheel
2. Column clamp
3. Steering column
4. Jacket tube flange
5. Rubber coupling
6. Steering gear
7. Gear arm
8. Cross rod
9. Side rod
10. Idle arm

810 steering assembly

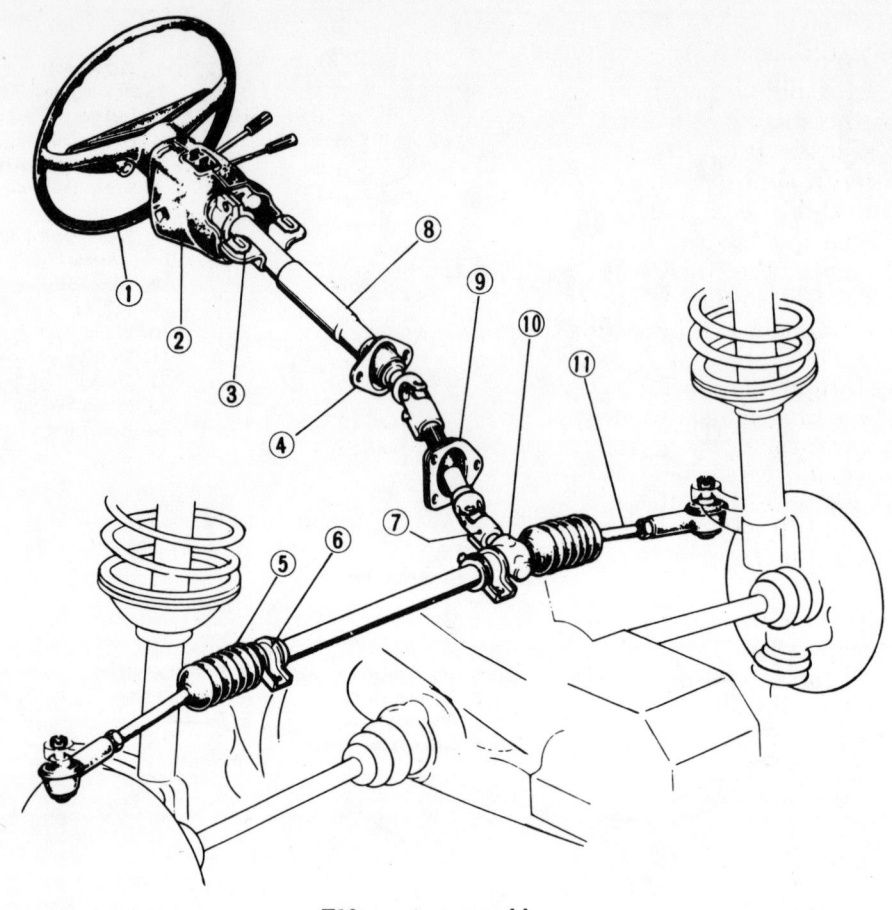

186 SUSPENSION AND STEERING

F10 steering assembly

1. Steering wheel assembly
2. Steering column cover
3. Upper clamp
4. Lower clamp
5. Steering gear boot
6. Steering clip
7. Column lower joint assembly
8. Steering column assembly
9. Column hole cover assembly
10. Steering gear assembly
11. Side rod assembly

Chapter Nine

Brakes

Brake System

ADJUSTMENT

Front disc brakes are used on all current car models, with drum brakes at the rear. All car models are equipped with independent front and rear hydraulic systems with a warning light to indicate loss of pressure in either system. The 610, 710 and B210 have a vacuum booster system to lessen required pedal pressure. The parking brake operates the rear brakes through a cable system.

NOTE: *Only the rear drum brakes require adjustment, the front disc brakes are self-adjusting.*

To adjust the brakes, raise the wheels, disconnect the handbrake linkage from the rear wheels, apply the brakes hard a few times to center the drums, and proceed as follows:

Bolt Adjuster—All Except 1973 510

Turn the adjuster bolt on the backing plate until the wheel can no longer be turned, then back off until the wheel is free of drag. Repeat the procedure on the other adjuster bolt on the same wheel. Some models may have only one adjuster bolt per wheel.

Bolt Adjuster With Click Arrangement—1973 510

The adjuster is located on the backing plate. The adjustment proceeds in clicks or notches. The wheel will often be locked temporarily as the adjuster passes over center for each click. Thus the adjuster is alternately hard and easy to turn. When the wheel is fully locked, back off 1–3 clicks.

After Adjustment—All Models

After adjusting the brakes, reconnect the handbrake linkage. Make sure that there is no rear wheel drag with the handbrake released. Loosen the handbrake adjustment if necessary.

Hydraulic System

MASTER CYLINDER

Removal and Installation

Clean the outside of the cylinder thoroughly, particularly around the cap and fluid lines. Disconnect the fluid lines and cap them to exclude dirt. Remove the clevis pin connecting the pushrod to the brake pedal arm inside the vehicle. This

187

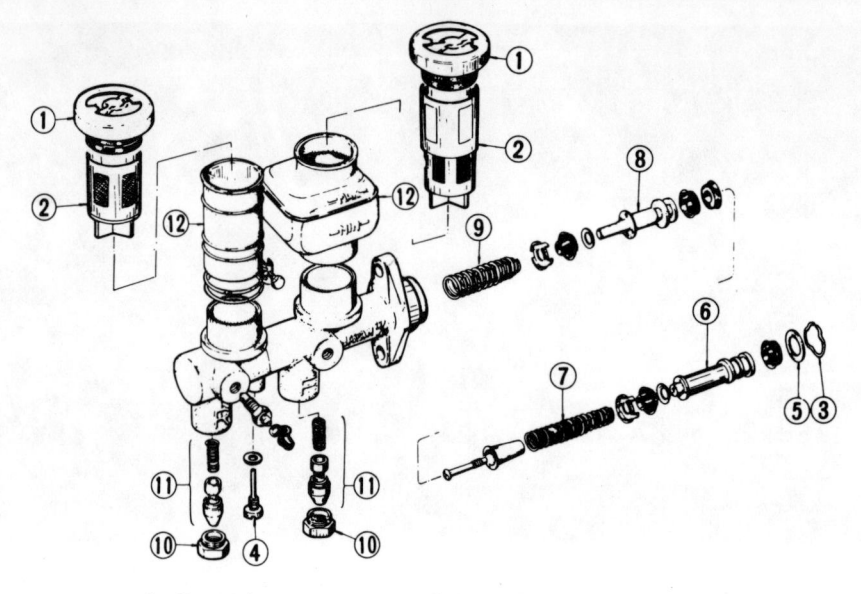

BRAKES

1 Reservoir cap
2 Filter
3 Stopper ring
4 Stopper screw
5 Stopper
6 Primary piston assembly
7 Primary piston return spring
8 Secondary piston assembly
9 Secondary piston return spring
10
11 Check valve
12 Reservoir

Exploded view of 510, 610, and 710 master cylinder

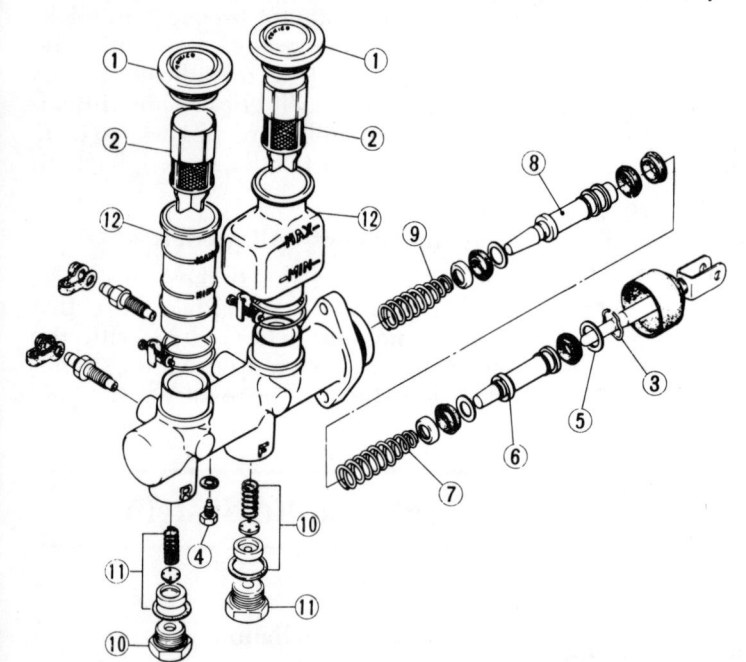

1 Reservoir cap
2 Filter
3 Stopper ring
4 Stopper screw
5 Stopper
6 Primary-piston assembly
7 Primary piston return spring
8 Secondary piston assembly
9 Secondary piston return spring
10 Plug
11 Check valve
12 Reservoir

Exploded view of 1200 and B210 master cylinder

pin need not be removed on models with the vacuum booster. Unbolt the master cylinder from the firewall and remove. The adjustable pushrod is used to adjust brake pedal free-play. After installation, bleed the system and check the pedal free-play.

NOTE: *Ordinary brake fluid will boil*

BRAKES 189

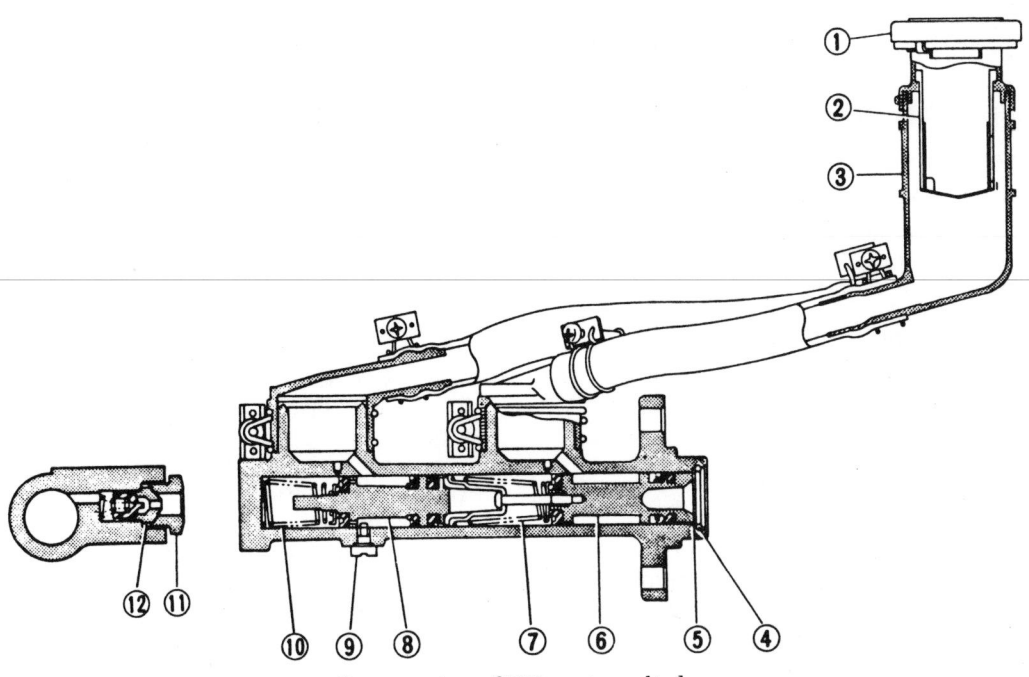

Cutaway view of F10 master cylinder

1. Reservoir cap
2. Filter
3. Reservoir tank assembly
4. Stopper ring
5. Stopper
6. Primary piston assembly
7. Primary return spring
8. Secondary piston assembly
9. Stopper screw
10. Secondary return spring
11. Plug
12. Check valve

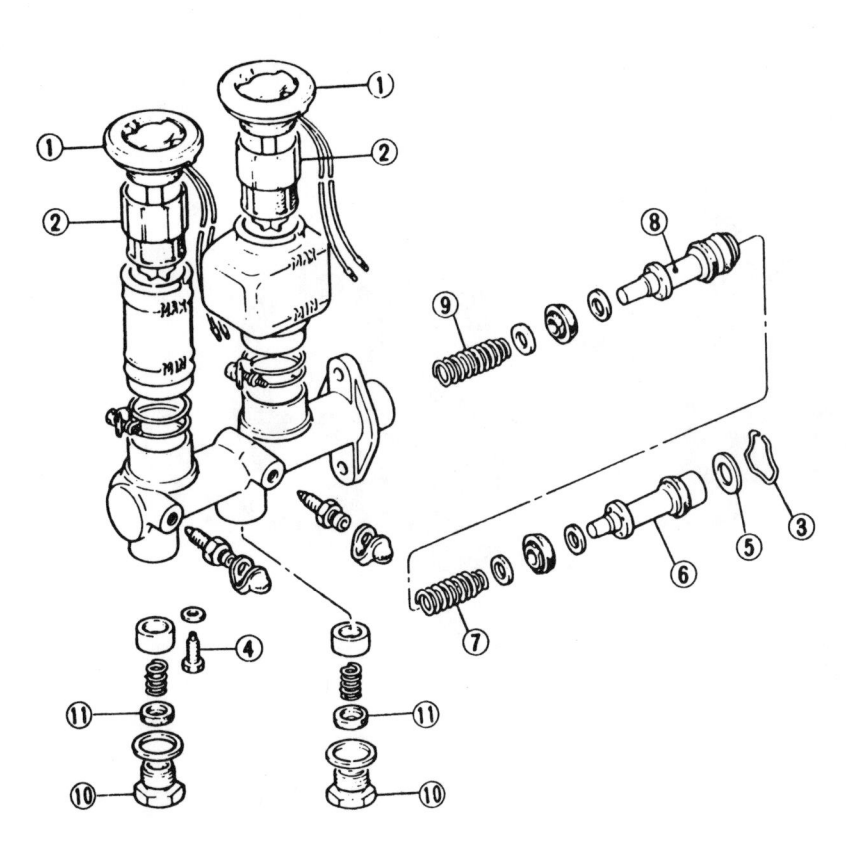

1. Reservoir cap
2. Strainer
3. Stopper ring
4. Stopper screw
5. Stopper
6. Primary piston
7. Spring
8. Secondary piston
9. Spring
10. Plug
11. Check valve

Exploded view of 810 master cylinder

190 BRAKES

and cause brake failure under the high temperatures developed in disc brake systems. DOT 3 or 4 brake fluid for disc brake systems must be used.

Overhaul

The master cylinder can be disassembled using the illustrations as a guide. Clean all parts in clean brake fluid. Replace the cylinder or piston as necessary if clearance between the two exceeds 0.006 in. Lubricate all parts with clean brake fluid on assembly. Master cylinder rebuilding kits, containing all the wearing parts, are available to simplify overhaul.

SYSTEM BLEEDING

Bleeding is required whenever air in the hydraulic fluid causes a spongy feeling pedal and sluggish response. This is almost always the case after some part of the hydraulic system has been repaired or replaced.

1. Fill the master cylinder reservoir with the proper fluid. Special fluid is required for disc brakes.
2. The usual procedure is to bleed at the points farthest from the master cylinder first.
3. Fit a rubber hose over the bleeder screw. Submerge the other end of the hose in clean brake fluid in a clear glass container. Loosen the bleeder screw.
4. Slowly pump the brake pedal several times until fluid free of bubbles is discharged. An assistant is required to pump the pedal.
5. On the last pumping stroke, hold the pedal down and tighten the bleeder screw. Check the fluid level periodically during the bleeding operation.
6. Bleed the front brakes in the same way as the rear brakes. Note that some front drum brakes have two hydraulic cylinders and two bleeder screws. Both cylinders must be bled.
7. Check that the brake pedal is now firm. If not, repeat the bleeding operation.

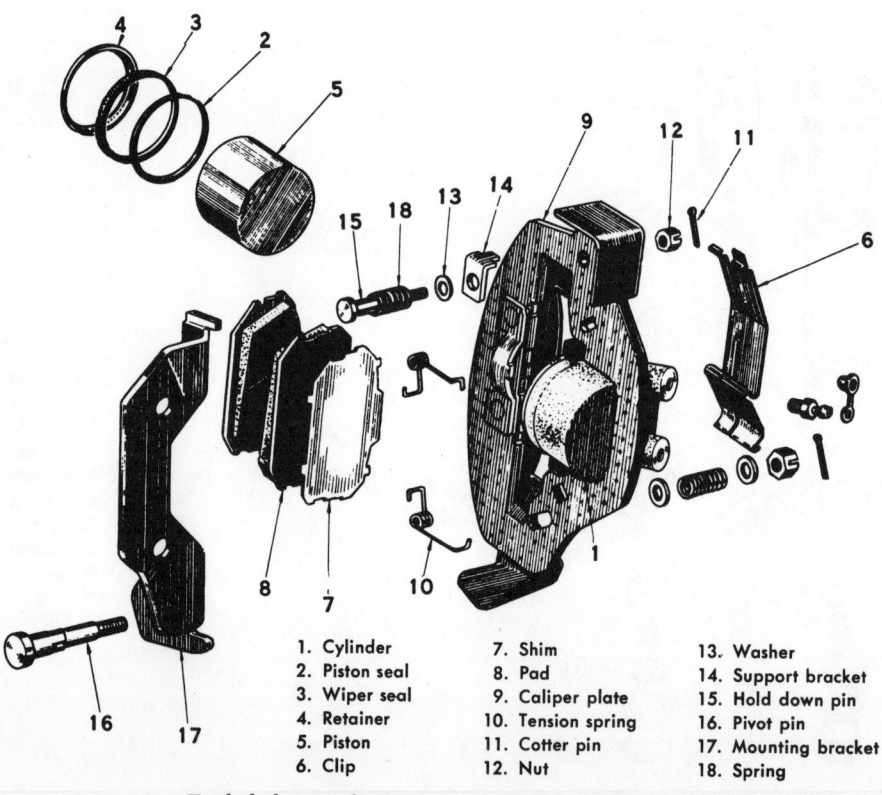

1. Cylinder
2. Piston seal
3. Wiper seal
4. Retainer
5. Piston
6. Clip
7. Shim
8. Pad
9. Caliper plate
10. Tension spring
11. Cotter pin
12. Nut
13. Washer
14. Support bracket
15. Hold down pin
16. Pivot pin
17. Mounting bracket
18. Spring

Exploded view of 510, 610, and 710 front brake caliper

Front Disc Brakes

DISC BRAKE PADS

Removal and Installation

All four front brake pads must always be replaced as a set.

510, 610, 710, AND 810

1. Jack up the car and remove the wheel.
2. Loosen the anti-rattle clip.
3. Loosen the bleed screw. Pull the caliper plate toward the outer end of the spindle and push the piston in 0.12–0.16 in. Be careful not to scratch the pistons or bores.
4. The outer pad can now be pulled out.
5. Pull the caliper plate inward and remove the inner pad.
6. Thoroughly clean the exposed end of each piston and the caliper assembly. Check the rotor (disc) for scoring. If it is badly scored, it must be removed for resurfacing or replacement.
7. If the piston has been pushed in far enough, the new pads can be installed.
8. Install the new pads. Tighten the bleeder screw.

1200, B210, F10, AND 200SX

1. Jack up the car and remove the wheel.
2. Remove the clip(s), retaining pins, and anti-squeal clips. Remove the coil spring.
3. Using pliers, pull out the pads and anti-squeal shims.
4. Thoroughly clean the exposed end of each piston and the caliper assembly. Check the rotor (disc) for scoring. If it is badly scored, it must be removed for resurfacing or replacement.
5. Before installing the new pads, the pistons must be pushed back into their cylinders. Be careful not to scratch the pistons or bores.

NOTE: *The master cylinder may overflow when the pistons are pushed back. The bleeder screw can be loosened to prevent overflow.*

Be careful not to push the pistons in too far or the seals will be damaged. The pistons need not be pushed in past a position flush with the edge of the cylinder. Install the new pads and tighten the bleeder screw if it was loosened.

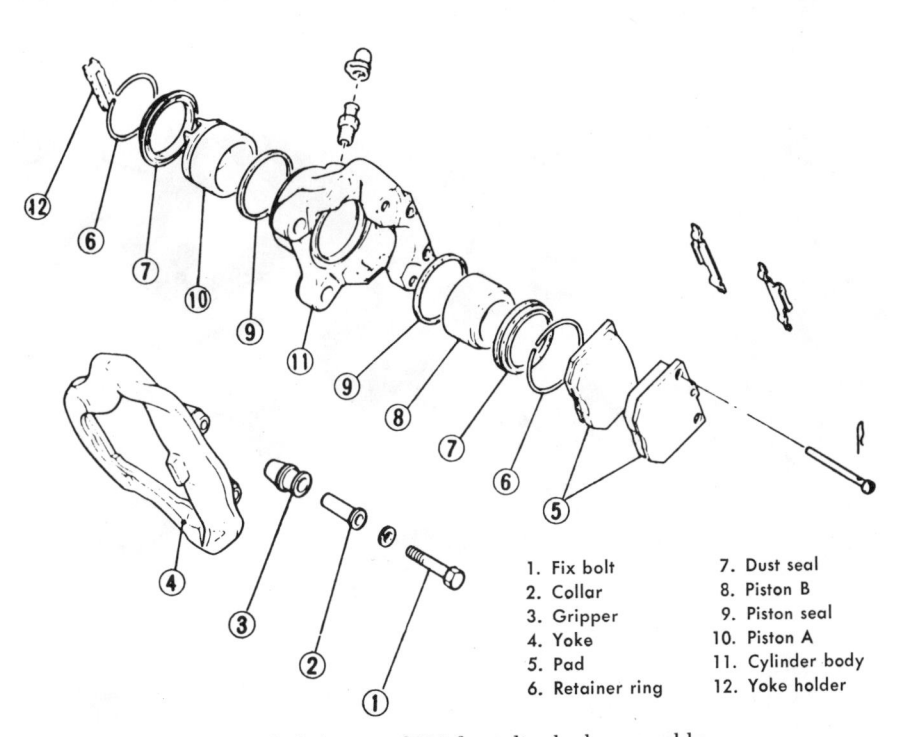

1. Fix bolt
2. Collar
3. Gripper
4. Yoke
5. Pad
6. Retainer ring
7. Dust seal
8. Piston B
9. Piston seal
10. Piston A
11. Cylinder body
12. Yoke holder

Exploded view of 810 front disc brake assembly

192 BRAKES

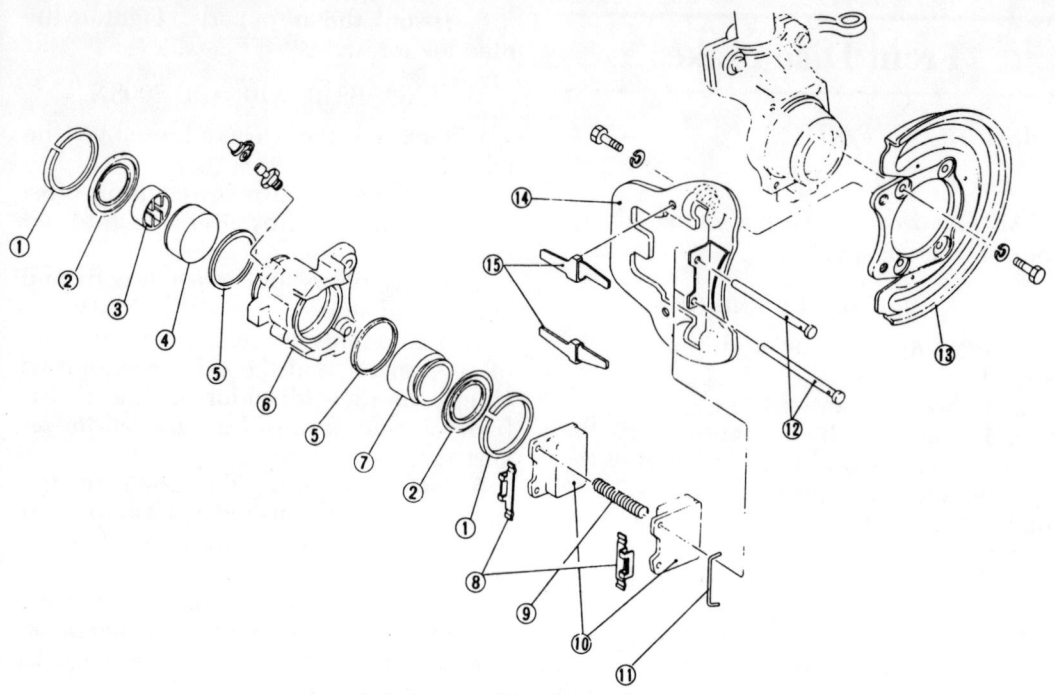

Exploded view of F10 front caliper assembly

1. Retaining ring
2. Boot
3. Bias ring
4. Piston A (inner piston)
5. Piston seal
6. Cylinder body
7. Piston B (outer piston)
8. Hanger spring
9. Spring
10. Pad
11. Clip
12. Clevis pin
13. Buffle plate
14. Yoke
15. Yoke spring

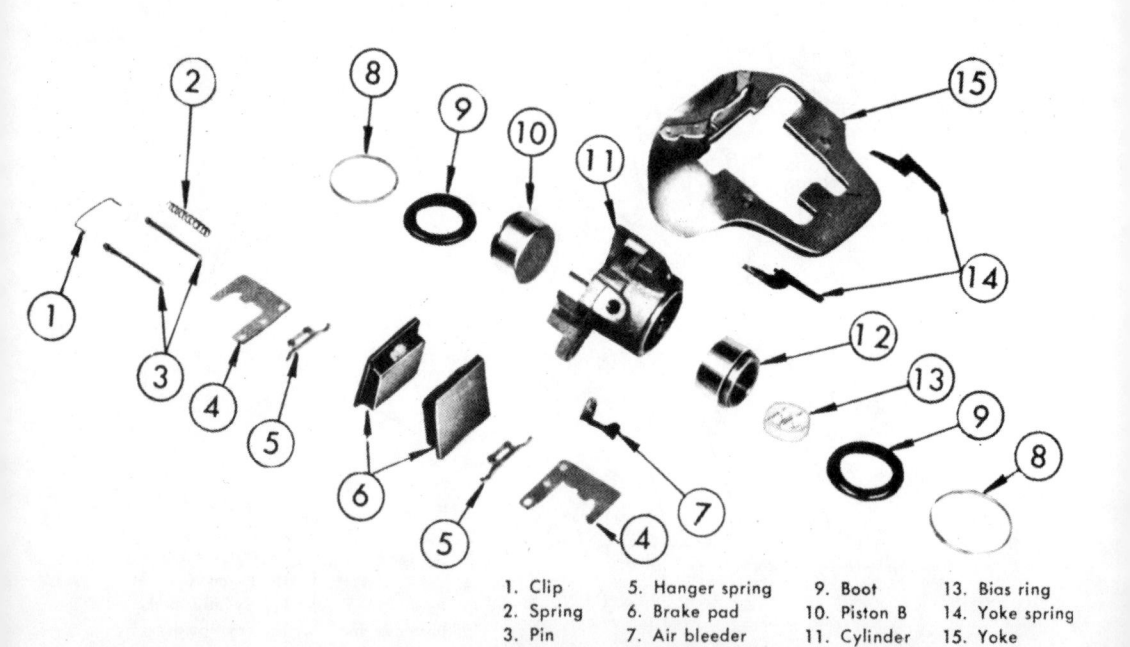

1. Clip
2. Spring
3. Pin
4. Shim
5. Hanger spring
6. Brake pad
7. Air bleeder
8. Retaining ring
9. Boot
10. Piston B
11. Cylinder
12. Piston A
13. Bias ring
14. Yoke spring
15. Yoke

Exploded view of 1200 and B210 front brake caliper

BRAKES 193

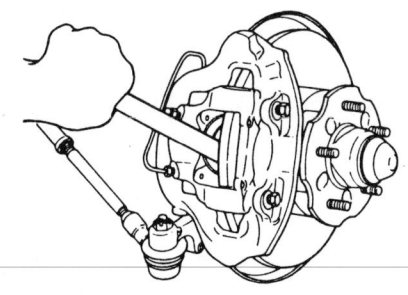

Pushing the inner piston in in order to install new pads

6. Install the anti-squeal shims with the arrow marks pointing in the direction of rotor rotation. The coil spring should be installed on the retaining pin farthest from the bleed screw.

7. Replace the wheels and pump the brake pedal a few times to seat the pads. This must be done before the car is driven.

CALIPERS AND BRAKE DISCS
Overhaul
510, 610, 710, AND 810

1. Jack up and support the car. Remove the wheel.
2. Disconnect and cap the brake hose.
3. Unbolt and remove the caliper assembly.
4. Remove the spindle nut and rotor with the hub.
5. Unbolt and remove the rotor from the hub.
6. Remove the pads. Remove the tension springs and pull out the cylinder. Apply air or hydraulic pressure to the inlet hole to remove the piston from the cylinder. Remove the retainer and seals. The piston seal also serves to retract the piston and should be replaced at every other overhaul.
7. If the rotor (disc) is scored, it can be machined. Minimum safe rotor thickness is 0.331 in. Rotor run-out must not exceed 0.004.
8. Wash all parts in clean brake fluid. Replace all seals. If the cylinder or piston is damaged, replace both.
9. Bolt the rotor to the hub, torquing the bolts to 28–38 ft lbs. Pack the bearings, install the hub on the spindle, and adjust the wheel bearing.
10. Insert a new seal in the cylinder groove and attach the wiper seal. Lubricate the cylinder bore with brake fluid. Insert the piston cautiously until the piston head is almost flush with the wiper seal retainer. The relieved part of the piston must face the pivot pin.
11. Install the cylinder into the caliper plate and secure it with the tension springs.
12. Install the hold-down pin, washer, and nut on the support bracket. Install a new cotter pin in the nut.
13. Assemble the mounting bracket and caliper plate with the pivot pin. Install the washer, spring, washer, and nut. Tighten the nut completely and lock it with a cotter pin.
14. Install the caliper assembly to the spindle, torquing the mounting bolts to 53–65 ft lbs. Make sure that the caliper plate can slide smoothly.
15. Install the pads and shims, making sure that they are seated correctly. Seat the inner pad first. Make sure that the antirattle clip is positioned correctly.
16. Reconnect the brake hose and bleed the system.

1200, B210, AND 200SX

1. Remove the pads.
2. Remove the brake tube.
3. Remove the two bottom strut assembly installation bolts to obtain clearance.
4. Remove the caliper assembly mounting bolts.
5. Loosen the bleeder screw and press the pistons into the cylinder.
6. Clamp the yoke in a vise and tap the yoke head with a hammer to loosen the cylinder. Be careful that piston A does not fall out.
7. Remove the bias ring from piston

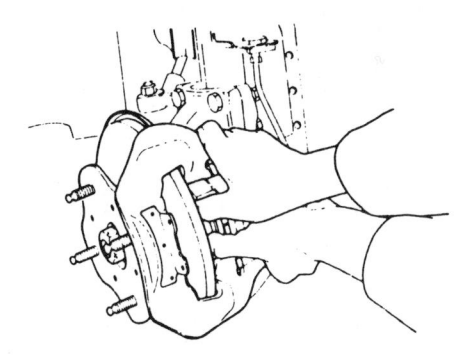

Pushing the piston in

BRAKES

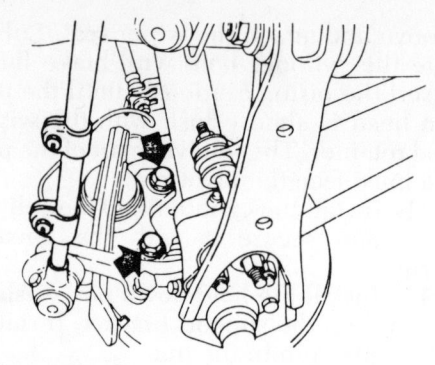

Caliper removal

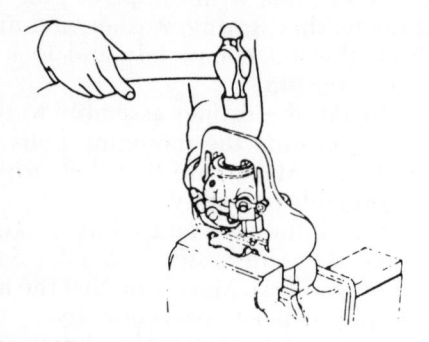

Tapping the yoke head with a hammer

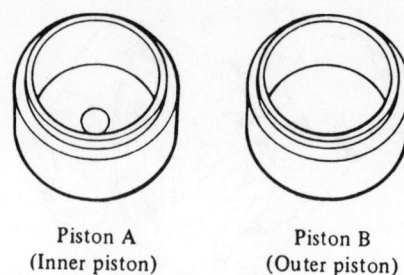

Piston A (Inner piston)

Piston B (Outer piston)

Piston comparison (inner and outer)

A. Remove the retaining rings and boots from both pistons. Depress and remove the pistons from the cylinder. Remove the piston seal from the cylinder carefully with the fingers so as not to mar the cylinder wall.

8. Remove the yoke springs from the yoke.
9. Wash all parts with clean brake fluid.
10. If the piston or cylinder is badly worn or scored, replace both. The piston surface is plated and must not be polished with emery paper. Replace all seals. The rotor can be removed and machined if scored, but final thickness must be at least 0.331 in. Run-out must not exceed 0.001 in.
11. Lubricate the cylinder bore with clean brake fluid and install the piston seal.
12. Insert the bias ring into piston A so that the rounded ring portion comes to the bottom of the piston. Piston A has a small depression inside, while B does not.
13. Lubricate the pistons with clean brake fluid and insert into the cylinder. Install the boot and retaining ring. The yoke groove of the bias ring of piston A must align with the yoke groove of the cylinder.
14. Install the yoke springs to the yoke so the projecting portion faces to the disc (rotor).
15. Lubricate the sliding portion of the cylinder and yoke. Assemble the cylinder and yoke by tapping the yoke lightly.
16. Replace the caliper assembly and pads. Torque the mounting bolts to 33–41 ft lbs. Rotor bolt torque is 20–27 ft lbs. Strut bolt torque is 33–44 ft lbs. Bleed the system of air.

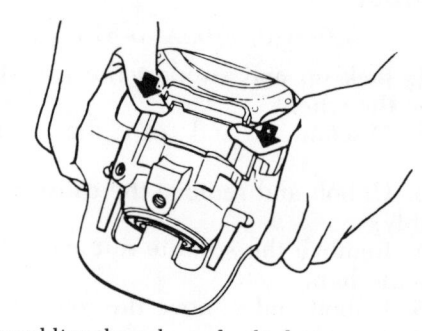

Assembling the yoke and cylinder

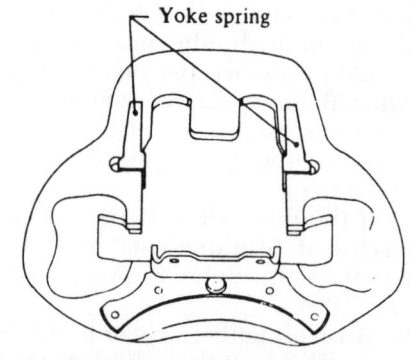

Yoke spring

Yoke showing yoke springs

F10

The F10 hub and rotor are removed as an assembly. See Chapter 8 for F10 hub removal. F10 caliper overhaul is the same as the 1200, B210, and 200SX.

BRAKES

WHEEL BEARING ADJUSTMENT

The factory procedure for wheel bearing adjustment is of little use to the backyard mechanic, since it involves the use of a spring scale, an inch pound torque wrench, and a ft lb torque wrench. For the following procedure, you will only need the ft lb torque wrench.

1. Jack up the car and remove the wheel.
2. Remove the hub cap and the cotter pin.
3. Torque the spindle nut to:

Model	Torque (ft lbs)
510, 610, 710, 200SX, F10, 810	18–25
1200 and B210	16–18

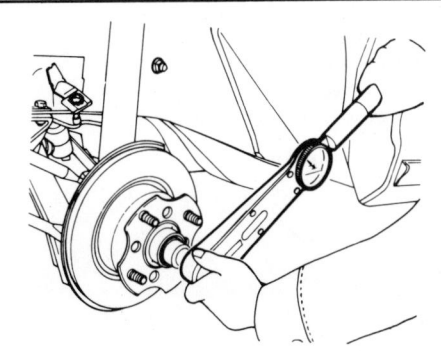

Tightening hub nut with torque wrench

4. Turn the hub a few turns in either direction and check the torque on the nut.
5. Loosen the nut to the nearest cotter pin hole and insert the cotter pin. Do not back the nut up any farther than 15 degrees.
6. Reinstall the tire and wheel and rotate the whole assembly. There should

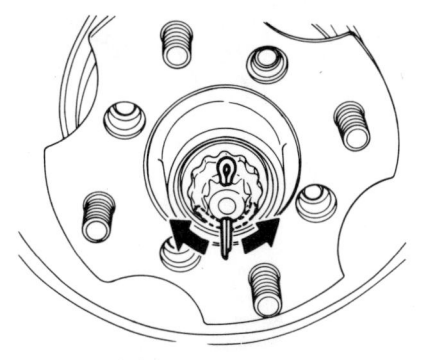

Split and spread the cotter pin

be no roughness or binding. Grasp the top of the wheel and move it in and out. There should be negligible play. If there is excessive play, the wheel bearing must be retightened. If roughness persists, check the wheel bearing condition.

7. Reinstall the cap and lower the car.

Rear Drum Brakes

BRAKE SHOES
Removal and Installation

510, 610, 710, 810, AND 200SX

1. Raise the vehicle and remove the wheels.
2. Release the parking brake. Disconnect the cross rod from the lever of the brake cylinder. Remove the brake drum. Place a heavy rubber band around the cylinder to prevent the piston from coming out.
3. Remove the return springs and shoes.
4. Clean the backing plate and check the wheel cylinder for leaks. To remove the wheel cylinder, remove the brake line, dust cover, plates, and adjusting shims. Clearance between the cylinder and the piston should not exceed 0.006 in.
5. The drums must be machined if scored or out of round more than 0.002 in. The drum inside diameter should not be machined beyond 9.04 in. Minimum safe lining thickness is 0.059 in.
6. Hook the return springs into the new shoes. The springs should be between the shoes and the backing plate. The longer return spring must be adjacent to the wheel cylinder. A very thin film of grease may be applied to the pivot points at the ends of the brake shoes. Grease the shoe locating buttons on the backing plate, also. Be careful not to get grease on the linings or drums.
7. Place one shoe in the adjuster and piston slots, and pry the other shoe into position.
8. Replace the drums and wheels. Adjust the brakes. Bleed the hydraulic system of air if the brake lines were disconnected.
9. Reconnect the handbrake, making

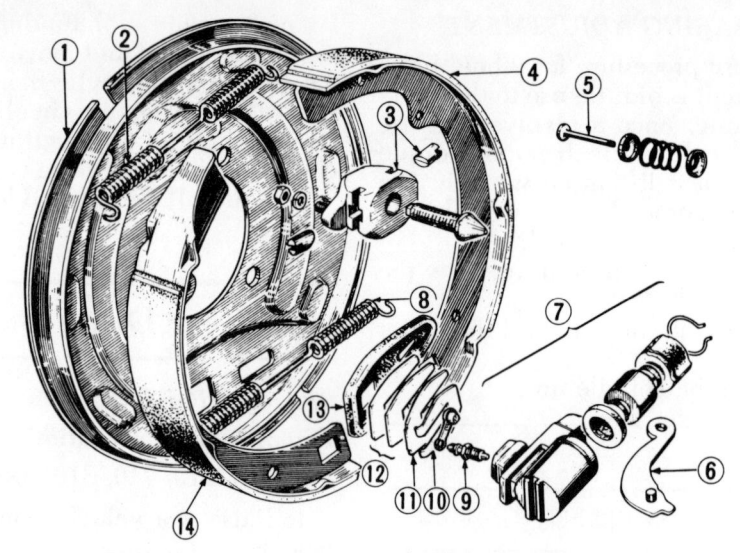

196 BRAKES

1	Brake disc	8	Return spring cylinder side
2	Return spring adjuster side	9	Bleeder
3	Brake shoe adjuster	10	Lock plate A
4	Brake shoe assembly-fore	11	Lock plate B
5	Anti-rattler pin	12	Lock plate C and D
6	Lever	13	Dust cover
7	Rear wheel cylinder	14	Brake shoe assembly-after

Exploded view of 510, 610, and 710 rear brake

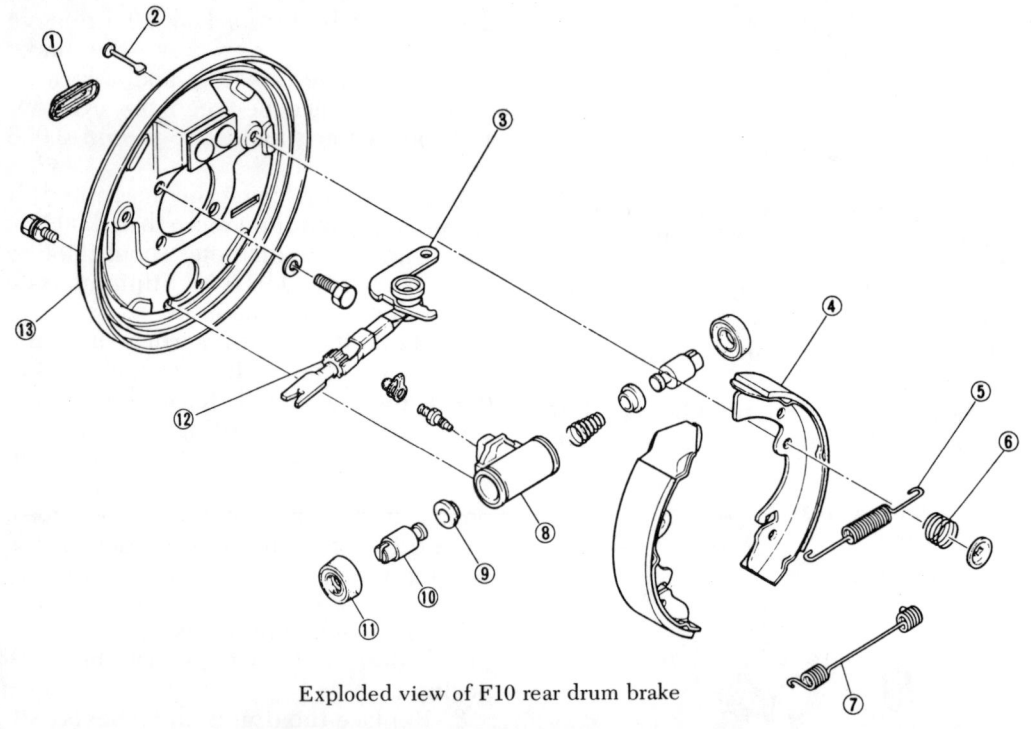

Exploded view of F10 rear drum brake

1.	Dust cover	6.	Shoe fixing spring
2.	Shoe fixing pin	7.	Return spring
3.	Lever assembly	8.	Wheel cylinder body
4.	Shoe	9.	Piston cup
5.	Return spring		
10.	Piston		
11.	Dust cover		
12.	Adjust nut		
13.	Brake disc		

BRAKES 197

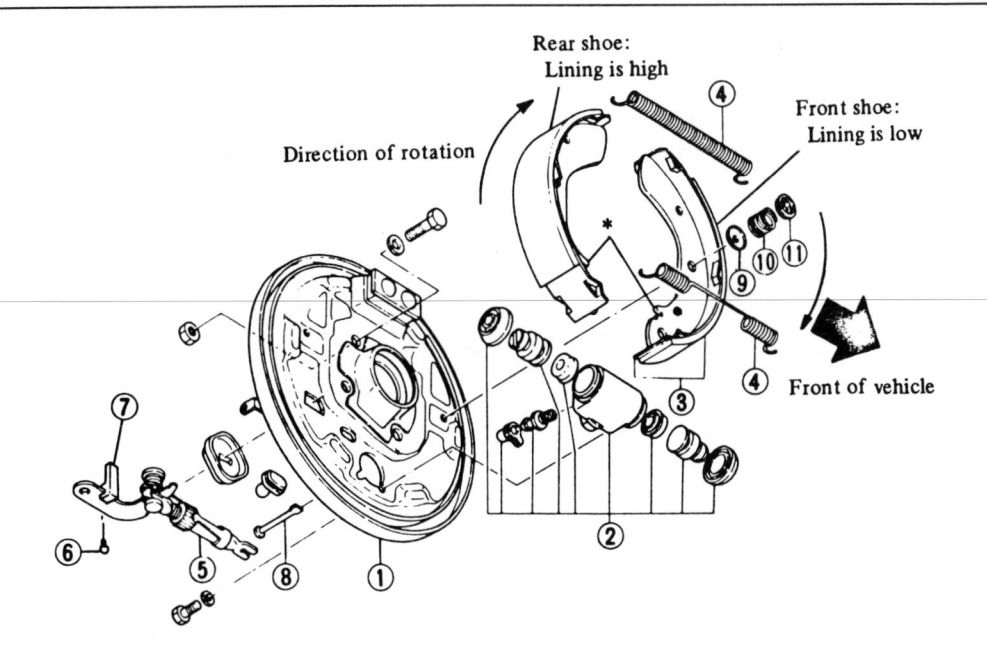

Rear shoe: Lining is high
Front shoe: Lining is low
Direction of rotation
Front of vehicle

*Both adjuster location holes are at the bottom

Exploded view of 200SX rear drum brake

1. Brake disc
2. Wheel cylinder assembly
3. Brake shoe assembly
4. Return spring
5. Adjuster assembly
6. Stopper pin
7. Stopper
8. Anti-rattle pin
9. Spring seat
10. Anti-rattle spring
11. Retainer

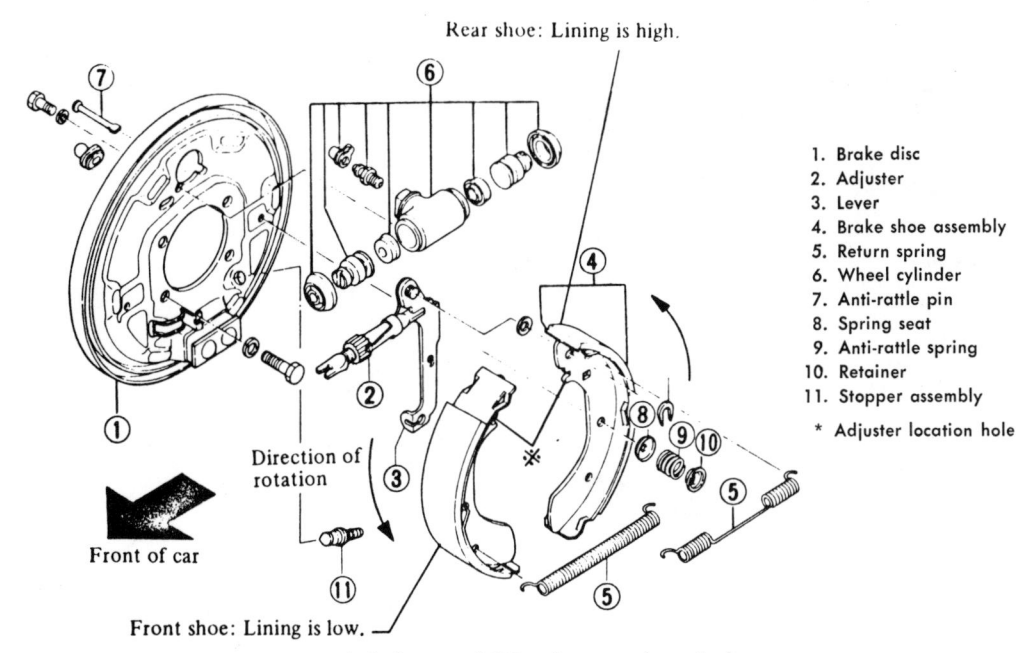

Rear shoe: Lining is high.

Direction of rotation

Front of car

Front shoe: Lining is low.

1. Brake disc
2. Adjuster
3. Lever
4. Brake shoe assembly
5. Return spring
6. Wheel cylinder
7. Anti-rattle pin
8. Spring seat
9. Anti-rattle spring
10. Retainer
11. Stopper assembly

* Adjuster location hole

Exploded view of 810 sedan rear drum brake

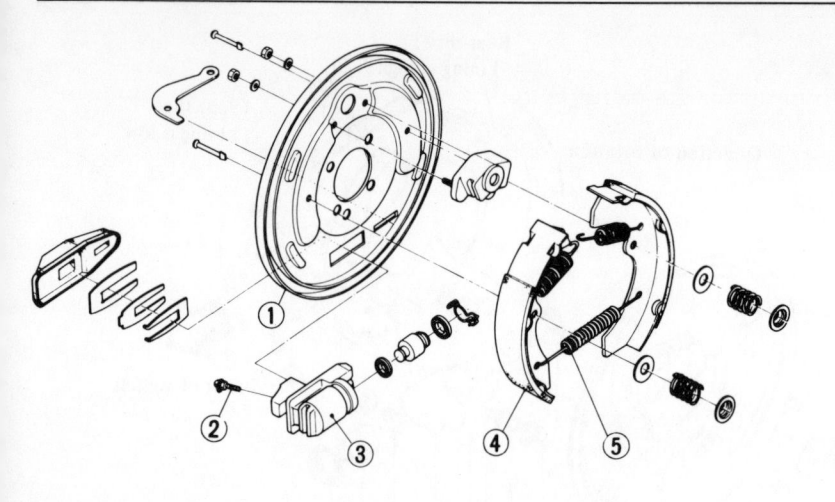

BRAKES

Exploded view of 1200 and B210 rear brake

1 Brake disc
2 Bleeder
3 Wheel cylinder
4 Shoe assembly
5 Return spring

sure that it does not cause the shoes to drag when it is released.

1200, B210, AND F10

1. Raise the vehicle and remove the wheels.
2. Loosen the handbrake cable, remove the clevis pin from the wheel cylinder lever, disconnect the handbrake cable, and remove the return pull spring.
3. Remove the brake drum, shoe retainers, return springs, and brake shoes. Loosen the brake adjusters if the drums are difficult to remove. Place a heavy rubber band around the cylinder to prevent the piston from coming out.
4. Clean the backing plate and check the wheel cylinder for leaks. To remove the wheel cylinder, remove the brake line, dust cover, plates, and adjusting shims. Clearance between cylinder and piston should not exceed 0.006 in.
5. The drums must be machined if scored or out-of-round more than 0.001 in. The drum inside diameter must not be machined beyond 8.04 in. Minimum safe lining thickness is 0.059 in.
6. Follow Steps 6–9 for 510, 610, 710, and 810.

Parking Brake

Adjustment

Handbrake adjustments are generally not needed, unless the cables have stretched.

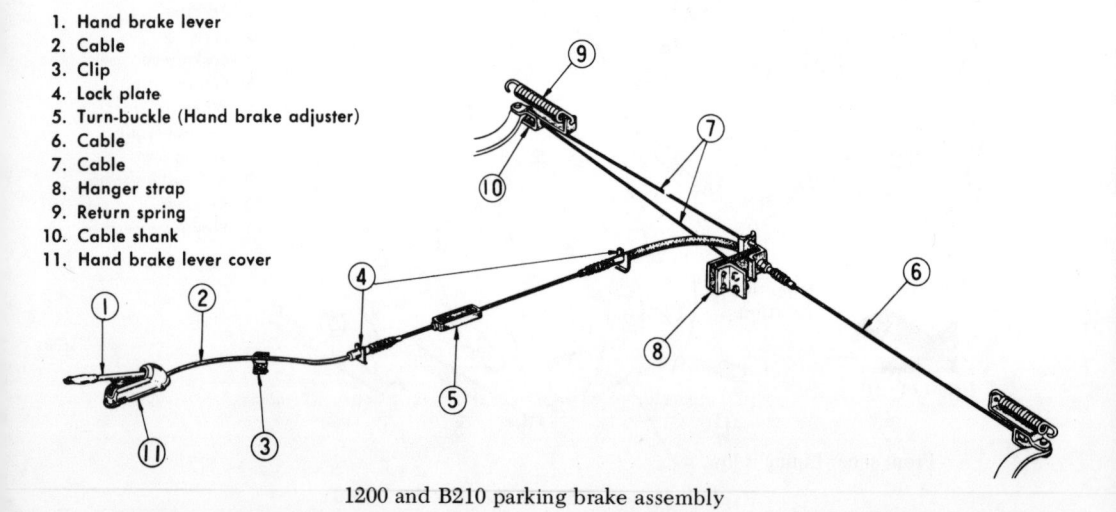

1. Hand brake lever
2. Cable
3. Clip
4. Lock plate
5. Turn-buckle (Hand brake adjuster)
6. Cable
7. Cable
8. Hanger strap
9. Return spring
10. Cable shank
11. Hand brake lever cover

1200 and B210 parking brake assembly

BRAKES 199

ALL MODELS

There is an adjusting nut on the cable under the car, usually at the end of the front cable and near the point at which the two cables from the rear wheels come together (the equalizer). Some models also have a turnbuckle in the rear cable to compensate for cable stretching.

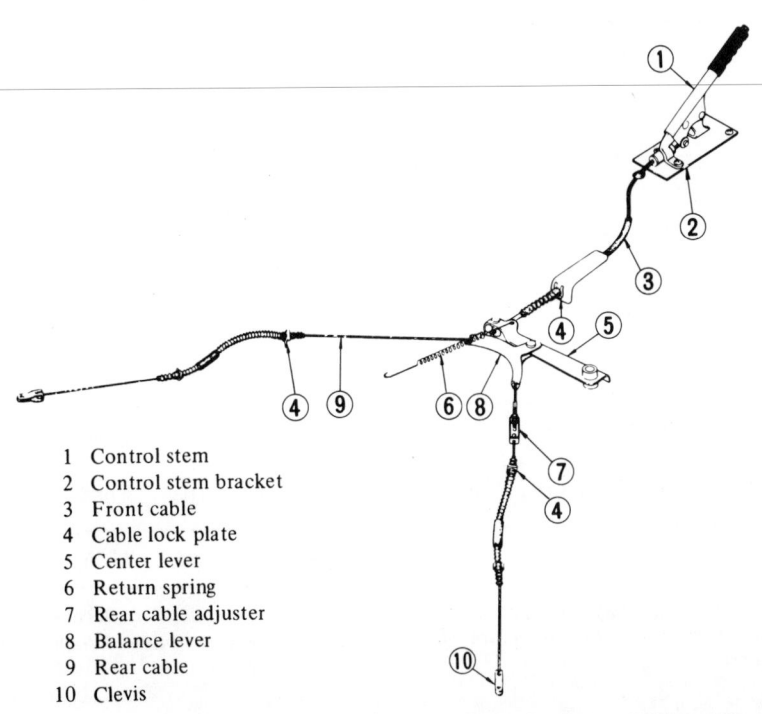

1. Control stem
2. Control stem bracket
3. Front cable
4. Cable lock plate
5. Center lever
6. Return spring
7. Rear cable adjuster
8. Balance lever
9. Rear cable
10. Clevis

510 and 610 (except station wagon) parking brake assembly

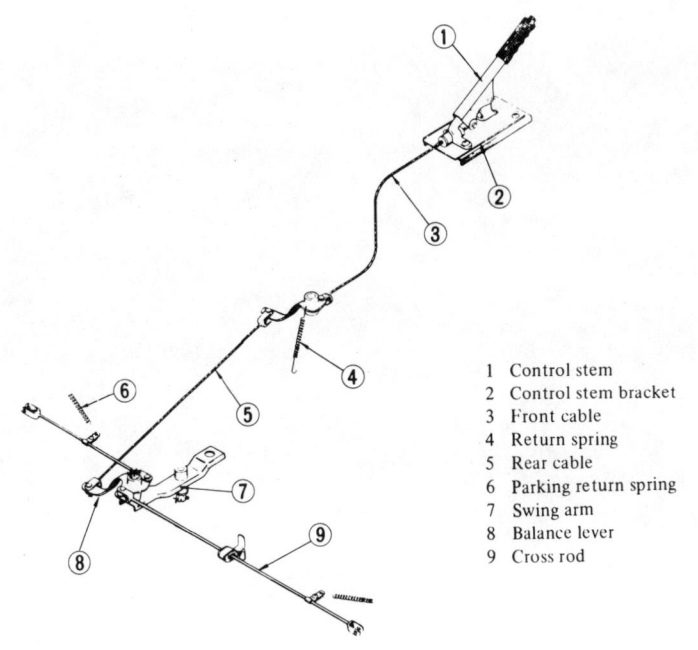

1. Control stem
2. Control stem bracket
3. Front cable
4. Return spring
5. Rear cable
6. Parking return spring
7. Swing arm
8. Balance lever
9. Cross rod

610 station wagon and all 710 models—parking brake assembly—others similar

Brake Specifications
All measurements given are (in.) unless noted

	Model	Lug Nut Torque (ft/lb)	Master Cylinder Bore	Brake Disc Minimum Thickness	Brake Disc Maximum Run-Out	Brake Drum Diameter	Brake Drum Max Machine O/S	Brake Drum Max Wear Limit	Minimum Lining Thickness Front	Minimum Lining Thickness Rear
1973	510	58–65	0.750	0.331	0.0047	9.0	9.04	9.093	0.059 (drum) 0.04 (disc)	0.059
	610	58–65	0.750	0.331	0.0047	9.0	9.04	9.055	0.079	0.059
	1200, B210	58–65	0.750	0.331	0.0039	8.0	8.04	8.051	0.063	0.059
	710	58–65	0.750	0.331	0.0047	9.0	9.04	9.055	0.079	0.059
	F10	58–65	0.750	0.339	0.0047	8.0	8.04	8.051	0.063	0.039
	810	58–65	0.8125	0.413	0.0059	9.0	9.04	9.055	0.079	0.059
1978	510	58–65	0.8125	0.331	0.0047	9.0	9.04	9.055	0.079	0.059
	200SX	58–65	0.750	0.331	0.0047	9.0	9.04	9.055	0.079	0.059

NOTE: *Minimum lining thickness is as recommended by the manufacturer. Because of variations in state inspection regulations, the minimum allowable thickness may be different than recommended by the manufacturer.*

Chapter Ten

Body

Doors

Removal and Installation

ALL MODELS

1. Remove the doors with the hinges attached.
NOTE: *On B210 models, it is necessary to first remove the front fender when removing the front door. On 610 and 710 models, it is also necessary to remove the front bumper, valance panel, windshield wiper blades, cowl top grille, and sill molding.*
2. Remove the package tray.
3. Remove the hinge access hole cover from the dash side trim on 1200 models.
4. Open the door and support it with a jack.
5. Remove the hinge bolts at the body side and remove the door.

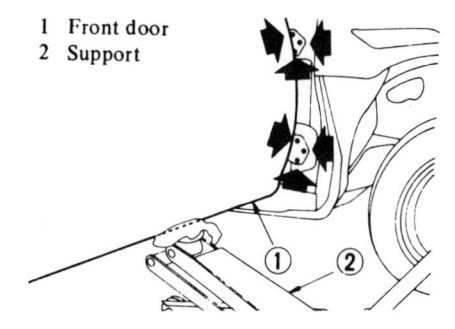

1 Front door
2 Support

6. Reverse the removal procedure to install the door.

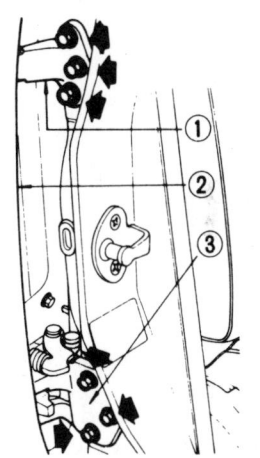

1 Upper hinge
2 Rear door
3 Lower hinge

Rear door mounting

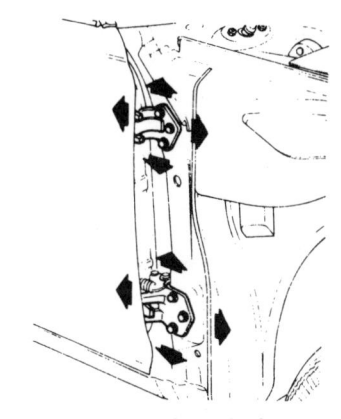

Door removal

Door adjustment is made at the hinges

201

BODY

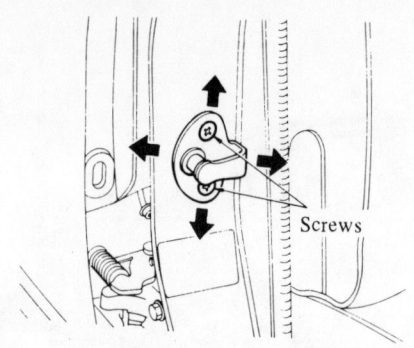

Door striker adjustment

Door Panels

Removal and Installation
ALL MODELS

1. Remove the door handle, lock handle cover, and arm rest.

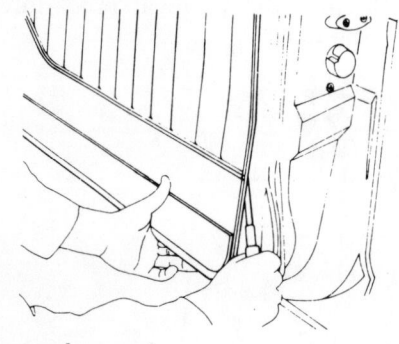

Door panel removal

2. Remove the ash tray outer case and the ash tray, if so equipped.
3. The door panel is retained by spring clips. Using a putty knife or other flat-bladed tool, carefully pull the panel toward you and release the clips.
4. To install the panel, reverse the removal procedure.

Hood adjustment

Hood, Trunk, and Tailgate

Alignment

All of these panels should be aligned in their opening by adjusting the hinge positioning and lock positioning.

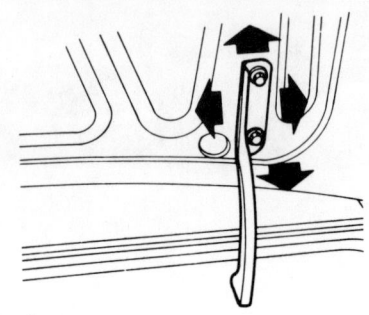

Trunk adjustment

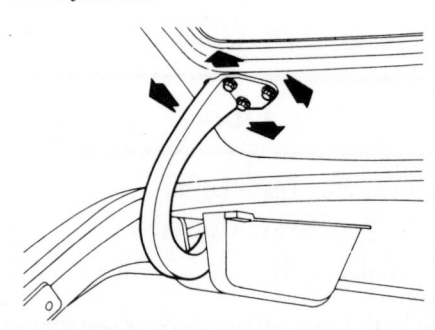

Station wagon tailgate up/down and side-to-side adjustment

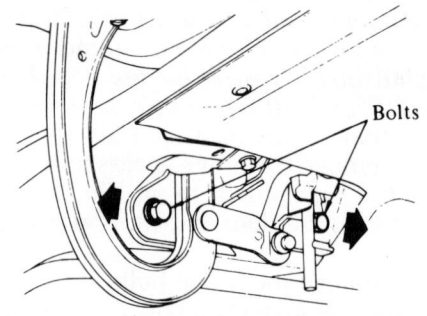

Station wagon tailgate fore-and-aft adjustment

Fuel Tank

Removal and Installation
1973 510

1. Remove the rear seat, seat back, and back trim. Disconnect the battery.
2. Remove the trunk finishing panel from within the trunk.

BODY 203

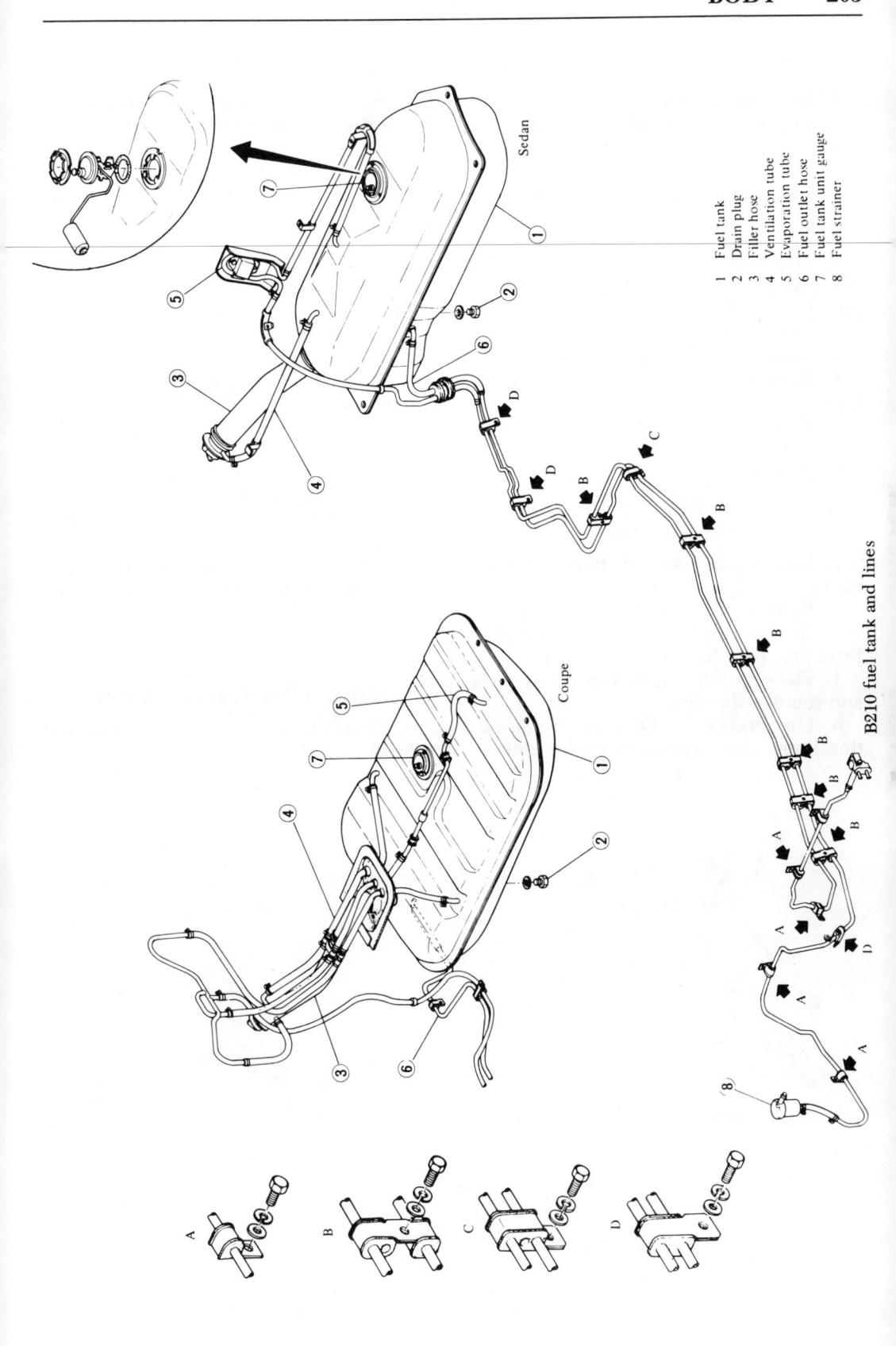

1 Fuel tank
2 Drain plug
3 Filler hose
4 Ventilation tube
5 Evaporation tube
6 Fuel outlet hose
7 Fuel tank unit gauge
8 Fuel strainer

B210 fuel tank and lines

BODY

3. Disconnect the gauge unit lead wire and drain the tank.
4. Remove the filler tube.
5. Remove the retaining bolts and disconnect the rubber lines for fuel outlet and return from the tank.
6. Remove the tank.

1200

1. Disconnect the battery. Remove the drain plug from the tank bottom and completely drain the tank.
2. Remove the fuel lines.
3. Remove the trunk finishing panel.
4. Remove the four bolts retaining the tank.
5. Disconnect the hose clamp and gauge wire.
6. Remove the fuel tank.

B210 SEDAN, 610, AND 710 SEDAN AND HARDTOP

1. Disconnect the battery ground cable.
2. Remove the front trunk panel.
3. Remove the spare tire and the plug from the spare housing.
4. Place a pan under the drain plug and remove the plug.
5. Disconnect the filler hose, ventilation lines, and fuel line from the tank.
6. Disconnect the fuel gauge wires from the tank.
7. Remove the rear seat cushion and back. Remove the front mounting bolts.
8. Remove the other two retaining bolts and lift out the tank.
9. Installation is the reverse of removal.

B210 COUPE

1. Disconnect the battery ground cable.
2. Remove the finish panel from the right-side of the trunk.
3. Place a pan under the drain plug and remove the plug.
4. Disconnect the filler hose, ventilation lines, and fuel line from the tank.
5. Disconnect the evaporative lines from the reservoir tank.
6. Remove the spare tire and then the inspection plate from the rear floor.
7. Disconnect the sending unit wires.
8. Remove the fuel tank mounting bolts and lift the tank out of the car.
9. Installation is the reverse of removal.

610 AND 710 STATION WAGON

1. Disconnect the battery ground cable.

Sedan and Hardtop

Station Wagon

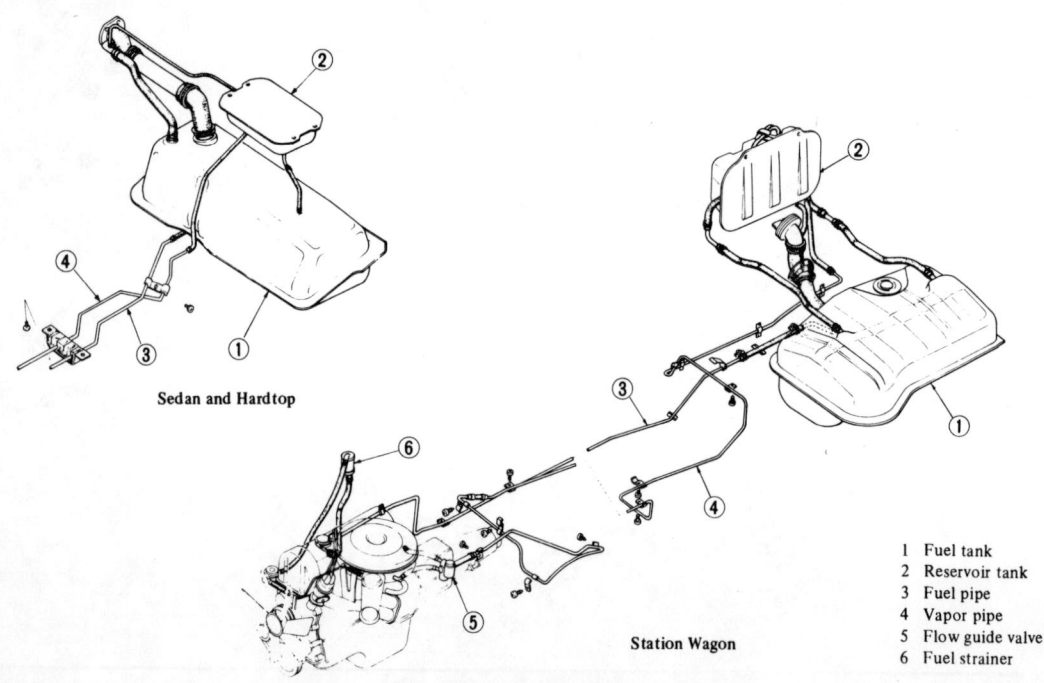

1 Fuel tank
2 Reservoir tank
3 Fuel pipe
4 Vapor pipe
5 Flow guide valve
6 Fuel strainer

610 fuel tank and lines

BODY 205

2. Remove the inspection plate from the rear floor. Disconnect the gauge wiring.
3. Remove the spare tire.
4. Place a pan under the drain plug and remove the plug.
5. Disconnect the filler hose, ventilation lines, and the fuel line from the tank.
6. Remove the retaining bolts and remove the tank.
7. Installation is the reverse of removal.

F10 Sedan and Hatchback

1. Disconnect the battery ground cable.
2. Drain the fuel into a suitable container.
3. Disconnect the filler hose, the air vent hose, fuel return hose, and fuel outlet hose.
4. Disconnect the wires from the sending unit.
5. Remove the bolts securing the fuel tank and remove the tank.
6. Installation is in the reverse order of removal.

F10 Wagon

The removal procedure is the same as that for the sedan and hatchback. However, when removing the fuel tank bolts, it is easier if you start at the three bolts at the front of the tank.

200SX

1. Disconnect the battery ground cable.
2. Remove the rubber plug located on the floor panel above the left side rear axle.
3. Remove the drain plug and drain the tank.
4. Detach the rear seat cushion, seat back, and rear seat backboard.
5. Disconnect the fuel hose.
6. Remove the two bolts which secure the fuel tank in the front.
7. Open the trunk, remove the trim in

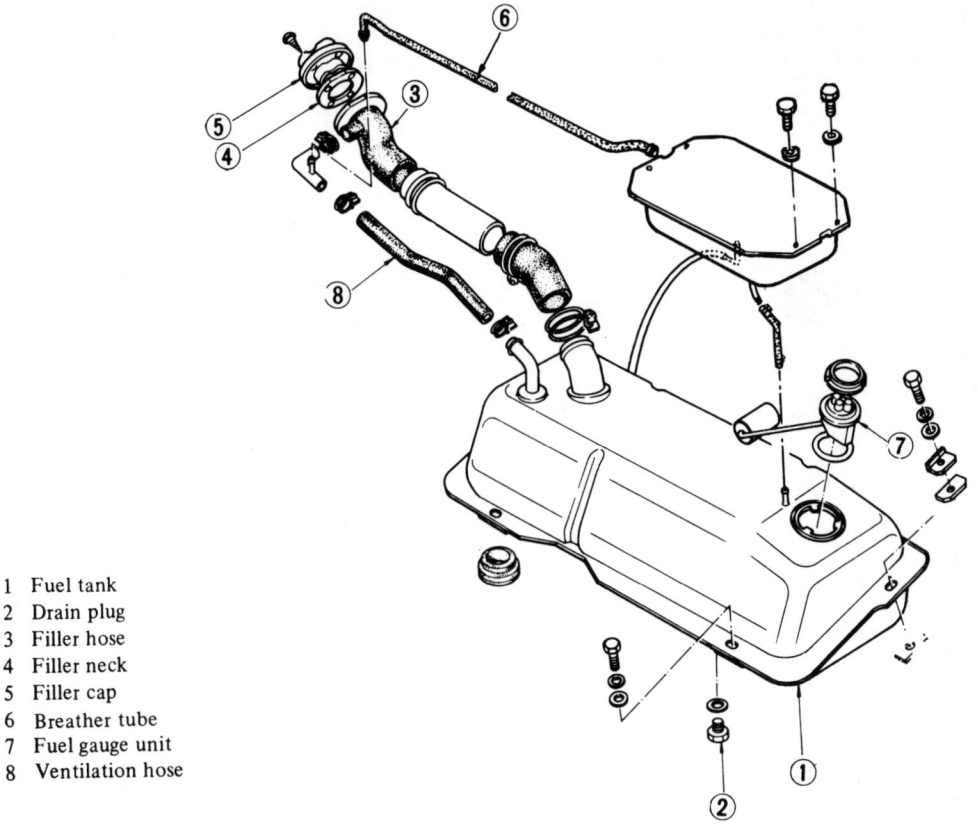

1 Fuel tank
2 Drain plug
3 Filler hose
4 Filler neck
5 Filler cap
6 Breather tube
7 Fuel gauge unit
8 Ventilation hose

710 fuel tank

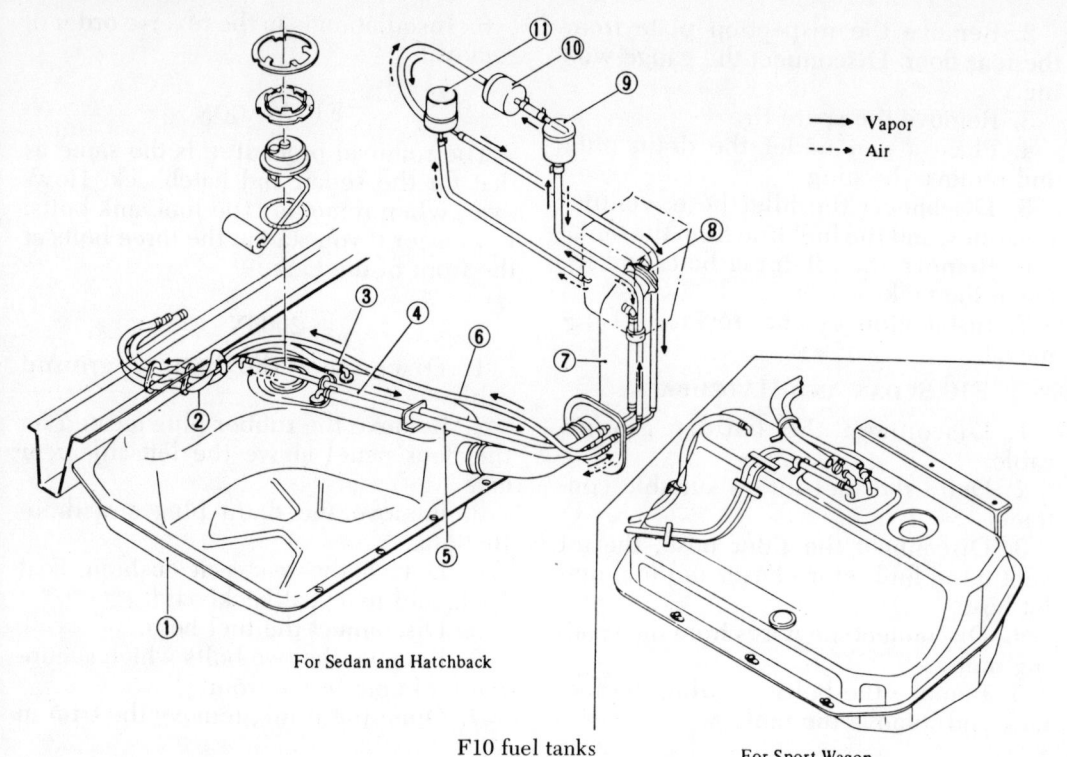

206　BODY

→ Vapor
---→ Air

For Sedan and Hatchback

For Sport Wagon

F10 fuel tanks

1. Fuel tank
2. Fuel outlet hose
3. Fuel return hose
4. Evaporation hose to fuel tank
5. Air vent line
6. Evaporation hose to engine
7. Filler hose
8. Filler cap
9. Separator
10. Limit valve
11. Vent cleaner

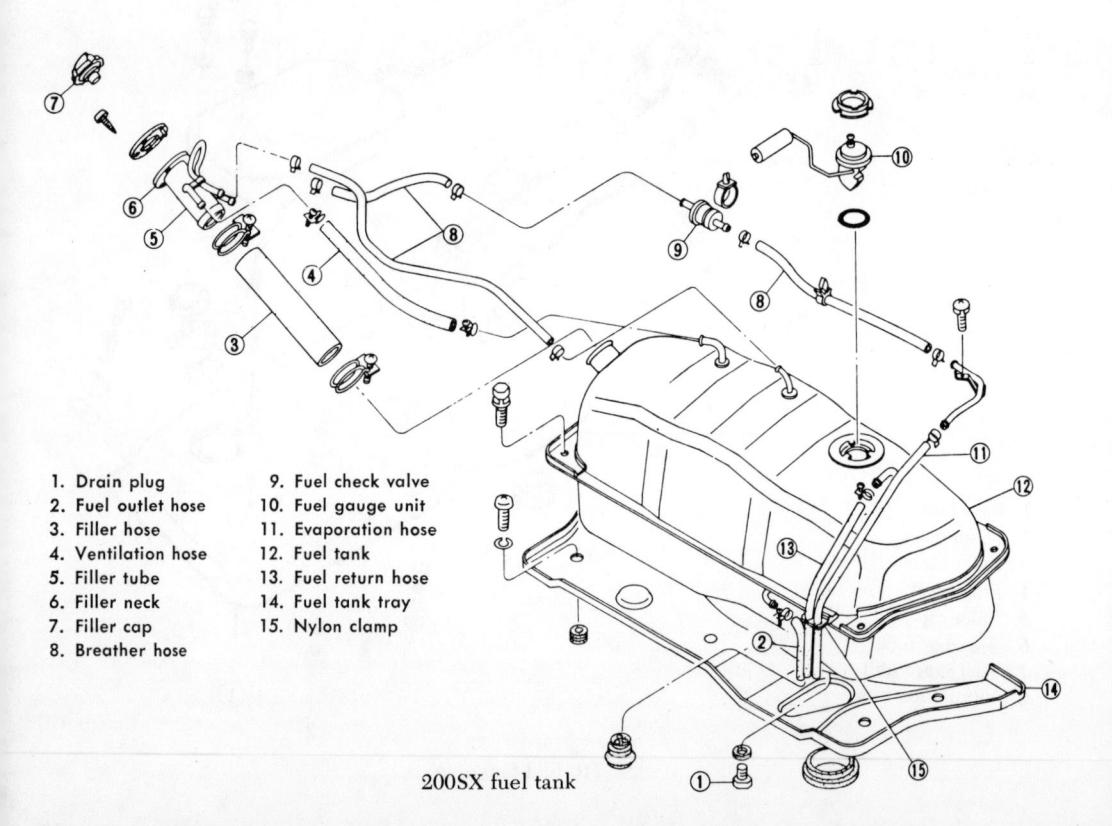

1. Drain plug
2. Fuel outlet hose
3. Filler hose
4. Ventilation hose
5. Filler tube
6. Filler neck
7. Filler cap
8. Breather hose
9. Fuel check valve
10. Fuel gauge unit
11. Evaporation hose
12. Fuel tank
13. Fuel return hose
14. Fuel tank tray
15. Nylon clamp

200SX fuel tank

BODY

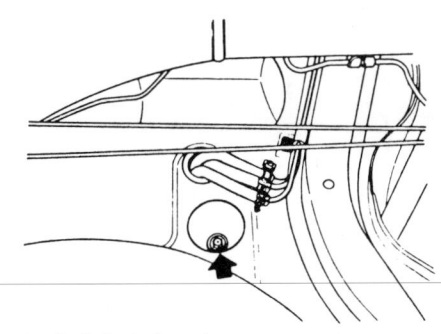

200SX fuel drain location

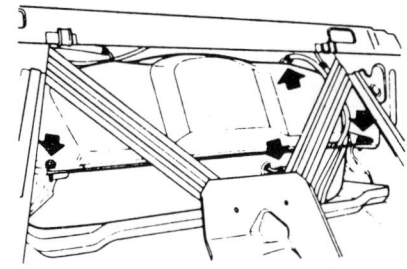

Fuel tank bolt locations—rear seat side

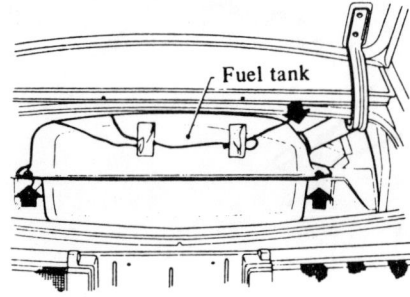

Bolt locations—trunk side

front of the tank, and remove all the hoses and lines.
8. Remove the two bolts which hold the fuel tank in the back and remove the tank.
9. Installation is in the reverse order of removal.

810 SEDAN

1. Disconnect the battery ground cable.
2. Remove the mat and the spare tire from the trunk.
3. Place a suitable container under the fuel tank and drain the tank. There is a drain plug in the bottom of the tank.
4. Disconnect the filler hose, the vent tube, and the outlet hose.
5. Disconnect the wires from the sending unit.
6. Remove the four bolts securing the fuel tank and remove the tank.

7. Installation is in the reverse order of removal.

810 STATION WAGON

1. Disconnect the battery ground cable.
2. Loosen the tire hanger and take out the spare tire.
3. Loosen the drain plug and drain the tank.
4. Disconnect the filler hose, ventilation hose, evaporation hose, and outlet hose.
5. Remove the tire stopper. Disconnect the wiring from the gauge.
6. Remove the four bolts securing the fuel tank and remove the tank.
7. Installation is in the reverse order of removal.

1978 510 SEDAN

1. Disconnect the battery ground cable.
2. Remove the back seat trim in the luggage compartment.
3. Drain the fuel in the fuel tank.
4. Disconnect all the hoses and wires from the tank.
5. Remove the bolts securing the tank and remove the tank.
6. Installation is in the reverse order of removal.

1978 510 HATCHBACK

1. Disconnect the battery ground cable.
2. Drain the fuel from the tank, then disconnect the fuel hose.
3. Remove the luggage carpet, luggage board, and fuel filler hose protector.
4. Disconnect all the hoses and wires to the tank.
5. Unbolt the fuel tank and remove it.
6. Installation is in the reverse order of removal.

1978 510 STATION WAGON

1. Disconnect the battery ground cable.
2. Drain the fuel from the tank. Disconnect all the hoses and lines.
3. Remove the spare tire and fuel tank support.
4. Unbolt and remove the tank.
5. Installation is in the reverse order of removal.

BODY

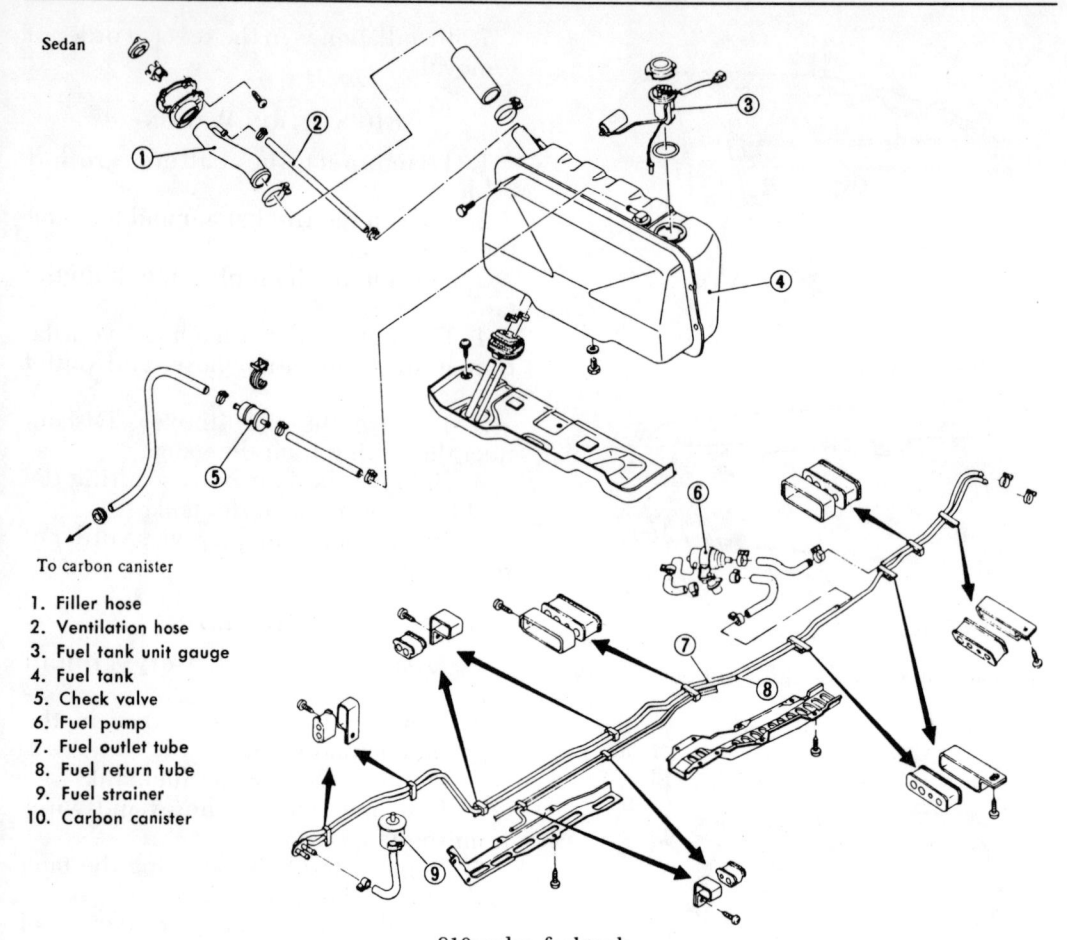

Sedan

To carbon canister

1. Filler hose
2. Ventilation hose
3. Fuel tank unit gauge
4. Fuel tank
5. Check valve
6. Fuel pump
7. Fuel outlet tube
8. Fuel return tube
9. Fuel strainer
10. Carbon canister

810 sedan fuel tank

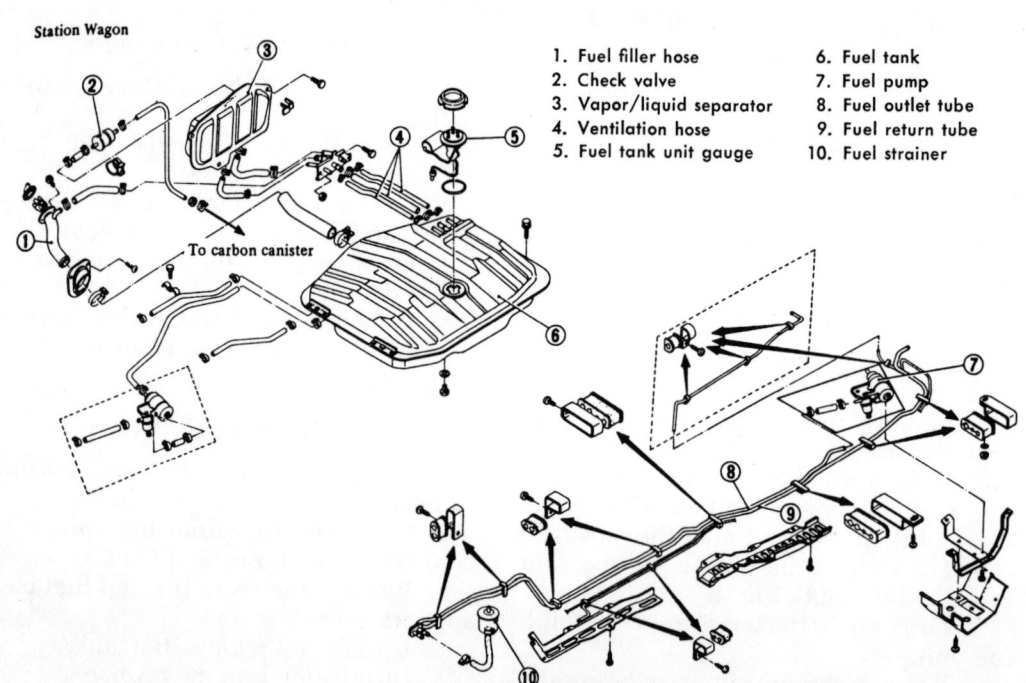

Station Wagon

To carbon canister

1. Fuel filler hose
2. Check valve
3. Vapor/liquid separator
4. Ventilation hose
5. Fuel tank unit gauge
6. Fuel tank
7. Fuel pump
8. Fuel outlet tube
9. Fuel return tube
10. Fuel strainer

810 station wagon fuel tank

BODY 209

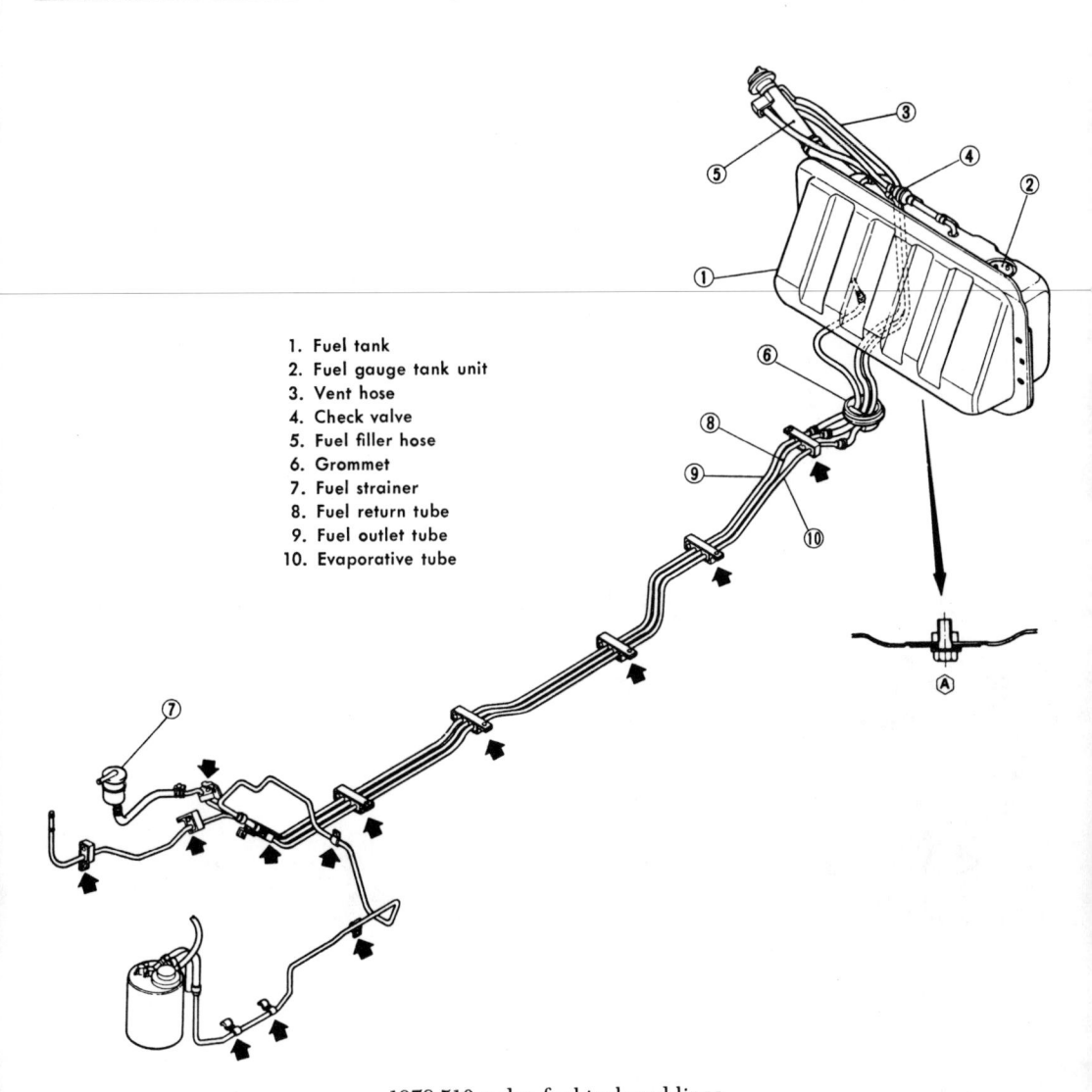

1. Fuel tank
2. Fuel gauge tank unit
3. Vent hose
4. Check valve
5. Fuel filler hose
6. Grommet
7. Fuel strainer
8. Fuel return tube
9. Fuel outlet tube
10. Evaporative tube

1978 510 sedan fuel tank and lines

210 BODY

1. Fuel tank
2. Fuel gauge tank unit
3. Vent hose
4. Check valve
5. Fuel filler hose
6. Plate
7. Fuel filler hose grommet
8. Fuel filler hose protector
9. Fuel strainer
10. Fuel outlet tube
11. Fuel return tube
12. Evaporative tube

1978 510 hatchback fuel tank and lines

1. Fuel tank
2. Fuel gauge tank unit
3. Vent hose
4. Check valve
5. Fuel filler hose grommet
6. Fuel filler hose
7. Fuel strainer
8. Fuel outlet tube
9. Fuel return tube
10. Evaporative tube

1978 510 station wagon fuel tank and lines

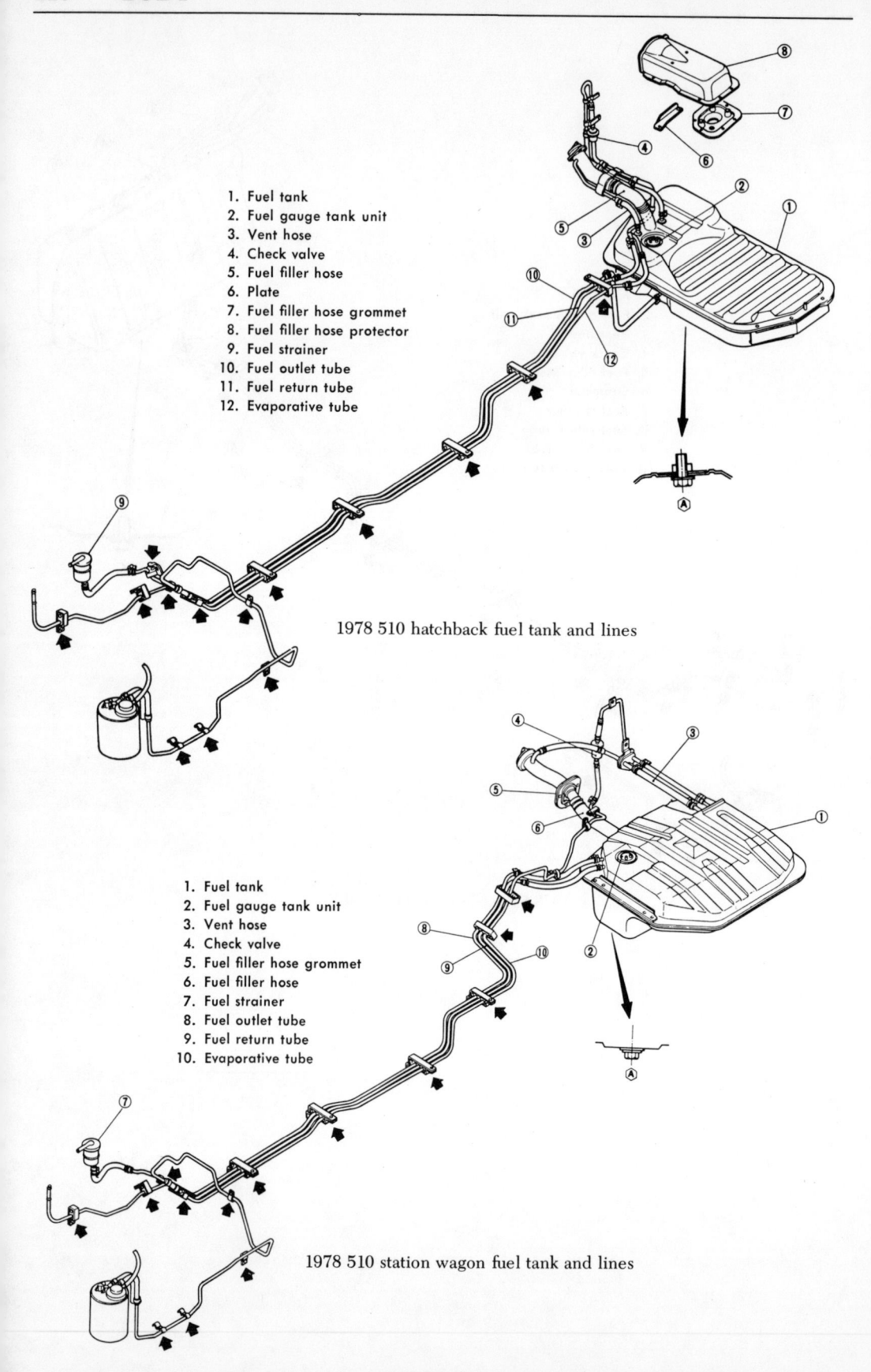

Appendix

General Conversion Table

Multiply by	To convert	To	
2.54	Inches	Centimeters	.3937
30.48	Feet	Centimeters	.0328
.914	Yards	Meters	1.094
1.609	Miles	Kilometers	.621
.645	Square inches	Square cm.	.155
.836	Square yards	Square meters	1.196
16.39	Cubic inches	Cubic cm.	.061
28.3	Cubic feet	Liters	.0353
.4536	Pounds	Kilograms	2.2045
4.226	Gallons	Liters	.264
.068	Lbs./sq. in. (psi)	Atmospheres	14.7
.138	Foot pounds	Kg. m.	7.23
1.014	H.P. (DIN)	H.P. (SAE)	.9861
——	To obtain	From	Multiply by

Note: 1 cm. equals 10 mm.; 1 mm. equals .0394″.

Conversion—Common Fractions to Decimals and Millimeters

INCHES

Common Fractions	Decimal Fractions	Millimeters (approx.)	Common Fractions	Decimal Fractions	Millimeters (approx.)	Common Fractions	Decimal Fractions	Millimeters (approx.)
1/128	.008	0.20	11/32	.344	8.73	43/64	.672	17.07
1/64	.016	0.40	23/64	.359	9.13	11/16	.688	17.46
1/32	.031	0.79	3/8	.375	9.53	45/64	.703	17.86
3/64	.047	1.19	25/64	.391	9.92	23/32	.719	18.26
1/16	.063	1.59	13/32	.406	10.32	47/64	.734	18.65
5/64	.078	1.98	27/64	.422	10.72	3/4	.750	19.05
3/32	.094	2.38	7/16	.438	11.11	49/64	.766	19.45
7/64	.109	2.78	29/64	.453	11.51	25/32	.781	19.84
1/8	.125	3.18	15/32	.469	11.91	51/64	.797	20.24
9/64	.141	3.57	31/64	.484	12.30	13/16	.813	20.64
5/32	.156	3.97	1/2	.500	12.70	53/64	.828	21.03
11/64	.172	4.37	33/64	.516	13.10	27/32	.844	21.43
3/16	.188	4.76	17/32	.531	13.49	55/64	.859	21.83
13/64	.203	5.16	35/64	.547	13.89	7/8	.875	22.23
7/32	.219	5.56	9/16	.563	14.29	57/64	.891	22.62
15/64	.234	5.95	37/64	.578	14.68	29/32	.906	23.02
1/4	.250	6.35	19/32	.594	15.08	59/64	.922	23.42
17/64	.266	6.75	39/64	.609	15.48	15/16	.938	23.81
9/32	.281	7.14	5/8	.625	15.88	61/64	.953	24.21
19/64	.297	7.54	41/64	.641	16.27	31/32	.969	24.61
5/16	.313	7.94	21/32	.656	16.67	63/64	.984	25.00
21/64	.328	8.33						

Conversion—Millimeters to Decimal Inches

mm	inches	mm	inches	mm	inches	mm	inches	mm	inches
1	.039 370	31	1.220 470	61	2.401 570	91	3.582 670	210	8.267 700
2	.078 740	32	1.259 840	62	2.440 940	92	3.622 040	220	8.661 400
3	.118 110	33	1.299 210	63	2.480 310	93	3.661 410	230	9.055 100
4	.157 480	34	1.338 580	64	2.519 680	94	3.700 780	240	9.448 800
5	.196 850	35	1.377 949	65	2.559 050	95	3.740 150	250	9.842 500
6	.236 220	36	1.417 319	66	2.598 420	96	3.779 520	260	10.236 200
7	.275 590	37	1.456 689	67	2.637 790	97	3.818 890	270	10.629 900
8	.314 960	38	1.496 050	68	2.677 160	98	3.858 260	280	11.032 600
9	.354 330	39	1.535 430	69	2.716 530	99	3.897 630	290	11.417 300
10	.393 700	40	1.574 800	70	2.755 900	100	3.937 000	300	11.811 000
11	.433 070	41	1.614 170	71	2.795 270	105	4.133 848	310	12.204 700
12	.472 440	42	1.653 540	72	2.834 640	110	4.330 700	320	12.598 400
13	.511 810	43	1.692 910	73	2.874 010	115	4.527 550	330	12.992 100
14	.551 180	44	1.732 280	74	2.913 380	120	4.724 400	340	13.385 800
15	.590 550	45	1.771 650	75	2.952 750	125	4.921 250	350	13.779 500
16	.629 920	46	1.811 020	76	2.992 120	130	5.118 100	360	14.173 200
17	.669 290	47	1.850 390	77	3.031 490	135	5.314 950	370	14.566 900
18	.708 660	48	1.889 760	78	3.070 860	140	5.511 800	380	14.960 600
19	.748 030	49	1.929 130	79	3.110 230	145	5.708 650	390	15.354 300
20	.787 400	50	1.968 500	80	3.149 600	150	5.905 500	400	15.748 000
21	.826 770	51	2.007 870	81	3.188 970	155	6.102 350	500	19.685 000
22	.866 140	52	2.047 240	82	3.228 340	160	6.299 200	600	23.622 000
23	.905 510	53	2.086 610	83	3.267 710	165	6.496 050	700	27.559 000
24	.944 880	54	2.125 980	84	3.307 080	170	6.692 900	800	31.496 000
25	.984 250	55	2.165 350	85	3.346 450	175	6.889 750	900	35.433 000
26	1.023 620	56	2.204 720	86	3.385 820	180	7.086 600	1000	39.370 000
27	1.062 990	57	2.244 090	87	3.425 190	185	7.283 450	2000	78.740 000
28	1.102 360	58	2.283 460	88	3.464 560	190	7.480 300	3000	118.110 000
29	1.141 730	59	2.322 830	89	3.503 903	195	7.677 150	4000	157.480 000
30	1.181 100	60	2.362 200	90	3.543 300	200	7.874 000	5000	196.850 000

To change decimal millimeters to decimal inches, position the decimal point where desired on either side of the millimeter measurement shown and reset the inches decimal by the same number of digits in the same direction. For example, to convert .001 mm into decimal inches, reset the decimal behind the 1 mm (shown on the chart) to .001; change the decimal inch equivalent (.039" shown to .000039").

Tap Drill Sizes

National Fine or S.A.E.

Screw & Tap Size	Threads Per Inch	Use Drill Number
No. 5	44	37
No. 6	40	33
No. 8	36	29
No. 10	32	21
No. 12	28	15
1/4	28	3
5/16	24	I
3/8	24	Q
7/16	20	W
1/2	20	29/64
9/16	18	33/64
5/8	18	37/64
3/4	16	11/16
7/8	14	13/16
1 1/8	12	1 3/64
1 1/4	12	1 11/64
1 1/2	12	1 27/64

National Coarse or U.S.S.

Screw & Tap Size	Threads Per Inch	Use Drill Number
No. 5	40	39
No. 6	32	36
No. 8	32	29
No. 10	24	25
No. 12	24	17
1/4	20	8
5/16	18	F
3/8	16	5/16
7/16	14	U
1/2	13	27/64
9/16	12	31/64
5/8	11	17/32
3/4	10	21/32
7/8	9	49/64
1	8	7/8
1 1/8	7	63/64
1 1/4	7	1 7/64
1 1/2	6	1 11/32

Decimal Equivalent Size of the Number Drills

Drill No.	Decimal Equivalent	Drill No.	Decimal Equivalent	Drill No.	Decimal Equivalent
80	.0135	53	.0595	26	.1470
79	.0145	52	.0635	25	.1495
78	.0160	51	.0670	24	.1520
77	.0180	50	.0700	23	.1540
76	.0200	49	.0730	22	.1570
75	.0210	48	.0760	21	.1590
74	.0225	47	.0785	20	.1610
73	.0240	46	.0810	19	.1660
72	.0250	45	.0820	18	.1695
71	.0260	44	.0860	17	.1730
70	.0280	43	.0890	16	.1770
69	.0292	42	.0935	15	.1800
68	.0310	41	.0960	14	.1820
67	.0320	40	.0980	13	.1850
66	.0330	39	.0995	12	.1890
65	.0350	38	.1015	11	.1910
64	.0360	37	.1040	10	.1935
63	.0370	36	.1065	9	.1960
62	.0380	35	.1100	8	.1990
61	.0390	34	.1110	7	.2010
60	.0400	33	.1130	6	.2040
59	.0410	32	.1160	5	.2055
58	.0420	31	.1200	4	.2090
57	.0430	30	.1285	3	.2130
56	.0465	29	.1360	2	.2210
55	.0520	28	.1405	1	.2280
54	.0550	27	.1440		

Decimal Equivalent Size of the Letter Drills

Letter Drill	Decimal Equivalent	Letter Drill	Decimal Equivalent	Letter Drill	Decimal Equivalent
A	.234	J	.277	S	.348
B	.238	K	.281	T	.358
C	.242	L	.290	U	.368
D	.246	M	.295	V	.377
E	.250	N	.302	W	.386
F	.257	O	.316	X	.397
G	.261	P	.323	Y	.404
H	.266	Q	.332	Z	.413
I	.272	R	.339		

ANTI-FREEZE INFORMATION

Freezing and Boiling Points of Solutions According to Percentage of Alcohol or Ethylene Glycol

Freezing Point of Solution	Alcohol Volume %	Alcohol Solution Boils at	Ethylene Glycol Volume %	Ethylene Glycol Solution Boils at
20°F.	12	196°F.	16	216°F.
10°F.	20	189°F.	25	218°F.
0°F.	27	184°F.	33	220°F.
−10°F.	32	181°F.	39	222°F.
−20°F.	38	178°F.	44	224°F.
−30°F.	42	176°F.	48	225°F.

Note: above boiling points are at sea level. For every 1,000 feet of altitude, boiling points are approximately 2°F. lower than those shown. For every pound of pressure exerted by the pressure cap, the boiling points are approximately 3°F. higher than those shown.

ANTI-FREEZE CHART

Temperatures Shown in Degrees Fahrenheit
+32 is Freezing

Cooling System Capacity Quarts	Quarts of ETHYLENE GLYCOL Needed for Protection to Temperatures Shown Below													
	1	2	3	4	5	6	7	8	9	10	11	12	13	14
10	+24°	+16°	+ 4°	−12°	−34°	−62°								
11	+25	+18	+ 8	− 6	−23	−47								
12	+26	+19	+10	0	−15	−34	−57°							
13	+27	+21	+13	+ 3	− 9	−25	−45							
14			+15	+ 6	− 5	−18	−34							
15			+16	+ 8	0	−12	−26							
16			+17	+10	+ 2	− 8	−19	−34	−52°					
17			+18	+12	+ 5	− 4	−14	−27	−42					
18			+19	+14	+ 7	0	−10	−21	−34	−50°				
19			+20	+15	+ 9	+ 2	− 7	−16	−28	−42				
20				+16	+10	+ 4	− 3	−12	−22	−34	−48°			
21				+17	+12	+ 6	0	− 9	−17	−28	−41			
22				+18	+13	+ 8	+ 2	− 6	−14	−23	−34	−47°		
23				+19	+14	+ 9	+ 4	− 3	−10	−19	−29	−40		
24				+19	+15	+10	+ 5	0	− 8	−15	−23	−34	−46°	
25				+20	+16	+12	+ 7	+ 1	− 5	−12	−20	−29	−40	−50
26					+17	+13	+ 8	+ 3	− 3	− 9	−16	−25	−34	−44
27					+18	+14	+ 9	+ 5	− 1	− 7	−13	−21	−29	−39
28					+18	+15	+10	+ 6	+ 1	− 5	−11	−18	−25	−34
29					+19	+16	+12	+ 7	+ 2	− 3	− 8	−15	−22	−29
30					+20	+17	+13	+ 8	+ 4	− 1	− 6	−12	−18	−25

For capacities over 30 quarts vide true capacity by 3. Find qu Anti-Freeze for the ⅓ and mult by 3 for quarts to add.

For capacities under 10 quarts multiply true capacity by 3. Find quarts Anti-Freeze for the tripled volume and divide by 3 for quarts to add.

To Increase the Freezing Protection of Anti-Freeze Solutions Already Installed

Cooling System Capacity Quarts	Number of Quarts of ETHYLENE GLYCOL Anti-Freeze Required to Increase Protection													
	From +20°F. to					From +10°F. to					From 0°F. to			
	0°	−10°	−20°	−30°	−40°	0°	−10°	−20°	−30°	−40°	−10°	−20°	−30°	−40°
10	1¾	2¼	3	3½	3¾	¾	1½	2¼	2¾	3¼	¾	1½	2	2½
12	2	2¾	3½	4	4½	1	1¾	2½	3¼	3¾	1	1¾	2½	3¼
14	2¼	3¼	4	4¾	5½	1¼	2	3	3¾	4½	1	2	3	3½
16	2½	3½	4½	5¼	6	1¼	2½	3½	4¼	5¼	1¼	2¼	3¼	4
18	3	4	5	6	7	1½	2¾	4	5	5¾	1½	2½	3¾	4¾
20	3¼	4½	5¾	6¾	7½	1¾	3	4¼	5½	6½	1½	2¾	4¼	5¼
22	3½	5	6¼	7¼	8¼	1¾	3¼	4¾	6	7¼	1¾	3¼	4½	5½
24	4	5½	7	8	9	2	3½	5	6½	7½	1¾	3½	5	6
26	4¼	6	7½	8¾	10	2	4	5½	7	8¼	2	3¾	5½	6¾
28	4½	6¼	8	9½	10½	2¼	4¼	6	7½	9	2	4	5¾	7¼
30	5	6¾	8½	10	11½	2½	4½	6½	8	9½	2¼	4¼	6¼	7¾

Test radiator solution with proper hydrometer. Determine from the table the number of quarts of solution to be drawn off from a full cooling system and replace with undiluted anti-freeze, to give the desired increased protection. For example, to increase protection of a 22-quart cooling system containing Ethylene Glycol (permanent type) anti-freeze, from +20°F. to −20°F. will require the replacement of 6¼ quarts of solution with undiluted anti-freeze.